Winner of the First Annual
Kenneth W. Mildenberger Medal
conferred by the Modern Language Association
for an outstanding research publication
in the field of teaching foreign languages
and literatures
1981

TEACHING LANGUAGES

A WAY AND WAYS

EARL W. STEVICK

Newbury House Publishers, Inc. / Rowley / Massachusetts / 01969

Library of Congress Cataloging in Publication Data

Stevick, Earl W
   Teaching languages.
   Bibliography: p.
   Includes index.
   1. Language and languages--Study and teaching.
I. Title.
P51.S856   407   79-27433
ISBN 0-88377-147-0

Cover designed by *Barbara Frake*.

NEWBURY HOUSE PUBLISHERS, INC.

Language Science
Language Teaching
Language Learning

ROWLEY, MASSACHUSETTS 01969

First printing: March 1980

Printed in the U.S.A.   6   5

To Betty Rae,
without whose love and support
I could not have become
who I am.

ACKNOWLEDGMENTS

Peter O'Connell and Madeline Ehrman have provided personal encouragement and professional companionship from the start of this project to the end of it.

The phrase A WAY AND WAYS is taken from a poem that my mother often quoted in my hearing many years ago.

Many of the distinctive ideas in this book have been passed to me from my children's generation. Becky and Lyman put me in touch with Gallwey and with Becker. Marian finally got me to read a little Dostoyevsky. Just before my last class in Honolulu, someone put into my hand a volume of Krishnamurti. Joel's ability to balance between living for the present and living for the future has been a continuing source of education for me. Laura has clarified some key points by letting me see them for a few moments through the eyes of a clearsighted bilingual.

The writing of the first draft of this book began unexpectedly at the 1977 Summer Institute of the Linguistic Society of America, at the University of Hawaii in Honolulu. I am grateful to members of the faculty of the University who invited me to teach two courses at the Institute, and to the students in those courses who provided a fertile environment for thinking and rethinking.

Jenny Rardin has been my principal contact person, guide, and adviser as I have explored Counseling-Learning. Her patient attention to some crucial chapters of this book has enriched them, and has clarified them for me.

I am grateful to Dieter Stroinigg, Irene Dutra, Dot Carhart, and Betsy Bedell for permission to include papers that they have written about their own experiences.

The School of Language Studies of the Foreign Service Institute has for nineteen years been my professional home, and a continuing source of contact with the day-to-day realities of teaching and learning foreign languages.

Not least, I hope that Esther Redmond, when she has read this book, will conclude that she did indeed win her bet with me.

I wish to thank the editors of *Modern Language Journal, Language Learning* and *Idiom* for permission to reprint material.

The following friends, colleagues, and students have contributed material that I have quoted, or they have given detailed reactions to one part or another of the manuscript. (Several have done both.) I regret any omissions!

Warren G. Yates
Fumiyo Yamanaka
Kruamat Woodtikarn
Dennis E. Wilkinson
Barbara Wiggin
Marc Wiederholt
Mark Wheaton
Taeko Wellington
Weldis Welley
Karen Waltensperger
R. Wade
Ken Vogel
Lianne Uno
Graham Thurgood
Edward Allen Thomson
Marcia A. Taylor
James W. Stone
Mira Soekias
Robert L. Smith
William A. Smalley
Roy Shelangouski
Willard D. Shaw
Sally Serafim
Sirinee Santaputra
Sima Rafiq
Karin Ryding
Christina Purdy
Sasha Platis
Ted Plaister
Tony Pfannkuche
Rhian Owen
Eulanda Opinaldo
Ralph Odom
Akimi Oda
Joy Noren
Noriko Nishi
Kalistus Ngirturong

Pat and Valerie Mills
Carolyn Miki
Charles Meding
John F. Mayer
Alan Maley
Wiktor Litwinsky
Edna Lennox
Donald N. Larson
Stephen D. Krashen
Daniel Koch
Annie Kobayashi
Ed Klein
Shar Klafehn
Gary Kissick
Judy and Guy Kirkendall
Sandy Kerns
Helen Jorstad and an
    anonymous group
    of her friends
Masachika Ishida
Meiko Inouye
Leslie Hopf
Joan Hildenbrand
Norris Henthorne
Seamus Haughey
Lee Gillespie
Yoko Fukushi
Barbara Fujiwara
John Egan
Barbara Jo Easton
Beverly Durham
C. Douglass
Tim Donahue
Ann Diller
Joel Diamond
Ellen deSzunyogh
Ruth Crymes

Jon Countess

Barry Cotton

Joe Chevarley, Jr.

Gean Cases

Marilyn Carpenter

Dot Carhart

Diane Butturff

Christopher Brumfit

J. Marvin Brown

Yvette Bretschneider

Kerry Brethouwer

Virginia Brennan

Bob Braithwaite

William Boyce

Larry Bott

Charles Blatchford

Bismoko

Fred Bennett

Paul and Betchen Barber

Romana Anastacio

Nobuo and Carol Akiyama

Mary Glenn Adams

And a warm "Thank you!" to the Newbury House production staff!

Arlington, Virginia
September 1, 1979

PREFACE

If I am soon to die,
Then I must give you this book now.
It will be a stone on which is written
All that is left from me.

If I have long to live,
Why, then, I will give you these words
As stones for the foundation
Of something new between us.

But if I gave you small words,
Easy for me to say and you to hear
I would be giving you sand — nothing
For us to build our house on.

CONTENTS

PART IV: A Third Way: Suggestopedia

PART V: Part I, Continued

PART I

A WAY
OF LOOKING AT
FOREIGN LANGUAGE
EDUCATION

CHAPTER I

ONE VIEW OF THE LEARNER

Some riddles have no final answers.

A few answerless riddles are still worth asking.

They are worth asking not for their answers, since they have none, but for what we do in struggling with them.

We may come to notice what formerly we had overlooked because it was too small, or too distant—or too large, or too close to us. We may see how pieces fit together within what we had always thought were units, indivisible.

Why do some language students succeed, and others fail? Why do some language teachers fail, and others succeed? What may the learners and teachers of foreign languages hope to succeed at anyway? How broad, how deep, how wide may be the measure of their failure, or of their success?

These questions have come to hold a greater and greater place in my thinking during recent years. In the early 1970s, I began to find some parts of some partial answers to these questions—answers that helped me and helped some of my colleagues (and our students) to succeed more often, helped us also to succeed in ways that went beyond mere learning of structures, sounds, and words. So I wrote a book about what I was finding out.

I found considerable satisfaction in writing that book. One thing I liked about it was that the bibliographical references covered eight pages of small type, and that the book itself contained hundreds of footnotes. I felt that this showed that I had taken into account the work of many other people, and that I had checked my own thinking against theirs.

I was therefore surprised by one letter that my publisher received from an anonymous person who appeared to have read my book with some care. This person seemed to like the book very much, but was impatient with the footnotes. He/she wrote, "I would like to see a book in which he speaks for himself entirely, instead of being a spokesman for others. He should write a book that is firmly and unequivocally himself." Another friendly critic wanted more "detailed descriptions of what the students actually do."

I cannot write a book just to please critics. Nevertheless, I hope that these two will feel that their suggestions have borne fruit in this one. The ideas that were growing in the writing of *Memory, Meaning, and Method* have been with me for these additional years. I have watched them develop with many additional language classes. I have worked through them with groups of language teachers from many parts of the world. So now these ideas are more fully integrated within me; they are more truly mine. Footnotes thus become less necessary, and less appropriate. This is not to say that I have originated all of this, however. The influence of Charles A. Curran permeates the book, and the first two chapters draw heavily on Ernest Becker and W. Timothy Gallwey. The thought of Caleb Gattegno and Georgi Lozanov is conspicuous in the chapters devoted to their work.

As these ideas have ripened, I think that their roots have gone deeper into whatever it is that lies underneath the process—the experience—of learning and teaching a foreign language.

At the same time, I have tried to keep these theoretical explorations in touch with reality, by drawing on materials of two kinds. First is a series of accounts of classes taught by me or by other people, telling what we did, and why, and how it worked. These are chronicles, not recipes; the reader is invited to learn vicariously from our experience, but not necessarily to copy what we did.

A second type of illustrative material consists of excerpts, some of them anecdotal, from papers written by language teachers in courses that I taught in the summers of 1976 and 1977. All quotations are used with permission.

There are of course many "ways" in language teaching other than the three that I have chosen for this book. All of these three are unconventional and relatively obscure. I do not mean to say that other methods are not equally worthy of attention. I do think that the conclusions reached in this book apply to the other methods—or at least to the methods with which I am familiar. But my purpose here is not to write a comprehensive treatise on methods. Neither is it to present the definitive solution to the complex issues of language teaching. What I hope my readers will find in this book is not a key or a compass, but only a little light. I will therefore leave my readers to decide what the ideas in this book might say in the reading method, the grammar and translation method, the audiolingual method, and all the rest.

These first two chapters will outline one view of the learning and teaching of languages—a view that is my own. In Chapters 3 to 19, I shall describe the work of three other people who have influenced me, and go on to show the shapes that their ideas have taken on in my own work as a teacher. Then, in the last two chapters, I shall come back to a further development of my own point of view. Because this point of view has emerged out of those same influences and experiences that form the subject matter of the intervening chapters, themes that I shall introduce in this opening chapter will recur, with further development, in a series of other contexts.

No, there are no final answers to the riddle with which I began this chapter. My earlier conclusion was that success depends less on materials, techniques, and linguistic analyses, and more on what goes on inside and between the people in the classroom. This seems to fit the experience of one teacher:

> Four years ago I was looking for any kind of job I could find. I happened to get one teaching ESL to a class of six women from various parts of the world who spoke no English. I had

never heard of ESL before. The salary was poor and I didn't know if I wanted to pursue a teaching career, therefore my approach was very casual and low pressure. My method usually consisted of thinking up a topic to talk about, introducing it, and encouraging each student to express her feelings.

In spite of my casual approach, the teaching job was extremely pleasant. I had a deep empathy for anyone who was facing a language barrier because I had just returned from a trip around the world alone as a monolingual.

They all started speaking English fairly well after the first two weeks of class. I remember a woman from Colombia telling me that she hadn't spoken English before because she was afraid of making mistakes. After being in class for a while, she spoke English and made mistakes but didn't care. I didn't attach much significance to the progress that the women made. I had no idea how long it took people to learn a language.

Gradually I became quite career-oriented, and made a conscious decision to try to be a top-notch ESL teacher. I had guilt feelings about the casual way in which I had taught those first six women, and my teaching evolved into the traditional authoritarian style with the text-book dominant. Over the years, it has gotten to where I feel frustrated if a student takes class time to relate a personal anecdote.

I can look back on these four years and see a gradual decline in the performance of my students. Until recently, I have been assuming that I needed to be more attentive to their mistakes in order to speed their progress. My present style of teaching bypasses the students' feelings and basic needs, and concentrates on method. I never see successes like those first six ladies.

I have not changed my mind about the fundamental importance of "what goes on inside and between," but I have been able to pursue this principle more deeply, and at the same time to practice it more broadly, than before. As a result, I have begun to suspect that the most important aspect of "what goes on" is the presence or absence of harmony—it is the parts working with, or against, one another. How such a thing may happen within and between the people in a language course is the subject of this book.

INSIDE PEOPLE

Only people use words.

We use words to stand for things which are absent, as well as for things which are present. Furthermore, we have a unique ability to put together highly complex strings of word-symbols so as to communicate with one another in detailed and subtle ways. (The ways in which we do all this make up the subject matter for the science of linguistics.) Because we are able to echo back and forth to one another both what we see now and what we remember—even what we hope for—we come to know that none of us is exactly like any other. This is one gift from language. We feel in ourselves uniqueness ("I am one of a kind.") not only in our bodies but in the way we use our symbols. And with this uniqueness, beauty: beauty around us but also inside us, beauty and irreplaceableness, therefore a kind of miracle. Like everyone else, I can realize that, out of a few resources, the human race has learned to make infinite uses, that because the possibilities are beyond counting, the choices I have made among them are my own, like no one else's. Uniqueness, beauty, choice, and power—I am a being like a god!

There is of course another way in which our race is different from all other animals: we know that some day we (or at least our bodies) will die. We learn this fact through words (a second gift of language). We learn it quite early, and the knowledge grows up alongside our experience of uniqueness and our sense of beauty. This is the Great Incongruity—the obscene paradox—with which we struggle, which churns within us, as long as we live. Ernest Becker told us that the unifying principle behind all that people do is not economic determinism, not sex, but "the denial of death."

We discover that physical death is something that we all will come to some day. Our only possibility of escape, then, seems to lie in identifying ourselves with something that is eternal—or at least, something that will last longer than we will—and that is universal—true for all people. The obvious examples are what we call the great religions of the world, and these examples are valid ones. But if religion were the only example of this reaction to the fact of death, there would be no point in bringing the matter up here. The struggle against death includes more than faith in life after death (or in "life after life"); it includes our identification with any value system—any set of choices—which we share with others, and which we and others mutually affirm to be true, right, good, and valid for all people. These may be patterns that run through our entire culture, or habits we share with people of our own age, schooling, or occupation, or precepts handed down to us by our parents. We therefore hold desperately to those patterns and those precepts. And/or, we look for new parent figures, new peer groups, new objects of allegiance which will assure us that what we have committed ourselves to—even if it is agnosticism—is truly of validity beyond ourselves.

We will see shortly how this principle makes itself felt in the language classroom. But there is another, a short-range way as well by which we fend off death: we put as much space and as much time as possible between ourselves and it.

Part of this is simple prudence: taking care of our health, looking both ways before we cross the street, and so forth. But another part consists in accumulating feelings that others are closer to death than we ourselves. This may be relatively benign—noticing that our classmates at the reunion have aged so much more than we have, for example. But these feelings of relative distance from death may also be manufactured. One way is to injure another person and get away with it. Another is to sit, successfully, in judgement on what another person is or does (or says!). Death-distancing is also one, though by no means the only, reason for wanting to outdo another person in any sort of competition.

So the fact that we inevitably know the world only through our own eyes—our own senses—coupled with our struggle against death, means that each of us has an ultimate need to feel that he or she is "an object of primary value in a world of meaningful action." (Becker quotes this phrase from Adler, and I have found it helpful.) This was beautifully and repeatedly illustrated in the movie *Siddharta,* which I saw while I was writing the first draft of this chapter: both the search for what is finally worthwhile, and the demand to be primary. The protagonist was not happy when he found himself the center of what he judged was not of ultimate value; on the other hand, when he concluded that a non-self-centered, nonseeking existence free of attachments was best, he found that it was virtually impossible not to attach himself to nonseeking.

Each of us, then, develops a self-image—a set of perceptions related to our body, but also to our personal style, to our actions, and to the values (the choices) that underlie them. But (and this is the key to much that goes on in the language classroom as well as outside it) if what reinforces your self-image contradicts or detracts from mine, then mine is threatened. And vice versa, of course. I believe that today's highly processed and chemically treated foods are unwholesome and avoid them; you eat them freely. Each of us secretly hopes the other will fall ill, not because we bear each other any malice, but just because we'd like to see our own choices vindicated. When you are the last person to leave a room in which the lights are on, you generally forget to switch them off, and I suspect you of rejecting not only this one rule, but also all of the values that I learned from my parents. One teacher believes in "accuracy before fluency," another in "communication" even at the expense of accuracy. What do they say about each other to parents, to students, to other teachers?

The preservation of the self-image is the first law of psychological survival. Therefore, in any social encounter, each person exposes for public scrutiny and public testing—possibly for intolerable undermining—the one thing that he or she needs most, which is the self-evaluation that he or she has so laboriously fashioned. This means that the stakes in any social encounter are incredibly high. No such encounter can be merely routine, therefore.

> My undergraduate major was French. I was even a member of the National French Honor Society. However, when someone approaches me in French, whether she is a native or a non-native speaker, I am unwilling (not incapable) to respond for the fear of making a mistake. This is true even though I usually understand what she is saying.
>
> Several years ago, I had the opportunity to live in Japan for six months, with the sole purpose of studying Japanese. Before I went, I had assumed that as my ability to communicate progressed, my involvements with the Japanese people would naturally increase. And what I wanted to avoid was what I felt I had often observed in young Americans going to Japan—becoming enchanted with things Japanese to the point of rejecting what is not Japanese. As it turned out, I did avoid becoming so enchanted, and I avoided it by practically avoiding all Japanese people. I hid in the intellectual study of the language and kept postponing a deliberate effort to use Japanese because I couldn't hold my own in conversation with a native speaker. But why did I feel it was necessary to hold my own in a conversation? And what, in fact, did I mean by "holding my own"? I think self-image was an important part.

And so a language class is one arena in which a number of private universes intersect one another. Each person is at the center of his or her own universe of perceptions and values, and each is affected by what the others do If the denial of death requires submission to something eternal and universal, then the teacher needs to appear strong, and competent, and self-confident. The textbook, in our culture at least, ought then to be the latest thing because the latest has had an opportunity to profit from the experience and the errors of all the others, so that it is presumably closest to the right method (immortal). If approval from one's parent-figures is an important reassurance, then it becomes urgent to please the teacher, and to have frequent tests, and to do well on those tests. On the other hand, it would be intolerable to find that our teacher, no matter how strong, self-confident, and apparently competent, used a style of teaching that contradicted the values that we had picked up from our parents or from earlier teachers.

> Graduate training in special education and three years' experience of teaching in a public high school that emphasized the need for a warm, humanistic learning climate caused me to become strongly committed to giving students plenty of latitude within which to develop their own inner resources. I carried these ideas with me to Taiwan, where I spent a semester teaching freshman and sophomore English at a university noted for the high calibre of its students. Emphasis was on developing the students' speaking ability. Yet despite my efforts to create the desired climate, the students remained inhibited and fearful for the entire semester. The key seems to have been the overwhelming difference between the two educational systems, for my students were products of a tradition that I did not understand—one in which the learner craves a paternal, assertive teacher. Though the students seemed to appreciate my "warmth, acceptance, and understanding," their needs were not being met.

If the denial of death draws support from those around us, then we will resist whatever there is in the course that asks us to violate the norms that we share with our peers. So we may resist the language itself, just for its foreignness, in the same way we resisted the native language teacher who tried to get us to say "he doesn't" when all our friends said "he don't." Further, a particular language may carry with it an undesirable stereotype of its speakers, as snobbish, lazy, dishonest, and so on. To become faithful to this foreign way of speaking would feel like being unfaithful to the group that nourished and supports us. The only time my father-in-law ever rebuked me was when he heard me pronouncing French too much like a Frenchman.

The need for support from those around us may also prevent us from achieving all that we could, just because we don't want to be regarded as the one who puts our classmates in a bad light.

> My second semester was in a different school, with a different textbook, and I was soon put into what was called "the slow group." In time, we began to stick together. We found a sense of security and protection with each other. We also had a feeling of belonging. Even though we were "the dunce group," we were able to form a bond and find comfort in each other's French inadequacy.

> Somehow, during the semester a pathological condition seems to have developed within the class. In a competitive recitation with another class, these students laughed at each other's every mistake, and as a group, they fell far short of the other class. The atmosphere in this class was the opposite of the warm acceptance which enables a student to perform confidently from the depth of his personality. In this environment, students couldn't give it all

they had, but fulfilled their class' expectancy for a low level of performance. The laughter was a social mechanism for enforcing this expectancy.

There is a third aspect of our "world of meaningful action" which makes itself felt in our response to a language course. This aspect consists of the intermediate and long-range goals that we have set for ourselves: academic goals, vocational goals, and the like. We know that we have only a certain amount of time available to us. We therefore become impatient with something which is presented to us as a new, separate goal in its own right, which does not contribute toward the achieving of other goals. Psychologically, we may react to it the same way our body reacts to a splinter of wood that gets into our finger. This may help to account for the popularity of language courses that are especially designed for people with particular occupational needs: English for airline pilots, German for organic chemists, and the like.

Our "world of meaningful action," then, draws on the power figures in our life, and on our peer groups, and on the more or less tightly integrated set of goals that we have set for ourselves. Other things being equal, we will respond better to a language course that fits into that system, and less well to a course that does not. But it also may happen that some language courses, for some people, turn out to have been integrating elements around which a previously ill-organized set of values becomes clearer.

This is most likely to be true when the student's experience of the language is relatively deep. For a "world of meaningful action" is not a flat, two-dimensional thing like a map. Its structure has many dimensions, and some of its parts are much farther from the surface than others. If what a student says makes little or no difference to him, it has little "depth," in this sense. But some things that he says, or hears, or reads, make a difference to him in many ways. This kind of experience is relatively "deep." It draws more energy from his "world of meaningful action," and in turn it helps to shape that world.

> While I was working for a large English school in Japan, the basic text used in the lower intermediate classes consisted of short dialogs followed by a great number of substitution and transformation drills. Many of the instructors were dissatisfied with these materials. We felt there was no meaningful communication taking place in the classroom. A committee was formed and after eighteen months, we produced what we thought was a better program. We had developed a series of lifelike, situationally defined dialogs on topics of relevance for today's world, followed by exercises that we hoped would elicit language that had previously been focused on in the study of the dialogs. The emphasis was on meaningfulness and communication. We were satisfied with the new materials in all ways but one: the students' final test scores were no better, and their actual use of the language did not improve perceptibly.
>
> Looking back, I think the trouble was that we did not recognize that a great amount of "communicative" activity does not necessarily lead to "depth." The new, more meaningful materials that we developed were used in the classroom just like the older, less communicative ones. The teachers' focus was still primarily on the language, and so the method was virtually the same. The learning process was aimed at the shallower levels. . . .

> Several months ago, I decided to try to get my class of eight intermediate students involved in group debates. After explaining the mechanics of a debate, *I allowed them to*

choose their own topic and the side of the argument that they wished to take, the only restriction being that there should be four persons on each side. They had a full week to prepare their arguments for each topic. I was to serve as referee, but I refused their request that I choose the winning team.

The results were even better than I had expected. The first few minutes of the first debate, the students were reluctant to speak, and I had to choose the first ones. In a very short time, however, they got into the spirit of it, and it was hard to get them to talk just one at a time. The students seemed to get lost in the debate and in their strong feelings about the topic, and to forget that they were speaking other than their native language. *The heat of the debate seemed to unlock capabilities they weren't aware they had.* They seemed to learn more during the Friday debates than they had in the previous four days. [Emphasis added.]

But, as Siddharta found out, we crave more than a "world of meaningful action"; we also demand a feeling of primacy, or at least strength, within that world. Hence the need for attention from teacher and from fellow students. Hence also the desire to compete, not only in order to draw out our own full potential, but also, often, to have someone to look down on—someone who is closer to academic "death" than we are. On a more positive note, there is also the need for a steady series of short-term successes and long-term achievements. "Depth" in a language course contributes to this sense of "primacy," at the same time that it enhances the meaningfulness of the action.

In addition (and this is true for other academic courses, not just for foreign languages), there is the fact that new information is being imposed on us from outside ourselves. At best, this requires us to do the intellectual and emotional work of integrating the new into what we already had. Worse, it implies that what we already had was in some way inadequate. Worst of all, we find ourselves in the power of the person who is imposing the new information and evaluating our mastery of it. We find ourselves in the position of being ignorant, powerless, and constantly evaluated—a clear denial of our primacy! For any or all of these reasons, we may feel more or less of general resistance just to the idea of being taught. This is true even when the teacher is tactful and kind, but with other kinds of teachers, it can become traumatic.

Eventually, the incessant corrections [were] perceived as an adverse attitude on the part of the all-powerful "mother." [I felt] fear of an unexpressed [homicidal impulse on the part of the teacher], pain, anxiety, depression, and desire to withdraw. . . . In the class of one pleasant female teacher, [I] experienced her implacable and incessant corrections so adversely that [I] was unable to converse with her, or even approach her either in or out of the classroom.

Foreignness, shallowness, irrelevance, and the subordinate position of the student—all may be obstacles to a learner's feeling of "primacy in a world of meaningful action." All of these originate outside of the learner. But there is another obstacle which originates inside the learner, and which may be even more troublesome than any of the external ones. This is the "divided self," which has been commented on by many writers over the years. Curran mentions it, Gallwey builds his "inner game of tennis" around this concept, and even St. Paul complained that, "I do not do the good I want, but the evil I do not want is what I do." The first of these selves is the Critical Self. This self tends to be calculating and verbal, and to impose its expectations on the second, the Performing Self. When the Performing Self fails to perform as the Critical Self thinks it ought, the Critical Self typically puts further pressure on it, or punishes it in some way: "I [Critical Self] don't know what's the matter with me [Performing Self] today." "I [Critical Self] keep telling myself [Performing Self] to try harder." Or the heel of the dominant hand comes up and smites the Body on the forehead. The trouble is that this kind of interaction between the selves usually produces additional anxiety, greater tension, and poorer performance.

One may guess that the expectations which the Critical Self lays on the Performing Self were acquired originally from parents and from early teachers, and so represent an attempt to identify with the powerful and the apparently eternal figures in the learner's early life. But these standards—or at least, this way of using these standards—are counterproductive for a situation that demands learning and performing. (This is especially true for speaking, where performance has to be rapid and spontaneous.) So the learner is put into a self-defeating bind.

Up to this point, I have listed a wide range of feelings which may have their origin in the struggle against death, and I have tried to suggest how those feelings may make themselves visible in a language classroom. It goes without saying that individual students differ among themselves in the relative strength of these feelings, and in the configurations which the feelings assume within each personality. I do believe, however, that this view of the language student is more comprehensive *and more down-to-earth practical* than a view which sees him only as a combination of language aptitude, learning style, vocational goals, and so on. The picture that I am proposing is one into which these others can be fitted, however, and I think it is particularly helpful in exploring what goes on inside and between the people in the classroom.

Clearly, this view accounts for/predicts a great deal of conflict, between student and teacher, between student and student, and also within the student himself. It also accounts for/predicts a great deal of aloneness—of alienation between student and teacher, between student and student, and even within the student himself. In general, the student cannot live up to the conflicting demands which he places on himself, and which he allows others to place upon him: "I want to achieve, but I mustn't offend my classmates"; "I shouldn't dislike the teacher, but she constantly leaves me feeling stupid"; and so on. To the extent that the student cannot meet demands which he recognizes as valid, his feelings of conflict and aloneness are capped by feelings of guilt.

So, instead of a student who is learning as a whole person, with body, mind, and emotions in harmony with one another, we have arrived at a quite different picture. We have a human being who started out to stave off death, but who winds up more or less conflicted, more or less alone, and more or less guilty—surely a sickness unto death! In defending himself from these feelings, the student may try to get away from what seems to be causing them: by dropping the course if he can, or by letting his mind wander, or by doing as little work as he dares. When he reacts in these ways, he only makes matters worse: his performance falls off, guilt and/or aloneness increase, and conflict between performance and expectation may become so unbearable that he lowers his expectation of himself.

> In a loud voice, we had to call out our failing grades for everyone to hear. We eventually became defensive against this humiliation by taking it as a joke and laughing it off.

> Having had a number of unsuccessful (or at least unsatisfying) encounters with language learning, I determined to take an introductory course in German. It was a "good" conventional class, replete with irrelevant textbook dialogs and irrelevant workbook exercises and irrelevant classroom drills. As the teacher went around the room, calling on student after student to recite, I would be in near panic by the time she got to me. Because of my status outside of the class, I *had* to perform well. And of course there were those inevitable "language whizzes" in the class to compare myself with. Well, whether I had programmed myself for it in advance I can't say, but the upshot was that I dropped out after a while—"too busy to continue just now"—and added another language learning failure to my record.

Or the student may react, not by withdrawing from the source of discomfort, but by striking out at it. He may come to hate all speakers of the language, or he may become very critical of the course and everything associated with it, or he may engage in disruptive behavior in the classroom, or he may mutilate books and equipment. Here again, of course, the result is poorer performance, increased conflict, and deepened alienation—a self-defeating reaction.

> One of my classmates seemed to take perverse delight in asking the teacher questions which she might not be able to answer about the grammar. Whenever he did this, the work of the class ground to a halt. I sometimes thought I saw a self-satisfied gleam in his eye.

> For the inexperienced teacher, it is sometimes appealingly tempting and secure to adopt an authoritarian approach, particularly with docile students. On the basis of my experience as a student of Korean, however, I can say that while the obedient learner may seem to thrive in such an environment, the less tractable individual is likely to become disruptive, at least socially or psychologically. Thus, there were frequent complaints concerning the nature of the drills, particularly those on tape. These complaints arose even though we were free to draw on whatever resources were available, and to make creative use of them. In addition, coffee breaks became protracted.

A third reaction is that of the good student, who tries harder, gets the right answers more of the time, pleases the teacher, and learns something. Depending on the particular pattern of feelings that the student started out with, this kind of reaction may in fact go far toward reducing the conflict and/or alienation and/or guilt that we have been talking about. But there are two things to remember about this kind of reaction. First, it is possible only for students who already possess a fair amount of internal strength and harmony, as well as native aptitude for languages. Second, the "learning" that results is likely to be of a piecemeal, intellectual variety that disappears soon after the examination is over. It may leave behind it a large amount of discomfort in the presence of the language, and even distaste for it.

> All through my schooling, I have had a tendency to be a teacher-worshipper, doing my best to please my instructors. Ethnic reasons excluded me from social acceptance among my peers at an early age, and for this reason my need and desire to be accepted by my teachers was doubly strong. I excelled scholastically and received praise from my teachers in course after course. I graduated with many high honors. Yet an overwhelming feeling of inadequacy as a student has bothered me for years—and still does.

> A couple of years ago, I was teaching English to engineers in the Persian Gulf. Most of the men had had English in high school, and used English grammar with some pleasant competence. But here, their careers were at least half conducted in colloquial English, at which they had no skill. Being inexperienced and eager to please, I taught to their strengths in grammar. Some of the students did ingeniously at transformation exercises. They soon became my star performers. But conversation in class remained stilted and hesitant.
> Outside of class, I saw a different social system forming among the engineers, and a happier one, in which one of my poorest, most reluctant students figured strongly. I did not know then that his spoken English was effective and rich, but delivered in a grammar so barely serviceable that after the first few days he had been shamed into barely opening his mouth in class. Eventually I found that I should talk less in class, look less keenly for learners' errors, and wonder a little at what my students really were. And this hitherto poor student began speaking. Impeded less and less by corrections, he brought out his conversational genius, and imparted a real spark to the class. He finally learnt considerable grammar, more from his classmates than from me.

When I was growing up, we sometimes played with box turtles. These little animals, five or six inches long as I remember them, could make amazingly good time as they moved along on their stubby legs, head fully extended from the shell. What we liked to do, of course, was to find one of them earnestly marching along somewhere, and touch it ever so lightly on the back. It would immediately retract its head *and* its legs into its shell, and remain motionless. Then we would pick it up and set it down again wherever we liked. (I have sometimes wondered whether, after it had recovered from its alarm and set out again, it headed for its original destination, or whether it had lost its bearings and had to devise an entirely new trip.)

I think we often see something like that happening in language classes. The engineer, for one, seems to have behaved in that way. Any student can arrive at a correct response in either of two ways: by using his own power, or by complying with the teacher's skillful lesson plan. If he does what he does on his own, and in conformity with his own timing and his own purposes, then he knows where he is, and why, and how he got there. If he merely lets himself be carried along by the lesson plan, then what he does will not be truly a part of him, and it may be lost all too quickly.

The analogy breaks down, of course. In a language class, it is possible for the student to travel by both means at the same time: some lesson plans provide opportunities for students to propel themselves along within the overall guidance of the teacher. What is unfortunate is that many lesson plans are based on the belief that we should get the turtle to the destination we have chosen for him as expeditiously as possible, even if we have to take him off his feet. Equally unfortunate, though less common, is the opposite extreme: "humanistic" techniques that place a premium on student initiative and student contributions sometimes fall flat. When this happens, it usually means that the turtle is being asked to come out of his shell in an environment which, for some reason, he finds alarming. Yet success in getting a new language, and especially in "acquiring" it (Chapter 21), requires the turtle's head and legs to be as far out of its shell as possible. For any method, but especially for the "humanistic" ones, there needs to be harmony between the two "selves" of each student, and a minimum of irrelevant tension among the people in the classroom.

The following account is typical of a dozen that I have heard from people who are language students and/or tennis players. It illustrates the effect of the relationship between the Critical Self and the Performing Self:

> I have been playing tennis for about four years. When I rallied with my friends, my hits were smooth, swift, and natural. But when I played a game, I usually tightened up. The goal of winning posed a threat to me, and games really "psyched me out." After reading *The Inner Game of Tennis*, I decided to put into practice the idea of "letting it happen." I relaxed and let my whole being flow. I did not concentrate hard or think of the many things that I should or should not do . . . and it really worked! My shots were smooth and well-placed. Nothing could have gone better! I have never played so well. I had a great feeling of inner satisfaction.

The turtle may retreat into its shell outside of the classroom also. The following is by a Japanese-American.

> In the past, I have usually been successful at whatever I set out to do. Although I welcome challenges, I tend to avoid situations which make me feel incompetent or inferior. In my many opportunities to interact with Japanese people, I have always been amazed at how my fluency in Japanese is affected by the other person's proficiency in English. I know two Japanese who can speak English fluently without any trace of an accent. I have generally used English in speaking with them. On several occasions when I did attempt to use Japanese, I found myself feeling uncomfortable and awkward, groping for words that I would ordinarily have been able to produce very easily. On the other hand, when talking with those who can speak little or no English, I am able to speak Japanese with great ease and fluency. I often surprise myself by coming out with words which I never realized I had in my vocabulary.

In this chapter, we have looked briefly at some of the anxieties that keep the Learning-Turtle's head back in its shell so much of the time—the attachments that preoccupy the prudent Critical Self and interfere with the potential of the Performing Self. They may contribute to a downward spiral, in which learning is severely reduced.

> I recall my first experience at learning a foreign language. I was in a private school for boys. The teacher faced his class of seventh-graders with an oversized paddle propped against his desk. He called it his "whacker," and he said he would use it on each of us sooner or later. The Latin declensions, conjugations, eventually whole passages, were assigned, memorized, recited on command. An incorrect answer brought the humiliation of at least the

teacher's scowl; enough correct answers brought only a good grade. However, no one doubted the teacher's skill at Latin, or his ability to get students to [absorb] vocabulary and structures.

Well, midway through the ninth grade, my family moved to another continent and at last I left that teacher's classroom forever. Today I remember him down to the necktie he wore on the first day of class. But when after a month or so in my new home I looked again at my Latin books, I discovered (to my residual terror) that my Latin had washed off me entirely.

What we hope, of course, is that language study will become an upward spiral, and not a downward one—an affirmation of life and not just a relatively successful "denial of death." Who, then, is to break, or to reverse, the spiral? Clearly, the student himself must assume some of the responsibility. Parents, friends, and academic counselors of various kinds may also be of some help. In the following chapter, however, we shall look at the role of the teacher. We shall do so for two reasons: First, this is a book for teachers, and the teacher is the only person over whom the teacher has direct control. Second, the teacher is the central and the most powerful figure in the classroom.

CHAPTER 2

ONE VIEW OF TEACHING

Teaching is part of life, or part of death; and learning is being born, or being stifled. It is gasping gladly for that next first breath, or being told, "Always breathe in, and never out."

Teaching and learning are two men sawing down a tree. One pulls, and then the other. Neither pushes, and neither could work alone, but cutting comes only when the blade is moving toward the learner.

At least that's how it should be. If the teacher pulls while the learner is still pulling, they work against each other and waste their strength. If, in her zeal to help the learner, the teacher pushes, then the blade will buckle, rhythm will be broken, both will become disheartened. . .

In Chapter 1, we looked at the classroom experience primarily from the point of view of the learner. It is in fact again becoming stylish to talk about "learner-centered" instruction. Jakobovits and Gordon have correctly pointed out that, while we know that "learning" takes place, and that people can do it, we are much less sure about "teaching." There can, after all, be "learning" without "teaching," but one cannot claim to have "taught" unless someone else has learned. This is what has tempted us to play down the importance of teaching.

There is an old story about a preacher in a revival meeting held in a big tent on the edge of town. When time came to pass the collection plate, a man in the congregation stood up and shouted, "Hey, Brother! I thought you said salvation is as free as the rain that falls from the heavens! Then why are you asking us for money?" To which the preacher shot back, "Yes, Brother, salvation *is* as free as the rain that falls from the heavens! But you have to pay to have it piped to you!"

Quite possibly our students, even our adult students, could learn languages without us if they were placed, under the right conditions, in the right cultural and linguistic environment. But with the world the way it is, these conditions and this environment are extremely rare. We may continue to affirm that the learner is in some ways "central" to what we do. But we should at the same time remember that there are other functions for which our society, and our students themselves, demand that we the teachers stand steadfast at the center of language education. I can think of at least five such functions:

1. Most obvious is the cognitive function: It is we teachers who possess the information which our students are seeking about the foreign culture and about its language. To say the same thing more bluntly, we have what caused them to come—or to be sent—to the course in the first place.

2. Almost as obvious is the classroom management function: Our students, and the society in which both we and they work, expect us to take responsibility for how they use their time while they are with us. In placing

this expectation on us, they rely on our training and experience with materials, schedules, and techniques.

3. A third function has to do with practical goals. Our students, and society, have certain overall goals for language courses. Sometimes these goals are listed very explicitly, and sometimes they are only half-conscious. We are supposed to take these long-range goals and translate them into goals that are weekly, daily, hourly.

4. The fourth function is personal, or interpersonal. Because of our near-monopoly of information, procedures, and day-to-day goals, and because of the great power which society invests in the giver of the final grade, the teacher is by far the most powerful figure in the classroom. Therefore (s)he, more than anyone else, sets the tone for the *interpersonal atmosphere*. That atmosphere, in turn, may mean that the students' nonlinguistic, emotional needs are met, or are denied, while they are in the language classroom.

5. Related to this fourth function, but centered still more closely on the person of the teacher, the teacher may radiate *enthusiasm for the task* at hand, and conviction of its value, or (s)he may not. I am talking here not so much about what the teacher says explicitly as about what the student infers from her/his manner. This is more subtle than the other four ways in which the teacher is "central" to the course, yet it is perhaps the most indispensable of the five.

These, then, are five respects in which the teacher may rightfully demand, and must rightly accept, the center of the stage in language instruction. The question now becomes, how can we reconcile the centrality of the teacher with the centrality of the learner? Do these two ideas not conflict? I think that we have in fact often assumed implicitly, if not explicitly, that such a conflict does exist. We have sometimes talked and written as though an increase in the learner's initiative necessarily requires some reduction in the degree of control that the teacher exercises, and vice versa. We have therefore concluded that all we can do is try for an appropriate balance, or trade-off, between control by the teacher and initiative by the student. In recent years, however, I have come to believe that this is not so. I believe that there is a way to define "control" and "initiative," not widely inconsistent with everyday usage, which will allow the teacher to keep nearly 100 percent of the "control" while at the same time the learner is exercising nearly 100 percent of the "initiative." This distinction has proved to be one of the more useful ideas that I have run across.

Some kind of "control" is necessary for the success of any human undertaking. As far as I can see, "control" *by the teacher* is legitimate even in "progressive," or in "humanistic" education. As I am using the term, "control" consists of only two essential elements. The first element is the structuring of classroom activity: What are we supposed to be doing? When is it time to stop what we are doing and start something else? In tennis, the teaching professional provides the court, explains the rules, provides suitable models, and sets appropriate goals. This part of the "control" function is tied in with the first three of the ways in which we have said that the teacher is "central" to a language class.

The other essential element of "control" consists in making it easy for the learner to know how what he has done or said compares with what a native would have done or said. In tennis, even the novice can generally see for himself whether or not the ball hit inside the line. In a foreign language, the new learner is not immediately equipped to know these things for himself. The second half of "control" is most commonly exercised through what we call "correction of errors," though the customary kind of correction is usually unnecessary and frequently undesirable. We will talk about some alternatives in Chapters 4, 11, 19 and elsewhere.

Seen in this way, "control" is clearly a teacher function, at least in the early part of any course. It is the teacher's necessary contribution toward making this new and bewildering corner of the student's "world of meaningful action" into a stable, well-lighted place in which to work (or play!). As time goes on, students may become able to assume some of the responsibility for the first (the "structuring," or "steering") aspect of control. Certain of my colleagues have been quite successful doing this in their classes, using a daily "chairmanship" that rotates among the students, and this can be very productive. But I would repeat that students need to feel that this sharing of "control" is voluntary on the part of the teacher, and fits within her overall plan. (They also need to accept it.) Otherwise, they will begin to feel that this corner of their world is not so stable after all. Furthermore, control in the hands of students must not be allowed to lead to much loss in the smoothness or effectiveness of the activity. If it does, it will damage the students' feeling of adequacy within that world.

I once witnessed a dramatic example of masterly delegation of this first element of control within the overall guidance of the responsible authority. In the summer of 1976, I was with a group of language teachers who were returning to Washington from Victoria, British Columbia, on the Washington State Ferry. It was night, and foggy, as the huge boat twisted its way among the hundreds of small islands in Juan de Fuca Strait. Some of us commented that under these conditions, we were glad the captain and all his navigational aids were hard at work on our behalf. A minute or two later, one of the men in the group was paged, and asked to come to the bridge. When he arrived there, he found that the person at the wheel was his own five-year-old son. The captain was standing several feet away, giving directions orally.

I don't know how far the boat was from the nearest island while all this was going on. I do know that, if I had been the captain, it would not have occurred to me to invite a small child to carry that responsibility under those conditions. In any event, this incident shows what can be done by someone who has an exquisitely detailed knowledge of the external medium (whether geography or language), and of the learner's skills and readiness.

Some teachers are in a great hurry to share the structuring responsibility with their students. They may do so because they take some kind of delight in seeing what they have enabled their students to do in this area (and/or in having their students and their colleagues see it). I myself tend to be this kind of teacher. Or they may rush to transfer the "structuring" aspect of control because someone has persuaded them that Being Nondirective is a Good Thing to Do. Whatever the reason, it is dangerous to turn this responsibility over to the students prematurely.

We said above that the second half of "control" in this sense consists of making sure that the student is not in the dark concerning his use of the target language: "Where is what I have said (or written, or understood) consistent with what a native would have said (or written, or understood) under the same circumstances, and where is it inconsistent?" This half of control is also a teacher function, at least in the beginning. It rests, of course, on the cognitive centrality of the teacher. It is the light, or the radar, by which the student begins to make out shapes of unfamiliar objects that lie in his path. When the light is dim, or intermittent, the student understandably becomes anxious, frustrated, and eventually hostile. If, on the other hand, this light glares too harshly, the student may be blinded by it, and flutter helplessly to the ground. We have seen in Chapter 1 a firsthand account of how that can happen.

The second half of "control," like the first, can be shared. In fact, looked at from one point of view, a primary purpose of any language course is to make the student independent of the teacher in knowing what can be said and what cannot. When this happens, the student may rightfully feel that he has become an adequate center in the universe of the new language, and can therefore accept the language itself as a part of his own personal universe. On the other hand, if this half of control is never adequately shared, the student is likely to wander through the big world outside the classroom permanently dependent on teachers and people whom he can treat as teachers—a perpetual alien in someone else's "world of meaningful action." But in the beginning, the second component of "control," like the first, is necessarily in the hands of the teacher.

"Initiative," as I am using the word here, refers to decisions about who says what, to whom, and when. These decisions consist of choices among a narrow or a very broad range of possibilities which are provided by whoever is exercising "control." Seen in this way, "initiative" and "control" are not merely two directions along a single dimension. That is to say, "control" on the part of the teacher does not interfere with "initiative" on the part of the student: when the teacher tightens her "control" of what is going on, she need not cut into the student's "initiative"; often, in fact, she will actually increase it. Similarly, insufficient "control" by the teacher may reduce or paralyze the "initiative" of the student.

The box turtle, which we mentioned near the end of Chapter 1, may help to show why this is so. When the student displays "initiative" in this sense, he is beginning to play an active, central, self-validating role in a "world of meaningful action." But if the "world of meaningful action" which the teacher has provided is unclear, or half-formed, then the turtle will keep its head in the shell; that is, the learner will stick to simple choices and safe alternatives.

Exercising clear and firm "control" is not the only way in which the teacher can help the learner to take strong and satisfying "initiatives," however. Earlier in this chapter, we said that the teacher is "central" for setting the interpersonal atmosphere in the class, and for conveying enthusiasm and conviction. These influence the turtle, and its readiness to venture from behind its defense system, even more than clear structuring can. And clear structuring in an uncongenial atmosphere will produce only limited "initiative."

> Using a set of sequentially arranged pictures, I was eliciting a story about them from the class. The students were expected to limit themselves to English that they could fully control. In this, I was following the theory that incorrect usages would establish themselves as habits. The story was well rehearsed orally, and then used as a dictation exercise. One student, however, flatly refused to follow this procedure. He would have nothing to do with the rather ho-hum little narrative that the rest of us were laboring over. I sensed that if I insisted that he participate, it would lead to class disruption far out of proportion to "John and Mary's Beach Picnic." So I suggested that he create his own story. The effect was amazing. His attitude shifted from withdrawal to intense involvement, which resulted in an imaginative, spicy version of the story that amused all of us.

This incident illustrates dramatically the different degrees and qualities of "initiative" which may be available from any one student at any given time. At the same time, it also illustrates how a change in the teacher's exercise of "control" can restrict or release a student's "initiative." The writer concludes his narrative by saying, "The experience was helpful to me as a teacher, though it was unnerving to be so directly challenged. I began encouraging this type of productivity and found the results beneficial to class community, and [therefore? EWS] to individual students' acquisition of English."

In exercising "control," then, the teacher is giving some kind of order, or structure, to the learning space of the student. In encouraging him to take "initiative," she is allowing him to work, and to grow, within that space. The trick, for the teacher, is not only to preserve this distinction; it is also to provide just the right *amount* of learning space. If there is too little, the student will be stifled. If there is too much, the student will feel that the teacher has abandoned him. Consider the spark plug which releases the power of the fuel in an engine: if the contacts are touching one another, there is a short circuit, and hence no spark; but if the contacts are too far apart, the spark again cannot jump.

What so often happens, of course, is that the teacher, in the name of "exercising control," also monopolizes initiative, telling the student which line of the drill to produce, which question to ask (or how to answer it), whom to talk with, and so on. The student knows that he has perhaps 3 to 5 seconds in which to respond, before the teacher reasserts initiative by repeating the question, giving a hint, prompting, or calling on someone else. To avoid this requires skill, and balance, and maturity on the part of the teacher. It requires the teacher to become aware of, and to control, her/his own personal needs.

Earlier in this chapter, we said that the teacher is "central" with regard to the cognitive content, the structuring of time, the articulation of goals, the setting of climate, and the final human validation of the whole undertaking. But the teacher's own urge to become "an object of primacy in a world of meaningful action" can lead her to carry any of these five legitimate functions to undesirable excess. Cognitive primacy may become an assertion of infallibility; the responsibility for structuring time may lead to a demand for omnipotence, and also to excessive defining of goals. Together, they are the principal ingredients of the evaluative manner that is so effective in stifling the initiative of students.

> I remember I was always reluctant to go to English class, in which the teacher was always asking us, hour after hour, to "repeat after me." One time while she was doing pronunciation practice, she had us repeat the word "pupil," first in chorus, then in rows, then individually. When I was called on, I repeated the sound I thought I heard, but she kept telling me to repeat, without giving me any explanation. Some of my classmates began to giggle, and I couldn't bring myself to look at them. Finally, I learned the sound that had been wrong, but after that embarrassing moment I was afraid to pronounce English in class. . . .
>
> Timid as I was in the English class, I felt quite at home with my Sunday School teacher, and could talk with her freely. In contrast with the regular school, Sunday School was free from the teacher's evaluation of the students.

The teacher's responsibility for keeping track of goals may similarly turn into an urgent need to see results, and therefore to a preempting of initiative.

> One day I had an opportunity to observe a teacher in an adult Basic English class of six people. I believe that this teacher entered the class with a set image of herself to be presented to the students: she was the teacher whose goal was to teach the completing of the simplest income tax form. As she began explaining how to fill in the different blanks on the form, it was apparent that the students were not understanding much. It seemed that her teacher-image was being threatened; so, sensing this, she set about to defend herself from this threat. For one thing, she did more talking and the talk became louder, perhaps with the notion that in this way the material would sink into the students' heads. Second, the teacher (in rapid English) told the students to write down what she said in the appropriate blanks without the students' really knowing why. Finally, after the students filled in the blanks with figures they did not understand, the teacher praised them with the classic "very good."

The teacher's concern to set a certain climate within the classroom may lead her to be uncomfortable and defensive when that particular climate is disrupted for any reason. And her commitment to the language and the course, which is so essential to the appearance of final validity for the course, can lead to great loneliness if the class does not respond in the desired way. There is also a potential for loneliness in the very act of committing oneself to transmitting a *foreign* culture and its language.

> I gave up teaching English composition [to natives], and began teaching literature. This was a little more satisfying, for I love it. But I am not very articulate, and my attempt to conduct lecture-style classes was a personal disaster. I felt very keenly the loneliness and vulnerability of the teacher. My tendency was to present the material as a given. When it was not accepted with gratitude, I felt rejected.

So the language classroom can be a place of alienation for student and teacher alike. Ernest Becker (1968, 1973, 1975) says that what any person needs is, first, an overall view of how everything fits together and, second, possibilities of action within that view. He defines "alienation" as the absence of that combination, and says that "the human self-contradiction is not a medical or a narrowly biological problem, but is always and at heart a social problem—a problem of what society will allow people *to know* and *to do*" [emphasis in original]. Becker, of course, was talking about human existence in general. Is it possible that within the confines of our profession, the two essentials that he is talking about are very close to what we have been calling "control" and "initiative"?

But, Becker says, no one human being can establish and maintain his own meaning, in a convincing manner, all by himself. And "the problem of conviction . . . is one of trying to get into contact with the full mystery and vitality of being." Quoting Martin Buber, he says that man can do this only in relation to another human self, even if the other self is just as limited and just as conditioned as he himself is. If we bring ourselves down, now, from the comprehensive viewpoint of these two philosophies, and into the relatively narrow back yard of the language teacher, we come again to the statement that what is really important is what goes on inside and between the people in the classroom.

What, then, can we as teachers contribute toward breaking the cycle of internal and external conflict, of alienation, of guilt, which accompanies so much of the academic experience that we call "language-learning"? Let's begin with three things which I think we should *not* do.

First of all, we must avoid letting the classroom become a power vacuum. I begin with this point because of widespread misunderstandings about some of the "humanistic" approaches that try to take into account the whole person of the learner. The silence of the Silent Way teacher does not mean that her hand is straying from the steering wheel. The patient, understanding, sometimes self-effacing teacher of Counseling-Learning does not "let the students do just whatever they want," in spite of the impression that many people carry away from their first experience with it. And the one most basic principle of Suggestopedia is the authority of the teacher. In the light of what we said earlier, we can see why this is so: A weak teacher would deprive the student of that stable arena for meaningful action that he so desperately craves. This is not to say that the teacher should never give the students freedom of choice in some areas. In fact, I think this should be done often—much more often than many teachers would imagine. But the student needs to feel that those choices, no matter how broad, are granted within the teacher's overall plan, by the teacher's own free will, and not out of weakness.

> In graduate school, I have met a few professors who promote equality while still providing strong guidance. By being treated as a colleague, I feel free to call upon their superior experience in ways which I never could have otherwise. But in all of my experience *before*

graduate school, I never saw a successful example of the "liberté, egalité, fraternité" model. Teachers who tried it were generally using it to cover up their inadequacies, or their disinterest in teaching.

Next, I think that we should not fill the power vacuum in the usual way. Most traditional classroom activity, in any culture that I know anything about, follows the Evaluational Paradigm, which consists of variations on a single formula. In this formula, the teacher says to the student—cynically or warmly, threateningly or reassuringly—"*Now try to do this so I can tell you how you did.*" Mistakes are pointed out—harshly or gently, immediately or after some delay—and the student's response to the task is evaluated. The student generally comes away feeling that he himself has been evaluated— negatively or positively—along with his product. We may be offering to the student a "world of meaningful action," but by our evaluation we deny his primacy in it. If our evaluation is negative, we also cast doubt on his adequacy within that world. At the time, our Critical Self calls his Critical Self into action, and together we harass his Performing Self.

Most teachers are willing to agree that negative evaluation may some- times be harmful to the student, but I have found few who are ready to see that *positive* evaluation is almost as dangerous a tool. It seems to be the evaluative *climate*, more than the content of the evaluation, that does the damage. Consider the following, an account by a middle-aged man:

> I learnt French in high school and in college. Outside the classroom I found numerous opportunities to use the language in valid social situations. The language flowed forth with a steadily increasing fluency. After a gap in usage from 1960 to 1975, I took an intensive advanced French course taught by a Frenchman, with success. Again the French flowed fluently forth and increased. Immediately following this intensive course, I returned to my home city, where a friend who was a native Parisian said, "Let's speak French now. I want to hear how well you do it." My heart did a highland fling, the cold sweat poured off me, goose pimples sprang out, breathing became hard, and the French section of my brain shut down with a bang. I could only answer (in English), "What do you want to test me for?" This friend and I have conversed quite satisfactorily on subsequent occasions, but not then.

I have had smaller-scale, but quite analogous experiences myself, with speakers of German. With one, we had just finished what I had thought was a reasonably fluent, *and mutually interesting,* conversation, when she said, "Oh, I like talking with you. You use such correct grammar [compared with most foreigners]." I avoided all further opportunities to speak German with this person, because just the memory of this remark would create an evalua- tive climate for me. Yet before, and after, with other speakers, I have thoroughly enjoyed using the same language.

> Languages which I have enjoyed studying are, of course, more available to me than those that were not enjoyable. Nevertheless, my ability to use even the former depends signifi- cantly on the cues received from native speakers. . . . In a situation where some specific communication is the goal, I used Japanese fairly fluently, but in big cities, the reaction to a sentence from me in Japanese was often, "Oh, do you speak Japanese?" followed by a

rather awkward exchange in English or Japanese. In a communicative situation, I am seldom at a loss for words, but if someone urges me, "Say something in Japanese," I tend to stick to formulas. Similarly, "I hear that you speak Japanese very well" is less satisfactory in eliciting a Japanese response than any non-evaluative conversational utterance in that language would be.

Gallwey, the tennis coach, tells us that if your opponent's forehand is giving you trouble, you may find it to your advantage to compliment him/her on it, saying, "Wow! Your forehand is really hot today! What are you doing?" This frequently has the effect, says Gallwey, of activating the other person's Critical Self, which immediately sets about interfering with his Performing Self.

I used the first draft of this chapter as the basis for lectures to a large class at the University of Hawaii. One of the requirements of the course was the writing of a pair of short papers. When the first few came in, I was so delighted with them that, thinking to encourage the class as a whole, I mentioned my pleasure at the next sessiosn. Although reaction to my announcement was mixed, it was overwhelmingly negative. Besides setting up an evaluative atmosphere, the students told me, I had given the rest of them the idea that they had a tough standard to *compete against.* Even those whose papers had been read and declared excellent felt that my public statement put them under extra pressure to *continue to perform.* What I had said left everyone feeling that I was *laying my own expectations on them.* Nothing that I was able to say had much effect in reducing their uneasiness.

This experience fits in with numerous other occasions on which I have tried to praise individual students, in as uncondescending a way as I knew how, only to have their performance drop off. I am not saying that one should never praise students, just as I would not say that a surgeon should never use a scalpel. But praise is two-edged, and very sharp, with more potential for damage than many teachers realize. Perhaps the beneficial elements in praise are the information it carries (comparable to a tennis player's seeing that the ball hit inside the line), and the feeling that one has given pleasure to another human being (the teacher). The negative elements are self-consciousness, and the expectation that the pleasure-giving performance ought to continue. The trick is to convey the positive without the negative, but this is a very subtle matter.

Finally, I am doubtful about the wisdom of trying to enclose the student in too much linguistic security. A few systems of instruction seem to have aimed at keeping the student's activity as risk-free, and his language as error-free, as possible throughout the length of the course. Some early programmed courses appeared to pursue this dream. This has generally proved to be too enormous a task even for the best-financed materials writers. Even if it were not so large an undertaking, however, full-time wall-to-wall insurance against error would run contrary to what I have been talking about, because it fails to call forth the student's full powers, and constricts the world within which he is permitted to take "meaningful action." It also gives "primacy" to the materials rather than to the student.

This is not to say that people do not "learn" under the traditional evaluative system, or by the super-secure methods that have been devised in recent years. I do question, however, whether much "acquisition" takes place (Chapter 21). I'm not even sure that most people "learn" as fast that way. Both styles of teaching provide the student's Critical Self with plenty of ammunition for keeping his Performing Self under a steady barrage of criticism. At the same time, they provide external Critical Selves to complete whatever the student's own Critical Self may have left undone.

On the positive side, I can see at least seven ways in which a teacher may work consistent with what we have been talking about. I will list them in order of increasing demands which they make on the teacher. This is *not* a chronological sequence of steps to be followed!

At the base of all else, the teacher may look closely, and steadily, at her/his own students in the light of what we outlined in Chapter 1. I am not saying that we are are to psychoanalyze our students or even that we can hope to gain a detailed knowledge of what each one is up against inside and outside of class. That would clearly be out of the question. But I do believe that we can be alert to this information as it becomes available. I also believe that we can try to tie it in with some relatively comprehensive and relatively deep framework like that of Chapter 1: what attitudes do the students have toward speakers of the target language, or toward language study, or toward study in general? How are they reacting to the course as it progresses? What general, and what specific, pressures do these students feel from their parents or from their employers, from us, from one another, and from themselves? Some of the answers to these questions will relate to individual students, while others will apply to whole groups.

Anyone who has ever seen an infrared photograph can understand what I mean here. The same terrain, photographed at the same time and from the same spot, looks quite different in infrared and in conventional color. It remains in some sense the same, yet features which are inconspicuous or invisible in the one become the most striking features of the other.

I would further urge that for the teacher to let her/his mind work in this way is not incompatible with any method, and that in itself it is not time-consuming. This first step, then, may be the only step that is open to all teachers.

This is not to say, however, that the first step is one that all teachers have taken. There may even be some who cannot take this step. A teacher may be so wrapped up in the academic substance of the course that she is oblivious to the other factors with which the student is dealing.

I am a teacher. I used to teach freshman composition and literature, but now I teach ESL. I stopped teaching composition because nothing in my B.A. or M.A. English programs had prepared me to cope with departmental regulations like 3 comma splices equals C or 3 comma splices plus 2 run-on sentences equals F. I didn't dispute the wisdom of such regulations. I didn't have the linguistic training which would have given me the confidence to reject prescriptive grammar, nor did I have the individual strength to encounter head-on my students' experiences or thinking. It was easier to add up comma splices, especially when the power of the whole English Department was behind me.

(This sounds very much like some of the teachers that my own children have had.)

Another way of failing to take that first step is the opposite of the first. The teacher may be aware of some of these nonacademic aspects of a student's experience, but use them as occasions to feel sorry for him, or to excuse him from meeting the subject matter of the course. Or, finally, the teacher may see what is bothering the student, but shrug it off as something which the student should resolutely put out of the way so that it will not interfere with his classroom responsibilities. In the second and third of these possibilities, the teacher's reaction is one of helplessness in the face of what (s)he sees—a helplessness that leads either to destructive sympathy or to destructive callousness. These second and third possibilities are perhaps more pernicious than simple blindness to what the student is going through.

It is for this reason that we need to do more than just notice some of the forces that are at work in or on the student. We need also to relate our observations to some general framework comparable to the one that was sketched in Chapter 1. When we are able to do so, they cease to be capricious, random bits of interference, and become parts of a comprehensible reality with which we are dealing. Walking through a darkened room, we stumble against the furniture. When the light is turned on, the furniture is still there, but our seeing it makes crossing the room easier, not harder.

A second step is also open to most of us. We can look at our lesson plans, and at our actual classroom activities, in terms of the "control" that we (or the students) are providing, and the "initiative" that the students (or we) are exercising. This distinction cuts across the distinctions among Hearing, Speaking, Reading, and Writing, or among Beginning, Intermediate, and Advanced, or among Mechanical, Meaningful, and Communicative—all of which are useful distinctions in their own right.

A third step is also generally available: The "control" provided by the teacher may lead the students to exercise their "initiatives" in ways that involve cooperation and mutual interdependence. This, in turn, improves the likelihood that a feeling of community will arise within the class. The "world of meaningful action" is thereby enriched. It no longer consists merely of me the student plus the more or less remote foreign culture, plus a teacher who is my social and linguistic superior. The things that we do in class, and the things that we talk about, begin to draw their reality more widely and more deeply from the here and now. Becker, speaking in the most general terms, observed that "man must seek the maximum of uplift in his relationships to another *concrete* organism." The language class, transient and limited though it may be, is no exception.

> My worst experience in teaching EFL was the year in which I taught first-year junior high school boys for five hours a week. At that time, I believed firmly that (1) language must be modelled and controlled by the teacher in order to avoid errors, and that (2) extensive oral practice was necessary to "set the language" into the students' heads. As the year wore on, I realized that my students were participating less and less in the artfully paced mix of oral drill activities that I had prepared for them. When I would say, "Turn to Chart 5," there would be little whines of "Mata ka?" ("Again??") I became very indignant at this lack of response and interest, especially since I felt that I had rescued these little ingrates through my modern techniques. Against this general background of frustration, I can remember one day on which things went well. I had given the students an assignment to work in twos and threes and write sentences about a picture in their book. That day, I walked around the classroom responding to questions, happily amazed at the transformation of my noisy, nonresponsive students into involved little workers.

At the same time, if I am the student, my place within the corner of my universe that is the classroom becomes more secure. The other centers (i.e., my fellow students) whose universes also include this classroom no longer appear primarily as competing for status, or for the teacher's attention. They now become welcome, even supportive, parts of this universe at the center of which I still sit. And when I am able to be helpful to my fellow students, I gain feelings of satisfaction and of status which can themselves become powerful sources of reward and motivation.

A subtle fourth step is possible for many teachers. That is to give off what in recent years we have come to call "good vibes." These are indications of confidence in oneself and in the student, of acceptance of the student, and of pleasure in the encounter. But they are not overt statements of confidence, or pleasure, or approval. Such explicit messages have their place, of course, but they are not parts of what I mean by "vibes." They are expressed in ways of which the student is not consciously aware, or of which he is only dimly aware. They take the form of facial expressions, body postures, tones of voice, and inferences which the student may draw for himself from what the teacher says and how she says it. These messages are all the more credible, and therefore more effective, because the student does not perceive them as being consciously directed at him by the teacher. In fact, an overt statement of "confidence" by the teacher may lead the student to infer, unconsciously and often correctly, that the teacher sees some reason why he the student should *not* be confident. He may also see in such a statement the teacher's way of imposing her own expectations on him. As we saw in Chapter 1, this sort of expectation may arouse resistance, or anxiety at not being able to measure up, or both. We will talk more about "good vibes" later, especially in the chapter on the work of Georgi Lozanov.

The extraordinary power of "vibes" lies in the fact that they sneak into the student's brain around the edges of awareness and so are not subjected to logical scrutiny. They can therefore play an early and profound part in setting the climate for language study—in building the student's idea of what this corner of his universe is like. This is particularly true for the way he will perceive that central, powerful, and awesome personage, his teacher. We have already seen that the overt part of the teacher's feedback is the light by which the student keeps track of his cognitive, his linguistic, progress. In the same way, the "vibes" that accompany that feedback are the light which tells the student where the teacher thinks he, the student, stands as a person within that universe.

This fourth step is one which a few teachers take by instinct, and which a very few are incapable of taking under any circumstances. Most of us can profit from watching ourselves on videotape, and from other help in becoming aware of how we come across to our students. And of course, none of this kind of teacher training is likely to help much unless our own genuine attitudes, which lie behind the "vibes," are wholesome and constructive.

A fifth possible step is to leave—to appear to leave—the Teacher role from time to time, and act the part of an Ordinary Person, a cordial, interested Fellow Human Being. There are many styles of enacting the Teacher role: demanding or gentle, sarcastic or constructive, calm or vigorous, and so on. Yet all of them convey to the student that "I am the *Teacher*, who is providing the "control" for this course, and in whose presence you as *Students* are to *perform* certain *tasks*—tasks of an *academic* nature which will lead you, by the end of the *course*, to *know* the language better, and to make fewer *mistakes*." The words which I have emphasized in the preceding sentence all contribute toward an atmosphere in which the student "learns" the language, rather than "acquiring" it (Chapter 21). The activities carried on while the teacher is in the Teacher mode may be as cut and dried as dialog memorization or substitution drills. But they may also consist of virtually anything else, emphatically including student-initiated free conversation. The essential feature is that the students feel they are performing under the teacher's—the Teacher's—watchful eye.

Yet I have seen a few teachers who are able to come out from behind this Teacher mask, at least during "free conversation." They have generally been among the best language teachers I have known. They escape the Teacher mask through changes in voice, posture, and facial expression. Their non-verbal behavior is the same that they might use at home in the living room, talking with guests: animated, engaged, apparently intensely interested in the other speaker(s) and in what is being said. When wearing the Ordinary Person mask, the teacher *appears* to be speaking quite spontaneously, at normal conversational speed, and saying whatever comes into her mind. In fact, of course, she is filtering what she says through her awareness of what the students are likely to understand. If she supplies a word, she does so in a tone of voice which says, "This may be the word you're looking for. I'm giving it to you so that you may go on with this interesting thing you're saying." If she repeats something that the student has said, it is in a manner which indicates a desire to verify the content, or simply to hear the phrase again because it has caught her interest.

This kind of mask-changing can be done at any time, from the first few hours of the beginning course, all the way to the most advanced levels. It may last for a few seconds, or for a whole hour. It may consume 5 percent of the total time, or almost all of it. With beginners, this kind of conversation must be teacher-initiated, but later on, the teacher may drop back and become just one of several participants.

I don't think that most teachers should—or would be able to—wear the Ordinary Person mask all of the time. .It is a supplement for the Teacher mask, not a replacement for it, and it *is*, after all, a mask. The requirement of play-acting within limits imposed by the students' ability may place this fifth step beyond the reach of some teachers.

Seen in the theoretical framework of these first two chapters, the "mask change" links the world inside the classroom with the world outside it; it can also give to the student an exhilarating sense of adequacy within that world. Conversations conducted in this way may contribute to "acquisition," as contrasted with mere "learning" through "conversation practice." At the same time, these conversations draw on, and are supported by, what has been recently learned.

A sixth contribution which a teacher can make is to provide the student with a model for his Critical Self—what Gallwey calls the "Self 1." Gallwey tells us that the best soaking up of skills, and the best performance, take place when the Conscious, Critical Self and the Performing Self are in a wholesome relationship with one another. In this relationship, the Critical Self notices what the Performing Self does, and how what the Performing Self has done compares with the goal; yet it notices without praising or blaming the Performing Self, or labeling what it has done as "good" or "bad." The Conscious Self also sets goals for the Performing Self, and exposes the Performing Self to good models of the skill that it has chosen to acquire. At the same time, however, it does not impose obligations on the Performing Self, or interfere with the Performing Self *while* it is performing by telling it *how* to perform.

If Gallwey is right that the best learning (in the everyday, general sense of that word) and the best performance takes place under these conditions, then it seems desirable that by the end of the course, the student's Conscious, Critical Self should have learned to help, and not hinder, his Performing Self. This would be an additional goal, beyond (or before?) the linguistic goals. How can the teacher contribute toward the realization of this goal? Perhaps the best way is through lending herself as a temporary Conscious Self, at the same time serving as a model for how the student's own Conscious Self may eventually come to act. Bringing the Performing Self into contact with appropriate models, setting goals, and noticing results are, after all, parts of the "control" function that we talked about earlier. The trick is for the teacher to perform these services in ways that will not confuse or inhibit the student's Performing Self, or throw it off its stride. How can a teacher get away from the evaluative, interfering style that is ingrained in academic traditions around the world?

One part of the answer lies in the area of technique—alternative ways of using familiar materials. We will look at a few such techniques at the end of Chapter 11. These extra techniques can be helpful up to a point. But if they are to have their full effect, and if their effect is to last, then they must come from a teacher who really is relaxed and detached, even while she is most vigorously active, most fully involved with the students and what they are saying—a teacher who really does see mistakes (or error-free utterances) for what they are, and not as occasions for generalization which leads to worry (or to congratulation). Much of the difference between this kind of teaching and the kind of teaching that I have most often seen lies again, as with the "mask change," in the nonverbal signals which the teacher gives out. Most of us are not by nature this kind of teacher. (I know I am not!) So this sixth step may cost us a change in our own personal style—a price that may be too high for some.

In the seventh and final step that I would like to suggest, the students are free to talk openly about their reactions to the course and to the language; about what works for them and what doesn't; about what delights them and what bores them; how they feel about the language and the people who speak it; what their fears are, and their frustrations. The teacher listens with interest, occasionally saying whatever is needed to verify for herself and for the student that she is getting the same picture that the student has in mind. In this kind of listening, however, the teacher does not reply to the student, or disagree with him, or agree with him, or try to set him straight, or tell him that he needn't feel the way he does. As the student hears his meanings being understood by the teacher, without the teacher's becoming defensive or evaluative, then he typically becomes better able to deal with whatever feelings he may have, and their ability to interfere with his study subsides. His mind is then left clearer to work on whatever issues may have been raised. At the same time, the teacher may gain valuable information about how things are going with the class. (This kind of listening will come up for further discussion in Chapter 8.)

This understanding can take place in regularly-scheduled teacher-student conferences. But if the teacher is alert, it can also happen when a student makes a chance remark, whether inside the classroom or outside it. Wherever this kind of understanding is found, it can go far toward reducing some of the kinds of "alienation" that we talked about in Chapter 1. Suppose, for example, that I as a student am having trouble in memorizing dialogs. If I cannot talk freely about this with my teacher, I am left feeling that I am cut off from her, and that I myself am in this respect inadequate. Around these two wounds, all sorts of secondary infections may grow up: tenseness and even poorer performance; feeling that my classmates resent me for holding the class back; dislike for the language and its speakers; lowered self-esteem; psychosomatic reactions, and so on. Bringing the difficulty out into the open and finding that the teacher sees but does not judge, tells me that I am not so unacceptable as I had feared. Insofar as my poor performance was due to anxiety and tension, even my classwork may improve.

This sort of thing, as described in the preceding paragraph, sounds great—like something that everybody ought to do. There are, however, three risks in taking this seventh step. One is that when the students' comments are negative, or even hostile, the teacher may be thrown off balance and engage in some kind of defensive behavior. If this happens, alienation is increased and not reduced. The second risk is that, as a result of what the students have said, the teacher may see that she needs to make some changes in what she has been doing. If she lacks the technical skills for making appropriate changes, both she and the class may be left with a new source of anxiety, even of guilt. On the other hand, and this is the third risk, she may accede too readily and too often to suggestions from the class. This can erode the feeling of firm "control" which we have said is so essential to student morale.

Taking this seventh and most demanding step, then, requires of the teacher both professional resourcefulness and personal resilience. It is not for every teacher, possibly not for every class. Yet without it, there will always remain—more or less broad, more or less pernicious—unnecessary areas of alienation among the people in the classroom.

The approach that I have sketched in these first two chapters is one which nowadays would be called "humanistic." This label arouses uneasiness in some teachers, just as it is somehow attractive to others. Those who find themselves drawn to this kind of teaching may be interested in a list of seven hazards inherent in it. I have compiled this list out of my own life and hard times, and have the scars to document each item.

1. In announcing that one is going to be "responsive" and "learner-centered," or that one is going to share "control," or invite the students' comments and suggestions, one may raise expectations that can't be fulfilled. After some initial euphoria, one may thus produce gripes that can't be dealt with. It is like throwing a paper airplane which is shaped wrong, so that it immediately rises sharply, and then suddenly plunges to the floor. This is likely to happen unless the teacher has that combination of personal resilience and professional resourcefulness that we were talking about.

2. In a well-meaning desire to be "democratic," or "nonauthoritarian," one may abdicate responsibility for content and/or for technique. We have already mentioned this danger repeatedly, so there is no need to discuss it further here. It is the little boy in the progressive school saying, "Please, Miss

Jones, do we have to do just whatever we want to again *today?*" It is throwing an unfolded piece of paper instead of an airplane.

3. Trying to copy the surface structure—the concrete techniques—of someone else's method is a common temptation, particularly when one has just seen a brilliant "demonstration" by a prestigious personage endowed with charisma. This is like folding one kind of paper airplane, and then using scissors to trim the wings into the shape of another style of plane. I have done this sort of thing often enough myself. Maybe it is a necessary first step in learning from observation of master teachers. Nevertheless, it means that the teacher does not fully understand what she is doing and why; it does not grow organically out of her self and the present situation. Therefore, if things do not go as expected, the teacher may become confused, disappointed, and upset. Then teacher insecurity quickly translates itself into insecurity on the part of the students.

4. A fourth hazard is that the teacher's verbal and nonverbal messages may conflict with one another. The teacher may say that she invites the initiative of the student, but clearly show that she does not like what she gets. She may tell the students that she invites their comments and suggestions, yet appear threatened by the ones they make. Again, confusion and general insecurity are the results.

5. The fifth hazard that I have encountered is that there will not be a proper balance between the students' opportunities to contribute to the course, and their opportunities to examine and work with what they have contributed. The most traditional kind of course goes to one extreme: the students spend almost all of their time examining and working with what the textbook and the teacher have set before them, and are allowed to contribute almost nothing. At the opposite extreme, one kind of "humanistic" course may so load the students down with self-generated texts that they can't move. This is a paper airplane with one wing much broader than the other.

6. The teacher may use the course as a new way to show off her virtuosity with techniques, or to demonstrate to students and colleagues what amazing results she is capable of achieving in a short time. As I said earlier, this is my own personal foible. But it is pernicious, for in this way the teacher is using the class for her own ego-needs, instead of seeing where the class is and working with it. The result is like taking a well-designed paper airplane and throwing it much too hard.

7. At the same time that the teacher does focus on where the class is, and on working with it, she must also focus on herself, and on her own needs. This is quite different from being the puppet of her own needs, as in the preceding paragraph. It is in fact one way of escaping that kind of slavery. As we saw above, she too longs to feel that she is an "object of primacy in a world of meaningful action." Her world is confirmed when others commit themselves even partially and temporarily to the same foreignness that she has invested herself in, or when she sees her own cognitive style at work in other human

beings. Her feeling of adequacy is strengthened when her students attend class regularly, behave themselves, learn well, and show personal respect/liking for her. All of these are normal needs, and legitimately pursued. My point is that the teacher needs to be able to see them for what they are, and to watch them in operation. Only to the extent that she is in full possession of herself can she give herself, in a nonexploitive way, to her students.

The first five of these seven hazards point out ways in which "control," as we have been using that term in this chapter, can be undermined. The fourth also indicates one of the most effective ways to erode "initiative." The last two move into fundamental issues relating to the need for focusing on the teacher, as well as on the students.

If we, in our zeal to be "humanistic," become too "learner-centered" with regard to "control," we undermine the learner's most basic need, which is for security. We may find that we have imposed our own half-baked anarchy on the class. Absence of structure, or of focus on the teacher, may be all right in certain kinds of psychological training, but not in our classrooms. In a task-oriented group like a language class, the student's place is at the center of a space which the teacher has structured, with room left for him to grow into. In this kind of relationship, there are two essentials for the teacher: *faith* that the student will in fact grow into that space, and *understanding* of where the student is in that space at any given moment. When both these ingredients are present, there is the possibility of true "humanism" in teaching.

And one last hazard: being so impressed with the first seven hazards that one becomes afraid to try!

PART II

ONE WAY OF TEACHING:
THE SILENT WAY

CHAPTER 3

SOME BASIC IDEAS
BEHIND THE SILENT WAY

How can one person know another's thoughts? There is no way—no path—that does not run through the mind of the one who would learn. Light from the face of the thinker, and from his hands, and from his marks on paper, may flow into the learner's eyes, and the air waves set in motion by the thinker's voice may strike his ears. But light and sound are only bits of energy. When they come to the brain, the brain may sort them out, but it is the mind that says what shall be done with them, and what they mean. Two learners may have heard a single speaker's words, but each one's mind must also draw from what it has already—choosing, comparing, understanding as it will.

What most thinkers think can be to us like grain, that nourishes (and some would say that others' thoughts are chaff). A few—a very few—think thoughts that we can better save for seed. Such is—for me at least, and for a growing number of teachers—Caleb Gattegno. I have found his thoughts to be like seed in another way, too: they require time and some energy to germinate and develop. This chapter, then, sets forth my thoughts about his thoughts. I do not undertake this lightly, for in what I write there are bound to be twistings, and omissions, from what he says; the best way to understand any author is to read him first, and last. It may be, however, that in between those first and last readings, there is a place for commentary from a stranger—from a fellow seeker whose style and viewpoint may be different from the reader's own. It is in that spirit that I write this chapter. At the same time, I know that my own readers cannot find my thoughts except through what they bring with them to reading me, and through their own painstaking work.

In Gattegno's view, as I have read him, the Actor is the Self, the Stage is the whole world outside the Self, and the Play is limited in Time. (This is my metaphor, not his.) The Self, the other actors, and the Stage, are Energy. Energy, as every schoolchild learns, is the "capacity to work." So the Self is energy that works on all that comes into its body through its eyes, its ears, its smell, its taste, its touch, to organize these inputs, forgetting them or holding them as new parts of itself. Moreover, as the Self works on these things that strike it from outside, it works also upon itself. The Self, as Energy, is not Work; it is "Capacity to Work." What it does or does not do within the time it has may lead—or may not lead—to freedom: freedom to "stop being lived, and live," as Gattegno puts it; freedom to enter the future fully human.

This, in one paragraph, is what I hear Gattegno saying. In the pages that follow, let me expand it just a little.

The Self begins its work at the very moment of conception, to build a body for itself. Here, as it will throughout its life, it draws on what it has within itself. The earliest inner resource is DNA—hereditary material provided by the parents. Working with what it has, it receives from outside itself things over which it has no control (the mother's nutrients) and builds them into itself. As it does so, it adds to what it has—to what it will be able to use in dealing with future inputs. This is the basic miracle that Gattegno sees recurring in one form or another throughout life: that what is not-Self becomes, through the Self's work, part of the Self.

The Self exists—work is done—in four realms at once: the electromagnetic realm of atoms and molecules; the cellular realm; the animal realm of the body and the instincts; and a fourth realm, "which makes him know his knowings." No one of these realms replaces, or denies the existence of, any of the others. So along with the body, the Self creates a Mind. The Mind may act on, may make use of the brain, but it is not the brain, for the brain is only one more organ in the body-realm. And because both Mind and brain are aspects of a single Self, we need not wonder how both can exist at once.

Much of Gattegno's writing is concerned, in one way or another, with how the Self responds when it runs into a new limit, or meets some new challenge from outside itself. Its best way of meeting this "aggression," as Gattegno calls it, is through learning. Learning means reshaping of whatever lies within its power to shape. This same continual and appropriate reshaping, in answer to whatever demands the here and now may place upon us, also defines full living (or full humanity), if living is more than animal existence. There is, of course, the choice of shutting out, ignoring these "aggressions," but to do so cuts off learning. The seeing Self, if it is to do the work of truly seeing, must see itself as seeing. When it does not see and learn, the Self may lose self-knowledge, and sink back into that universe which it will never reach, and never learn to deal with, within the time it has.

Just as the Self must "see itself as seeing," so it must also use itself in its working with other things, and reshape itself in its reshaping of other things. Learning, for Gattegno, is not so much an accumulation and recognition of facts, as it is the learner's coming to use himself better. This is true for what we ordinarily think of as the learning of new material. But it is also true for what we call "the correction of errors." Errors are corrected by the learner, who uses for this purpose the system that he has already built inside himself. They are not "corrected by" outsiders. All that an outsider—a teacher, or a parent—can do is bring to the learner's attention the fact that a difference exists between what he says (if the error is in language) and what is said by those around him. This information then becomes for the learner a new "limit," "challenge," or "aggression" from outside. The learner must decide, as with any other new "aggression," whether and how to work with it.

The Self, then, may come to see that what it has known, or what it has been doing, is in some way not good enough, or that it does not fit as the Self would like it to fit into the world outside. When this happens, the Self may begin to talk with itself about what it is doing, and try to change—reshape—what it is doing in a way that will fit better, and be more adequate. This dialog is what Gattegno calls the functioning of intelligence. Intelligence is that part of the total Self which works with whatever concerns the Self at this place and this moment. It works knowingly on those parts of the Self that are directly involved in any situation, and only on those parts.

The word "knowingly" is, I think, one of the features of Gattegno's thought that sets him apart from many others. The Self, through its intelligence, not only *works* at the beginning of the learning process; it also works *consciously*. A goal of teaching in general, and of his own research in particular, is to make learning a more conscious activity.

The intelligence deals consciously with two sets of things within the Self. Most obviously, it deals with the images which the Self has formed within itself in response to what has recently come in from outside. But it also guides the Self in "putting itself into"—activating, bringing to consciousness— certain of its earlier memories and capabilities. It brings them to consciousness, holds them there as long as needed, and examines them. These are the first parts of its work. The last part of the work of this intelligence goes beyond marshaling and considering. Its role ends when it directs the will into some kind of mental action. This choice of an action is the best that the intelligence could come up with, based on whatever resources it found within the Self. The action may prove to have been right, or wrong, but it is at least an action—an action from and of the Self. Even if the action does not succeed in conquering the Outside Unknown, at least it recognizes that the Outside Unknown exists, and even failure to conquer, in itself, brings in new information. Therefore, for Gattegno, trial and error is an intelligent way of meeting the unknown. Only through using intelligence can we escape from being slaves to the way things—and we ourselves—have always been. (I have found Gattegno's books and Krishnamurti's *Freedom from the Known* to be mutually illuminating.)

The first part of the learning process is completed with this commitment of the Self to mental action. If the trial is successful, the next step is retention. There are two kinds of "retention." For Gattegno, most retention is something that the Self does for itself without any cost in energy. If, for example, I have once clearly seen that my hotel is on one side of the avenue and the marketplace is on the other, I will hold onto this fact without having to work on it. Suppose, however, that I wish to remember the street address of the hotel. That, as we all know, is quite another kind of retention. Here, it is no longer a matter of retaining a relationship among things that I have known with my senses. Now I must hold onto an *arbitrary connection* between a thing and its label. In merely reading or saying the address, I am making ordinary use of language. At the cost of very little energy, I shape the words, but when they have been shaped, and when they have fulfilled their function, the energy that went into them flows back into my Self, ready to be used again. Think of shaping bread dough. It is easy to mold, but if some arbitrary shape of the dough is to become permanent, we must hold it in that shape while we apply to it, in the oven, energy that far exceeds what was required to shape it for the moment only.

Gattegno has his own term for what the Self must do if it decides it wants to hold onto some new arbitrary connection, such as is involved in adding a word to a foreign language vocabulary. He creates a unit which he calls an "ogden," and says that the learner must "pay an ogden" for that connection. The learner must "pay" because he is getting something that he could not have provided from within himself. When retention involves what the learner could not provide or invent out of his own resources, Gattegno says that the material is being "remembered." This retaining of what the Self has done consciously and voluntarily is the second step in learning.

This distinction between simple retention and retention that includes "remembering" is the key to one of Gattegno's oft-repeated statements. He likes to say that "No one remembers his native language." This statement is obviously not true in the broad everyday meaning of "remember." Yet it is true in the sense that speaking our native language does not require mental energy of the kind that speaking a foreign one requires. The reason, of course, is that the words and structures of our native language have become parts of ourselves, and so we can provide them at will, from our own inner resources.

And yet, while we were learning it, even our native language was not part of what we could invent for ourselves, from resources that existed already inside us. It came, bit by bit, from outside of us; we must have "paid thousands of ogdens" for it. This observation shows us that same miracle that we remarked on in the Self's first life within the womb, making a body for itself: working with what it has already, the Self receives from outside itself things (energy) over which it has no control except to respond by building these things, in its own way, into itself. That which was non-Self becomes, through the Self's work, part of the Self.

To develop further the bread metaphor (which comes from me, and not Gattegno), it is as though the Self had taken food into its mouth, chewed it, swallowed it, digested it, and assimilated it. At the end of that process, the Self has a new source of energy within itself. It may even have used that energy for building within itself a new mechanism for dealing with future inputs. In any event, the new element is no longer alien, no longer requires the Self to use energy in dealing with it.

But the Self may still forget words that it has "paid ogdens" for. Gattegno remarks that we seem to take for granted that we should be able to recall things, and assume that when we forget, there is something wrong. Not so, he says. Forgetting is just as natural, and just as necessary, as retaining. Here again, the food analogy may apply. Not all food that goes into the mouth is chewed and swallowed. What is swallowed may not have been chewed enough to make digestion possible. Some of what we eat disagrees with what is already there to such an extent that it is violently ejected. And in any case, the natural metabolism of the body requires elimination as well as eating. But in general, going back to language now, the Self assimilates a new word into itself by using it repeatedly. What at one time had been a series of successive and separate moves of the Self working through its creature the mind has now been transferred, transformed, into more permanent changes in the cells of the brain—which is, as we have seen, one part of the Self's other creature, the body. This, to use the expression once again, is the central miracle. It is the basis for Gattegno's title, *The Mind Teaches the Brain*.

All of this forming, assembling, examining, sorting, recasting, and assimilating of images requires time and a great deal of energy. Moreover, the work is delicate. Most of us find it hard to carry out this work successfully at a time when new inputs are constantly coming in through the senses. For this reason, the mind does much of this work during sleep. The mind needs sleep at least as much as the muscular system of the body does. Gattegno even goes so far as to say that the Self has to be willing to live a double life: while it is awake it is "social and bound" because it has to respond to, and please, other people. In sleep, it can become "human and free." He seems almost to say, without quite saying it, that whenever one is interacting with other people, one is less than one's true self.

To summarize, learning involves two steps. The first is a conscious and deliberate act of the will, guided by the intelligence, which results in some mental action. The second is the process of assimilating the results of that action, through formation of new images or reshaping of old ones. Much of the first step takes place while the learner is awake, but much of the second happens during sleep. Once this process has taken place, a certain amount of meaningful practice (not rote repetition) may still be necessary to ensure fluency and permanence.

The result of the process is a new resource—new information or even a new way of functioning—which is now available to the Self from within itself, just as the native language is. When the Self acts on the basis of this resource, it does not need outside confirmation that it is right, any more than it needs outside confirmation that it has used the words for "two" or "three" correctly in its native language. It now possesses within itself criteria which are new, but which are nonetheless reliable. An additional thing to be learned in the Silent Way, on a deeper level than language or mathematics or other subject matter, is that one does possess these "inner criteria" and that one can trust them.

By undertaking this process—this kind of learning—the Self has been working on its own limitations, and has pushed them back a little. It is less under the control of outside forces, and of what its own brain had learned earlier for use in other circumstances. It is therefore more free; it has new choices available to it.

Drawing on the theory that we have summarized up to this point, Gattegno identifies three qualities of the Self which he thinks education should recognize and encourage. One is "Independence," which stands for the fact that we can make use of whatever we have already inside us, and that we can count *only* on what we have inside us. Students begin to experience "independence" in this sense as soon as they notice that they can use knowledge of their own language to open up some things in a new language, or when they take their knowledge of the first few words in the new language and figure out additional words by using that knowledge.

The second of these three qualities is "Autonomy": the making of choices among equivalent expressions in a given set of circumstances, and the exercise of initiative in attacking new material. The teacher cultivates the student's "autonomy" by deliberately building choices into situations.

The third quality is "Responsibility." We are "responsible" first of all because we have a will, and this will is essentially free—incompletely determined by heredity, history, and environment. Any set of linguistic choices provides an opportunity for "autonomy," but the choice to choose or not to choose among them, and the ability to choose systematically and carefully, are evidences of "responsibility."

These three qualities are especially conspicuous in Gattegno's second book for language teachers, *The Common Sense of Teaching Foreign Languages,* from which my descriptions of them have been drawn. For further clarification, the reader is referred to that source.

What Gattegno has produced, then, is much more than an educational technology. It even goes beyond what we think of as "education" in the usual academic sense. There is good reason for speaking, not of the Silent "Method," but of the Silent "Way." It is a "way" not only for the teacher, but also for her students. Any Self is "an evolving system endowed with awareness and the capacity for self-education." By developing his awareness, the learner becomes more and more free, able to live "more respectful of the truth in Reality." The evolving Self creates "new forms that integrate [its own] past," and so it finally "contributes to collective evolution." As he becomes more fully human, the learner discovers that those two worlds, the Outer and the Inner, are, after all, intertwined.

The long goal of such development, then, is that the Self should add its own unique contribution to its world. A goal within but at the same time beyond that one is "to recast [one's] world in a manner that makes more sense to more people and leads [them] to accept that [they] were not 'seeing' outside reality as it is." I think that this last sentence describes what Dr. Gattegno himself has done for many of us.

CHAPTER 4

THE SILENT WAY AS A METHOD FOR TEACHING LANGUAGES

I said in Chapter 3 that the Silent Way is not primarily a set of techniques. Nevertheless, a number of techniques and materials derived from the theory have come into use among practitioners of the Silent Way. These help to illustrate that theory. At the same time, the description of concrete classroom procedures has a direct, instinctive appeal for readers who are serious teachers. Two warnings are therefore necessary at this point. First, my own exposure to silent teaching and learning has been only partial, and it is not completely up to date. Second, I do know, from what experience I have had, that the techniques without the theory are incomplete. In this chapter and in Chapters 5 and 6, I am like one of the blind men who described the elephant, one comparing it to a wall, one to a rope, and so on according to which part of it they had touched. My hope is that what I have set down here, together with independent examination of Dr. Gattegno's writings, and her/his own experiences with the method, will enable the reader to form a fuller, sounder idea of the Silent Way.

The things that any outsider notices first about any language teaching method are its materials and its techniques. In this chapter, I will describe briefly—or better, I will enumerate—some materials and techniques which are commonly used in foreign language courses taught by the Silent Way, and then try to show how they are related to a series of principles derived from the theory of Chapter 3. Superscript numbers in the description are cross-referenced to parenthesized numbers in the list of principles.

DESCRIPTION

The teacher commonly begins by pointing at meaningless symbols on a wall chart.[1] These symbols stand for the syllables of the spoken language. The students read the appropriate noises—syllables, etc.—aloud, first in chorus and then individually.[2] Where possible, this activity begins with a chart in the students' native language, or in some other language in which they are literate.[3] This chart, called a "Fidel," contains all of the spellings for all of the syllables of the language. The symbols on the chart are printed in various colors, in such a way that symbols which are to be pronounced alike are colored alike. In this way, students are able to ignore the shapes, at least temporarily, and depend on the colors. They are therefore unencumbered by anxieties about the shapes, and left free to concentrate on the new sounds. The students first use their knowledge of familiar shapes to learn the phonetic meanings of the colors. Then, switching to the Fidel of the new target language, and guided by the teacher's gestures they use their knowledge of the pronunciations of the colors[4] in order to read the syllables aloud from it. Where the new language contains sounds that are absent from the familiar language, the teacher may silently focus the students' attention and then give them a single clear audible example[5] of the sound. Otherwise, the teacher may up to this point have remained completely silent. During this first phase, the teacher shapes the students' pronunciation[6] of the target language by means of her (largely) silent reaction—or lack of reaction—to their efforts.

After the students can pronounce the sounds of the new language well enough so that no native would misunderstand them,[7] the teacher moves on to a second phase. This phase centers around a second set of charts, which contain miscellaneous words carefully selected from among the most common words of the language,[8] including the words for numerals. Using these words, together with written numerals, the teacher leads the students to produce long numbers up to a million, a billion, and beyond.[9]

In the third phase, the teacher typically puts into use a set of colored wooden (or plastic) rods a square centimeter in cross section, ranging in length from 1 to 10 centimeters. Each length has its own distinctive color. Using the charts, together with gestures and perhaps a few spoken words, the teacher leads the students to talk about various configurations and uses of the rods.[10] At first, work is on numbers and colors, but soon it moves into relative locations, and beyond that to virtually any and all grammatical structures that the teacher thinks the student needs.

(There are other materials which are used later in the course. I will not describe them here because my purpose is only to show examples of how the basic principles of the Silent Way are realized in practice. The later materials and techniques embody the same principles as the three phases that I have already described. Readers who are interested in accounts of the later phases, and in fuller, more authoritative treatment of the first three, should carefully consult Dr. Gattegno's book *The Common Sense of Teaching Foreign Languages.*)

Throughout at least the initial phases, the students meet one clearly delimited new element of the language at a time.[11] The students know that they are expected to work only on this point,[12] using whatever resources they already have at their disposal. They feel that what they have done has moved them toward their long-term goal in an efficient way,[13] and that they have worked both well and thoroughly.[14] The teacher is matter-of-fact[15] both about the students' successes and about their errors, but she always shows by her manner that she accepts the students as persons.[16]

The teacher generally exercises the initiative[17] in deciding which syllable or word the students will work on at any given moment, or which rod structure will be built. Within her initiative, however, she provides frequent situations in which the students have more than one correct response available to them.[18] Students are engaged in a constant series of trial-and-error approximations to the language.[19]

When the students respond correctly to the teacher's initiative, she usually does not react with any overt confirmation that what they did was right.[20] If a student's response is wrong, on the other hand, she indicates that the student needs to do further work on the word or phrase;[21] if she thinks it necessary, she actually shows the student exactly where the additional work is to be done. Sometimes points which have not been completely mastered are left to clarify themselves overnight.[22]

The teacher is almost always silent.[23]

The teacher uses a collapsible metal pointer[24] to guide the students' attention to the charts or rods, even when they are within easy reach of her hand.

Students frequently help one another,[25] and learn from overhearing one another.

There is no memorization,[26] no translation,[27] and no repetition for its own sake in the absence of meaning.[28]

PRINCIPLES

A. *Learning is work.*   It is not primarily a display of ability, or of erudition, or of moral character on the part of either the student or the teacher. *Therefore,* it is natural for the teacher to show a matter-of-fact attitude toward the student's performance (15), and to treat the student as an accepted human being regardless of how fast or how slow he may be.

Because learning is a continuing and living process, rather than a one-time event or a passive process of submitting to inculcation, partly wrong pronunciation and other phenomena of "interlanguage" are seen as stages in that process, rather than as micro-disasters and causes for alarm.

B. *The work is done by the student.*   The student is necessary to the process, and so (in a language course) is the language he is learning. The teacher is potentially very useful, but is not absolutely necessary. *Therefore,* teaching must be treated as subordinate to learning. The question is not so much, "How can I teach?" as it is, "How can I help these people to learn?" The teacher whose work is subordinated to the work of her students must be continually learning from them about where they are—must be constantly "learning them," so to speak, at the same time that the students are learning the subject matter. But it is hard to listen to someone else closely while at the same time one is trying to produce something for the other to listen to. This is one of the reasons why the teacher tries to remain silent as much as possible (6, 23)

I suspect that the subordination of teaching to learning may also be one reason for using the pointer rather than the teacher's hand for so many purposes (24). The pointer can be brandished as though it were a birch rod, or it can be used like a conductor's baton, to order people around in an imperious way. Neither of these styles is obviously consistent with the subordination of teaching. But it can also be used deftly and gently, as a way of keeping the student in contact with the work at hand, while at the same time keeping the teacher as far out of the picture as possible. (A masterly example of this last style is to be seen in a series of videotapes which show a pair of ESL classes conducted at Educational Solutions, Inc.)

C. *The work must be conscious.*   The chief implication of this principle is that the student should meet one challenge at a time. *Therefore,* pronunciation is taken up before meaningful expressions. Otherwise, students would have to try to cope with new sounds and new words at the same time (1 to 3). For the same reason, new lexical and structural material is meticulously broken down into its elements, with one element being presented at a time (11). In this way, the teacher is able to fulfill her implied promise to the students, that they will always know exactly what is expected of them at any given moment (12).

D. *The work takes place within the learning student.*   "Nobody hears words; ears hear sounds." Even the "words" are a result of work which the Self does on the sound waves. The chief implication of this proposition is that learning can use whatever is inside the student, and only that. *Therefore,* the work on pronunciation usually begins with a Fidel from a language that the students already know how to pronounce (3). In the same way, the newly acquired ability to respond to the phonetic values of the colors becomes an inner resource to be used (4) in work with the Fidel of the target language.

What is found within one student may not exist—or may not be readily accessible—within another. The emphasis on students learning from listening to each other, rather than listening only to the teacher, shows the students (a) that they are not absolutely dependent on a single authoritative voice; and (b) that their inner resources enable them to take in, refine, and profit from even inferior raw material (25). It is of course understood that the students filter the inputs from each other through their knowledge of the teacher's reaction (or lack of reaction) to each effort.

A further implication of the ideas that work takes place within the learner (D) and that it is conscious (C) is the great emphasis placed on concentration of mental energy. This is not the kind of concentration that one attains by tightening one's muscles, furrowing one's brow, and telling oneself, "Now, I must concentrate!" It is rather the concentration that happens when distractions are absent. This kind of concentration may in turn be one reason for the visually simple, brightly colored rods (10). It may also be one reason why an audible model is usually given only once by the teacher (5), and why the teacher remains silent as much as possible. The students learn, in addition to the sounds, words, and patterns, that it is in their interest to listen.

E. *The work requires the learner to relate the linguistic signs to truth that he perceives with his senses.*   Words are only a secondhand report of truth. This must be a large part of the reason for so much reliance on the rods and pictures as ways of generating "truths" to which a whole roomful of people can relate (10). It is also the reason why translation from the student's native language is not used in the oral, early stages of the work (27).

When the students are working with public, visible truth, it is relatively easy for the teacher to set up situations where the students have a choice among two or more equivalent expressions (18). This dramatizes a very important aspect of the relationship between language and what language talks about.

This principle also explains why in the Silent Way there is no drilling of forms in the absence of meaning (28). There is systematic practice of similar sentences, but always accompanied by rod structures or some other direct "truth."

F. *The learner does the work in order to adjust better to the unknown world outside himself.*   The teacher represents this outside unknown to the student by translating it into a series of challenges. She selects and times the challenges in accordance both with her knowledge of the language and with her perception of where the student is at any given moment. *Therefore,* the teacher initiates many of the exchanges (17); the student's trial-and-error behavior is an essential source of current information for the teacher as well as for the student himself (19); the teacher points out when and where the student needs to do more work (21); as he succeeds more and more in meeting the teacher's challenges, the student feels that the course is being effective (14) in moving him toward his chosen goal.

G. *The work adds new resources to the self.*   Each time the student comes to feel that he now knows something from within himself, and not from echoing the teacher or from memorizing rules and paradigms, he has developed a new "inner criterion." The student must learn to notice these "criteria," and to trust them. It is apparently for this reason that the teacher seldom confirms a correct response on the part of the student (20). By not overtly approving a correct response, the teacher leaves the student alone to take note of it, and to learn to trust himself more.

H. *The student must not only learn through this process; he must also learn to be aware of the process and to control it.*   This is an additional reason for withholding confirmation of correct responses (20); and for giving the student at the very beginning of the course the experience of learning and immediately using the colors as a phonetic transcription (4); and for insisting that students produce sentences for themselves as much as possible, rather than falling back on their ability to repeat after the teacher (26).

I. *The time available for the work is limited.*   Teaching that constantly monitors and is subordinated to learning will waste less time. The selection of the words in the charts, to yield maximum power in the language in return for minimum memorization, also conforms to this principle (8). Memorization of sentences and dialogs is avoided (26) because it is so expensive in ogdens, particularly in comparison to what it enables the students to do in the language. Because the student is conscious of the limits on his time, he has a right to expect a feeling of efficiency (13), as well as effectiveness, from the course.

J. *Much of the work takes place during sleep, or when the mind is apparently idle.*   This is why some matters that are not yet clear or language that is not yet fluent are allowed to carry over until the next day (22).

* * * * * *

We have looked first at the Silent Way in terms of some of the theory on which it is based (Chapter 3); then we listed some of its most frequent and characteristic practical manifestations and related them to principles derived from the theory; we will now take a third and final look at it from the point of view of Chapters 1 and 2.

The godlike characteristics of the learner are conspicuous in Gattegno's thinking: the ability to make infinite use of finite resources, and the ability to transcend one's animal nature by seeing oneself as seeing, seeing oneself as seeing that one sees, and so on. The mortality of the learner is equally clear in the urgency which Gattegno feels for efficiency in learning—for being sure that we "exchange time for experience" rather than wasting it. And the picture of the Self creating itself even from the moment of conception, on physical as well as intellectual levels, certainly affirms the heroic aloneness of a Self at the center of its own universe.

Going on now to Chapter 2, the Silent Way is anything but a power vacuum, and it emphatically rejects any idea of trying to protect the student from making errors. It is much closer to the Evaluative Paradigm: "Now try to do this so I can tell you how you did." It differs, however, in three important ways from most teaching that is conducted on that basis. First, there is very little "positive feedback" from the teacher, in the sense of telling students (in words or silently) that their responses were "right" or "very good." Second, although the teacher's overt reactions are mainly to mistakes, they are given in a totally matter-of-fact way. The student is supposed to feel that his wrong response (or his *right* response!) is *not being "corrected," but is being accepted and worked with.* Third, the teacher learns the student at the same time that the student is learning the language. This means that the teacher does not merely present the student with a prefabricated series of challenges, but that she also provides new challenges as she sees they are needed.

No one who has read *The Mind Teaches the Brain* can doubt that Gattegno has taken a deep and very steady look inside the learner. The people in his classes are whole, complex persons, and not simple few-dimensional simplifications. In his two books that are directed especially to language teachers, he is very clear about the learner's need to feel secure in three areas: in knowing what is being asked of him at any given moment; in knowing how his performance compares with what is expected; and in being accepted as a person without regard for any linguistic difficulties he may have. On the other hand, it is not clear to me how much importance Gattegno attaches to the kinds of resistance, conflict, and alienation that we sketched in Chapter 1: to the learner's attitudes toward speakers of the target language; or to the learner's reactions to being "ignorant, powerless, and constantly evaluated"; or to his reactions to pleasant or unpleasant experiences with his fellow students. Gattegno's position may be that if the teaching is done well enough, those factors will fade from the picture of their own accord.

The Silent Way certainly provides clear, firm, and continuous "control" of the learning process, in the sense in which we have been using that term. Within this control, it is possible to leave room for an exciting amount of "initiative," and even creativity, on the part of the students. I have seen two Silent Way teachers who vigorously exploited the opportunities to give initiative to the students, even while they (the teachers) maintained tight control over what was going on. The other teachers I have seen have given much less initiative to the students, at least in the early stages.

In its emphasis on the ways in which students learn by listening to one another's efforts, the Silent Way not only allows interdependence, but also requires it. There are also endless opportunities for cooperation among the students, under the close monitoring and control of the teacher. But I am uncertain, just as I am unclear concerning "initiative," about exactly how far the teacher is supposed to follow up on those opportunities.

As far as I am aware, Dr. Gattegno has said nothing to language teachers about "vibes." I believe, however, that "good vibes"—an air of the teacher's competence, and of confidence in herself and her students—are important for success in using the Silent Way, just as they are in using any method.

The Silent Way does not provide for the teacher to lay aside her Teacher mask and replace it with an Ordinary Person mask. It may at least allow such an exchange as long as "control" (in my sense) is not lost. I am not certain.

A Silent Way teacher sets short-term goals for her students, and lets them know when "the ball lands outside the court." She does this in an alert, matter-of-fact way, without either praising the students or reproaching them. She thus acts the way Self 1 (the Conscious, Critical Self) ought to act.

In doing do, she often finds herself in conflict with the students' own Self 1's. The Self 1's of most students are in the habit of dealing in praise and reproach, and of having teachers who provide a continuous supply of one or both. For this reason, students sometimes experience conflict and anxiety at the beginning of instruction by the Silent Way. Once they adjust to the new style, and begin to let their own Self 1's work *the way the teacher is working*, they frequently have a feeling of elation, and their learning rate leaps to a level that they would not have thought possible.

Between activities or between sessions, the Silent Way teacher from time to time allows students to ask questions, or to talk about the experience, in their native language. At these times, the teacher does not remain silent, but in other respects she remains true to the principles of the Silent Way. Thus, when she is asked a question, she may choose to avoid giving a direct answer. Instead of a direct answer, she may say something that directs the ques- tioner's mind toward work which may enable him to find the answer for himself, within himself. In the same way, if a student expresses confusion or discomfort, the teacher may try to reply in a way that will give the student a hint at where or how to work within himself, rather than giving him the kind of supportive understanding that we talked about in Chapter 2. In their first experiences with the Silent Way, students and other people sometimes regard this kind of reply as ill-mannered.

Perhaps the chart on page 51 will be useful in relating the work of the learner and the work of the teacher to a few of the terms we have used.

In dealing with the theories and generalizations of Chapters 3 and 4, we have been like birds looking down on a fertile valley far below us. In Chap- ters 5 and 6, we will leave our remote vantage point to scratch and peck our way among a bit of the underbrush in that same valley.

Principle	Learner	Teacher
LEARNING IS WORK FOR THE PURPOSE OF ADJUSTING TO THE OUTSIDE WORLD	In meeting a new challenge,	The teacher provides challenges
INDEPENDENCE	I use resources from within myself	relative to the student's present resources,
RESPONSIBILITY	in order to decide for myself	but remains silent, noninterfering,
AUTONOMY	among the choices	while the student works to choose
INDEPENDENCE	offered by the resources within myself (for no other resources are available).	among the resources that we have guided him in developing.
REMEMBERING ("LEARNING"?)	The result of this work	This kind of teaching
RETENTION ("ACQUISITION"?)	may become a part of myself.	frees the student.

CHAPTER 5

SOME OF MY OWN EXPERIENCES IN USING THE SILENT WAY

Over the past eight years, I have had many opportunities to use the Silent Way. Most of these opportunities have been one-hour brief experiences for groups of language teachers, but a few have been longer, and have involved real students. The language has almost always been Turkish for people who had a native, or at least a good, command of English. I will describe some of these episodes here, in the hope that my trial-and-error encounters with the Silent Way will be of help—sometimes negatively, sometimes positively—to my readers.

The One-Hour Experience (Prior to 1976). I have conducted essentially the same brief experience with the Silent Way at least 15 or 20 times, for language teachers of many kinds, in many countries. Until recently, I have thought of them and allowed my audiences to think of them as "demonstrations." But the word "demonstration" brings with it the kind of thing that a salesman does with a new car. It is understood by both parties that the salesman is trying to persuade the customer to buy the car, and that the customer's natural contribution is to look for reasons why he should not buy. A "demonstration" of teaching methods also seems to say, "You can/ought to be able to do in your classes what you have seen me do here, and what you have been doing hitherto is certainly old-fashioned, probably inferior to what I am showing you." If the audience feels that the "demonstrator" is working on this basis, they are almost certain to become defensive. Their reactions are likely to take either of two forms, both of which begin with "Yes, but. . . ." The first "Yes, but . . ." is "Yes, but this would never work in large classes like mine / with students who are not language teachers in disguise / in a course with a prescribed textbook, etc., etc." They are usually at least partly right: the exact techniques they have just seen probably would be unusable in their own classrooms. But this kind of reaction on their part also excuses them from learning anything at all from the demonstration. Teachers can sometimes be as resistant as students to the idea that there is something new that they need to learn.

The second "Yes, but . . ." is "Yes, but I'm already doing this." Again, the partial truth of this reply often blinds the spectator from seeing something new in the demonstration.

To get back to my "demonstration," however, it always worked quite smoothly and provoked discussion which made me feel effective as a demonstrator. So I kept on doing the same thing time after time. Nevertheless, two things began to bother me about my little routine: I felt that the "yes butters," through their reactions to the details of technique, were too often depriving themselves of the opportunity to see the underlying principles from which the technique flowed; and there were a few recurring snags in the language learning that went on during the "demonstrations." At the same time, I began to suspect that even my underlying principles were not entirely consistent with the Silent Way.

Since 1976, therefore, I have been very emphatic in describing this same routine to my audiences as "an experience, not a demonstration." I tell them that what I am about to do is exactly what I would do if their only purpose in participating were to learn as much Turkish as possible; that I am working with these students "here and now," and not trying to show them what to do in their own classes "there and then"; that I hope that the experience will be something they will open themselves to, and assimilate, and draw on in their own ways when they find themselves in quite different situations later on.

The routine to which I have been referring went like this (as in Chapter 4 superscript numbers in the description are later cross-referenced to parenthesized numbers):

I invited six people to sit around a table, in view of the rest of the audience.[1] When they were settled, I opened my bag of rods and dumped them onto the center of the table.[2] Then I picked up rods of various colors, one by one, and looked at them.[3] Finally, I picked up one of the longer rods,[4] motioned for everyone to listen and remain silent,[5] and pronounced the word *çubuk* ("rod").[6]

After this dramatic event, I held the learners silent for a few seconds,[7] and then motioned them to say the word in unison.[8] When they had spoken the word chorally a few times, I picked up the same rod time after time, and had individuals produce the word.[9] If one learner's pronunciation was very far from what native speakers would have understood, I had him try it again.[10] If that didn't work, I used silent gestures,[11] or my own silent mouthing of the word, or I silently elicited a new model from one of the learners who had pronounced the word correctly.[12] In one or another of these ways, everyone soon developed a good pronunciation of *çubuk*.[13]

When I felt that the pronunciation had been established, I pushed all of the rods toward one of the learners,[14] and motioned that he or she was to speak. Invariably, the learner came out with the word *çubuk*.[15] Most frequently, he also picked up a rod of the same color that I had used.[16] If he did not pick up a rod, I motioned to him that he should.[17] I sometimes gave unobtrusive but clear confirmation that the learner had in fact done what I had had in mind.[18] I continued in this way, going from learner to learner, until someone picked up a rod of a different color.[19] Sometimes that person said "*çubuk*?" and I would nod matter-of-factly.[20] Sometimes the learner only looked at me in a questioning way. Then, I silently replied that he already knew a word for it.[21] In either case, it soon became clear to everyone that *çubuk* applied to all of the rods, and not just to those of one color.[22]

This may be a good point to stop and look back at what the learners and I had accomplished so far. Some of the desirable things that they had learned, or at least begun to learn, were the following: They could develop good pronunciation (13) on the basis of a single audible model from the teacher (6); they could learn from each other, as long as the teacher guaranteed that they would not go astray (12); they could successfully explore beyond the exact data that had been given to them (4, 9, 19, 22).

My reasons for doing some of the things that I did were the following: I held the students silent for a few seconds after the audible model (7) because I wanted them to have time to play the sound back in short-term memory and work with it in any ways they liked. This is something like throwing a pebble into a quiet pool and then watching the ripples as they move across the surface. It is impossible to watch the first set of ripples if someone tosses in a handful of gravel immediately after the pebble.

I shoved all of the rods to one person after another (14) because I wanted to establish, even within this minimal vocabulary, the idea that individuals could take "initiative" (Chapter 2) under my "control," and that they would be required to do so as a regular part of the lesson.

I stayed with rods of one color (9) because I wanted the students to be able, later on (19 to 21), to have the experience of having discovered for themselves the fuller range of meaning for *çubuk*. In this way, I felt that I was guiding them toward beginning to explore, for and within themselves, the mental resources that they had brought with them to the task of learning.

Nevertheless, a few things happened that were not what I had hoped for. The one I noticed first was that, while most of the learners seemed to find the experience enjoyable, a few were made tense by it. Other than the fact that they were serving as "students" in a public "demonstration," there were at least two possible grounds for their tension. The more important was that they were being required to cope with many different kinds of new data all at once: the sounds, the combination of sounds that made up the word, the meaning of the word, and the unfamiliar way in which the class was being conducted. In later stages of the same demonstration, they would also encounter the beginnings of the grammar of Turkish. A second source of tension was the absence of any written representation of the word. All of these sources of tension would have been reduced if I had followed the present-day practice of most Silent Way teachers and begun with pronunciation and the charts (see Chapter 4).

From time to time, I would also find people who came to the end of the demonstration confused about the meaning of the word *çubuk*. They realized, of course, that it applied to all of the rods, but they also wondered whether it might extend to other wooden objects such as the table, or to other long, thin articles such as a pen. I tended to think of those people as worrywarts, who were seizing on this marginal unclarity as an excuse for sidestepping real engagement with the language. I felt that they ought to become more ready to abandon themselves to the trial-and-error process of learning. Perhaps I was right. I notice, however, that when Dr. Gattegno introduces the word "rod" for the first time, he is careful to pick up and name rods of several different colors. Similarly, I have now adopted the practice of pointing to tables and pens and silently making clear that we do not yet know the words for these objects. Maybe in trying to get people to use their inner resources for exploring this matter, I was doing a right thing at a wrong time.

Even this first brief bit of the demonstration contained the seeds for another undesirable effect that sometimes came to the surface by the end of such a short demonstration: one person would appear to be much better (or worse) at this sort of thing than the rest were, and feelings would begin to build up around the difference. This sort of anxiety cannot be avoided altogether, of course. I think, however, that I contributed to it by eliciting new models *from* one learner *for* another (12). I now think that it is better to leave, for the moment, the student who is having difficulty, go on to another student, and *do something else* with that other student. Then, not really very long after leaving the first student, see to it that someone does correctly what the first student was unable to do. Then, *but not immediately,* go back and give the first student a new opportunity. This maneuver avoids direct comparison of students: the teacher is less likely to seem to say, "See? He can do it! Why can't you?" The student who has not yet been able to say what he is supposed to will have less occasion to think, "What is the matter with me? Am I holding the others back? Are they becoming impatient with me?" On the positive side, that student's mind will be kept busy watching for the next suitable model, instead of just sitting and having it handed to him.

Giving control of the rods to one person after another (14) probably did have the positive outcomes that I hoped it would have. But it was also time-consuming, and so reduced the students' linguistic achievements in the amount of time that was available. It may also have kept me from coming across as the brisk, all-competent teacher into whose hands they could comfortably surrender themselves.

Finally, my positive feedback (18), however muted, was probably sufficient to confirm what the learners expected on the basis of all of their past language classes: that they can and must depend on the teacher in order to know when they are right.

Now to resume the description of my routine Turkish demonstration. After introducing çubuk in this way, I went on to the numbers 1, 2, and 3. I did not begin with colors because in Turkish one cannot join an adjective to çubuk without a numeral or some other word to go with them.

First, I set out six rods: one by itself, two together, and a group of three. I placed them on the table with obvious deliberation and fairly loudly. Having done so, I made a great show of counting them with my finger. The idea that I wanted to convey was, "Now we are going to work with numbers."

Then, motioning for the students to listen and remain silent, I pronounced the first numeral. In the earlier demonstrations, this was the word for "one," but I soon learned to start with "two." The reason is that the last consonant of *bir* "one" when the word is pronounced by itself has a sound that is unfamiliar and very confusing to speakers of most other languages. The word *iki* "two" poses no such difficulty. By starting with *iki,* I can go immediately to the phrase *iki çubuk* "two rods," and then *bir* can be substituted with a much easier *r*-sound, for *iki.*

Once I had introduced *çubuk, iki,* and *bir,* I followed a three-step formula which had appeared in embryo even earlier: "Teach, then test, then get out of the way." That is, I presented the new material, quizzed the learners silently with the rods to be sure they had gotten it, and gave each of them control of the rods for a minute or two so that they could decide what to say and when. In this way, they were able to work with their own inner resources and inner readinesses much more sensitively than I could hope to. At the same time, they were gathering experience at taking initiative, always within the very clear framework which I had established. I felt that this three-step formula was consistent with the Silent Way; it was, in fact, one of the features that first attracted me to the Silent Way. Now, as I indicated in Chapter 4, I am no longer so certain about the relation between the formula and the Silent Way. (But I still like the formula!)

As I pushed the rods from student to student, they used them in several different ways. Occasionally, someone would enact the Teacher role which she/he was so accustomed to playing, and use the rods to quiz the other people around the table. I did not leave the rods under the control of such people for long. More frequently, the person who had the rods would pick up one combination of rods after another, recite the words that went with them, and watch for reactions from me. My feedback to them rapidly became less and less clear, until finally I might break off eye contact altogether. Quite dependably, the rest of the group moved in to fill the vacuum. As this trend became clearly established, I often moved away from the table, or even left the room for a short time. My purpose was to dramatize to the learners what in fact was true: that *as a group* they were as infallible as I was *on the clearly limited matters* that I had left them to practice among themselves. I also intended it as a way of leading them to develop a feeling of responsibility for careful listening and for mutual support. I cannot remember it ever failing. In fact, it was a consistent crowd-pleaser. (Not least, I had the fun of leaving the audience impressed with how skillfully I had enlisted personal and interpersonal resources in the shared task of learning a language.) Once again, however, I suspect that the amount of time used, and the dilution of the role of the teacher, may have made what I did inconsistent with the principles of the Silent Way. Perhaps it is possible to subordinate teaching to learning without breaking the subordination of the learner to the teacher.

One effect of the way I conducted those early demonstrations was that the people around the table often remarked on how within the twenty or so minutes they had come to feel a warm sense of community among themselves. This always made me feel good. But while interaction among students is clearly a goal of the Silent Way, I am not sure that an early feeling of community among them is.

At about this point, I would silently wave the six people away from the table and indicate that their places were to be filled from among those who up to this moment had assumed that they would be merely spectators. Without giving any new audible models, I had the new people reproduce what their predecessors had been doing, and then went on to present some new material. Depending on the length of the demonstration and the size of the audience, I often summoned a third team in the same way. The value of this was that it made people realize how much "spectators" can learn, and left them less pessimistic about using techniques of this kind with larger classes.

At the end of the session, I invited questions and comments. Generally, I asked first for comments that were drawn from the participants' experiences as learners of Turkish. Only later did I accept questions and comments based on their role as teachers-watching-a-demonstration. In either case, however, I first "understood" what had been said (see Chapters 7, 8) and then, if I thought necessary, gave some kind of reply. My overall manner was supportive and cordial. If I had followed the principles of the Silent Way at this point, I might not have given so many direct answers, or given "counseling responses" (Chapter 8) to so many comments. Instead, I would have tried to respond at least to some speakers in ways that were intended to stimulate them to work toward building within themselves their own replies to whatever they had said. In so doing, I would have carried the Silent Way to still another level for them. Or at least, such is my current reading of Dr. Gattegno's works.

Two Intensive Weekends as a Student.   My next significant contact with the Silent Way consisted of two 20-hour weekends as a student, about three months apart. The languages on the two weekends were different. They were equally foreign to me. Both used nonroman writing systems. The classes were similar in size and composition. From the point of view of my own learning of the languages, one weekend was an unprecedented success, the other a total failure. Yet the weekend from which I learned no language was the one that I came to with higher hopes, and the one during which I felt that I remained physically relaxed, intellectually hopeful, and stubbornly optimistic until the very end. I even came away feeling good about the teacher and the method.

It would be a waste of time to examine these two episodes too closely. I will only list four hypotheses which come to my mind whenever I look back on the two weekends. In chronological order, they are: (1) Perhaps it is dangerous for a teacher to appear to lay some of her own personal expectations of success onto one or more students. (2) When the directing is done by one person and the audible models are supplied by another person, as sometimes happens in Silent Way classes, it may be dangerous for those two people to appear to be out of harmony with each other. (3) When a student is having persistent difficulty with a point, he may sometimes be able to do the necessary internal work faster and better if he is given control of the rods for a minute or two. This contrasts both with having the teacher work on him, and with trying to pick out appropriate new models from a flow of classwork that for him has become only a blur. (4) Negative feelings conveyed from a faster student may make a slow student still slower.

Bellingham. I conducted 6-hour experiences with Silent Turkish for two groups of secondary school language teachers in Bellingham, Washington, in the summer of 1976. Each experience consisted of four sessions. There were twelve people in the first group, sixteen in the second.

What we did was clearly billed as "an experience, not a demonstration." With exceptions which I will describe below, the actual procedures that I followed were similar to what I had used in my "demonstrations." The longer time, however, allowed us to go much farther into Turkish. We were able to do a fair amount with reading and writing; and with regard to grammar, I led them straight into and through the worst thicket in Turkish structure. As one part of the final session, we experimented with learning a short dialog of the type found in the textbooks that they teach from, using a technique derived from the Silent Way. A number of features of the Bellingham experience deserve comment.

Twelve people were too many for me to deal with around the table at one time. I knew from the demonstrations that spectators can learn along with active participants. My first thought, therefore, was to have two teams, or "shifts," of six learners each, who would alternate between the active and observing roles. I decided, however, to have each of the spectators stand behind one of the people who was seated at the table. I mentioned the possibility that this "support person" might want to place his or her hand lightly on the shoulder of the person being "supported," and many people did so. The role of the support person was to give any assistance requested by the person at the table. In the beginning, I directed the teams to exchange places about every ten minutes. Later, when I saw that the learners had a feel for these two roles, I allowed individuals to trade back and forth as they felt the need.

This feature of the experience was warmly received, and was the subject of much favorable comment. For one thing, it contributed to the security of the learner in two ways. The person in the "support," or "backup," role was sure of not being called on by me. Perhaps for this reason, the support person was frequently better able to produce the phrase I was calling for than was the person I was directly "teaching" at the table. At the same time, the person at the table had the security of knowing that there was always someone to fall back on when needed. The only difficulty that we encountered in this rela-tionship was that sometimes the support person would give help before it was requested. In doing so, he deprived the other person of the opportunity to work through things for himself. If the course had continued, I think this wrinkle could easily have been ironed out.

Although this innovation was apparently successful, it may have run counter to the spirit of the Silent Way. If the essence of the Silent Way is to affirm the individual learner in his self-contained independence—one might almost say, in his existential aloneness—and to guide him through work that he must do on himself, then whatever dulls that awareness of self-contained independence may distract, delay, or even defeat the deeper kinds of learning. An atmosphere of too much support and solicitude may therefore be inappropriate from this point of view, even if it does, in the short run at least, produce more right answers more comfortably. This is an issue that I myself need to explore further.

At any rate, I have found it easy to teach in this way, one at a time, all of the grammatical endings of the Turkish noun. After doing so, and after the students have met several nouns, I then use the rods in a quite different way. The long orange rod stands for the noun, while other rods stand for the endings. In Turkish, a noun may have a plural ending, plus one of a series of endings that show the person and number of its possessor, plus one of another series of endings which carry other grammatical meanings. So the orange rod is followed by three columns of rods lying on the table.

I begin with just the noun plus the rod that stands for "plural." The students must choose between two forms of this ending, according to the last vowel of the noun stem. When I tap the orange rod with the pointer, a student gives a noun. When I tap the "plural" rod, the same student gives the same noun with the appropriate form of the plural ending. If there is an error, I wait, or tap the "plural" rod again. We go around the class rapidly in this way. The steady rhythm, the visual effect of gazing at the rods, and the gentle, non-demanding tapping of the pointer combine, I think, to make relaxed concentration easier for the students.

As the activity continues, I add one suffix at a time (there are eleven altogether), identifying each by a word (e.g., "to," "from") if necessary. Each suffix has from two to sixteen forms, depending on what precedes and/or follows it. I direct each student in producing about three forms of his chosen noun. Just which forms these are depends on what I think the student needs to work on at the moment. Mistakes are dealt with in a way calculated to allow the student to do as much of the work as possible without disrupting the shared sense of moving ahead together in a way that gives learning in exchange for the time spent. So, if I think the student will catch an error himself, I give no indication that one has been made. If that is not sufficient, I lift my hand, usually from the wrist and not from the elbow or the shoulder. The purpose here is to convey the necessary information with minimal emotional impact. If I think that more information is needed, I tap again the rod—or the part of a rod—that shows *where* the error is located. Only if that is insufficient do I bring my hands and face into the picture. The total elapsed time for these "repair" activities of mine is only a few seconds.

I think that I am learning *not* to ask another student to provide a correct form for a student who still cannot come up with the desired form. To do so inevitably carries the impact of comparison, and comparison leads to an atmosphere of relative evaluation. When all students give and receive this kind of help with equal frequency, this leads to a beneficial sense of community. But a student who feels that he is always or almost always on the receiving end may become discouraged. He may then decide that he lacks the ability for this kind of thing. He may also conclude—usually wrongly, but sometimes rightly—that the other students are impatient with him for "holding them back."

Another reason for not having students supply each other with correct responses in this activity is that to do so allows them to fall back on their ability at mimicry, and to miss out on the mental work that is at the heart of learning by the Silent Way.

This way of dealing with errors could of course be cumbersome and turn into a prohibitively great burden on the teacher's memory if there were many times when students were unable to come up with the desired form on their first turn. This is why the teacher must "learn" the students as she is "teaching" them the language.

In this activity, I maintain complete "control," in the sense in which I used that word in Chapter 2. That is to say, I tell the students what to do at all times, and how to do it; in addition, I keep them informed as to the relation between their answers and the language as native speakers use it. Besides "controlling" the activity, I assume part of the "initiative" when I specify which endings a student is to add to his noun. If I were also the one who decided which noun each student was to work with, I would be exerting 100 percent of the "initiative," as well as 100 percent of the "control."

For reasons that we do not need to go into here, some Turkish nouns are easier to add endings to than others are. An argument in favor of my exerting 100 percent of the "initiative" in this way is that if the students are left to themselves, they may shy away from the more difficult nouns. An argument against full teacher "initiative" is that when the students put even a small bit of themselves into a drill, the drill is less likely to go dead on them. This second argument assumes that when people feel reasonably safe, they will not simply stagnate in the easiest options, but will reach out and explore further. When they do so, they know more precisely than even the most sensitive teacher can, just what they are ready for at any given moment. Here is an additional reason for sharing the "initiative" in this particular procedure.

As a variation, I sometimes allow the students to choose their own suffixes, as well as the noun itself. This is of course a further sharing of "initiative," still completely under the teacher's "control." It seems to work best when the students use their fingers or the pointer to touch the rods as they pronounce the endings.

This way of using the rods has drawn a large amount of student comment, virtually all of it favorable. The only class that did not enjoy it consisted of people whose concept of grammatical abstractions such as "second person singular" was not strong and clear. It seems to be especially appreciated by those students who find it hard to work with "just words." Such students have often said how thankful they are that they can have something to work with that they can see and touch and move around for themselves, to correspond to the grammatical noises that they are learning. One is reminded of Gattegno's dictum: "There is no truth in words."

There are several ways in which the teacher can keep this procedure from working well. One is to overuse it, and run it into the ground. I have already said that I think the sharing of a little "initiative" may lengthen the students' attention span. A second way is to give the students their individual tasks according to some plan or schedule which does not require the teacher to be constantly "learning" the students. This will produce tasks that are frequently inappropriate—too hard or too easy. A third way is to appear to be patient with a student who is having more difficulty than the others. It is all right to *be* patient, but the teacher who *acts* patient may cause some of the same anxieties as the teacher who acts *impatient*. A fourth way is to remain silent while presenting the task, but to become "helpfully" vocal as soon as the student hits a snag. If the tasks have been chosen by a teacher who both knows the language and is continuously "learning" the students, these snags will not destroy the forward momentum of the class. On the contrary, they are invaluable occasions for real learning, which the vocal teacher spoils.

In the brief "demonstrations," I had not bothered with reading and writing at all. In Bellingham, I wrote the first words on the board as soon as the learners were able to pronounce them. Later, when the learners had met all of the features of Turkish spelling that were unfamiliar to them, I had them do the writing I felt that this was consistent with the principle of making people aware of what resources they had inside themselves, and of not doing for learners what the learners can do for themselves. This part of the work went smoothly, and people seemed to enjoy it.

Beginning with the second session, I set aside a few minutes now and then for the learners to write out their own phrases in Turkish, and correct them among themselves. They were able to do so with only an occasional silent indication from me that something was still amiss.

As a part of the last session, I wrote on the board a brief greeting dialog in Turkish. The format was one that is well known in many published courses: individual words followed by full sentences, with a translation in a parallel column. The first step was to have the learners read the Turkish aloud. They seemed pleased with themselves to discover that among them, they could do so fairly readily. Again, the only help from me was an occasional silent indication that they needed to look again at one letter or another.

As the second step, I erased the first word (*gün*) from the board. Since that word happened to have one syllable, I set a one-centimeter rod on the table, pointed to the rod, motioned to them to speak, and they said *gün*. The second word (*aydın*) had two syllables, so I next replaced it with a two-centimeter rod on the table. I had the learners "read" first one rod and then the other until they were comfortable with them. In this way, we gradually replaced the entire five-line dialog with rods whose lengths corresponded to the numbers of syllables in the words. I also spent a little time jumping back and forth at random among the wooden "words" and found that this seemed to pose no particular difficulty for the students.

The third and last step consisted of having the learners, as a group, copy the dialog from the rods back onto the board. The discovery that they were in fact able to do so was exciting to all of us, though I pretended not to heave a sigh of relief.

Later, in other settings, I have used this same technique for text memorization in two other languages. Most recently, I have had the students themselves set up the rods. After they have gone through the dialog word by word, I sometimes have them shove pairs or triplets of rods together according to how they feel the words clump together into phrases.

Response to this way of using rods for memorization has generally been quite enthusiastic.

The only really negative experience that I have had in trying to use the Silent Way was with a group of "real" students: people enrolled in a regular language course who were not language teachers by profession. This may seem to vindicate the opinion which some people have expressed, that language teachers are a separate breed of human, so that what works for them will not necessarily work in ordinary classrooms. I think, however, that the reasons for my partial failure in this situation are more complex than that, and that such a conclusion is not justified by the facts.

In cooperation with the regular teacher, I worked with this class for two hours out of each of the first ten 6-hour days of a long course in which all students expected to go to Turkey as part of their professional careers. I started out by saying that for this part of the day we would be playing a "game" together which would prepare them to deal in a relatively independent way with the language. The techniques that I used were approximately those which I have already described, and which appear in Chapter 6. The linguistic results were highly satisfactory from my point of view, comparable to what I had gotten elsewhere with groups of language teachers. About once an hour, I gave people an opportunity to talk about the experience and to ask questions. Nothing in what was said at those times alerted me to the presence of serious trouble.

Yet about three months later, I began to overhear among the students references to the Silent Way experience. These references were humorous, but with an amount of emotion that was surprising after so long a time, and the humor was clearly tinged with bitterness and sarcasm. I therefore arranged for a series of individual interviews with the students.

Not all of the reactions that came out in these interviews were negative. One person, in fact, had liked the Silent Way very much. A few people had enjoyed the opportunities to "intuit" what was going on, and the necessity to think vigorously. One person mentioned that it was good to be able to see physical objects and to move them around during practice, and that retention had been good.

Nevertheless, the word that was used most often in describing the experience was "frustrating," with "horrible" coming out once or twice. Most troublesome was the feeling of not knowing in advance what the linguistic goal of a particular sequence of activity was going to be. Similarly, many people were unhappy when their errors were not quoted to them complete with explicit grammatical labels. They sometimes had the feeling that they had learned something, all right, but that they could not talk about what that something was. Or they felt that they frequently made the right noises for the wrong reasons, anxiously choking something out just to get their turn over with, but essentially "working in the dark." [I remember feeling this way myself in the less productive of my two intensive weekends as a student.] It was also frustrating not to be given written material for study between times. One person wanted to have some "relevant" nouns, rather than sticking so long to "rod."

The most obvious explanation for these disappointing reactions is that my teaching was defective. I may have followed wrong techniques, or I may have followed correct techniques too inflexibly, or my pacing may have been off. I would not deny any of these, and I am especially suspicious of my pacing. Remember, however, that there was nothing wrong with the *linguistic* results, and that comparable linguistic results had produced strongly positive morale in other classes.

One possible explanation that makes sense to me is that this class was generally much less secure than the others. To begin with, they had much more at stake, both in length of the total training and in career urgency. On the other hand, two important sources of security were unavailable to them. The newness of the method, in contrast to the expected "dialogs-drills-and-tapes" format, meant that they could draw no reassurance from past experiences. Perhaps even more important, I was a complete stranger to them, without the reputation that has sometimes enhanced my impact on groups of language teachers. So these students could neither develop positive expectations based on my mere presence, nor open themselves to my explanations of what we were doing and why. I had no "aura." And I did not take this fact sufficiently into account. I believe that a strong positive "aura," far from being a spurious gimmick close to charlatanry, is both a legitimate and the most fundamental factor in success, with this or with any other method.

CHAPTER 6

THE SILENT WAY IN HONOLULU

In the summer of 1977, I taught a course for language teachers at the University of Hawaii, which began with ten 75-minute sessions devoted to the learning of Turkish by my best approximation to the Silent Way. The physical conditions under which we worked were new to me. First of all, there was only one table in the room. Second, the chairs were all of the type used in many classrooms, with an arm on the right side for writing. Third, and worst, the chairs had been joined three abreast by boards attached underneath them, so that the formation of small groups of six students was extremely awkward. At the beginning of each session, we had to move the seats so that one group of three faced another, and at the end of the session we moved them back again. At best, it was difficult for the people sitting at opposite corners of this configuration to see and hear one another well. The course met at 7:20 a.m. There were 44 students, about 60 percent of them native speakers of English. In addition, visitors were required to participate in one or another of the seven groups.

Because this was a university course, I was able to ask the students to take turns in writing up the daily sessions. The papers they wrote were generally careful and thoughtful, describing the procedures themselves but also their own reactions to the procedures. Thanks to my students, I am able to document this experience with the Silent Way relatively fully.

First day. About 50 students were present. I had been hoping for about 20, but was prepared to accept as many as 32. A quick rollcall revealed, furthermore, that several of the people who had signed up for the course were not present, while many who had not preregistered wished to take the course either for credit or as auditors.

In my opening statement about the course, I said that it would consist of learning a little Turkish with my approximation of the Silent Way, followed by a little Swahili with Community Language Learning; that I would teach them, not as language teachers who were participating in a "demonstration" but as though they were students who merely wanted to learn as much language as possible in the time available; that this would not be a course "about" the methods, but "through" them—an experience which they would reflect on and assimilate, to draw on it later each in his or her own way. I also urged as many people as possible to drop the course, and announced that auditors would be required to participate and hand in papers just like students who were taking the course for credit.

My purpose in this opening statement was fourfold; (1) Most obviously, I wanted to convey certain information, and forestall certain misunderstandings. (2) Also obviously, I wanted to get the size of the class down to a more manageable number. (3) This was my first opportunity to set the climate for the course. My overriding concern was therefore that the students should begin to feel secure in the course and with me. I tried to achieve this in two ways: (a) by showing that I knew how I was going to organize their time ("control"); (b) by sounding self-assured but at the same time relaxed and gentle. (4) I had in mind a bit of a Gideon Effect (*Judges* 7), by which those who did stay in the course would feel more committed to it.

My conduct in this opening statement, and the reasoning behind it, were drawn not from the Silent Way, but from what I knew of Counseling-Learning. I then continued in a Counseling-Learning style by asking for a few volunteers to talk briefly about some of their earlier experiences with foreign languages. As they spoke, I responded to them in ways which were intended, verbally, to verify for them and for me that I was following what they were saying, and nonverbally, that I accepted them in what they were saying, without imposing on them either my own standards, or my sympathy, or my reassurance. I did this for two reasons. First, I wanted to contribute to the students' security by showing that I could and would listen to them nonjudg-mentally. This would enable them to be less defensive in their learning later on, and would also produce more frankness in their daily reaction papers. Second, I assumed that as these individuals spoke about their experiences and found themselves understood and accepted, the emotional freight which those experiences carried for them would be at least partially unloaded. I also assumed that even those people who did not actually speak would feel some of this same effect, on a vicarious basis.

These preliminary remarks concerned with administrative matters and climate-setting lasted about 40 minutes. When they were completed, and with another request that as many people as possible drop out at the end of the session, I announced that I would give them a brief sample of Turkish.

I wrote ten words on the board. Then I silently asked people to read one of them aloud (*iki*), and gave silent indications of how close they were to the pronunciation that I was after. I chose this word because it is pronounced in about the way that most users of the roman alphabet would expect it to sound. I chose students first from a row about two-thirds of the way toward the back of the room so that the first tries could be heard by everyone. I worked with one row at a time so that the people in the other rows could have a temporary feeling of safety. I went beyond just indicating when a pronunci-ation was inadequate, and gave some low-key positive feedback. I did so partly out of habit, but partly because the seating and the acoustics in the room were so bad that students were not able to learn from what people across the room said, or even to see my reaction to it.

We treated three or four more words in this way, all of them relatively easy for native and nonnative speakers of English to pronounce. Then we went on to *üç, dört,* and *altı,* all of which contain "new" vowels, which are the only difficult sounds that Turkish has for speakers of English. I worked rapidly, so that each person had a chance to try each word at least a few times.

About eight minutes before the end of the period, I stopped this activity and invited the students to express their reactions *as learners, not as teachers.* As I had done earlier in the hour, I gave responses that were intended to convey nonevaluative understanding. As I said earlier, I believe that in so doing I may have been departing from the Silent Way.

Finally, about two minutes before the end of the hour, I asked the students to sit silently for 60 seconds, closing their eyes if they liked, and allowing their minds to go into neutral. At the end of the minute, I dismissed the class, using a very quiet tone of voice. My purpose in this silent period was that the students' brains should have at least this brief opportunity, immediately after the end of the lesson, to begin the kind of work that Gattegno finds to be such an important aspect of sleep. I also hoped that this final bit of time-structuring, which made no demands on the students to perform, would contribute further toward their feeling of security.

Student reactions.   The reactions to this session, like the reactions to all but one or two of the other sessions, were overwhelmingly favorable. In this account, I shall report the critical reactions in full, and provide a sample of the favorable ones.

Two people were uncomfortable because they had still not heard any of the words pronounced by a competent speaker of the language. One felt "frustrated and cheated" at this point, while the other reported only a "nagging desire" to hear an authoritative model. Both wrote that in spite of their misgivings, they were willing to withhold judgment on the method. Their misgivings presumably show how strong is the need for security about the value of what is being learned, which manifests itself even in a course where everyone knows very clearly that the language itself is only a vehicle for experiencing a method.

One person reported that she had enjoyed the class itself very much, but that when she left the room, she found that she was not sure she could pronounce all of the words correctly from memory, and also that she was not clear about what I had expected from the class for that day. In the Silent Way, the teacher tries to leave the students with the feeling, "Now I am as good as the teacher on such-and-such a point." The teacher should also make expectations clear. Obviously, I had not fully succeeded in doing either of these things for this student on this day. But the Silent Way also recognizes that students frequently leave class with some loose ends that still need working on. And it does take time to become used to a new and very different set of expectations.

One student reported, "I felt no inadequacies by the end of the period. I was reasonably happy with my pronunciation (and the teacher seemed to accept it), so what more could I have expected from the first half hour?"

Another: "I felt very much at ease because it was not difficult to guess what the teacher wanted us to do [N.B.: Security resulting from clear "control." EWS.].... I enjoyed [it] so much that I was quite surprised to find that my attention did not wander at all."

The comments of three other people bear on Gattegno's thesis that adequate security can come from shared concentration on a series of clearly defined tasks: "Because the teacher was silent, all were paying very close attention. ..." "The nonthreatening atmosphere and mutual support stimulated by necessary total concentration on the part of the learner and her peers deemphasize the 'I can't do it' feeling. The feeling of 'Let me try again' is delightful." "A lot of effective learning took place because I felt relaxed and comfortable. My mind wasn't concentrating on my inner fears, but on what was actually going on in the classroom."

The informative but nonevaluative responses of the teacher contributed to security for at least one student: "I was afraid of making a mistake—afraid of making a fool of myself. But when I saw that others were also making mistakes but were not punished, I began to relax. ... I felt that it seems natural (at least during this class) to make errors. Because of this, I wasn't afraid to speak up and guess at the pronunciation of the words."

Second day.   I began by having the students move the seats so that one three-seat unit faced another. In this way, we created seven groups of six students each. In two groups, a seventh person sat at the end.

As I remarked earlier, this seating arrangement was extremely awkward, both because the seat-moving interfered with a smooth beginning and ending of the hour, and because people sitting at opposite ends of such a configuration had trouble in seeing and/or hearing each other. I made only minimal comments on this inconvenience, however. Instead of drawing attention to it, I tried to give the impression that it was really a minor matter that I was quite accustomed to dealing with. At the same time, I hoped that this small shared hardship, and the cooperative labor needed to overcome it, would contribute a bit toward group spirit. I think it did.

First, I asked the students to take paper and write as many words as they could remember from the preceding day. I assured them that the paper was not to be handed in. After about a minute, I had them cooperate with the person sitting opposite, to try to come up with a complete list. Then I had them cooperate in the same way in larger groups.

Then, I wrote all ten words on the board in a new order, and guided the class in working on pronunciation, in the same manner as on the first day.

Although the students did not know it yet, these words were the numbers for one through ten. I now wrote the numeral 1 opposite the first word (*bir*) and had the students read it aloud. Then I wrote a telephone number on the board, pointed to the digits one by one, and without any difficulty obtained vocalizations of them from people in the class. Then I wrote "12," and quickly found someone who guessed that the way to express it in Turkish is literally "ten two." From there we went on to larger numbers.

This maneuver was successful in that I turned out to have been right in guessing that I would be able to obtain the words I wanted, and that I could obtain them quickly. But it also shows the tendency that I have come to distrust in myself as a teacher: I was trying to impress my audience with how much I could get them to do, how quickly, with how little input from me. In short, I was showing off. I succeeded with some of the students, but too many of the others were lost and discouraged—left so far from what was going on that for the time being they had no basis even for working effectively. Although a class is always and legitimately an audience, it is an audience to be led, not to be exploited. I paid for my irresponsibility with a temporary faltering of the class.

When many of the class were able to handle numbers in the hundreds of thousands, I called one student to the board to serve as secretary in writing down numbers that were called out from the floor. This was another calculated risk, but worked out better. In the words of the student who was put into this position:

> I felt that I was chosen because I had an obvious look of confusion on my face. Much to my surprise, however, I was not panic-stricken as I have been under similar circumstances before. I do not feel that this ease was due to the method. I have had a brief experience with a similar method before and it was a terrible strain because of the competitiveness. The calm feeling was probably due to the fact that the class is relatively relaxed and friendly, and that the teacher's personal style is very soothing.

Finally, I had the students practice among themselves in groups of three.

The period ended with a few minutes in which people expressed their reactions and I understood them, followed by a minute or two of silent relaxation, as on the first day.

Student reactions made clear that I had committed one tactical error which I could have foreseen. I had chosen the numbers 1 to 10 for the first day's pronunciation work because they happened to include all of the vowels and almost all of the unusual spelling conventions of Turkish. This meant that we could get into the meaningful work of the second day without having to add new words. But the use of alphabetical order on Monday left many with the feeling that *altı* should mean "1," *beş* should mean "2," etc. They were eventually able to work this out, but the work was unnecessary and irrelevant, and caused a number of negative comments.

One student wrote that my silent cues were not always clear. (Others, however, disagreed with him.) He also felt that there was a certain inefficiency in relying on models provided by other students instead of the teacher. Another, with a different reaction to the same aspect of the session, wrote, "I was surprised that the material was presented so silently and smoothly. Because of the silence, I felt more eager to try and to learn than if the teacher had talked. I wasn't afraid to make mistakes because I knew that the other students were concentrating on pronunciation, rather than on each other's mistakes." Two others made similar comments about the teacher's silence. There were also favorable comments about the small-group practice, and about the brief silence at the end of the period.

Third day.   First, I checked individual pronunciation of the words that contained the vowels *ü, ö,* and *ı,* so that people could know where they still had work to do, and so that they could carry that work forward by listening to themselves and each other and by noting my reactions. Because of the size of the class, I worked very rapidly, skipping from one part of the room to another, but keeping track of who I still had to spend time with.

Then I wrote some long numbers on the board and had the class pronounce them, largely in chorus.

Third, I had individuals come to the board one at a time and write numbers dictated by other students. My purpose was to provide for "initiative" on the part of the students, and for interaction among them. This was carelessly executed on my part, however, because people were never quite sure who was supposed to•dictate the next number. That is to say, I did not provide sufficient "control" in organizing that aspect of the activity. When I saw that it was beginning to drag, I discontinued it. Instead, I had the students practice dictating numbers among themselves in their groups. This size group was large enough so that errors were unlikely to go undetected, but small enough so that there was plenty of time and space for everyone to get more practice. They also began to discover how much they could do for one another, and how nearly infallible a group consensus was, in the absence of the Authority Figure.

While this was going on, I noticed that some people were making use of notebooks, and asked the class not to do personal writing during group sessions. This kind of writing, I feel, merely perpetuates the anxious, individualistic style of learning which is the only one that many students have ever experienced, and which blocks them from experimenting with something new.

I placed the table in the middle of the room, and had four people come and sit around it. Then, by lifting up rods of various colors, I made it clear that this word could apply to any rods at all. I also remembered to make clear that it did not apply to other objects, such as pencils or chairs.

Then I picked up a blue rod, because it is a large rod and because the Turkish word for "blue" is fairly easy to pronounce. I put it next to other blue objects in order to show that what I was interested in was its color. I had the students read aloud the words from the board until they came to the right one. Then I led them to say "one blue rod," "two blue rods," etc.

At this point, I replaced the students at the table with other volunteers and continued, adding two more colors and practicing more three-word phrases. At first I selected the rod configurations for them to describe, but later had them select them. Because the linguistic possibilities were still extremely limited, I was not really relaxing "control" in doing so, but I was providing the students with a chance to exercise a little "initiative" and to interact with one another. Finally, with a third group of volunteers at the table, we completed learning the colors that were listed on the board.

Having the students guess which words went with which colors may have seemed a little cute on my part. On the other hand, I did not want to do for them what they could easily do among and for themselves. There were, after all, only a few words to choose among. And this way, when the students read a new word aloud, the reading was not an end in itself, but a means toward the larger and slightly deeper goal of finding out its meaning.

As before, we ended the period with a few minutes for student reactions, and a minute or two of silence.

There were no unfavorable written reactions to this session. There was some evidence that two aspects of this new style of learning were beginning to be felt: "I had plenty of time to practice everything, and time to make *internal assumptions* about how the language works." [Emphasis added.] "I especially like hypothesizing about the language from the very beginning." "Personally, I feel extremely comfortable." "I felt anxiety when the notebook had to be closed; but this left quickly when I realized I did not need it." "I experienced quite a variety of feelings. I was pleased with the progress I was making learning the numbers. I was even gaining a feeling of confidence. That confidence was greatly diminished when I went to the table to work with the rods and suddenly found that I didn't know the colors. After an initial sinking feeling, I was able to go on and try because I felt I had the support and help of the rest of the class. I really like the feeling of togetherness and team work I get in this class."

There was also one account of the results of work that went on during sleep: "When I was talking with friends Wednesday night, I said that I couldn't remember the colors, but when I got to class on Thursday, I discovered that I did remember them."

Fourth day.   I began by asking the students not to use notebooks during the whole-class and small-group work, and to avoid English in the small groups. I also distributed a set of rods to each group.

As I had done on the third day, I began with a review, giving every individual at least a few chances to verify his/her pronunciation of the three unfamiliar vowels.

Then I invited the class to practice numbers in groups of three students. While they were doing so, I left the room for a minute or two. I left the room for two reasons: first, to allow them to feel more free to experiment with their voices; second, to say in action what I had already said in words: that by now the consensus of even a small group was close to infallible.

After about 5 minutes of small group practice, I had a few students come to the board one at a time, either to take dictation from the class, or to write things for the class to pronounce. My purpose was to give them experience in helping one another, and in making choices within the limits that I had set.

Finally, using the small table as I had used it on the third day, I introduced the remaining colors, and had the class pronounce the words. I pointed to or modified the written word in order to show where additional work was needed and, if necessary, to make clear exactly what that work was.

After the introduction of each new item, I allowed time for small-group practice. As I had earlier, I left the room briefly during each of these occasions.

I then invited student reactions. After a few minutes of understanding these reactions, I invited the members of the small groups to introduce themselves to one another. My reason for waiting until the fourth day rather than doing this earlier, was that I felt that now the class was past the shakedown phase; now the students were beginning to recognize one another, and to become familiar with how they were like and unlike one another. To have done introductions too early, I felt, would have come across as a hollow and perfunctory maneuver out of a catalog of techniques for "building group spirit."

I also invited the students to call me by my first name if they felt comfortable in doing so. I would estimate that about half of them—mostly Americans—did so by the end of the course. I did not insist on this point, particularly because I knew that the cultural backgrounds of many of the students forbade it.

The class ended with silence.

Reactions were more varied than on the first three days. One student found himself to be the only person in his small group who had been present at the earlier sessions. All of the responsibility for remembering and correcting therefore fell on him. In a negative way, this verifies the value of the consensus which I mentioned above, as well as the support which the small groups can provide for their members. As two other comments put it: "Small groups are good for making reticent speakers open up. No one minds being corrected by a group member." "Our group works well together. To verify each other's pronunciation, we just listened [to one another] and pronounced any word that we thought sounded strange. The speaker then said the word again: nobody 'drilled' anybody else." One person, however, "had mixed reactions to peer corrections. When there was disagreement, . . . I didn't want to admit right off that my version was incorrect. I wanted outside confirmation."

Perhaps related to this last comment, one person reacted negatively to the way another student had acted while at the board: "She/he seemed to be 'drilling' the rest of the class" in what came across as an "aggressive manner."

I, too, had noticed this element in the style of the student at the board, and for that reason had terminated the activity as soon as I thought I could do so gracefully.

One person commented that listening to other students during the verification of pronunciation, and noting my reactions to them, was effective for her because it enabled her to know "what to aim for. I keep that in mind and then let my pronunciation happen."

There was also evidence of the development of "inner criteria" in another person's statement: "Although I missed the first three classes, I was able to catch up with the others. I am aware that I didn't have all of the sounds right, but the knowledge of the words stabilized in me. . . . Outside the class, I found that I was naming colors in Turkish."

One person said that choral reading of numbers written on the board was frequently ineffective for her because she couldn't hear parts of the answers. I had intended the choral work to provide a safely anonymous occasion for people to make noises. But whatever that may have contributed to "security" was more than offset, for this person at least, by the insecurity of not knowing what the right answer was—a failure on my part to maintain the second aspect of "control" (Chapter 2).

One person reported "some boredom with the lengthy group practice of colors and numbers—even though I needed the practice." This could perhaps have been prevented if I had used a greater variety of techniques, particularly techniques with more involvement of emotions. But changing techniques too often can become confusing. I had to strike a balance.

Another area in which I had to balance advantages against disadvantages was in the announcement of objectives. One person said she would have liked to know whether the primary goal of the week was just pronunciation. The fact is that I did have a rather clear series of goals: security with me, security with each other, pronunciation, vocabulary, and awareness of their own functioning as learners. Perhaps I could have been more explicit about these goals. But there would have been two dangers. Instead of concentrating on what was going on from moment to moment, people might have found it harder to keep from worrying about those goals and their progress toward them. And I would have had less freedom in responding to events as they unfolded in class.

One person reported that he was at first uneasy when I left the room, but that he soon came to see it as my way of expressing confidence in the class.

One person reported what I have also experienced as a student, and have observed in many others: "One minute I knew that *kırmızı* means 'red,' the next I had forgotten it, but still later I recalled it again," with alternating feelings of frustration and satisfaction. I suspect that becoming aware of this flickering of new words, and learning to accept and work with it, may have been among the more valuable things that have been learned up to this point in the course.

Two people said that, although they themselves had found the method enjoyable and effective, they doubted that it would work with students the age of the ones that they teach. These comments are evidence of how hard it is, in practice, to keep clear the difference between a "demonstration" and an "experience."

Fifth day.   This was the last day of the week. The last 30 minutes were set aside for questions asked by the class members in their capacity as language teachers, rather than as my students of Turkish. The Turkish learning was therefore abbreviated. The separation of student-reactions from the teacher-reactions of the same participants has proved to be of the utmost value in keeping an "experience" from degenerating into a "demonstration." Keeping these kinds of reaction apart requires from the leader a certain amount of resoluteness, as well as tact.

Like the preceding sessions, this one began with review of old material, with emphasis on verification of pronunciation. We then moved to small-group work on the same material. As I had on the fourth day, I left the room briefly at the beginning of this step.

I then asked for a volunteer to come to the table in the center of the room. After setting out a few groups of rods and having the volunteer name them, I said in Turkish, "Take one pink rod." When, as I had expected, there was no response, I took his hand and guided it in the action. In this way, the meaning came across fairly quickly. Then I had someone else write it on the board, with the help of the class. This was followed by small-group practice.

Finally, the phrase "Give me . . ." was introduced, followed by practice in the small groups.

Some of the papers that were written after this session went beyond the events of this day, and talked about the writers' views of the Silent Way in general. One of these papers was generally negative. For one thing, the writer pointed out, the Silent Way is so different from conventional instruction that students are "initially insecure about how they should be acting." He therefore suggested that such a course ought to begin with a description of the method. It is true that I kept my own introductory remarks to a minimum with this class. I am not sure, however, that I would not do so again. To spell the method out in detail at the beginning would probably mean that students would learn the *linguistic* part of the course with a little less initial stress. But this might also cut the students off from any chance of learning some of the more general, more essential facts about the method, and about themselves as learners.

The same writer felt that there was a good deal of "inefficiency" in the Silent Way, at least as he had seen me use it. For one thing, he felt that people were having to divert too much energy into figuring out what my gestures and other silent signals were supposed to mean. He would have liked to have these explained "at the beginning of the lesson." This reaction contrasts with some of those that I have already quoted, or with another person's state-ment that while this "might be frustrating for some students, for me it was [just] suspense. It did not bother me." The negative reaction is just as valid as the others, of course. The teacher should certainly try to be clear in structur-ing the activity and in providing feedback, and I apparently failed to do so, at least for this student.

It would be possible to comment aloud to the class on the meanings of some frequently used conventions. But a complete inventory of the nonverbal signals to be used in a particular lesson would be impossible; worse, I think it would violate the overall approach by depriving the student of an opportunity to learn more than just the language.

The method also seemed inefficient because it appeared that, by not giving the model, the teacher is forced to "wait for the correct pronunciation to emerge almost randomly from the whole range of trials." For me as a teacher, this is definitely *not* what I do. I will not gamble on a correct pronun-ciation coming up soon unless I know that the cards are stacked in my favor—that is, unless I know that at least one student in the group has had earlier experience with the sound, or a similar one. Thus, I withheld models of ü and ö from this class, but did pronounce ı once. In a class with no experi-ence in French or German, I might have provided models of all three.

It also is inaccurate to believe that "the larger the number of students, the greater the number of wrong responses the teacher has to endure." From my point of view, the *larger* the number of students, the *better* the chance that at least one of them will come up with the desired response. And I do not feel that wrong responses are something that I must "endure." They are invalu-able evidence—my best evidence, in fact—about where the students are in their work with the language.

Another writer, also commenting in general, found this kind of learning to be "active, productive, and . . . effective." Having to correct himself without a further audible model "makes the student very attentive to what is going on."

One student who joined the class on the fourth day had a full range of negative feelings, but in practice was able to climb beyond them: "I was shocked at first to see how little the instructor said. I felt a need to ask ques-tions, but realized that I wasn't supposed to. I wanted to drill the instructor [sic] on some sounds, but that was impossible. I had doubts about what the standards for correct pronunciation were. I had misgivings about the amount of time spent in reconstructing what the instructor had said . . . I felt a little frustrated. Nevertheless, the general experience was pleasant for me. I felt I was participating in a profitable game. . . . I was forced to contemplate, grapple with, and test out the language I was learning. . . . I feel I get a firmer grasp on [the] language this way." This feeling of a "profitable game" is exactly what I would like to create in all the students I teach by the Silent Way.

One student said that he would like to have more practice than had been provided, and another wished that there were more chances for students to speak. One said he was quite happy with the experience in class, but was not sure how much he would remember over a long period.

Another student had two things to say about lapses of time. She reported that on the day following this class, at the beach, "I picked up a small stick, and quite unconsciously uttered the word *çubuk*." She also felt that the minute or two of silence at the end of the period allows "each person [to] leave class with a mental summary of the language" that had been used in that session.

One person provided a detailed account of what happened in his small group. There was disagreement as to whether "take" should be *alın,* or *allın.* The "strongest member" thought it should be *allın,* but there was "no real confrontation," and when I provided the correct form (*alın*), there was "no gloating," and the group "quickly picked up and practiced" the correct form.

The same writer reported that there was some confusion about the meaning of *bana* "to me," and that this confusion drove the group to using English. I think that this resulted from my failure to follow the principle of "one thing at a time." The element that paralleled *alın* was *verin* "give." I introduced *bana . . . verin* "give . . . to me" almost simultaneously. I should not have been surprised, therefore, when *bana* caused trouble both with regard to its meaning and with regard to its position.

Sixth day. We began with the students working in small groups to review what they remembered from previous sessions. The security of the small group, as contrasted with performance in public under my direction, seemed particularly important because today was Monday following two days away from Turkish.

I then did the usual checking of pronunciation, with special attention to the three unfamiliar vowels.

When that was completed, I summoned three or four students to the table. First, I gave them familiar directions: "Take _____" and "Give me _____." Then I said, "Give him/her _____," and caused them to act accordingly. This gave them the word "to him/her" as a contrast and clarification for "to me." Finally, I had someone write it on the board. The visible form provided another channel for the input and also increased the security of many people. Since the Turkish word (*ona*) was very easy to write, letting a student do it with help from friends was a safe way of demonstrating, and expressing confidence in, their own inner resources at this point.

The principal new material for the day consisted of the postpositions (which in Turkish are actually nouns) "top/over," "bottom/under," and "(be)side." Using my hand in exaggerated gestures above and beneath the table, I said *alt* "under" and required the students to be silent for a few seconds in order to assimilate the sound. Then I had them repeat it twice in unison. Third, I had someone write it on the board. In the same way, I presented *üst* "above" and *yan* "side."

Then I took an orange rod and silently led the class to say *turuncu çubuk yanı* "orange rod side," which was not fully correct. Next, I motioned for silent attention and said *turuncu çubuğun yanı* "the orange rod's its side," which is correct Turkish. After a pause and group repetitions, I silently asked for this phrase to be written on the board.

Here, I felt safe in drawing on the little reservoir of confidence that I had built up in the students by letting them write relatively simple words like *ona* and *alt*. In their cooperative version of the new phrase, I knew that there would be some errors. Wrong vowels and consonants could be easily set right by merely pointing to the spot where further work was needed, and letting the group process operate. I of course served as guarantor of the final accuracy. But the silent letter *ğ* was something that *I* had to write, pantomiming the fact that it has no sound.

In the same way, we learned *turuncu çubuğun üstü* "the top of the orange rod" and *turuncu çubuğun altı* "the bottom of the orange rod," and wrote them on the board. This new structure then became the subject of practice in the small groups.

Next, I summoned volunteers to the table I placed a red rod on top of a blue rod, and led the students to say what they were able to say: *kırmızı çubuk mavi çubuğun üstü* "red rod blue rod's its top." Then, in the same way in which I had introduced *turuncu çubuğun yanı* (above), I said, *kırmızı çubuk mavi çubuğun üstünde* "red rod [is] at the blue rod's its top," which is one Turkish way of describing this configuration. This was followed by small-group practice.

The session ended with the usual silence.

One person said she was surprised at what she had been able to learn, and at the pleasure with which she had learned it. At the same time, however, she noted that the teacher's gestures were sometimes complicated, and that they left her uncertain about what the class was supposed to do.

Two others, uncertain about the precise meanings of the new endings, felt themselves wishing for traditional translation equivalents. Another person liked the presentation because it focused her entire attention on the new material so that she was able to remember it on the following day.

Two other reports raised special issues. The first writer expressed his general pleasure with the session, but said that "I knew Turkish was Altaic and therefore probably had vowel harmony, but I could not figure out what the phonological features were that governed the vowel harmony." This concern is a relic of the usual academic approach to language learning, at variance with that kind of relaxed concentration on the material at hand which the Silent Way calls for.

The second writer reported that a newcomer to their group had disrupted their practice by being bossy and talking too much, even though his ability was high, and even though from a purely linguistic point of view he did not hold the others back. This experience highlights the crucial importance of "what goes on inside of and among the people in the classroom."

Seventh day. The day began with small-group practice. However, as soon as the groups had settled down to work, I had everyone stand and rotate one seat clockwise in the group. This was so that the same pairs (for face-to-face work) and triplets would not become permanent. At the same time, rotating within the existing groups was less costly both in time and in emotion, compared with a random reshuffling of the whole class. I had the students rotate again from time to time throughout the rest of the course.

Group practice was followed by a quick pronunciation check.

The only new material for the day was the Turkish expression for "between." I felt that without something new, the students might feel that their forward progress had stopped. On the other hand, the new material of the previous day had been so complex that I thought it needed additional work. I chose "between" because it fits with the other locations, but represents an additional morphophonemic complication beyond "vowel harmony." (Although I still think that this was a right decision with regard to most of the class, one person reported that he would have liked to have more new material.)

The practice consisted in having the students build and describe rod structures. For this, we alternated between the demonstration table with the whole class watching, and small-group practice. For additional variation in technique: (1) A student built and described a structure with the rods, and the others said *evet* "yes" or *hayır* "no," to show whether they thought the description was right or wrong. (2) One student described while another built. (3) Using a vertical notebook as a screen, I built a simple structure which one pair of students could see, but another pair could not. The first pair described, while the second pair built a duplicate structure. The reason for working with pairs, rather than with individuals, was partly that in this way I could involve twice as many people. More important was the moral and linguistic support that the partners were able to give one another. This increased their security, but it also made things move more rapidly because most uncertainties and mistakes were caught and dealt with immediately, without having to wait for me or other outsiders.

The session ended, as usual, with expressions of people's reactions as students, and with a minute or two of silence.

Three people wrote that they were unclear, not about what had been presented, but about the further ways in which the new construction could be used. Another wrote, "I am beginning to experience a great amount of pleasure at finally being able to make longer, more complex sentences in Turkish. I feel I am beginning to get the hang of things."

One person expressed a preference for working in groups of two rather than in groups of three, provided that there was frequent rotation, and provided that the dyads could call on one another for help when they needed it. In this way, there was more time for practice.

There was evidence that some of the general, nonlinguistic goals of the Silent Way were being realized. One person commented that "the student's independence is indeed being trained." Another reported, " I was having trouble with the meanings of the new forms because I was thinking about their English translations and trying to pay attention to the demonstration at the same time. Then I realized that I wasn't doing the right thing, and started to pay more attention to [what was going on]. After that, I learned [the new material] readily."

Eighth day.   Today was to have been a repeat of yesterday as far as procedures were concerned. The new material was a suffix meaning "from," which in form and function is exactly parallel to the suffix "in, on, at" which had been introduced and practiced earlier. The purpose was to consolidate previous learning through addition of the sentence "Take _____ from on/top of/underneath/beside _____ ."

After practice got underway, however, I noticed that people were saying things like "Take two red rods from on top of the blue rod" when there were in fact *only* two red rods on top of the blue rod. It occurred to me that the usual thing to say under those circumstances would be the Turkish equivalent of "Take *the* two red rods. . . ." This required only the substitution of *çubuğu* for *çubuk*. I therefore went ahead and tried to teach this distinction, superimposing it on the "from" pattern, with which most of the class was still working.

As will be clear from some of the comments quoted below, this was a large and costly blunder on my part. It was also an obvious one—so obvious that I still cannot understand how I could have fallen into it. In the first place, it violates the principle of "one thing at a time," and of working with students where they are at the moment. In the second place, my experience in Bellingham had nearly run afoul of this same "definite direct object" ending, and I had at that time worked out a way around it. My best guess is that I was intoxicated by the success of the first seven days, and gave in to the temptation to impress someone—myself and possibly some of the students—with the method and/or with my own virtuosity in it.

The oral reactions at the end of the hour indicated dismay, anger, and other negative feelings. Nevertheless, of the six written reports, two reported positive feelings. One wrote, "After the new material was introduced, the class was faced with the task of delimiting the possible combinations of the structures we now knew. . . . This was naturally a confusing process, during which certain patterns became clearer through trial and error. I was surprised when I found out how far we had jumped. . . . This one experience more than any other seemed to demonstrate the effectiveness of the technique to me, in the sense that the period of doubt worked itself out into a clear ability to use the structures, although I was not 'linguistically certain' of all that was going on."

The other favorable report mentioned the absence of any "pressure or anxiety," and commented that, although I was trying to withhold positive feedback, my reactions were still visible enough to help him toward a correct pronunciation. It may be that this reaction indicated that I had slipped into a crowd-pleasing deviation from the Silent Way, achieving pleasant short-term results at the expense of deeper long-term effects.

A third writer directed negative comments against his group, which he felt did not provide sufficient "care and attention" to its members on this day. (I would guess that any falling off of group spirit came from anxiety, which came in turn from the faulty presentation on my part.) On the other hand, the same writer continued, "During the silence, many things came to my mind, and they seemed to come quite naturally. . . . I was more interested in the art of concentration and in controlling myself, than in learning the language. It was a kind of Zen practice."

The other three writers were directly critical of the way the session had gone. One failed to realize at first that the difference between *çubuk* and *çubuğu* was not just a variation which I was for some reason letting go by. Then she had trouble figuring out what the difference stood for. "I constructed several theories, only to have them destroyed. I wanted to demand that you rescue us from our confusion, yet at the same moment, I did not want to be helped."

Another writer commented that "after 20 minutes of groping, it appeared that most of the students left today's class in a state of total frustration."

The last writer also mentioned "frustration," and also a loss of confidence in her grasp of Turkish. She continued, "Wednesday's experience was the first really jarring one in the two weeks that we've been doing this. I feel that the Silent Way really lulls one into a false sense of security. In class, I feel that I'm speaking Turkish and am very proud and pleased. But when I think about it, I really know very little. I expect that Wednesday's experience, by emphasizing my limited competence in the language, may have made it a positive experience, rather than a negative one." The fact that these words were written by a person who in the course of the summer proved to be an unusually strong and self-reliant learner shows how fragile learners can be. Her *linguistic* security had not really been dealt such a blow; what had suffered was her confidence—in herself, in me, and in the Silent Way. I, in turn, was jarred by realizing how grave was my responsibility to the Silent Way as well as to these students when I claimed to be representing it to them.

Ninth day. The new material for today consisted of only three new postpositions: "in front of," "behind," and "at the end of." These posed no new structural problems at all. I introduced them only so that people would have the feeling of some forward progress. My primary goal for the day was to work through the unresolved issues of the preceding day and restore confidence. The techniques were similar to those used on the eighth day except that when someone produced a correct sentence, I often had that student or the whole class repeat it.

This was to be the last day of learning Turkish by the Silent Way. At the end of the learning segment, and before the time for student comments, I decided to give the class an example of a contrasting way of teaching the same material. I summarized, in linguistic terminology, the many grammatical features of the language which they had come to control in nine hours, and assured them that this was very difficult indeed.

There was no time for silence at the end of this session.

The written reports were generally favorable again. Four people commented specifically on the recovery since yesterday. A typical account was, "Feelings of frustration and doubt began to give way to more confidence, through the rod work and observation of the rod work, though some doubt remains. Speed and complete facility are still lacking, but we are getting a 'handle' on the material. My own time at the center table was exhausting, but at the same time exhilarating with discovery."

One person commented that the repetition of the correct sentences had been very helpful, but that he would have liked more of it. Along the same line, another person suggested that, in the absence of printed charts, the correct sentences might have been written on the board. I think that both suggestions were highly appropriate.

Someone else wrote, "I am particularly impressed with the learning which occurs in small-group exercises. Group work requires each student to become an active participant in learning. Furthermore, a student who makes an error receives direct and immediate attention. While students are working among themselves, the instructor is available to verify questionable structures."

A sharply contrasting view of group work was expressed by another writer: "I felt some annoyance at the other members of the group. Generally the others would work first, only asking me for verification. I didn't feel right mentioning it to them, but I did feel I was being taken advantage of. I also felt considerable resentment when I was corrected by other members of the group. Despite the fact that I consciously realized that group teaching is an important part of the Silent Way, I think that subconsciously I resented having my 'equals' correct me." [I don't think group teaching *is* an essential part of the Silent Way, though the size and arrangement of the room made it almost inescapable with this class. EWS]

The same person also expressed frustration at not having learned any "basic conversational Turkish"—what Gattegno calls "luxury vocabulary." Another person, however, reported that "I feel I am 'speaking' the language. I can't ask for what I want in a store, or tell someone what I think, but I feel I'm getting a base for doing those things."

The issue of how a Silent Way teacher should deal with correct responses from students, which one person discussed yesterday, was addressed by another person today. (Both writers referred to experience with other Silent Way teachers.) Today's commentator took issue with my use of the expression "matter-of-fact" in describing the style of feedback that I was trying to achieve: " 'Matter-of-fact' has negative connotations: indifference, maybe smugness. If a teacher projects these feelings, students will react negatively to them. . . . Actually, I feel that a teacher shouldn't be . . . truly neutral when giving feedback. It's not human! The teacher should strive to be nonevaluative, while projecting interest and concern for students as learners and as fellow human beings." [This is, in fact, quite consistent with what I do mean by "matter-of-fact." EWS]

My little lecture on what the students had accomplished drew mixed reactions, all of which made me feel that it had succeeded in its purpose. "I liked your description of what we've learned so far. . . . I strongly feel that any such explanation before or even after your introduction of new material and our practice *would have confused me.* It would have been *a barrier* between me and my using the language. I really like being able to figure things out." Another writer: "The comments on Turkish shed *too much light,* and contributed to a great *let-down.* Granted, it's a complicated language, but to go into detail doesn't seem necessary, and in the long run *may even be discouraging.* To look back at the progress we have made is revealing, but to look at the whole picture is frightening." [Emphasis added.] A third writer commented in a similar way.

Tenth day. The experience of the first nine days had all used a single family of techniques, as close as I could manage to the standard procedures of the Silent Way. On this tenth and last day, I broke the continuity by using two quite different techniques, still teaching Turkish. I had two purposes in doing so. One was to show how the principles of the Silent Way might be applied to an audiolingual or a grammar-oriented course. Second, and more important, I wanted to help the teachers who were acting as my students to separate, in their own minds, the principles from the concrete techniques.

The two procedures that I used were the one for teaching dialogs and the one for teaching inflectional endings. Since I have already described them (Chapter 5), I will not give an account of them here. They were well received. One person reported that three days later she was surprised to realize that she could still remember all of the words and sentences that she had learned in this way. Another person felt that "using the rods for words and phrases was effective because they were clear mnemonic aids. They made it easy to remember all the words in order, yet didn't make me dependent on writing, the great enemy of memory." One person's report indicates that I could have been clearer in getting across the idea that the length of each rod corresponded to the number of syllables in the word. Another felt that "presenting the meaning of a new word in the student's first language visually even for a very short time is a good way to give the student a feeling of security, [but] to have him exposed to written words too long may lose the whole significance of the Silent Way, mainly because he will just try to produce automatically what he sees written, without activating his mind."

One person was "impressed with everything about the Silent Way except the [teacher's? EWS] silence." At the same time, he felt that some strong students might be able to learn as much or more in the same amount of time by doing response drills with a native speaker. He also said that he had observed a group of Peace Corps Volunteers being trained by the Silent Way at the intermediate level in the Kigeni language, and had not been reassured, even though Peace Corps officials had told him that PCVs trained in this way generally test higher at end of training than PCVs trained audiolingually.

Another report presented a contrasting view: "In group activity, I sometimes felt like asking for an English equivalent of a new Turkish word, but my peers kept me from it. In learning a completely exotic language, I found myself to be more mentally productive through trial and error than I had been before."

Postscript.   To me personally, this ten-hour experience with the Silent Way was intensely enjoyable and satisfying. My only regret was that I ended the experience according to my original schedule, instead of continuing it for an extra day or two. In this way, I might have consolidated the recovery from the trauma of the eighth day. This would have left the students with a more favorable, and to my mind also a fairer, impression of the method. I said this to the class near the end of the course.

Two weeks later, in a lecture course on teaching methods, I conducted a one-hour experience with beginning Turkish for a class of six volunteers. This time, I started with a set of words on the board which included numbers, but also some other words. The words were grouped by their vowels. I was even more careful than before to reduce positive feedback. Also, when someone had trouble with a sound, I did not elicit a model from someone else directly. Instead, I went on around the circle, as though forgetting about the student's difficulty, but making sure that the necessary information was present in what I asked the second or third student to do. This hour was the best I had ever conducted, both with regard to the amount learned (by spectators as well as by the six participants) and with regard to the comments afterward.

PART III

A SECOND WAY: COUNSELING-LEARNING

CHAPTER 7

THE BEGINNING OF A LETTER

Dear B _____ ,

· You have already seen, from the thickness of the envelope, that this is not an ordinary letter to you. It is, in fact, the first draft of the missing chapters of the book that I told you of in September. Chapters 1–6 were ready a year ago, and the other chapters lie at hand almost completed. But, as you know, writing stopped last spring with Chapter 7, which was to introduce the accounts of what some of us have done with Counseling-Learning and Community Language Learning. In the two months since our last conversation, I have been turning over in my mind how I might say more clearly what I was trying to say at that time. Then, a few days ago, I began to write this chapter, but as a letter to you. I could not have done it in any other way. Come to think of it, this fits in well with Curran's deep belief that even what we call "scholarly communications" are, first and last, embedded in the give and take between whole persons.

One reason why I can write this letter to you is that I know you have read Curran's books about Counseling-Learning and Community Language Learning, and also the things that I have written. You worked through a week-long institute in 1975, and you have watched me as I did my best to show various groups of language teachers what I thought CL and CLL were all about. You have used some of the ideas from CL and CLL in your own classes, and I believe you have used them both wisely and well. Yet the last time we talked about these matters, I saw that your understanding of them was unlike mine. I am not sure just *how* unlike, or exactly *where* the unlikenesses are. But, with your patience, I will set before you now, in this letter, my own understanding. I do this, at the same time, because I hope that other people besides you will take in, through their own eyes, what I have written first of all for yours.

In the preceding paragraph, I have three times used the words "CL and CLL," instead of "CL/CLL." This is a departure from the usage of much that Curran and others have written about his work. The form "CL/CLL" emphasizes the essential unity of that work, and the fact that "Community Language Learning" has its roots in—is one manifestation of—the overall approach to education called "Counseling-Learning." Certainly we must recognize this unity and this continuity. Yet the longer I work with CL and CLL, the surer I am that we must *also* see them as separate from each other. If we do not, we may fall into a confusion of the general with the specific, and demand that CLL do what CL is supposed to do, or vice versa. What I mean by this will become clearer in this chapter and Chapter 8.

Even though both you and I are language teachers, B _____ , and though most of the other people who are likely to read this are language teachers, I hope you will stay with me through these next pages, which will be about "counseling" as Curran used that word, and about Counseling-Learning, and not directly about language teaching. Other readers should skip this chapter entirely, unless they want to get at what lies beneath the chapters that follow.

I think I can best set forth my understanding of CL under four headings:

1. Getting It All Together (The Chaos Within)
2. Holding It Together (The Chaos From Across the Room)
3. "Loving" and Stillness
4. Sharing in What Is There

Young people of the past ten or fifteen years have talked about "getting it all together." With these words, they have come near to one of the insights at the heart of Counseling-Learning: the insight that doing and feeling and knowing (what scholars sometimes call the "somatic, affective, and cognitive aspects of living") cannot be fully untangled from one another; we may choose to look at only one or two of them, but then we will not see the whole; in some kinds of research, we may cut them apart artificially, but in so doing we cut ourselves off from life. This is true for one learner at a time, and also for all of the people in a classroom as they work with, on, and through one another.

But as you well know, there is more to "getting it all together" than "unity of body, mind, and spirit," whatever that may mean. We also have a need— even a strong drive—to get our *expectations* together. I know that "getting expectations together" is a clumsy way to put it, and that it sounds as if I am making up my own private jargon. So let me try to spell out what I mean by it.

In simple English, my "expectations" are whatever I think is likely to happen. What I think will happen—the way I think things are going to be one year, one hour, one second from now—is built up out of all the things that I have learned to tell apart from one another, and from the ways in which these things have fitted themselves together in my mind. Rain is not snow, but when spring comes, both will run downstream as water. Red is not green, and a motorist faced with a red light almost always stops. Girls are not boys, and margarine is not butter, and irony is not quite sarcasm. These things, and more subtle things, and more complex things—these things and the ways in which I have seen them fit together in the past, make up my picture of the world. One might even say that they *are* my world—the only world I know. This, in one sense, is that "world of meaningful action" that Adler, and after him Becker, talked about: the very world in which, at the end, my life will have been worthy or will have been lost. What I am—the world in which I have meaning—is made up of what I have learned to expect.

A well-known example of what I mean is the fact that where English has the word "snow," Eskimo has fifty or more words for different varieties of white frozen water. The Eskimos have learned to *tell one* "kind of snow" *from another.* They also know what to *expect* from each, in terms of heaviness, ability to bear the weight of a snowshoe, and so on.

A striking example came up one time when I was talking with a group of people from Northern Europe. During the conversation, they said that many of their American colleagues did not greet them, or acknowledge their greetings, when they met in the hallways or the elevators. This did not meet their expectations of how people show courtesy to one another. I then raised my eyebrows, and asked them whether *that* would be enough to make them feel that another person had acknowledged that they were there. At first, they were not even aware of what I was talking about. Then they saw the raising of my eyebrows, but were not able, without a little practice, to distinguish it from a wink. I suspect that, most of the time, the Americans who they thought had ignored them had actually greeted them silently by a friendly raising of eyebrows. These Northern Europeans and I were different from one another in what facial movements we could *tell apart,* and in what we *expected* other people to do.

A language is also a complex network of telling things apart and knowing what to expect of them. The most obvious examples are "phonemic" distinctions: speakers of one language hear and use the difference between r and l, or between nasalized and nonnasalized vowels, while speakers of other languages do not use them, cannot hear them, and so ignore them. Another example which was first described a quarter of a century ago but which is receiving increased attention these days is "cloze" testing, in which a person's strength in a language is measured by his ability to fill in blanks where words have been left out of paragraphs. And to say that a person has "communicative competence" in a language/culture is to say that he has the same expectations as the natives about what a person may try to do when, and about what means are appropriate for what ends, and so on.

But, useful as expectations are, there are several ways in which my "expectations" can get me into trouble. First of all, my expectations may not always agree with one another. To take the simplest and most trite example, someone may set an extra piece of pie in front of me. I can safely expect that if I eat it, my taste buds will send me happy messages, but I may also expect that eating the pie will make me weigh more than I want to weigh. So my expectations pull against each other; whatever I do, whether I eat the pie or not, will contain those expectations within it, and will be shaped by the conflict between them.

Conflicts are found in all parts of life, of course, and not just at the dinner table. If I write what I really think, I can look forward to a good feeling that comes from knowing that I have been straight with myself and with my readers. But I may also have reason to expect that saying what I mean will make some people turn away from me—people whom I do not want to lose.

There is no end to the examples that we find in the foreign language classroom. I set some of them out in Chapters 4 and 5 of *Memory, Meaning, and Method*: pronouncing the language well may please the teacher but lead my friends to feel that I am disloyal to our native land and language; succeeding through methods that are different from, and easier than, what my first teachers used may leave me both feeling good and feeling that I have cheated someone and will soon have to pay for it; saying, in the foreign language, something that is important to me may be at the same time satisfying and risky. Even when the student does outwardly only what the teacher, or the textbook, or the tape tells him to do, these inner conflicts twist, in great ways or in small, his doing of it. We sometimes see this twisting literally, in the microphone cords of our language laboratories: I know of at least one university that went so far as to install worry beads in its booths, just to drain off the nervous energy that was causing nonmalicious damage to its equipment. Side remarks inadvertently recorded on the student tracks of lab tapes sometimes give us amusing, yet also sobering, glimpses into what is going on inside the student. But even when we cannot see the twisting, it is there: feelings, attitudes, and the conflicts among them are parts of the whole act of learning. *They are therefore stored in the student's memory, intertwined forever with the word or sentence or rule or paradigm that he has learned.*

As I write, I see that the preceding paragraph is itself an example of conflicting purposes. Because it is about learning languages, I can hope that it will help to keep the attention of other people who may read this—most of whom I expect will be language teachers. At the same time, however, it may take a reader's mind away from the general groundwork that I am trying to lay for telling you what I understand by "Counseling-Learning."

A series of diagrams may make my meaning clearer. In the diagrams, I will be using the same capital letters that appear in the acronym SARD, of which Curran made great use. For the present, I will give my own meanings to the letters. Then, in Chapter 8, I will speak directly about SARD as Curran used it, and interrelate it with my own interpretation.

DIAGRAM 1

Here, S stands for one person's Self. The A may stand for "action," or "assertion"—anything that comes out of the Self and into the world. But what I have been saying is not so simple as this diagram. What runs between S and A is not like a single wire; it is more like a cable with many strands.

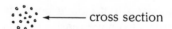

Some of the strands of this cable may carry the effects of rational, intellectual thoughts; others may carry the effects of various emotions and needs and desires. Some of the strands carry messages that we are not even aware of. And these messages may disagree among themselves: what goes out along one strand may work against what goes out along another. To say that someone "has got it all together" would be to say that all these messages are in harmony with one another. I don't suppose that any human being ever "gets it together" 100 percent, or not for long anyway. Some people are closer to it than others, and each of us is closer to it at some times than at others.

In any event, lack of harmony among the many parts of the Self can keep the Self from doing what it wants to do as well as it would like to; too *much* conflict within the Self can bring real trouble, or may even tear the Self apart. So the Self instinctively abhors the chaos within, and has a deep drive toward healing itself—toward making itself whole and harmonious. As I have said, it never completely succeeds at this, partly because it is a prisoner of those very same expectations which are in conflict with one another. Or it is like a woman trying to apply makeup without being able to see her face in a mirror. Or it is like a person who is trying to straighten out a bureau drawer that is completely full, with no way of leaving some of the contents outside the drawer for a short time so he can sort them out and rearrange the other things in the drawer.

But Becker showed us that the Self's drive to put itself into the best order it can has another and deeper source. It does not come *only* from the desire to do well whatever it wants to do. It is also more than a wish to have fewer internal stresses and strains. There is the strong need to feel that we are somehow consistent with the way things finally are (whether that "final reality" be what orthodox Christianity teaches, or what another religion teaches, or whether it be the "reality" of materialism, or of humanism, or of nihilism).

Some years ago, I came across a game that caught, in a way that is easy to see, something of this inner drive to bring harmony into one's self, or to get the pieces of one's self to fit together. I think the game was called "Spill and Spell." It consisted of nothing but a plastic cup and a set of 15 dice. Instead of spots, the faces of the dice carried letters of the alphabet. The first player puts the dice into the cup, shakes them, and spills them out onto a tabletop. The player then tries, within a limited period of time, to fit the dice together so as to spell words with whatever 15 letters came up. The words may cross each other as in a crossword puzzle, or in Scrabble. Each letter scores a certain number of points when it is used, with the rarer letters scoring most, and the very common letters counting least. Normally, it will be impossible to use all 15 letters at once; so the player must decide which letters to leave aside.

It seems to me that this game is true to life in at least four ways. First, things seldom or never come out entirely even. Second, the choices that the player makes depend on what he thinks the rules are. If one religion, or one culture, or one philosophy, or one outlook on life says that the letter *j* is worth more than the letter *z*, and another says that *z* is worth more than *j*, then two players who follow different philosophies will make different decisions, and starting out with the same 15 letters they may end up with quite different configurations of words. Third, once a player has begun to build up one particular pattern of intersecting words, he would rather look for more words to fit into that pattern, than start all over and try to use his 15 letters in an entirely new way, even though the new way might bring an even higher score. Fourth, if a player does not know a particular word, he cannot use it. But if he learns a new word, he then becomes able to use it. Fitting the new word into his configuration of words may take work, but it may also change his score, upward or downward. The player must decide whether, within the time that he has left, he is willing to do the work, and run the risk, that the new word would cost him. The worst thing—the lowest score—would be if time ran out after a player had torn up one arrangement and before he was able to put a new one together. Life in this respect is harder than the game, because we never know how much time we have left.

What I have said so far, then, is this: that what each of us does (the S⟶A line in the diagram) begins in the Self; that what looks like a simple act has many parts: some parts are physical movements of the body, other parts have to do with purposes, emotions, attitudes, expectations, and so forth; that each of these parts of an act has its roots in some part of the Self; that the various parts of the Self are more or less in harmony with one another; that the Self wants to organize its parts so that they work smoothly with one another; but that it never succeeds completely at this task, and sometimes has real trouble with it.

Up to now, I have been talking only about the Self, and about how its parts work together (or fail to work together) as the Self acts outward on the world round about it, and on other people. That, of course, is only the beginning of the story. The world round about also acts on the Self, so that we need a second arrow in our diagram:

DIAGRAM 2

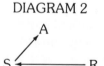

For the time being, let's let the R stand for "round about."

Now, the Self sends out hundreds or thousands of S⟶A arrows every day. And of course, it is hit by R⟶S arrows of one kind or another many times in every minute, as long as it is awake. Like the S⟶A arrows, the R⟶S arrows may be complex:

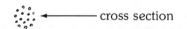 cross section

with physical, aesthetic, emotional, intellectual, and other kinds of things all bound up together, and acting on one another in ways which we only partly understand. The Self is aware of some parts of many of these arrows, but some parts run beneath or outside conscious awareness.

The R⟶S arrows bring in information from the outside. As the information reaches S, much of it fits readily into the network of expectations which the Self has already put together. Some of the information, however, does not fit. Perhaps two things which the Self has always seen as alike now need to be treated as two different things: for example, a belief that all members of a given race act alike may not hold up if one is willing to look at what two or more members of that race actually do. Or, to take an example from language study, English speakers, as long as they are speaking English, do not need to hear the difference between the vowels in French *pure* and *pour*. But in using French, we need to reshape our expectations so that they will be able to handle that difference.

Other information, perhaps, does not fit because it says that the Self needs to give more weight to something than it has given to it in the past. In an everyday example, the Self may have been aware that regular visits to the dentist are important, but a visit after a lapse of three years may bring results which cause the Self to come back sooner and more frequently in the years that follow. Here, the Self is not asked to make a new distinction, but only to change the weight it gives to something that it already knows about. A language example may be the speaker of a Western European language who has distinguished all his life between masculine and feminine in *third* person pronouns, but who starts to learn Arabic or Hebrew and suddenly finds that those languages have separate masculine and feminine forms also in the *second* person.

Going back to the player of "Spill and Spell," when this new information comes in, it is as though someone had suddenly changed the game, either by adding new letters or by taking some letters away, or by changing the number of points that each letter is worth. It is easy to understand why the player might become annoyed, might tell the other person to go away, or might try to pretend that the other person was not there at all.

A player of "Spill and Spell" needs to feel that he knows the rules, and that at least some of the other players will give him credit for the words that he puts together by following those rules. If one part of his life tells him the rules are this way, while another part tells him they are that way, and if he cannot in some way decide when to follow one set of rules and when the other, then he may with one sweep of his hand knock all of the dice onto the floor. Or if he knows the rules, but sees that with his letters (e.g., G, Q, Q, V, V, V, X, Z) he can put together nothing that is acceptable by the rules, he may do the same thing. Even a player who has usable letters may fling the dice away if he cannot make a score that gives him the status he seeks with the other players.

Here is a paragraph from a story by Michael Dobbs in the *Washington Post*, May 21, 1978:

> N _____ was one of the most successful women in Hungary. She had a large circle of friends, ran a smart fashion salon in Budapest, and made frequent trips abroad. Last year she killed herself at age 70 by jumping from a highrise apartment building. . . . According to her family, the reason . . . was that a pair of false teeth implanted in her gums had started to rot. For most people, that would not have been the end of the world. But for a woman who had made a highly successful career in the beauty business, it was impossible to bear.

By contrast, some players find that their arrangements of letters are valued even more highly than they had dared to hope, and are judged by exactly the rules that they had been working by. Vice President Mondale said of Hubert Humphrey:

> In looking back over Hubert's life, it seems as though all the disappointments that were visited on him were suddenly settled in his favor in that last year, when everyone wanted him to know they appreciated what he had done for them and for their country.

This morning, I listened for about ten minutes to a sonata for mandolin and harpsichord. I didn't particularly enjoy it, and I finally turned it off, but my reasons for listening at all fitted in with what I have been saying about "expectations." If I am to enjoy music at all, it must fit in somehow with my overall system of expectations. But it may do so in several ways. Most simply, at any point in a piece of music, I like to feel that if I had two, or at most a dozen guesses, I could predict (in my mind's ear) what is coming next. In a piece that I have heard many times, I don't even need two guesses, of course. I know exactly what is coming next. Listening to that piece of music, then, leaves me feeling comfortable because it confirms my expectations one note at a time. Listening to a piece which I have never heard before, but which is in a style that I am familiar with, does not confirm my expectations on the same simple level, because I cannot predict every note exactly. But the notes are ones that I might have guessed on my second, or seventh, or eleventh guess. In this way, it reassures me that my overall *system* of expectations is adequate to handle new material. If the music is too modern, however, I have no idea what the composer might choose to put next, and so I become confused and then annoyed. The musicians are asking me, as a listener, to spend time in a "world of action" whose meaning I do not see.

In the case of the sonata for mandolin and harpsichord, my expectations were at work in still another way. I generally enjoy the music of plucked instruments, but I have not had much experience listening to mandolins. Because I think of myself as a person who appreciates that kind of music, and because I expect to hear more of it in coming years, the experience of this morning's listening contributed toward filling a gap in the system of expectations that I had already built. Some people go at the learning of new languages in much the same way: a person who has a strong interest in Scandinavia and knows Swedish and Danish will get special pleasure from ingesting Norwegian and Icelandic as well. More generally, an experienced and expert language learner may find in each new language learned a renewed confirmation of the value of what he has inside him. To learn a language on this basis is sometimes just good clean fun, and harmless.

Perhaps the music that gives me greatest pleasure is music that meets and confirms a set of expectations that bring with them good feelings from my past, but which also opens up to me new combinations, new possibilities, which still fit into my familiar pattern, but which I have never heard before.

In those of our expectations which lie next to the rock on which our safety rests, we may find even the slightest changes to be unbearable. Here is the small child, whose bed is his best replacement for the womb, listening to a familiar bedtime story read by a parent, who is his all-powerful protector. He will object to, and correct, any syllable that strays from the original.

The same thing comes out in two stories, both of which happen to be about Bostonian ladies. (They might even be about the same woman at different times in the history of Boston!) In the first story, the lady is asked whether she has ever traveled, and she replies, "Why should I? I'm already here!" This is a person who is in an enviable position. She has her expectations and her differentiations pretty well sorted out. She is in harmony with herself and with all that she sees. She knows *where* she is and so, within that solid and dependable framework, she can know *who* she is. The idea that she should put all of this in danger by traveling surprises her. If someone offered her a free trip to Chicago, she would probably find some excuse to turn it down.

The second story was a cartoon showing two middle-aged women driving toward Boston. The passenger has apparently been away for some years. The driver turns to her and says, "I think I should warn you. They're tearing down Boston and they're putting up something else." New R⟶ S arrows have forced a reorganization of the expectations that make up the driver's S! She is preparing her friend for the shock of having to do the same thing.

So these new inputs from R ("the chaos across the room!") mean that, even if we manage to "get it all together," we can't stop there. We have to *hold* "it" together against a steady stream of new R⟶ S arrows. We can do this by hiding from them, or we can try to fight them off, or we can use them in a constant process of rebuilding "it." This rebuilding takes work, of course, but fighting the new arrows off takes work, too, and so does hiding from them. Sometimes hiding may be the best way of reacting, and sometimes fighting back may be. Most often, perhaps, the best reaction would be to rebuild, but this may require more energy than hiding or fighting, in the short run at least. Furthermore, to change one's habitual reactions away from hiding or fighting and toward rebuilding is itself, on a deeper level, an act of rebuilding. (Some readers of the first draft of this letter have wondered what it is that determines which way we react in any given situation. I do not know.)

Now let me take a third step in drawing my diagram. When two people come together, we have two Selves; that is to say, we have two memories, two sets of expectations, two systems of values. Not least, we have two bodies, each with its own eyes, ears, and tongue, its own heart and lungs and arms and legs, its own will to go on living and to cheat death. All of this lies behind this little diagram of only four lines:

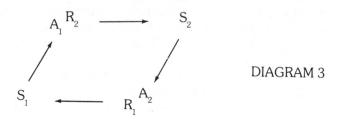

DIAGRAM 3

(Enlarging the diagram to include two people has made my notation more complex. I have been able to think of nothing better than capital letters with subscript numerals. The usual reading for S_1, in my dialect is "S-sub-one," and R_2 would be "R-sub-two." I think that reading Diagram 3 in this way would confuse even me. May I suggest something like "the Self of the first person," and "what comes to the second person from round about him"?)

The diagram says what we already know: that what comes from and fits one Self ($S_1 \longrightarrow A_1$) is a part of the new input to another Self ($R_2 \longrightarrow S_2$), into which it may or may not fit. If it does not fit S_2, then S_2 will have to work either to fight it off, or to pretend that it is not there, or to rebuild its own system of expectations so as to make a place for the new input.

(The diagram, to be complete, needs additional $R \longrightarrow S$ arrows that come toward S_1 and S_2 from other directions. They would stand for the input that comes, not from the other person, but from other sources, animate and inanimate, round about each S.)

We all learn about Diagram 3 at a very early age. We learn that certain kinds of $S_1 \longrightarrow A_1$ from us will cause an S_2 to punish us by spanking us, or by turning its back on us or even leaving us altogether. We also learn that other kinds of $S_1 \longrightarrow A_1$ from us will force the other person to produce $S_2 \longrightarrow A_2$ arrows which become $R_1 \longrightarrow S_1$ arrows which fit in with our system as it already stands—or that some $S_1 \longrightarrow A_1$ from us will at least keep S_2 from putting out $S_2 \longrightarrow A_2$ which lead to $R_1 \longrightarrow S_1$ that are troublesome for us. The other person, S_2, has of course learned the same things. Therefore, when two people come together, each must decide how much of his Self he had best hold back out of the sight of the other, and, in general, how to act so that the other will behave to fit his expectations. There may be a power struggle, which may last for just a few seconds or may even go on for years.

So the English word *expectation* has two separate meanings, which in their effect on other people are quite different from each other. One kind of expectation is something that ones thinks is likely to happen: "I expect it will rain tonight." The other kind places someone else under pressure to fulfill it: "I expect you to answer this question correctly (and you'd better not let me down!)" "I expect you to do the dishes before you watch television!" These expectations can be conveyed either with or without words. The unspoken sentence, "I expect you to do well/get this right" may be either the first kind of expectation or the second. The first lifts the student's spirits, while the second is a warning to defend himself. *To recognize and control this difference within her own behavior is one of the most delicate tricks a teacher can master, but it is also one of the most useful!*

There is more to men and women than what I have told up to now. If there were not more, then the human race would be unlucky indeed! But let's suppose that there *is* no more. What if all of us are bound to live by Diagram 3 and by nothing else? What will two people do when they meet? First, if I am S_1 and you are S_2, I will find many things that I know, and see, and perhaps would like to say, about which I know I must not talk to you. You likewise know that there are certain things about which it would be unwise to talk to me. So we are partly cut off from each other. There may be some things which I feel I must not talk about with anyone. I may feel this way because of something that happened many years ago, between me and other people. So it is not only that I am cut off from you. Even worse than that, I feel that those parts of myself which I think others are not willing to look at or hear about are "bad", I feel shame for them; I myself may not be able to look at them steadily; not being able to look at them, I am unable to deal with them, to set them right. The "bureau drawer" (page 89) is a mess. Some of the things in it are pretty badly mildewed, and no one wants to make other people smell something unpleasant. In these parts of my life, I am lost; I am alone; I am cut off not only from other people, but even from myself. This is the first of three things that happen when people meet one another according to Diagram 3: We may hide from each other.

The second thing that may happen is the opposite. Instead of hiding from you, I may use whatever strength I have, and whatever cunning, to get you to act in ways that will tell the world, and will tell me, that my system of expectations is right, and good, and worthy of being held by all people. Perhaps you will yield to me altogether, and set about rebuilding your own acts, your own habits, your own system of expectations, so that they will fit what I seem to want. Or perhaps you will fight back, using your own strength and your own cunning to reshape me, just as I have been trying to reshape you. Or, finally, you may be careful to put out $S_2 \longrightarrow A_2$ arrows that you think will not displease me, yet without really changing your S_2. To do this, you must build yourself a little model, s_1, of what you think my S_1 wants from you. Moreover, you must give to this s_1 a place within your own S_2. But the shape of this foreign s_1 will not agree with your S_2, and so the two will rub and pull against each other. After some time, the two may become more like each other, so that one of them or both of them have changed. Or perhaps they go on forever, chafing and pulling at each other. Then the S ⟶ A's that they put out may show the effects of that conflict.

There are so many ways in which we lay our expectations onto one another! Direct orders and open criticism are only the most obvious. If a student says he is discouraged at the end of the first week, and if I tell him, "There, there! You shouldn't feel that way!" I am laying my own expectation onto him. If I explain the formation of the past tense, using a tone of voice that says, "Now, always remember . . . !" I am doing the same thing. If I give someone a suggestion about how to get rid of his headache, and then an hour later ask if his headache is better, I am probably more interested in vindicating my own suggestion than I am in his physical state. A driver who follows too close behind the car ahead of him, along a road where there is no possibility of passing, is using a nonverbal way of laying his expectations on the other person. Compare also the knowing, reproachful fluttering of eyelids by the actress in a television commercial, as she informs us that she takes a patent diet supplement "*every day*—and so should you!"

But Diagram 3 does not always bring disagreement and conflict. Sometimes one person's acts, A_1, become exactly the kind of R_2 that another person needs in order to fill out what is missing within his own S_2. In the physical realm, sexual attraction may provide examples of this. In the realm of food and eating, Jack Spratt and his wife are an example from folklore. If a person who very much needs to see his own solution of the "Spill and Spell" puzzle confirmed by how faithfully other people copy it meets someone whose inner Self has been a howling wasteland crying out for order, then each may find in the other exactly what he/she had been looking for. In all of the examples that I have mentioned in this paragraph—sexual attraction, dietary complementation, the relationship of guru and disciple, the relationship of master and slave—the people who are involved may describe their relationship by saying that they "love" each other. If a third person comes along and tries to break the partners away from each other, they will fight that third person, and in this fighting they will do things beyond what they or anyone else would have thought them able or willing to do. Likewise, if one of the partners turns away from the other, terrible things may happen. By the very fact that this other person—this S_2—had shared so fully and so deeply my S_1, I find it all the more frightening to watch that S_2 go off and leave me, and succeed in doing without what both of us had once agreed was both good and necessary. All of us, because we are human, need and use and appreciate from other human beings the kind of support that I have pictured in Diagram 3. But insofar as we depend on that kind of support, what we call "loving" and "being loved" can become clutching, and holding, and controlling.

In life according to Diagram 3, then, the acts (S ⟶ A) of one person may become for another person an input (R ⟶ S) which is welcome and helpful, or unwelcome and unhelpful, or welcome but unhelpful, ,or unwelcome but helpful. When should one act, and when hold oneself back? In a religious or ecclesiastical context, this is the question of the ethics of evangelism:

> The impatient gate, that swings both in and out,
> Whose work is lost when no-one passes through;
> The faithful fence, that marks off false from true—
> No time for hanging back, no room for doubt—
>
> Exist, not in the world, but in the mind,
> Yet God forgive if what is there for me
> I either hide, or try to press on thee,
> To shout thee deaf, or leave thee lost and blind.
>
> This dreadful choice sets brother against brother,
> Either to injure, or to fail each other.

This same dilemma is equally present in contexts which are not religio-ecclesiastical. So we organize our existence and institutionalize it against the dread of these choices, and against the dread of chaos and oblivion. Society then consists of

> chain-link lives
> twisted tight,
> even, stout,
> to keep Us
> In,
> Them and It
> Out.

("It," I suppose, is the chaos, oblivion, and knowledge of death about which I have been talking.)

Is Diagram 3, then, all there is? Maybe not. Someone once gave me a quotation from Rilke which puts into words the difference between two kinds of "love." He said that, "Once the realization is accepted that even among the closest human beings infinite distances continue to exist, a wonderful living side by side can grow up, if they succeed in loving the distance between them which makes it possible for each to see the other whole against the sky." I think Rilke is telling us here, if we can understand it (and I would not claim *I* understand it completely), that something is possible which Diagram 3 cannot account for.

[Please be patient with me, B _____ , that I, certainly amateur in both thinking and writing about these things, have for so many pages been pressing on you, one after another, this long series of insights that so many others have spoken of before me. But without them as a foundation, I know of no way to set before you what I understand by "Counseling-Learning," and that is the task I have undertaken in this letter.]

The heart of this sentence, I think, lies in the way Rilke sets next to each other the words "closest" and "infinite distances." In our everyday use of these words, both of them cannot be true at the same time concerning the same two people. In saying that they cannot be, and yet are, true at the same time, Rilke is trying to lift us out of our everyday reality, for our everyday reality is made up of the same hiding and fighting and controlling and holding on that I have already described. In everyday reality, we have no way of knowing others, or of being known, except through those same S→A→R→S lines of Diagram 3. These lines are the tubes through which we have been nourished, the cables through which we have received the messages that have shown us how to grow into whatever we are, and the messages also which reassure us day by day that we are who we think we are. But what we do not always see is that these lines are not threads which are all that keeps us from a fall into nothingness. To put the same thought into other words, if S_1 is lucky, it may someday see, for an hour or for a minute, that it is more than just a place where R→S lines and S→A lines converge. It has its own being, and if it has its own being, then S_2 may likewise have a being of its own. When S_1 sees S_2 and itself in this light, then it becomes able to treat S_2 in a new way. The S→A→R→S lines have not disappeared. They are still there, but now they are no longer as they were before, because S_1 is no longer as it was before. Now the word "love" can take on a new and deeper meaning. In this new relationship, S_2 may in its turn see what S_1 has seen—it may see itself partaking in, yet at the same time free of, the web of S→A→R→S lines; it may know it has been loved, and so it may know that love is possible. With this vision comes a stillness to which great philosophers and spiritual teachers have through all ages borne their witness. Only, I think, from within that stillness can the vision turn itself to flesh and blood—to S→A arrows which carry it, the vision, to another human being. It can be bedrock above which is built great teaching regardless of method.

In life, of course, we "play Spill and Spell" on many different levels at once. We may challenge, and even break up, one another's configurations, and we may do so on one or more of these levels. Thus, you may call into question the *words* I have spoken, or the *deeds* I have done. Or you may attack the *purpose* that I had in my speaking or acting. Deeper still, you may say (or show without saying it) that in your eyes the *kind of person* who would give himself to these purposes of mine has no worth—that the world would be better off without such people. Any of these attacks may frighten me into hiding or fighting, or it may not. What I do will depend on where I feel secure, and where I do not. When I have that stillness at the center, then I see that all these games of "Spill and Spell" are only games, and that I, the player, stand outside them. Then you may do your worst: you may prove my words wrong, you may show that my purposes work against each other, you may even cast scorn upon the kind of person I have tried to be, and I can still "understand" you—"see you whole against the sky." When I do not have that stillness, then if you attack my purposes, I need to have you tell me that you still see worth in the kind of person I am. Otherwise, I may panic. When I am not sure within myself about the kind of person I have chosen to be, then if you attack my words or criticize my deeds, I need to believe that you at least agree with my purpose. And if I am not at one with myself even in my purposes, all I have to hold onto is your approval of my words and deeds. Then, if you do not take and use my words, if you do not praise my deeds, I feel great threat, and I may run away, or fly at you, or fly apart.

CHAPTER 8

COUNSELING, COUNSELING-LEARNING, AND COMMUNITY LANGUAGE LEARNING

Now, at last, I have the vocabulary that I need in order to tell you what I understand by "counseling" as I heard Curran use the word. Once I have done that, I will be able to move on quickly to "Counseling-Learning," and from there to "Community Language Learning." Let me remind you that my goal here is not to speak for Curran, or to tell you what he said. That you can read for yourself at any time. My goal is to speak for myself, to show you what has grown up in my mind from the seed that he planted.

In "counseling," as in normal conversation, there is a constant stream of $S \longrightarrow A \longrightarrow R \longrightarrow S$ from the person who is being understood (the "understandee")* to the person who is doing the understanding (the "understander"), and back again from the understander to the understandee. But "counseling" is unlike normal conversation in at least five ways.

First, the understander sees himself and the understandee in the way that Rilke described: Although they are in close, perhaps intimate communication with each other, still each one has his own wholeness, his own worth, which is unlike the wholeness and worth of any other person, and is independent of any other person. It is this view of the understandee, *and also of himself,* that enables the understander to listen, without turning a deaf ear, to anything that the understandee says, and without judging it as good or bad, and without trying to reshape the understandee's S_2 into a pattern that comes out of his own S_1.

Second, the understander (S_1) as he listens, tries to form in his own mind a picture (s_2) of the Self (S_2) of the understandee, or at least a picture of that part of S_2 that the understandee has shown to him. As I said earlier, a picture or a model (s_2) within the understander's Self (S_1) is not in a watertight bag. There is a real chance that some part of it will leak out and make changes in S_1. But in the stillness that I talked about earlier, and in the knowledge that he is who he is and belongs to himself, the understander can take that risk without hiding or fighting back. (Since no human being is in perfect stillness all of the time, it would be more accurate to say that *insofar* as we have that

---

*I dislike concocted words like "understandee." But "counselor" and "client" have too much the sound of a professional relationship in which one person is always in one of the roles, and the other person in the other. "Person-doing-the-understanding" and "person-being-understood," on the other hand, are just too cumbersome.

stillness and self-steadiness, *to that degree* we will be able to be open and nondefensive in our listening.)

We are all familiar with how hard it is to listen to—or to talk about—certain drastically painful topics. One of a group of teen-aged cancer patients reported that "When they told me I had Hodgkin's disease, . . . they never said the word cancer. Then one day I looked the disease up in the encyclopedia and saw the word cancer, and I nearly fell over. It was six months before anyone else said the word." But as a language teacher I can remember brushing aside much less serious things that my students were trying to tell me, simply because what they were telling me would have caused me pain or inconvenience. Perhaps I was not always wrong to do so: each of us has a limit on what he can carry. But I *did* turn away.

In "counseling" also (and this is the third difference), much of what the understander says has as its purpose to be certain that the understander's s_2 really does fit the understandee's S_2. This is at the heart of this kind of "counseling" for at least two reasons. First, as in ordinary conversation, there is no use in two people talking about two different things when they think they are talking about the same thing; that only leads to wasting time and to frustration. So the understander needs to check out his own understanding by telling the understandee what he thinks he is hearing.

Some people, however, have gotten the idea that in this so-called reflective listening the understander simply repeats or paraphases the other person's words. If that were true, then this sort of "counseling" would be nothing but a technique, and a rather superficial one at that. (Curran himself was quite emphatic on this point.) When I am trying to give this sort of understanding, however, I find that most of my words are descriptions of the s_2 that has been taking shape in my mind. The words of the other person serve me first as a source for (much of) that picture. The paraphrasing of words into other words plays only a secondary role.

But there is a second reason for "reflective listening," which is even more important than verifying what the other person is saying. When the other person feels that the understander has truly understood him, and yet has not turned away in boredom or disgust, or tried to change him, then he feels less cut off. He is not alone. He sees that he is not, or does not appear, unworthy, foolish, ugly, horrible as he had feared.

This holding back, this self-discipline on the part of the understander is the fourth way in which this kind of "counseling" is unlike the conversation of a sympathetic, solicitous friend. The "counselor" avoids criticizing what the other person says, of course. But he is equally careful to keep from agreeing with it or praising it. To do *either* would be to put himself into the position of a judge. The other person, perhaps without knowing it, would then try to please that judge, or try to overthrow him, or both. In any case, the other person could no longer work and speak out of his own wholeness, which is unlike the wholeness of any other person. Instead, he would become entangled in the $S \longrightarrow A \longrightarrow R \longrightarrow S$ web of the *understander's* expectations.

The fifth and last point has to do with the understander's own contributions to the conversation. A person who is trying to give this kind of understanding holds back from asking questions, and from telling about his own experiences, and from making suggestions. Again, the reason is that he has faith in the other person's ability, working freely within his own wholeness, to come up with what he needs. Questions, suggestions, or the understander's own experiences would only lay onto the other person the understander's own expectations; which is to say that it would be like pulling the other person into the understander's world and asking him to conform to it.

What the understander is trying to do is in fact exactly the opposite. He is trying to see the other person's world through that other person's eyes, without reaching into it and changing it. If he can do that, he can then reflect that world back to the other person. In doing so, he uses a very special kind of $S \longrightarrow A$. He tells the other person what facts and what feelings he sees in that world, but the understander's own feelings as they come through on this kind of $S \longrightarrow A$ do not copy, and do not react against, the feelings that he sees in the world of the understandee. For example, he does not weep with one who is weeping. If the understandee is angry with him, he does not become angry or defensive or conciliatory in return. He talks *about* the other person's feelings, but the feelings that he himself sends out are *whatever kind of support is appropriate to the situation.*

But to say that in this kind of "counseling" the understander holds himself back, or to say that he does not react directly, in the usual way, to the feelings of the understandee, is not to say that he is just an uninvolved observer. On the contrary, the understander is involved with the other person *more* deeply than is usual in normal conversation. This brings us back to the paradox in the Rilke quotation: infinite distance in greatest intimacy.

When the $S_1 \longrightarrow A_1$ of the understander follows these rules, then the $R_2 \longrightarrow S_2$ that the other person receives is also unlike most $R \longrightarrow S$. Because the emotional tone of the understander's $S \longrightarrow A$ is neutral and supportive, the understandee does not have to defend himself from it. He is therefore free to hear more clearly what the understander is saying, and to see how it fits together. To go back to the picture of the cluttered bureau drawer, the understander is providing to the understandee a table top on which he can lay out some of the things that have been all tangled in together, and untangle them, and sort them out, and see them in a new and clearer way, and decide what he wants to do with them. He recognizes the same *facts* that he had been describing to the understander; but he also finds that his own *feelings* are coming back to him from the understander as *facts*—factual statements about what the understander has seen and heard of his feelings. And all of these facts, as they are carried in the understander's $S_1 \longrightarrow A_1$, are accompanied by the understander's own feelings of nonjudging, unquestioning, supportive interest. The understander is providing a rack on which the understandee can hang some of his mildewed clothing in the sunshine and fresh air for a while.

After being listened to in this way, an understandee often finds that he is "hearing himself better" than he had before. He may feel less cut off, not only from the understander and the rest of the outside world, but even from himself. He may still have the same basic feelings that he started out with, but his *feelings about those feelings* may be less bad. The fresh air may take away some of the mildew. And it is often those feelings-about-feelings that led into the vicious circle that left the understandee feeling cut off, a prisoner of his own uniqueness. Another of the teenage cancer victims tells us, "People with cancer don't want you to talk. They want you to know what they have to say. They want someone who lets them talk about what it's like." Again, the examples in language classes are less dramatic. But I remember clearly how much better I felt, *and* how much more easily I learned, in a demonstration class in Chinese when someone successfully "understood" how I felt about the study of tones.

As a representative of the outside world, then, the understander has power over the understandee, either to tighten the circle around him, or to make a little break in it. Through using this power, he can reward the understandee or punish him, and so shape what the understandee does, and even what he thinks. It is therefore important that the understander not use his power in order to sell the other person life insurance, or change his religion, or otherwise exploit him. But even in a nonexploitative relationship, the understander's choice of words and images can lead the other person subtly, therefore compellingly. The good understander needs to watch out lest in this way (s)he distort what the other person is saying.

If I may oversimplify the picture of the S $\longrightarrow$ A arrows, the understander communicates to the understandee through two channels: most obviously through words, but also through body posture, facial expression, tone of voice, and so forth. It would be misleading to say that the word channel carries what the understander has understood and nothing else; or that the other—the nonverbal—channel carries the understander's attitudes and nothing else. Certainly the main use of the word channel is to carry, and to verify, what the understander has heard. At the same time, however, subtle choices of words or of phrasing—the kind of thing that would show up even in a typewritten transcript of the conversation—can also carry hints about how the understander feels toward the understandee and what the understandee has said.

In much the same way, it is true that the main use of the nonverbal channel in $S_1 \longrightarrow A_1$ is to carry the feelings of the understander. At the same time, however, it can be used in very specific ways, which can let the understandee know that the understander is following in detail what he is saying. On two occasions when the situation was one in which I was not permitted to speak, I have—with apparent success—conveyed understanding through the nonverbal channel for periods of over 15 minutes. This is quite different from just sitting silent with a benign look on one's face. (Someone did that to me last week, for just 5 minutes, and I found it unsettling.) Normally, of course, the understander uses both channels at once.

Nevertheless, if I had a choice between bungling the verbal or the nonverbal side of communication with someone to whom I was trying to give this kind of "understanding," I would without hesitation choose to get the nonverbal part right and let the words go. The words are the precise lines of a fine pen, but the nonverbal communication is the surface on which they are drawn.

I have said that the supportive nonverbal communication from the understander should be of "whatever kind is appropriate" to the situation in which the two people find themselves. Some of us first learned this kind of listening by watching psychological counselors at work, and then trying to imitate them in our practice sessions with each other. This worked very well while we were in training. It also worked very well outside of the training institutes, with colleagues, students, friends, and family as long as there was a clear agreement, spoken or unspoken, that this was what the other person wanted: that he or she welcomed, for the time being at least, a series of responses from an understanding person which consisted of little or nothing except reflections of what (s)he has said, and which carried with them feelings of warmth, acceptance, and support. We found that by responding in this way to people who wanted us to respond in this way, we could often be helpful in ways that had been closed to us before. This new skill was not only helpful to our friends and students, however. It at the same time opened to us new and deep sources of satisfaction. I can remember three such sources especially. Most obvious was the feeling of having been helpful. Alongside that was seeing that the people to whom we had given this simple help often had good feelings toward us: warmth, gratitude, admiration, and the like. Not least was the pure joy of craftsmanship: like an artist who has caught a likeness truly, or a bowler who has just made a difficult spare. So, for all of these reasons, we sometimes acted like the child who received a new carpenter set for Christmas, and who went around pounding nails into the piano and sawing the leg off the dining table. We looked for every opportunity to do this kind of "counseling," whenever anyone expressed anything but the simplest fact. We did so even though we had been clearly told that this sort of understanding relationship would probably take up no more than 10 to 20 percent of our daily activities. I'm quite sure that we never did anyone any damage in this way—one of the things that I like about this kind of "counseling" is that it does not push, or probe, or tell people what to do, or look for emotional blisters that it can lance. But we did, every now and then, make our chosen "understandee" pretty annoyed with us.

I can remember two kinds of annoyance that came up more than once. The first was that we were trying to work some kind of psychological trick—to play psychiatrist with them. So they felt manipulated, and nobody likes to feel that way. The other annoyance arose from the fact that in this kind of "counseling" the understander gives himself entirely to hearing what the other person is saying, and reflecting it back faithfully. A person who is "understood" in this way for a long time without wanting it may begin to feel that the understander is holding himself out of sight, or that he is even running away from him. (And I suppose it is true that this kind of "counseling" can be used for that purpose.) At any rate, the people who trained us had warned us that "counseling without a contract" could get us into trouble, and they were right.

At the same time, we saw people react in exactly the opposite way. A person who had been well "understood" for three or four sentences, even without a contract, might flash a "hurt" look if the person who had "understood" him suddenly began to talk about his own related ideas, or to offer advice, according to the conventions of ordinary conversation.

So, while I accepted the rule against "counseling without a contract," I could not get away from the idea that skill in this kind of disciplined understanding had a place outside of the "counseling contract," and that my reasons for feeling this way went beyond my personal needs to receive gratitude and to have a sense of craftsmanship.

I have gone off on this detour about how some of us used and overused our "counseling" skills because I think that what happened to us sheds light on the kind of feelings that the understander should send to the understandee. We were taught that the "counselor" should show "warmth, acceptance, and support," and we also picked up, without anybody telling us to, a sort of professional, consulting-room air which sometimes came across fairly plainly. For people who had asked for this kind of understanding, the faintly professional "warmth, acceptance, and support" proved to be reassuring and clearly welcome. It was appropriate to the setting. To others, it could be objectionable. In their situations, it was inappropriate. In some situations, an appropriate feeling is intense personal interest in the factual side of what the understandee is saying. In some situations, it is appropriate to agree, to commiserate, even to raise objections. All of these were discouraged (and with good reason) by those who trained us in the formal "counseling" relationship. They also discouraged us from taking the center of the stage and telling stories about our own experiences or our sufferings. Yet I have found that telling an understandee such things about myself can be highly appropriate and effective, *provided* that the story is not too long, and *provided also* that the end of my story ties back in to where the understandee left off.

In his last, posthumous book, Curran made it especially clear that "counseling" is not just a form of "spiritual soothing syrup." The "counselor" does not spend all of his time in understanding the other person. He some-times takes a stand of his own. When he is "understanding," he may occa-sionally sandwich in a bit of "standing." When he is "standing," by the same token, he may sandwich in a bit of "understanding." But one of the skills which a good counselor offers to a client is the ability to serve up these two roles as the bread and meat of a sandwich. By contrast, the well-meaning friend who is listening sympathetically but without this skill is likely to flit back and forth haphazardly between "standing" and "understanding." The result is less like a sandwich, and more like hash. It destroys the clearness and cleanness that can be so welcome to an anxious understandee.

When the counselor does take a stand of his own, he may simply express his own views. Or he may force the other person to come face to face with how what he does and what he has said contradict each other. He may even engage in "creative destruction," just as a dentist may drill a hole in the patient's tooth to take out what is rotten in order to fill the tooth and save it. The dentist does not passively accept the patient's teeth as they are, or merely reflect an x-ray picture of them back to the patient. On the other hand, he is careful to be certain, before he begins work, that he has seen the patient's teeth *as they actually are*. As he works, he watches the patient care-fully to see where the areas of pain are, and to be sure that the pain does not become too great. So the skilled "understander" moves back and forth between "understanding" and taking stands of his own. "Destruction" can be "creative" only when the understandee is in the fourth stage of relationship with the understander. Otherwise it will be truly destructive, and therefore irresponsible on the part of the understander.

All of this is true when the understander is in the role of therapist. But I am finding that it is equally true in any ordinary conversation except the most trivial: people want a certain amount of opinion, or narration, or whatever, from me (or from you, or from anyone else), but if they get too much, they soon begin to feel crowded, annoyed, resentful. So the understander needs his skill on two levels: first, to hear what the other person is saying; second, to see when the other person needs that first kind of understanding, and when he needs something else. But there is yet a third level: the understander needs to be aware of his own needs, his own interests, and his own resources. Being aware of them, he does not entirely keep them out of the picture; rather, he draws on them and controls them, both while he is "understand-ing" and while he is "standing for himself."

So the second kind of "love"—the kind that Rilke was talking about—is as simple as the paradox of closeness and infinite distance. At the same time, it is complex, because putting that kind of love into action must be done with sensitivity on several levels at once. There may be a few people who do this instinctively, but many who think they do so are (in my experience) not fully aware of how they are coming across to the people they are "understanding." Most of us can profit from systematic practice followed by frank feedback from the persons we are trying to "understand."

What I have said about this kind of "understanding" comes, then, to only three points:

1. *See and hear* the other person as he or she is, without turning away, without fighting back, and without trying to control the other person.

2. *Believe* that the other person has the desire, and much of the wisdom, to straighten out what is within his or her S_2, and to make it more harmonious.

3. *Speak and act* in ways that flow out of what you have seen and what you believe, and out of what is appropriate to the situation in which you find yourself.

Looking back now, I find myself asking whether one can become very adept at giving understanding unless one deeply understands the need for understanding; and whether one can understand this need unless one accepts its existence within oneself; and whether, as one understands more deeply the need for understanding, one feels more pain when it is withheld— whether from others or from oneself.

And that is all I have to say about "counseling," as Curran uses the word. "Counseling-Learning," then, is a way of learning and teaching in which one or more of the persons involved acts as a "counselor" to the others, in order that the work of the other(s), whether that work is learning or teaching, may be fuller, smoother, more satisfying.

In Counseling-Learning (CL), as in any approach to education, one person knows something that the others want to (or have been sent to) learn. This person is usually called the "teacher," but Curran preferred to call him/her the "knower." A "teacher," I suppose, is one who carries responsibility not only for "knowing," but also for managing or directing the learning of the others. The teacher in Counseling-Learning takes on a third responsibility: that of "understander" to her students. A teacher who does not feel ready to take on this third responsibility may still use techniques which have grown out of Counseling-Learning, and these techniques sometimes work very well outside of CL, at least for a while.

In most CL classes, it is the teacher who takes the "counselor" role at the outset. An experience of one of my daughters shows, on a small scale, that the learner may be the one who is the first "counselor." In the summer before her senior year in college, she was taking a literature course. The lecturer seemed to know his subject matter well enough. His knowledge, however, was a battleground on which the professor and several of the students waged a continuing power struggle. The students scored points by proving that they knew something that the professor had not known, or by asking him questions that he could not answer, or by pointing out flaws in what he said. The professor defended himself and his status by using learned words, by general obfuscation, and by patching up one statement with two others so as to make it less open to attack. The result, of course, was a series of lectures that were almost impossible to follow. My daughter tried giving to the professor what Curran would have called "understanding responses: 'What you are saying is...'" and so on. This did not transform the whole class into a "learning community," of course. She did find, however, that when she did so, the professor began to speak more clearly, with more apparent self-confidence, and with fewer of the defensive devices that he had been using before.

This incident shows how threatening a classroom can be for the teacher, and not just for the students. In some schools these days, teachers fear for their physical safety. But there are so many other questions: Will the knowledge that I have put together at so much cost within my S_1 find a welcome and useful place in their S_2, S_3, ... ? (This is part of what Curran called "the sickness to teach.") Will my students regard me as superior to them in knowledge, or will I come out looking ignorant? Will they accept me as superior to them in authority, or will I have a "discipline problem"? Will my students admire me, and will my colleagues regard me as competent? Will I continue to have enough students so that I can make a living for myself and my family? As I teach my students more and more, will they give me less and less respect because the difference between their knowledge and mine is smaller? Will something that a learner says show me that this part of my S_1 needs to be taken apart and put together again, perhaps with some new pieces? These are some of the issues with which a *learner*-counselor can help the *knower* to deal.

A teacher's unmet needs may show themselves in many ways. A need to feel that one is an able teacher may lead to pressure on the students to perform beyond what they are ready for—forcing the correct sounds out of them at a time when those sounds are for them little but noise. The same need may lead to the awarding of overgenerous grades, and then allowing oneself to believe that those grades were accurate. (The same grades may also serve to impress colleagues, pupils, parents, and administrators.) In quite the opposite direction, one may exalt the subject matter (and, indirectly, oneself) by grading very harshly. I have wondered whether the tendency of some teachers to emphasize the difficulties in their own languages ("*My* language has a difficult spelling system / irregular verbs / lots of inflectional endings," etc., etc.) may sometimes have a similar function.

But most often, it is the teacher who starts out as the "counselor," or "understander" to the students. In classes of this kind, Curran talked about the students being in one of five "stages." In "Stage 1," the learner desires as much security as the knower/teacher can provide for him. As he gains a bit of knowledge, and some confidence, the learner enters Stage 2 and begins to take small risks by trying things out on his own. The knower is close at his side, however, to provide security when the learner seems to want it. In a swimming lesson, the Stage 1 learner keeps his feet on the bottom of the pool. The Stage 2 learner tries floating, with the teacher's hands an inch or two beneath him. The Stage 3 swimmer has great fun jumping into the water and paddling around with his friends. All he needs is a lifeguard to warn him when he is getting into a dangerous area, and to rescue him in case of real trouble. The Stage 3 swimmer, however, has little patience with the expert who wants to show him the fine points of swimming faster or more gracefully. The would-be teacher may therefore feel considerable frustration and pain, of the kinds that I listed above. He feels this way both because he feels rejected by the student, and because he sees all that the student is missing by refusing to learn more.

In Stage 4, the roles of the knower and the learner are reversed. In Stages 1–3, it was the knower who provided security; the learner was free to stick his neck out or not, according to the amount of security that he felt. The knower had to be very cautious not to destroy that security, whether by the wrong kind of correcting of mistakes, or by loading learners down with more than they could handle. In Stage 4, on the other hand, the learners are secure enough so that they are able to take care of their own anxieties. They are also able to see some of the anxieties of the knower: his fear that what he has to offer will not be valued by the learners, his pain at the way they are mangling his language (or whatever he is teaching), and so on. They are also able to help the knower with his anxieties—and at the same time to help themselves learn better—by welcoming his corrections and suggestions. In an ideal Stage 4, the knower continues to have an "understanding" attitude toward the learners, so that the relationship is one of mutual support. Each side puts into the learning enterprise what it is able to supply, whether knowledge of subject matter, or knowledge of what it is ready to take in next, or appreciation of the contribution of the other, or awareness of its own reactions of perplexity, elation, anger, or fatigue. Each side also accepts the contributions of the other freely and nondefensively.

Curran often spoke of his approach to education as an "inseminational model." He made much use of metaphors both from human reproduction and from the planting of seed in a garden or a field. The former is clear in the relationship which I have just described, in which the living knowledge is passed between persons who are intimately bound to one another in mutual "love" (as Rilke used the term). The agricultural metaphor brings out the lapse of time and season between planting and reaping, and reminds us that the one who cultivates the plants, or who reaps the harvest, may not be the same one who planted the seed. And, as in the Parable of the Sower, it is a convenient frame of reference for thinking about all of the things that can happen to the seed from the time it leaves the hand of the sower until it finally bears fruit.

But frequently the knower is intent only on getting his subject matter across, or on fulfilling various personal needs. A patient, understanding learner may still enter into a "Stage 4" relationship with such a knower. I have already told of my daughter's experience in doing this. (Large parts of the Counseling-Learning Institutes are conducted on this basis, partly for training purposes.)

In Stages 1 to 3, the knower-counselor's concern for the security of the learners kept him from correcting many of the learners' smaller errors. Now, in Stage 4, the knower is free to deal with these errors, and the learners are able to overcome them.

Stage 5 is like Stage 4, except that now most errors are behind the learners, so that both the learners and the knower can turn their energy to polishing and perfecting the new skill of the learners.

These five "stages" are not an inflexible series, and a learner may shift from one of them to another from moment to moment. But they do show how the relationship may grow and become more mature. In the first stage, the learner is locked into himself, his own purposes, and his own anxieties, and sees the knower either as a source for getting what he wants, or as a threat, *or as both at the same time.* He is in the situation of Diagram 3. The knower-teacher, however, sees the learner, not according to Diagram 3, but "whole against the sky." In Stage 4, the learner has left Diagram 3 behind, and also sees the knower "whole against the sky." These two ways of seeing are really quite different from each other. Therefore, moving from one of them to the other—from Stage 3 to Stage 4—may prove to be a very emotional experience, bringing with it pain, anger, and confusion. In Counseling-Learning, the knower who has served as counselor through the first three stages now has the opportunity of continuing to provide understanding support through this period. The knower-counselor's job is made more delicate and more difficult by the fact that some of the learner's anger and aggression may be directed against him. So this is the part of Counseling-Learning which requires of the teacher the greatest strength and deepest stillness—the surest maturity.

These five "stages," then, are five modes in which knower and learner(s) may relate to each other. The stages differ among themselves in various ways. The central, or the most basic difference is not in the degree of security that the learners feel; the *goal* is that learners should feel a high degree of security in *all* of the stages. The difference lies, rather, in where that security comes from. In the first stage, the knower makes considerable positive effort to *provide* security to the learner; by Stage 4, he may simply watch out not to create irrelevant or unnecessary *insecurity.* Curran, of course, was neither the first writer nor the last to emphasize the fundamental importance of security in limiting—and in making possible—what people do. But he took this concept of "security" and made it the starting point for a formula which I have found to be immensely useful as I try to understand what is going on around me. Curran's name for this formula was SARD. For my own purposes, I sometimes think of it as SAARRD.

The formula begins with the letter S. This means that on the first day of class, a teacher who is following this formula is concerned first (in time) and most urgently (in emphasis) with establishing a climate in which the student feels *secure*. It also means that this concern for, or awareness of, security continues to carry top priority in the teacher's work throughout the course. It emphatically does *not* mean that the student is kept throughout the course wrapped in a warm, soft cocoon of personal solicitude and linguistic protection.

In fact, the whole CL system is built on the assumption that when people feel secure, they will not just curl up and fall asleep in their security, but that they will push out from it—"burst the cocoon," if you like—and look for something new to bring into their growing selves: R ⟶ S arrows, as I put it in Chapter 7. Here, too, is the turtle that I am always talking about, sticking his head and legs out of his shell and setting forth on new adventures.

And this is the meaning of the first *A* in the SAARRD formula: the learner begins to *assert* himself into the class, by asking questions, by making suggestions, or in general by contributing to choices about what he is going to say, and when, and with whom. (You will recognize this "assertion" as what elsewhere I have called "exercising initiative.")

The second *A* of the formula stands for the assumption that when something—a word, a sentence, or anything else—is the result of a learner's having asserted himself, then that student will give fuller and deeper *attention* to it.

The first R of the formula stands for *reflection*: even after giving full attention to something new, learners usually need to look at it again, separated now from the feelings and the other miscellaneous sensations that surrounded it during the Assertion-Attention phase out of which it was born. The counselor-teacher provides two different kinds of "reflection." One kind is a chance to reexamine the content of what the learner has done: to hear his own voice on tape, to watch himself on video playback, to see a written summary of what he has done, and so on.

But the teacher-counselor reflects back to the learners more than just the content of what they have done. Counseling-Learning, historically, grew out of the belief that in the learning experience knowing and feeling are closely intertwined with each other. Accordingly, the teacher-counselor also reflects back to the students their feelings, whether of pleasure or frustration or discouragement or triumph. The teacher does this in the manner that I have already referred to: the students' *feelings* become the *facts* that the counselor describes and verifies, but the feelings that the counselor sends along with this message are calm, patient, and supportive. Giving this kind of reflection obviously requires a certain balance and security on the part of the teacher, just as giving the first kind of reflection demands that the teacher be able to choose among many different techniques.

As he works again with the new material, the learner sees it from new angles and forms a rich set of associations with it. In this way, the new material comes to be tied in with the learner's entire network of memories, so that he finds he can hold onto it more easily and get it back when he needs it. The second R of the formula stands for *retention*.

The D at the end of the formula stands for *discrimination*: after the learner has retained a new item, he can then compare it with other things that he knows, and learn to tell them apart. Or, more generally, he can take the new item and work it into an appropriate place within the total of what he already knows. This kind of "discrimination," coming at the end of the SAARRD sequence, can be subtle and intimate and lasting in its effect. (It is quite another thing from the way I used to take students on the first day of class, and put them through minimal pair drills so that they could begin to hear and make the phonemic distinctions of their new target language.)

That, then, is *my* summary of *my* understanding of Curran's SARD formula. There are five points within it that I think are worth further comment.

1. The concern for security (S) is not confined to the beginning of the sequence. In the "reflection" activities especially, the teacher's techniques, or the teacher's personal style, or both, may build, or may destroy or at least damage the learner's security. If the latter happens, the student is in effect punished for his "assertion" (the first A in the formula), and the "turtle" will pull its head and legs back into its shell.

2. One essential part of the initial "security" (the S of the formula) is the providing of clear *structure* within which the learner is to assert himself and make choices. (It happens that the word *structure* also begins with S; perhaps the formula should be SSAARRD!) This structure need not be detailed; in fact, if it is too detailed, it may even block the learner from assertion. The important thing is that the structure be clear, and gentle. As Jenny Rardin once put it, the learner fares best when the knower-counselor is "confidently and sensitively directive."

3. The first two points, taken together, show why Counseling-Learning teachers talk so much about "learner space": structuring that space, first of all, but also respecting it by leaving the learner room in which to work without unnecessary interference. This is very close to what I have meant when I have talked about "control" and "initiative."

4. "Security" is not a simple concept. The same thing that makes one person feel very secure can make another person feel insecure and even angry. Some people, for example, are perfectly happy to create their own sentences, watercolor paintings, computer programs, or whatever, within only the most general guidelines. Others very much want to be told exactly what to do, and then to be told immediately whether they have done it right. What is warm support to one person may seem like oversolicitude and crowding to another. Some people become upset if they are asked to mem-

orize something, while to others, memorizing gives them something to hold onto and depend on. Some people are content to talk about anything at all in a language class, while others feel that they are wasting their time if they are not talking about something that has a direct bearing on a future examination or a future job. "Security" in general, I suppose, means getting back R⟶S arrows that fit into the needs of one's own Self. And Selves are so very different from one another! The teacher needs to "understand" the students on at least three levels at once: their language, their hour-by-hour reactions to what is going on in class, and their longer-term needs and readiness.

5. In Chapter 7, I began by saying that my "Self" is built up out of all the things that I have learned to tell apart, and all the things that I have learned to expect. In this sense, the "discriminations" that come at the end of the SARD formula are actually newly acquired, and newly accepted, parts of the Self. Now, in Chapter 8, in my discussion of the SARD formula, I have given new meanings to the letters in Diagram 3, *but these letters follow the same path.* So the SARD formula can be written as:

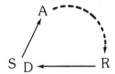

but since Discriminations become parts of the Self, we can rewrite it once more, either:

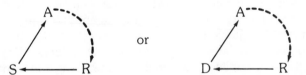

The dotted lines stand for the fact that the R depends partly on the A, and partly on other people or other things which lie outside the learner and outside these diagrams.

Turning the SARD formula into a circle, or better yet into a spiral, brings it, I think, closer to life. A secure Self which learns in this way is constantly growing, reorganizing itself, and renewing itself. An insecure Self which equates Security only with Stagnation brings forth, not new Discriminations, but (in Curran's words) a kind of living Death. (One thinks of the Parable of the Talents, *Matthew 25.*) Sometimes the security which the teacher provides is what makes the difference for the learner between one of these patterns and the other. It was in this sense that Curran saw the role of the teacher as potentially a "redemptive" one—bringing the learner back toward a life-giving harmony with himself and with the world around him.

Notice, however, that Counseling-Learning does not rule out any techniques which existed before it, or which had their birth in theories of learning which are quite different from Curran's. I have already mentioned that the memorizing of dialogs may, for some learners, be a very welcome—a very security-giving—addition to the "Reflection" phase of language study. Another example is programmed instruction, which is based on the assumption that people (and animals in general) learn principally by doing things right and then being rewarded in some way for doing so. In programmed instruction, the learner meets one tightly structured bit of learning space (one "frame") after another, and is invited to assert himself into it in some very clearly defined way—perhaps by pushing one of four buttons. From a CL point of view, this kind of "assertion" is of course very narrow and shallow. Even so, it can be of great use within CL for following up and developing points on which the learner finds that he needs practice. And, for those students who are able to work with language outside of the context of genuine communication, programs offer a degree of security that few conventional types of instruction can match. What *is* essential is not the procedure itself, or the theory out of which the procedure arose; it is, rather, that the technique be chosen, and be used, within the kind of relationship which I hope has appeared in my discussion of the five "stages" and of "SARD."

This brings to an end what I have to say about Counseling-Learning. Anyone who wants a fuller and authoritative account of it should read Curran in the original. Such people as Jenny Rardin and Dan Tranel worked long and closely with him, so that they are vastly better able to speak for him than I would be. As I said at the beginning of this letter, I am really speaking only for my own understanding of him, which is quite another thing.

"Community Language Learning" (CLL) is a term that has met with a great deal of partial understanding and partial misunderstanding. In general, I suppose, it can be applied to any method of teaching and learning foreign languages which follows the principles of Counseling-Learning. To "describe" it, except by examples, would be impossible, unnecessary, and misleading. Chapters 12–15 and 17 contain accounts of some actual experiences, from the point of view of students as well as teachers. None of them is intended as an example to be followed. I would like to make only two brief points about CLL, and then this letter is finished.

1. I have found it *very* useful to distinguish between Community Language Learning (CLL) in general, and what I call the "Classical Community Language Learning" (CCLL) method in particular. CCLL was the first CLL method, which was developed by Curran and his associates in their research seminars in Chicago. Most of the learners and most of the knowers in those seminars were actually graduate students in counseling. For them, the primary purpose of the language-learning sessions was to develop and deepen their understanding of themselves, and of how human beings interact with one another; the language learning was secondary—a vehicle for

experience. This method is the one in which learners sit in a closed circle, with the knower(s) outside. The learners say in their native language whatever they want to say to one another. As they do so, the knower stands behind the speaker and gives the corresponding expressions in the target language. During the conversation, the target language sentences of the learners, and nothing else, are recorded on tape. After 10 minutes or so of conversation, the tape is played back and used in various ways. I give this brief description only in order to identify which method I mean by "CCLL." The description is incomplete, and applies only to the beginning level. Curran described the basic techniques in his 1972 and 1976 books, and there is no point in repeating in this chapter what he said there. Accounts of three of my own adaptations of it appear in Chapters 12–14.

A certain amount of inevitable misunderstanding arose when Curran and his associates began to show their work to those of us who were language teachers from outside of their circle. Since at that time CCLL was the only existing form of CLL, we did not distinguish the one from the other. I'm not even sure how clearly Curran and his associates saw this distinction in those days. And the difference between CL and CLL was very fuzzy for me at first. So we tended to confuse the range of applicability of CCLL (a method or a technique) with the range of validity of CL (a way of looking at how people behave). Those of us who were impressed by CL tended to claim that CCLL was more widely usable than it was. Others, who more quickly saw the limitations of that one method, may have thrown away with it some valuable insights of the underlying theory.

2. The word "community" means that power is more evenly distributed between knower and learner than it is in a conventional classroom. But in a community, "power" is itself subordinated to "responsibility." Both knower and learner are responsible for bringing to the task the resources that they alone possess. This is a relationship with constantly shifting equilibrium, not a relationship of fixed roles.

Some people have seemed to assume that in CLL the students therefore run the class and design their own training. I suppose that might happen in a class of very mature students. But Curran saw the role of the knower-counselor as far more than just being flexible and "understanding." The knower-counselor, by virtue of his knowledge, also "stands for" the subject matter of the course. By virtue of his expertise in teaching, as I said earlier, he establishes and maintains as much structure as the learner needs. By virtue of his skill in understanding and seeing, he may from time to time confront the learners with differences between what they think they are doing and what they actually are doing. He may even insist that the learners live up to the best that he sees that they have in them. This is of course very different from insisting that one's students perform according to some standard that comes from the teacher's own desires.

Well, B _____ , this has been a long letter. I have enjoyed writing it, I think I have learned something from writing it, and the writing has been ever so much easier for having you as the specific addressee. I do not dare to hope that you or anyone else will read it straight through from start to finish. I do hope, however, that what you and other readers get out of it will help you to make better sense of the other chapters in my book.

This is where the original letter ended. I will add one bit of verse which hung on the wall of Curran's study. We will never be sure exactly why it hung there, but its pictures, taken together, match one part of what I think Curran was about:

Over the way of walking is the way of flying;
It is faster, and much smoother, but it is not for me.

The unbruised foot does not know where it has been;
In April I drink the scent of the lilacs one at a time.

This is the earth that I rose from,
And the ground on which I shall sleep.

Therefore I do not envy the swallow,
Or even the eagle.

They have their kingdom in seeing,
But mine is in touching, and waiting.

CHAPTER 9

CAN WE AFFORD TO BE RELEVANT?

This paper was delivered at Fairleigh-Dickinson University in 1971. It contains in embryo some of the ideas and the emphases which appear in more fully developed form elsewhere in this book. I reprint it here for three reasons: (1) The metaphor of the plug, with all that lies behind it and all that it leads to, may put into perspective the materials and equipment that we use. (2) The series of questions about "relevance" are still today a reminder to me not to be too facile in saying, "Oh, yes, of course we must be 'relevant'!" (3) The concept of "relevance" ("strength," in my 1971 book) was still only a rough sketch of what in *Memory, Meaning, and Method* I called "depth." In the present book, through the use of the Becker and Adler materials in the first two chapters, and the Rilke quotation in Chapter 7, I have tried to push the "depth dimension" a little farther. I have also added some detail and organized more clearly my picture of what goes on in the "depths."

Let me begin by saying that I am not here today as an expert in what you are doing. I have never taught a language to anyone under eighteen, and most of my students have been over twenty-one. Furthermore, my recent experience has been with seldom-taught languages like Armenian and Swahili, which are taught under conditions and for reasons which are vastly different from what most of you are accustomed to. What I hope is that a few of the ideas that have developed out of my kind of work will be of some interest in yours.

I am not here, then, because I am an expert, and only partly because I am a linguist. My own principal reason for wanting to talk with you today is that I am a parent. Two of my children have gone through five years apiece of foreign language study in what I believe to be one of the best school systems in the country, and I am gravely concerned lest my third—and thousands like him in all parts of the country—have an experience like theirs. My first two, though their grades were very high, almost dropped their languages after four years; they did drop them after five, and I must say that I can't blame them. The principal shortcoming in their high school instruction, I am convinced, was lack of relevance. That is what I'd like to talk with you about this afternoon.

Here in my hand, I have an ordinary two-pronged electrical plug. If life were an electrical system, this plug would be a language, and the process of assembling this plug would be the subject matter for a language course.

This plug, as you see it here, is related to nothing: *and* it is totally "irrelevant." But suppose now that I have a socket into which I can fit the plug. Now the plug is no longer related to nothing. It is closely and appropriately *related* to the socket. But it is still just as *irrelevant* as it was before. Suppose I go on and relate the socket to a wiring system, and the wiring system to a fuse box, a power line, and ultimately to a generator. The plug is still irrelevant, even at the end of this long chain of relatedness. We still need a wire from the plug to a switch, and something for the switch to turn on, and finally we have to have somebody to eat the toast, or read by the light, or listen to the radio. Then and only then does this plug become in any useful sense "relevant." If the chain is broken anywhere, the plug immediately reverts to irrelevance.

In this sense, "relevance" is an all-or-none proposition. In the context of language teaching, if what goes on in class does not make sense in terms of at least one of the student's interests, and that interest make sense in terms of a pattern of wider and longer-term interests—in other words, to what is for him reality—then relevance breaks down after the plug. Just a picture of Buenos Aires or Berlin, or just talking about the day's events, or race relations, or the war, or ecology, or just playing dominoes with each other in French does not guarantee relevance. Any of these may be helpful, but none is sufficient, and none is necessary. And if on the other hand there is a lack of an authentic model to follow, or lack of coherent materials, then the power is not getting even as far as the socket.

Much of what has been said and written about language teaching, particularly in recent years, has concentrated either on getting the power to the socket, or on devising faster, more efficient, cleverer ways of assembling the plug. We're pretty good at that. Sometimes I think we're much better at that than we need to be. But we are much less adept at tying into the total need-and-interest structures of our students.

Can the hard-pressed classroom teacher, who meets over a hundred different students every day, hope to have time and energy enough to fire up a toaster for one, drive a radio for another, and light a reading lamp for yet another? Can we be expected to do more than get the 110 volts up to the socket? Or, in the words of my title today, can we afford to be relevant?

The obvious reply to a question like that is, Relevant to what? In that connection, I'd like to list for you several kinds of relevance which I have observed over the years, but particularly within the past year as I've been traveling around, talking with all kinds of language teachers, and pulling together some of my thoughts for a report to the Office of Education.

A relevant lesson or activity may of course relate to *present* reality—to the here and now—what is physically present in this classroom, during this hour. Or it may relate to *prospective* reality—something that will or may happen in the future. This is valid as long as we remember that the literal meaning of "prospective" is "looking forward," and that the person whose imagination must look forward to these things in the future is the student, and not just the teacher and the textbook writer. In the same way, a relevant lesson may have its immediate relationship to something in the past—last week, last year, or a thousand years ago. This we may call *retrospective* reality, and again, when we say "spective" we are referring to the mind of the student, not only the teacher or the textbook writer.

This is the chronological dimension of relevance, past, present, and future. Scattered along this dimension we find the student's experiences, we find his use of language as an instrument to do other things, all of these in their external aspect, in terms of his relationships with the outside world, and with other people. All of these, then, involve what we may call extro-spection. This outward-looking kind of relatedness may in the long run be necessary for relevance, but it is not by itself sufficient for relevance. Because running at right angles to the horizontal chronological dimension is the vertical dimension which goes beneath extrospection to introspection—to what the student sees when he looks inside himself. Does he see himself as a success, or as a failure? As apt, or as inept? As a docile internalizer of "phonetics, basic vocabulary, and grammar," who is striving to meet the teacher's expectations and so receive a passing grade? Or as a contributor of necessary insights and valued expectations? Whose activity does he see as primary, the teacher's or his own? Is he, in his own eyes, a mover or a pawn?

Emphasis on the introspective end of this vertical dimension is, to my way of thinking, the most interesting feature of what Dr. Gattegno calls his "Silent Way" of teaching languages. Exploitation of the horizontal dimension is reduced to what must surely be its very narrowest minimum. During the first part of the course, all talking is about a set of cuisenaire rods. As you know, these are small wooden blocks which differ from each other only in length and color. They are little more than concrete abstractions. These are followed by a series of pictures which portray other things, but which again are about as unrelated to the horizontal kind of external, interesting reality as it is possible to get and still depict real objects. But it is this very annihilation of the horizontal dimension, coupled with the almost complete silence of the teacher, that allows and indeed forces both student and teacher to focus their attention on the introspective—on what resources are available from within his mind, and what he is ready to do at any given moment. Having seen this kind of thing in action, I am no longer willing to deny that, in the short run, and with a teacher who can focus his attention on the inside of the student's mind, the vertical dimension may be sufficient. In the long run, of course, it is not. In fact, the essence of relevance is that it connects something on the horizontal dimension of external experience with something on the vertical dimension of the student's appreciation of himself. It is the vertical dimension, however, that language teachers talk and write about least.

So we have discovered that the essence of relevance lies in forming a bond between the exterior and the interior. Very pretty. We still come back to our original question: Can we *afford* to be relevant? And a second obvious retort to this question is, Can we afford *not* to be relevant? Put that way, it is almost like asking whether we are against motherhood or goodness. How can anybody, these days, say publicly that he believes we can afford *not* to be relevant? But be that as it may, I'm afraid that even the stoutest certainty that we can*not* afford to be *ir*relevant does not guarantee that we *can* afford to be *relevant.*

So let's try again. Maybe the question, instead of Can we afford to be relevant? should be How relevant can we afford to be? This sounds like asking

How much individual attention can we give students? To what extent can we dispense with a printed textbook? To what extent do we dare put ourselves into the position of often responding to the initiative of the students, as contrasted with only evaluating their responses to ours? These are fundamental questions, all right, and they do have to do with relevance, but to the hard-working and overworked classroom teacher, they may also be alarming questions. So let's select a question that is a little less formidable. Instead of inquiring about the limits, as in the question How relevant can we afford to be? let's start from where we are and look in the direction we want to go. The question then becomes *How can we afford to be more relevant?* That is the question that I am going to explore with you today.

Before trying to answer it, though, let me state one hunch that is on its way to becoming a conviction: that a small-scale relevance—relevance now and then, whenever we can make time for it—is going to turn out to be prohibitively expensive. Maybe it's true that we cannot afford to be irrelevant, but we can't afford relevance, either, if we have to pay for it at retail prices. We can afford it, though, if we can get it wholesale, on a regular, habitual, pervasive basis. This for me has required a drastic change in outlook—in some ways a reversal of much of my thinking of ten years ago. What I am suggesting to you today is that such a change is possible, and I would like to tell you what I think it involves.

We have often said that "language is behavior," and so it is. Some of us have gone on from that statement, though, and concluded that what we must therefore do is first of all to describe that behavior and its internal structure, and cause students to produce that behavior, and further that the way to get them to produce that behavior as a whole is to start by having them reproduce small samples of its external manifestations: this is where we get close mimicry, dialog memorization, and the like. Others have quarreled with the emphasis on pronunciation and surface structure, but even they have left unchallenged the assumption that description of the language, and particularly of its *deep* structure, is a matter of top priority.

But let's go back to our original three-word premise and draw a different set of conclusions from it. "Language is behavior." Well and good. But it is behavior that normally accompanies other behavior, and all these kinds of behavior are related to one another like strands in a cable: none will carry much weight by itself. It seems to me that in our everyday, week-in-and-week-out ordinarily irrelevant language teaching—mine at least, and the kind that has been inflicted on my kids in high school—we have placed almost all the weight on the linguistic strand. No wonder it so often sags or even snaps in two!

Language is only one strand in the cable of total behavior, and furthermore, that cable is usually attached at both ends: behavior is normally purposeful. This leads to two conclusions: (1) that the teacher should know *what* is being done, by teacher and students, in the greatest possible detail, and (2) that the teacher should also know *why* it is being done, and should see the "why" on the widest possible scale.

Going on to look at the lesson itself, as it stands in the book, I would like to suggest a simple but useful way of analyzing its *content,* and a simple but useful way of analyzing its *form.* Content may be inventoried from a linguistic point of view: what words and what structures does the lesson contain? A second point of view is social: who might use this kind of language in talking with whom? A third point of view is topical: what is being talked about? Having made an inventory from each of these three points of view, the teacher is in a better position to hold the structures constant and supplement the vocabulary, or to hold the language relatively constant but change the social setting, or to make other conscious changes that are demanded if we're to have controlled adaptation.

Even more important, to me, is analysis of the form of the lesson. I have just about concluded that a complete, well-balanced, nourishing lesson must have four components and needs only those four. Let's skip the first for a moment. The second component is the one that is the most conspicuous in many language courses today. It is what I call the sample of language in use: a basic dialog, or a reading selection or something like that. The third component consists of one or more ways of exploring the structure of the language, usually departing from something in the sample of language use. These are drills, exercises, grammar notes, and so forth. And the fourth component consists of one or more ways of exploring the lexicon—again usually starting out from the sample of language use. The first component—the one that I think should be first in the mind of the textbook writer and the teacher, and at the same time the *res ultima,* the destination which the student reaches at least once in every lesson—this component is the one that receives the least attention from most writers whose books I have seen, and from most teachers whose students I have interviewed. This alpha and omega of a good lesson, this source and goal of all the other components, can be stated quite simply in one word: "payoff." What will the student be able to do, as a result of the lesson, that will enhance his appreciation of himself, and/or enable him to make a favorable impression on people whose opinion he values, and/or get information that he really wants, and/or do other things that he genuinely wants or likes to do? And it is particularly the interpersonal and intrapersonal kinds of payoff that so seldom get mentioned among us language teachers.

"How can we be *more* relevant?" If a high school teacher in a fourth year course spends day after day reading aloud to his students, and another, whose command of the language is somewhat better, sees fit to lecture over a period of weeks about details of the architecture of a series of cathedrals, both are obviously dealing with classes of students who could be engaged in all manner of interesting projects, either individually or in groups. Those are easy examples, but drawn from actual classrooms. The point is that neither of them could have happened if the teacher had looked first at the payoffs that could be expected to result, or not to result, from his performance.

Here's another example of what I mean. Lesson 1 of a well-known beginning text in French (*La Clef,* by Yvette de Petra, Holt, Rinehart, and Winston, New York, 1970) a text that illustrates more than most do the kind of attitude that I think we ought to be encouraging. The author, in the introduction, speaks to the student about ways to "restore your confidence in yourself and in what you are doing" (vi) and encourages them to use their imagination and their intuition (viii). She enjoins the teacher to "encourage any initiative, provided that French is the medium used" (19). On the very first day of class, when only half of the first dialog has been presented, the teacher is advised not to worry about finishing it, but to "use the rest of this period for reviewing or conversation" [21]. On the fourth day, the teacher's manual observes that " 'free' conversation is a very useful exercise which can be resorted to whenever time permits." (25) On the eighth day, the teacher is instructed to "adapt the questions in the book to fit your specific class. . . . Try to make this as much of a 'real' conversation as possible, not just a series of questions and answers on a text they had to prepare." (30) Later on in Unit 1, which covers 17 class meetings plus lab, the students do two compositions, one on describing the classroom and the other on describing a picture; they do this first orally and then in writing. The purpose of the composition topics is to "force the students to use the French which they are learning, in relation to their own experience. . . ." (15f) Now, what could possibly be closer than that to what I am recommending?

Let's take another look at this book. The teacher's manual is a wonder of thoroughness, even to the point of suggesting specific gestures and quips for the teacher to use, but the exhortation to make conversation as real as possible is about the only one in the book that is not supported by detailed examples. Even where free conversation is described as "useful," it is not the focus toward which all other parts of the lesson converge. No, it is something to be "resorted to," and when? "Whenever time permits." This lesson has all the right components. Its faults are mainly in focus and emphasis.

But we can go beyond free conversation. Let's look only at the simplest visual aids, such as travel posters or large magazine pictures. Items in each picture can be marked with numbers, as they are in the book itself. The vocabulary can be made available on a single tape or cassette. Individual students may then contract with the teacher to prepare an oral or written description of one or more pictures. Going one step further, students might provide their own pictures of rooms or buildings, marking with a number each new item for which they don't know the name. The teacher, or some other speaker of French can then read the vocabularies onto a tape, which is then made available to the students. This gives an opportunity to use French-speaking paraprofessionals in a controlled way. Going one step further still, the French speaker might describe each picture in three or four sentences.

Students could understand what was already in their textbook, guess at some of the rest, and incorporate it into their own compositions. Meantime, they would have the satisfaction of partially understanding something done impromptu in response to their own pictures, and at the same time they have a good excuse for not worrying about whatever they *can't* understand.

I'm afraid we don't have time for further examples. The thought that I would like to leave with you today is this: that the total meaning of a language course for any one student is the net effect it has on him. He may conclude that language learning consists in assembling and adjusting an especially complicated plug. Or he may have learned to handle the language somewhat, but believe that he owes it all to a gifted teacher, or a well-written textbook, or even a teaching machine, and fail to appreciate his own part in the process. He may think that the main object of speaking a foreign language is to avoid making mistakes. I would rather have a student come out of a course with a vocabulary of 500 words and a weak grasp of the subjunctive, but with the skills and confidence that will enable him to go on and get more of that language (or some other) when he needs it, than to have him come out with 5000 words and flawless control of the subjunctive, but with the conviction that he cannot—or doesn't even want to—learn more on his own later on. Yet lack of self-confidence in language matters is what we see in too many college graduates who come into the Peace Corps or the Foreign Service. And lack of interest is what my oldest daughter's high school teachers built into her—at exactly the same time they were qualifying her for her membership in the French Honor Society!

CHAPTER 10

ON GOING FROM ONE LANGUAGE INTO ANOTHER: SOME FIRSTHAND EXPERIENCES

To say that something is "alive" is to say that it is able to take into itself new things that it needs, and to use them, and to get rid of what it no longer needs, and to grow (in size or in other ways) into the world around it. In doing all these things, it continues to be itself even as it changes.

Whenever two people meet, each comes away with less life, or with more. The same is true for the Spanish-speaking, and English-speaking and Korean-speaking, and other selves that dwell together within one and the same body. If my command of Sarkhanese is new, or if it is old and rusty, then my Sarkhanese-speaking self will be particularly vulnerable. When it shows itself, the way people react to it may cause it to bloom or to wilt.

I felt this power of the other person very keenly in a conversation last week. What Portuguese I know came from a little reading of grammar books and a lot of talking with people. That was 20 years ago, but for some reason, Portuguese remains one of the languages that I most enjoy using. Two years ago, on a flight within the United States, I happened to be seated in the midst of two dozen tourists from Brazil. Even after so many years, I was able to talk at length with two of them all the way from Oklahoma City to Washington (with intermediate stops at Tulsa and Chicago!). I had no real difficulty with fluency or vocabulary, and even my grammar seemed to hold up rather well. On two or three occasions, thinking that my friends might like either to practice their English or to escape my Portuguese, I switched to English, but they continued in Portuguese. The point I wish to make is that my Portuguese was still quite serviceable then, and that there is no reason to think that my neurochemical storage has suddenly deteriorated in the last two years.

In recent months, I have had several occasions to speak with a Portuguese-English bilingual whose first language was Portuguese. Most of our conversations had been in English, but the Portuguese conversations had seemed to me to be quite satisfactory.

Our conversation last week was by telephone. It started out in Portuguese. After a few sentences, I made a huge error of elementary grammar—one which I certainly would not have expected myself to make. I corrected myself immediately, but from that point on, the other person kept replying to me in English, even though I continued in Portuguese.

This experience raised several questions within me. On the linguistic level, I asked myself, "Has my Portuguese suddenly left me? Or have I been deceiving myself all along about how serviceable it is?" On the personal level, I wondered, "Have I been imposing myself on this person (and on other speakers of Portuguese)? Have I been selfishly exploiting this person's obligation to be polite to me?" On the practical level, I began to think, "Maybe I'd better stop using Portuguese except with people, such as teachers, who are paid to deal with that sort of thing. Maybe I should go back and learn some more before speaking to ordinary people."

Which is to say that my Portuguese-speaking self died a little in that encounter. Some hardy souls will say that I should not have been so easily intimidated—that I should have shrugged it off. The fact is that I did feel as I did. But I would not trouble myself to write this experience down, or allow people to read it, if many other people had not related to me similar experiences of their own.

Then, just two or three days ago, I had another encounter which cast light on the Portuguese phone call, and also on some other things which have happened recently. This encounter was in the corridor of the building where I work, with a speaker of Bulgarian. I know no Bulgarian, and the Bulgarian speaker knew that I knew none. Nevertheless, she greeted me with "Good day!" in Bulgarian. The bit of Russian that I remember from college enabled me to know what she was saying. I said the greeting back to her, and then added in English, "And many of 'em. I often think how true it is." Both of these are stock phrases in English, which I was quoting as empty formulas. She looked startled, not so much at me as at herself, and then said, "I don't know why I spoke to you in Bulgarian. I just did it on impulse." With that, we continued on our separate ways.

A few steps down the hallway, however, I suddenly realized what had happened. I turned back, caught up with her, and said, "I'd really like to know your reaction while it's still fresh. What effect did what I said have on you? Did it make you more likely, or less likely, to speak to me again in Bulgarian?"

"Well," she replied, "I probably *will* speak to you again sometime in Bulgarian, but I did have the very clear feeling that you were shoving me away." Here, unlike me in the Portuguese phone call, it was a fully competent native speaker who was being pushed back into her shell.

By coincidence (or was it coincidence?) the original Bulgarian encounter was almost word-for-word a replay of one I had had with a speaker of Polish only a week or two earlier. In that encounter, however, the light did not dawn, and so I did not follow it up with a question about the effect of what I had said.

I cannot be certain why the Polish and Bulgarian speakers had the impulse to greet me in their native languages. Looking back on the two incidents, my only feeling is that they honored me by doing so. I would like to feel that there was something about me that made them want to invite me into their linguistic home for a moment. But that would be speculation.

I do, however, have clear recollection of how I myself felt, and why I rebuffed them. First, I sensed that here was an intimacy—a very minimal intimacy, but still an intimacy—which was not under my control. So, with my addition of the two stock phrases from English, I in effect replied with a wisecrack. In so doing, I converted a human greeting into a dead linguistic object. At the same time, I pulled the conversation back into English, which is my home ground. That was certainly the principal motivation for replying as I did.

There was a second motivation, quite different from the first, but which pushed me in the same direction. I sometimes give brief experiences in learning Swahili, as part of a workshop for language teachers. Occasionally weeks or months later, someone who has been in one of those workshops will come up and greet me with a hearty "Hujambo?" I do not like it when they do so. I don't mind people practicing their Swahili with me in any other way, but I do react against the greeting by itself. To me it feels like an empty promise of something which the greeter knows he/she cannot fulfill. Or it hits me as a demand for an approving pat on the head. The actual motivations of these enthusiastic "Hujambo" sayers may be quite different from how they seem to me. I am only trying to explain *my own actions, not theirs*. But the feeling of futility at knowing we could not go beyond the simplest greeting was, I believe, one part of the reason why I rebuffed the speakers of Bulgarian and Polish. As a result, in defeating them I also defeated my own desire to know them better.

Again, there is no excuse for recounting my own experiences unless they are very much like the experiences of many other people. I suspect that they are.

The point of this chapter, as illustrated in these two anecdotes, then, is this: that when two people speak with each other in a language other than the one they usually speak together, there is risk. The risk may bring great gain. Or, as in these two incidents, it may bring a loss.

Another kind of negative outcome from even the simplest greeting in a foreign language appears in the incident reported in Chapter 12, in which I as the stronger speaker of Swahili imposed myself on someone who had had only an hour or two of the language. The result was panic for her, and a feeling on my part that I had blundered professionally. This was like the panic of my other friend (Chapter 2) when a native Frenchman said, "Let's talk French so I can hear how well you speak."

This kind of thing doesn't always lead to panic. My college German has, in recent years, proved to be about as serviceable as my Portuguese. Three years ago, I had several occasions to converse in German with someone at work. I enjoyed it, and he appeared to enjoy it also. The following year, I found another German speaker and we talked for about five minutes. Again, I enjoyed it and thought that she had also. But at the end of the conversation, she said, "Oh! I like talking with you! You speak so correctly!" Obviously she meant "correctly compared with many foreigners." Still, I believe that what she said was intended as a sincere compliment. Nevertheless, from that time I avoided speaking German with her. She had turned human communication into a linguistic exhibition for which she was judge and scorekeeper. The kind of person who would enjoy putting on such exhibitions was not the kind of person that I wanted to become. In the terminology of the Levertov Machine (Chapter 21), I was "turned off." (Remember that I am describing *my own reaction only*. I am not even guessing at how she felt, or what she was trying to do.)

On another occasion, a person with whom I had formed a cordial relationship in English suddenly asked me, "Wie gut ist Ihr Deutsch?" ("How good is your German?") Then he sat back and waited for a sample. I did not panic, but I did find that my German, which a few months before had flowed fairly freely, suddenly dried up.

All of these anecdotes illustrate the laying on of "expectations" (Chapter 7) from one person to another, and show what can happen to one or both parties when the expectations are not met. The laying on of these expectations may cause the other person to feel that he/she is being treated as a linguistic object and not as a human being. Some seem not to mind that, and a few apparently enjoy it. Others, however, are made self-conscious by it, or worse. In this relationship, more or less "learning" (Chapter 21) may take place, but effective "acquisition" is probably impossible. The person on whom the expectation has been laid comes away with less life rather than more.

Yet how often language teachers do this to their students! Of the hundreds of teachers whom I have watched over the years, I suppose nine out of ten treat their students as full-time linguistic objects, even when playing games with them, or during sessions of "free conversation" with them. So this is not a matter of "technique" in the usual sense. One and the same question from the teacher—even something like "What did you see on TV last night?" may have this effect, or it may not. Everything depends on how it is asked: on timing, tone of voice, ,and so forth.

All of the examples that I have given so far have been negative. A very positive example of the same principles comes out of my first experience in a Spanish-speaking country. Except for a very ineffective semester of Spanish 27 years earlier, I had had no exposure to Spanish. Then suddenly, for one wonderful week, I was consultant to a program in which several dozen people were studying the language. Some already knew various amounts of Spanish, but many were beginners. I was a beginner in Spanish, but knew some Portuguese.

The most conspicuous *"expectation"* was laid on us in the form of a *demand*: that we use no language but Spanish at any time, in or out of class, day or night. People actually conformed to this rule to a surprising degree. The weak helped the weaker, the strong helped the weak, and the staff helped all of us. I left at the end of eight days about half as fluent in Spanish as I had been in Portuguese, and having had in the meantime those days of continuous and intense experience, all of it in Spanish. The one large "expectation"—that we stick to Spanish—had taken the place of, had blotted out, all of the petty ones that might have soured the atmosphere. Even the times of formal "learning" thus became experiences which led to "acquisition" (Chapter 21).

The results showed themselves in two interesting ways. The first was an incident on my way home. When I changed planes in Lima, a cabin attendant asked me, in English, whether I spoke English, or Spanish. I very firmly replied, in Spanish, "Both!" This did not mean that I thought of myself as anything remotely approaching a complete bilingual. What it did mean was that I felt quite comfortable in my Spanish, limitations and all, and that I would have welcomed being seated next to a Spanish-speaking person.

The second result has shown itself over the years. The Spanish that I heard in Chile was pronounced differently from the Spanish of Spain and many other parts of Latin America. This is especially noticeable with the consonants spelled y and *ll,* and with s when it is not followed immediately by a vowel. Normally, when I speak Spanish these days, I use the more widespread, non-Chilean, pronunciations. But when I feel that someone is exerting personal force on me and I want to exert a counterforce, I more or less consciously switch back to the pronunciations of that one group of Spanish speakers who accepted me for a few days as almost one of them.

The high point of my Spanish came six years later, at the beginning of my first trip to Spain. During the first day or two, a few people very kindly volunteered to let me limber up my Spanish by conversing with them. I had hardly used the language since Chile, but I was looking forward to continuing from where I had left off. I was not disappointed in this hope. I found that I was able to converse for a half hour or more at a time, on a wide range of topics, in a most pleasurable way. By listening to the other person's Spanish and comparing it with mine, I was able to pick out and correct a number of errors without either of us disturbing the flow of conversation.

That, as I said, was the high point in my use of Spanish. Unfortunately, when I got out into the street, the Madrileños were not so patient as my friends had been. When I did not understand them the first or second time they said something, they pretty consistently cut me off. As a result, I lost the feeling that I was not imposing myself on people by using Spanish with them. So my range of speaking shrank to match the range of my ability to understand. All in all, my Spanish had pretty well collapsed by the end of my first week in Spain, and it has never recovered in the four years since. The only evidence that it still exists somewhere inside me has come in conversations with two friendly monolingual taxi drivers (both of whom I tipped munificiently at the end of my rides with them!).

Most recently, I have begun to learn another language. After my first 25 or 30 hours, I became acquainted with two speakers of the language. When, on separate occasions, I told them that I was beginning to study their language, their reactions could most optimistically be described as "noticeably uninterested." This was not what I had hoped for, or what I would have expected on the basis of experiences with speakers of other languages that I have learned.

My earlier experiences had led me to expect one or another of two reactions. The first would have been to reply to my announcement with some simple phrase in the language, possibly inviting me to practice it with them either then and there or at some later time. When two people meet with nothing special to say to each other, the bilingual may actually be glad to enter into this kind of conversation just because it serves as its own topic. We have already seen that this kind of welcoming behavior can be dangerous to some new speakers of a language even though other new speakers enjoy it. It can also be costly to the established speaker, most obviously in loss of flexibility and fullness of communication, and in the time and effort needed in order to find the right words to use with the neophyte. The neophyte is asking the established speaker to give up some of his/her freedom so that the neophyte may gain a bit of new freedom. This is not a request to be made lightly. At the same time, and perhaps even more troublesome, by artificially maintaining the conversation in the language that the other person wants to practice, the bilingual assumes a position something like that of a right-handed person who is steering a bicycle with the left hand: the kind of attention which it requires threatens to unbalance the ongoing relationship between the two people, and this destroys its integrity. (I suspect that this may be a large part of the explanation for the disappointing experiences that I have recounted in this chapter.) It is not surprising, therefore, that many people avoid this first alternative. Instead, they say something like "Wonderful!" and follow it with almost any general, cordial-sounding remark. The conversation can then continue on some other topic, in the learner's native language, without the learner feeling unwanted.

As I said, neither of my acquaintances reacted in either of these two ways. I was left feeling that, for the time being at least, I had intruded myself into an area which was more private or more precious than I had expected, or which held some particular kind of pain. So in later meetings with them I avoided any attempt to use even one word of the language.

Native speakers differ widely in their reactions to errors. (1) They may ignore all errors except when they are not sure they have understood what the neophyte is trying to say. (2) They may use "counseling responses" (Chapter 8) as carriers for corrections, which the other person may or may not pick up. (3) They may supply the correct form in a soft, almost apologetic voice, like a parenthesis in what the other person is saying. (4) They may treat an error as though it were a fly crawling on the other person's forehead, pick up a flyswatter, and smash it. In this, they have no ill will against the person who made the error. They simply assume that no one would want a fly crawling around on his face, and so they reach out and swat it for him. The verbal equivalent of the flyswatter is to take the tone of voice that one's own secondary school teacher used in correcting mistakes, and suddenly intruding that into what had been a friendly conversation. (5) They may react with real annoyance against the person as well as against the mistake.

Of these reactions, the fifth is obviously the most destructive. In my experience, the fourth is almost as hard to take, though I have heard it used by people who apparently thought they were being cooperative and hospitable as conversation partners. I use the third in conversation with people (nonstudents) whose English is generally excellent, but even then I find that it sometimes throws them off. On the other hand, I have a colleague who makes excellent use of it with students at all levels. The first may make some people very comfortable, but if it leaves a speaker with the feeling that he is being allowed to strengthen his bad habits, then it can destroy security rather than increase it. The second is the safest, but it does require more skill, and more concentration on the part of the native speaker.

Whatever ability I have to speak Swahili was developed not in East Africa (which I have only visited), but in the United States. I owe it to two speakers of the language who, at different times, voluntarily related themselves to me through the medium of Swahili, using a combination of (1), (2), and (3) in reacting to my errors.

It seems, then, that when two people speak with each other in a language that is foreign to one of them, either or both may be laying their lives on the line—at least their lives as speakers of that language. Such an undertaking therefore calls for sensitivity on both sides. Sensitivity here means more than just seeing the dangers and shying away from them. It includes sensitivity to what the other person is able to do, and is ready to try. But even the most "sensitive" person sometimes guesses wrong. So the undertaking demands on both sides not only sensitivity, but also courage. This sensitivity and this courage are quite a bit to ask of a layman. Perhaps we should not expect even the professional language teacher to display these qualities at *all* times. Yet I think that here lies an important area of our professional commitment.

CHAPTER 11

SOME USES OF CUISENAIRE RODS IN COUNSELING-LEARNING*

In Chapters 7 and 8, I set out my own understanding of Counseling-Learning and Community Language Learning, but without saying much about what goes on in a CL/CLL classroom. Chapters 11 to 15 and 17 will describe actual classes and will preserve much of the complexity that we find in any class with real students and a real teacher. Those chapters contain descriptions of many techniques, but at the base of all CL/CLL methodology is the teacher's ability to make what Curran (and others as well) have called a "counseling response." The present chapter starts from one very simple but practical technique, and discusses the "counseling response" in relation to that technique. I hope that in this way it will be a bridge between the theoretical and the practical chapters on Curran's work.

In a well-known training film, the teacher introduces her class to the French words *la viande* by unwrapping a pair of real lamb chops. Now, 20 years later, the price of meat is such that most of us have found less expensive visual aids for that particular vocabulary item. Shrinking budgets have forced us to other economies as well, so that we think twice before investing in even modestly priced equipment. This, then, may be an appropriate time to take a look at visual aids in general, to try to figure out how they work, and why.

This article will describe only one visual aid—an extremely simple one—and will describe only one way of using it. The technique happens to be a favorite of mine, which I have found relatively successful. My purpose here, however, is not to recommend this technique to others. My purpose is rather to use the technique as a vehicle for exploring some of the things that happen inside and between the people in a language classroom. (This is what I mean by "psychodynamics.")

The visual aid itself is a cuisenaire rod—a light green block of wood three centimeters long, with a cross section 1 centimeter square. A bagful of these rods sells for about five dollars. They have often been associated with Gattegno's "Silent Way" of teaching, (Gattegno 1972), but the technique to be described here is only partially consistent with that method. It is suitable for use with students at any time after the first semester.

THE PROCEDURE

1. *The teacher places the rod between himself and a student, on a horizontal surface which has been cleared of all other objects.* The teacher

*The first part of this chapter appeared as an article in *Language Learning*, Vol. 25, No. 1.

should appear relaxed and self-assured. He avoids a mysterious or threatening air. Nonverbally, he tries to communicate two ideas: "This is something we're going to enjoy together," and "I know you're apprehensive, but everything is going to be all right." In doing so, the teacher recognizes and accepts the student's anxiety, at the same time trying not to add to it. These two nonverbal statements are promises, which the teacher must keep in the steps that follow.

2. After a few seconds, when he feels that this communication has gotten across, *the teacher says, in a matter-of-fact voice, "I'd like you to look at this rod, and picture it as some kind of building."* He then pauses for a few seconds to allow the student to form a mental image.

3. By his own looking at the rod, the teacher conveys the idea "What we are talking about has my full and undivided attention." By not looking at the student, he avoids one channel through which he might inadvertently convey doubt or disappointment. This also permits him to concentrate more attention on his own audio output.

Continuing to gaze at the rod, then, *the teacher says, "I'd like to have in my mind the same picture that you have. Will you tell me about it?"* The teacher's manner and tone of voice are those of a sympathetic, interested conversationalist. They must not be those of a teacher, however kindly, giving an assignment to a student. (This dramatic feat may require a little practice, but most teachers can learn to bring it off.) The teacher's verbal and nonverbal communication support each other in expressing faith rather than doubt, and delight as each new feature of the student's picture is conveyed through words.

4. The crucial part of this procedure lies in the way the teacher reacts to whatever the student says. Fighting, if necessary, against nature and his own habits, and *continuing to gaze at the rod, the teacher remains in the role of sympathetic conversationalist and repeats or paraphrases what the student has said:* "Oh, it's a warehouse!" "Ah, I see, it's 12 stories tall!" and so on.

If what the student says contains a linguistic error, the teacher reacts in the same way as to a correct statement, except that he himself speaks the language correctly. If, for example, the student says "It's a 12-stories building," the teacher might reply, "Ah, a 12-story building!" There is nothing in the teacher's manner or tone of voice that says "That's wrong," or "I've caught you!" The student is still likely to notice the discrepancy.

Another way of responding when the student has made a mistake is to pretend (perhaps not immediately) to have been inattentive: "I'm sorry, did you say a 10-story building, or a 12-story building?"

On paper, repeating or paraphrasing the student's statement may look a little like what Rowe (1974:209) calls teacher "mimicry" of student responses. Two examples, taken from an actual science class, are the following:

Student: There's hot air around it.
Teacher: *Hot air.* Why is there hot air?

Student: Because there is no room for the new clean air to get in. No space for oxygen.
Teacher: *For oxygen,* that's right . . .

In "mimicry" of this kind, the teacher seizes on something that he has been looking for. The purpose of doing so is either to evaluate the student's response (second example), or to use it as the basis for a further question, designed to draw the student further into the teacher's world (first example). The teacher's responses in Step 4 must serve neither of these functions.

The same principle applies when the student falters: the teacher remains in the role of conversationalist, rather than authority or critic. If the student gives a native-language word, or if it is obvious what he is trying to get across, the teacher supplies the word in the same tone of voice that he would use with a native speaker of the target language who was momentarily groping for it. The nonverbal message is, "I'm giving you this word because I'm interested in the conversation and want to keep it moving." Similarly, if the student produces a correct form that he is unsure of, and looks inquiringly at the teacher for confirmation, the teacher's reply—nonverbal and/or verbal—is "Yes, yes, of course!" rather than "Very good! You're a fine student!"

The same principle applies again if the student makes a nonlinguistic error. The student must come to feel that his image is accepted by, and of interest to the person to whom he is talking. For example, someone once told me that the rod was a 55-story building in Washington, D.C. I repeated the statement acceptingly even though I knew that such a structure is nonexistent and would be illegal.

As in Step 3, it is absolutely essential that the teacher continue to act and sound like an interested conversationalist, and not like a teacher directing and correcting a student. This is not easy for every teacher, but I have seen teachers who had learned the trick. Observers—experienced language teachers—who did not understand the language being taught either assumed that no correction at all was taking place, or grossly underestimated the number of corrections that the teacher made.

5. If, as is usually the case, there is more than one student in the class, *the teacher occasionally asks another student to repeat the information contained in what the first student says.* The first student still remains the focus of attention. Step 4 still applies: the teacher is participating in a conversation, not conducting a quiz. The nonverbal message is, "Oh, I'm sorry. I seem to have forgotten. What was it that he said?" It is *not,* "Let's see if *you* are able to say that sentence," or "Let's see if *you* were paying attention," or "Now it's time for *you* to get a little practice."

In a full-sized class, several students may receive rods of various lengths and colors, and the class may deal with several images. But each rod should be visualized and described by only one student.

After the procedure has been completed, the material which it has generated may be fed into any number of other standard techniques, such as written composition, dictation, grammatical analysis of selected sentences, or ordinary drills, but those possibilities are outside the scope of this paper.

PSYCHODYNAMIC ASPECTS

The overall purpose of this procedure is to bring about a relatively "receptive," rather than "defensive," style of learning (Curran 1966; Curran 1972; Stevick 1973; Stevick 1974a). I have suggested (Stevick 1974b) that if receptive learning is to be possible, the student needs to be able to say a number of things about whoever and whatever he is learning from ("the teaching figure"):

6. This figure is strong in relation to me: (a) It knows something that I want to know; (b) It can give me access to something that I want; (c) It is always able to control my actions, even though it may not always choose to do so; (d) It can provide me an opportunity to work without unwelcome distractions.

7. This figure is strong in relation to itself: it is at peace with itself; it has and knows its own purposes. (cf. Steps 1 to 5, and especially Step 1.)

8. This figure is on my side.

9. This figure will pay attention to me no matter what.

10. This figure does not conflict seriously with the powerful figures (parents, early teachers, adolescent peers, etc.) who have already molded my feelings about how things ought to be.

11. Dealing with this figure somehow makes me feel better about myself.

Turning now to the procedure (1 to 5 above), and looking for what happens inside and between the people involved in it, we can make a number of observations:

12. In its shape, color, feel, and sound, the small green rod is nonthreatening, even reassuring and a bit pleasant. I believe that in these respects it is more suitable for these purposes than the 2-centimeter rod, which is bright red, or the 4-centimeter rod, which is pink. But any cuisenaire rod has the further advantage that it is not covered with details (painted doors, windows, and the like) that preempt the function of the student's imagination, and may present him with features that he does not know how to describe. (cf. 8, 10 above.)

13. The rod is visually clear, simple, and small. Focusing my gaze on it for a period of time helps me, the student, to block out distractions. In a very mild way, it is something like the hypnotist's gold watch. This is part of what Gagliardo (In Gattegno 1972:132) meant when she said that the rods can be "mesmerizing." (cf. 6d above.) In this very special way, the small green rod relates to the student's "need for security" (Maslow 1970:45f).

14. I, the student, can project my own vision onto the rod. What we talk about is going to be something that I already understand, and that makes sense to me because I created it. The teacher is helping me to talk about it. (cf. 6b, 8, 10 above.) This removes one whole area of threat on the level of esteem, or status, and at the same time opens up opportunities for positive experiences on this level (Maslow, ibid.).

15. In visualizing the building, I can draw on material from any period of my life that I choose, preferably from a period in which I was relatively

content and secure. In psychological terminology, this opportunity makes it easier for the student to achieve a desirable amount of "regression" (cf. 6d above) (Whitman 1964:314).

The subject of "regression in the service of the ego" is treated by Schafer (1958), in an article that is of interest to all language teachers even though its author was not aiming his words at the field of pedagogy.

Schafer (1958:122) described "regression in the service of the ego" (RSE) as "a partial, temporary and controlled lowering of the level of psychic functioning to promote adaptation." It is "a process which increases the individual's access to the preconscious and unconscious contents [of his personality] without disruptive anxiety and guilt" (p. 123). It thus can make learning into more of a "whole-person" experience (Curran 1972). In RSE, "central controlling functions in the ego may suspend some other functions, such as defensive functions and logical functions, and may emphasize genetically primitive mechanisms, such as projection and introjection" (Schafer 1958:123). We may thus expect RSE to assist in the achievement of the receptive, nondefensive kind of learning that we have said is the aim of this procedure.

Schafer (1958:125) quotes Freud's description of some of the differences between the "primary process" and the "secondary process." "*Thinking,* under the domination of the primary process, tends to be unreflective, timeless, and concrete; under the domination of the secondary process, it is reflective, shows time perspective, and uses abstract concepts corresponding to reality relations." There are also differences with regard to *perception:* under the primary process, there is "disregard of total external content," while under the secondary process there is "adaptive selectivity and organization." RSE permits the primary process to have relatively free play, but the products of the primary process are then subjected to productive working over by the secondary process. This combination may become, in a special and very important sense, a kind of "whole-person learning" (Curran 1972).

16. The rod forms a physical link between me and whoever else I am talking to. Students using the Silent Way frequently comment on how they prefer talking with the rods in front of them, instead of attempting to go directly from one person's imagination to another's without benefit of the visual aid. (Maslow's "need for belonging," or companionship with other people.) This simple physical link helps the procedure to become more fully a community learning experience (Curran 1972:11).

17. Whatever I say becomes the occasion for a warm, supportive, and understanding reaction from someone else (4 and 5 above). This demonstrates that the authority figure pays attention to me (9), and that it is on my side (8). This frees my imagination as well as my tongue, so that at the end of my turn I am surprised and pleased at what I have been able to do (11). This in turn further enhances my confidence in the teaching figure (6).

18. There may be important effects for learners who are observing, as well as for the one who is speaking. One colleague of mine, who is herself at an intermediate stage in the study of Italian, acted as learner in the presence of two relative beginners. She hesitated and repeated herself a bit more than was actually necessary for her, but otherwise acted as she would have acted if the beginners had not been present. They understood virtually everything she said, and after a few minutes began to join in voluntarily. In the security of their position as "overhearers," they were able to absorb and also to produce on a level beyond what might otherwise have been possible.

GENERALIZATION

Readers who are familiar with work in the field of interpersonal relations will recognize that at the heart of this procedure lies a "counseling response" on the part of the teacher. As I am using the term here, a "counselor" is one who "assume[s], insofar as he is able, the internal frame of reference of the [person he is listening to],to perceive the world as [that person] sees it . . . and [tries to communicate to that person] something of this empathic understanding" (Rogers 1951).

Curran has applied this kind of counseling in the field of foreign language learning. As he describes this relationship, the teacher-knower, as counselor, brings to the student "a deep understanding of the student's anxieties, insecurities, and feelings of inadequacy" (Curran 1961:81). He listens without evaluation (even when he is "correcting errors") and without going off on tangents of his own. At all times, he appears to the student to be more interested in the student and what the student is saying than in the mechanics of language.

In this way, the teacher-counselor helps the students to become increasingly aware of their worth as persons. As a result, "the learners, like clients related to a counselor, grow confident and secure in their ability to trust the knower and to abandon themselves to the knowledge which he represents" (Curran 1972:5).

The relationship that results may help to remove at least two blocks to RSE. Schafer (1958:130) says that one factor which makes RSE easier is "a history of adequate trust and mutuality in interpersonal relations." Schafer was referring particularly to the early mother-child relation, but the same principle may apply to current and intermediate associations.

Another factor which is thought to promote RSE is "meaningfulness to the larger community," which leads to a feeling of "personal and effective communication to others" (Schafer 1958:130). Again, Schafer was thinking on a larger scale both of time and of space than a simple classroom exchange between student and teacher. Again, however, the principle seems valid.

In fact, the technique is powerful enough so that it should be used with care. Students sometimes create for themselves a picture so real, and in which they have invested so much of themselves, that if the teacher abruptly breaks off the relationship before the essentials of the gestalt have been transmitted, the student may feel a sense of letdown or even betrayal.

Inexperienced counselors—or teachers trying to use this approach—often tend to alternate between being overly protective and reassuring, and being too abrupt. Their first aim is supposed to be to communicate empathy, and later to help the learner to move toward independent language adequacy (Curran 1961:81).

The giving of "counseling responses" is not easy, or even congenial, for everyone. It apparently requires a certain amount of RSE in the teacher, as well as in the student. Probably no one can continue it indefinitely. The teacher must temporarily sacrifice a normal urge to control what is said, or even to inject his own ideas and personality into it (Curran 1972:93). In his questions, he must abandon any attitude of doubt or disapproval toward the student (Curran 1972:52). But he must also withhold the kinds of approval that well-meaning teachers so often like to dispense. A teacher who wishes to experiment with this procedure must be prepared to find his own rewards solely in the response of the student, rather than in the handing down of "correct"/"incorrect" verdicts on the sentences that the student produces, or in the display of his own cleverness as a conversationalist.

But a teacher who both knows how to give "counseling responses" and is willing to do so will find many uses for them outside of the single procedure described above. There are many other inexpensive visual aids, and there are techniques for the use of each. I will not take space here to remind readers of these familiar procedures. I would only like to point out a few of the choices that a teacher may make, and their effect on the "counseling" quality of the resulting interaction.

Pictures are certainly among the most common of visual aids. I used to enjoy *Saturday Evening Post* covers, both because they were clear and realistic, and because they frequently told a story that was hidden from most people who were not natives of my culture. My students were therefore totally dependent on my perception of the picture. I could quiz them to my heart's content over the story that I made up about it, as well as about details of the picture itself. If I had adopted a "counseling" point of view in those days, I would have chosen pictures that were simpler, more ambiguous, and less bound to one culture.

Real objects are another part of the panoply of most language teachers. A counseling approach would be able to deal with relatively complex and culture-specific items such as a stapler or a tire pump, but it would look first for simpler and more universal items such as a leaf, a stone, or a piece of bread.

The author of a recent discussion on visual aids works on a premise that is similar to the one with which I began this article. He says that teachers who use visual aids "run the risk of turning their students off unless . . . they ask themselves why they are using visual aids and how they are using them"

(Carter 1974:324). That article may help to clarify what I have been trying to say in this one because, while it begins with the same question, its author and I look in opposite directions for our answers.

The article to which I am referring gives numerous and very usable examples of pictures and other simple visuals, together with techniques that are appropriate for them. One stated goal is "economy," which means getting many sentences from a few images or cues. Another goal is that the teacher be as imaginative as possible. The sequence of activities moves from "teacher-guided" to "stimulus-free." The examples of "stimulus-free" expression have the student either taking a role that the teacher has established and vacated, or retelling something from memory, or responding to nonverbal cues.

The differences between the approach of the article which I have cited here and the approach which I am recommending are clearest at three points: (1) The concern for getting foreordained sentences from the student. (2) Greater attention to the imagination of the teacher than to the imagination of the student. (3) The relatively narrow meaning that seems to be attached to "stimulus-free." Nevertheless, these apparently contradictory approaches are not necessarily mutually exclusive. They may be combined in at least two ways. Most obviously, they may be used in alternation with each other. But it should also be possible to include one within the other, the noncounseling style being included within the counseling style as a temporary expedient.

Over the years, I have had occasion to give workshops and other inservice training to many groups of language teachers. The "Little Green Rod Technique" has been the nucleus for a gimmick that people seem to have found particularly eye-opening. I ask for a volunteer to come forward and assist me, with the assurance that it will be my own behavior, and not the behavior of the volunteer, that we will discuss later on. The volunteers are either native or extremely good nonnative speakers of English. I follow the "Little Green Rod" procedure exactly with this volunteer. After two or three minutes, I break the conversation off and ask the volunteer a few very openended questions about the experience. As he/she replies, I continue to give "counseling responses." Then I invite the spectators to tell the volunteer how the experience looked to them, and see whether he/she agrees. (I emphasize that in this matter, the volunteer is the "expert" on his own reactions, who is by definition always right.)

I then ask for a second volunteer, and have this person look at the same rod. But now my manner is quite different. If with the first volunteer it was what Transactional Analysis would call "Adult," now with the second volunteer it is very "Parental." My opening instructions are in the voice of a teacher giving instructions for a new activity. After each of the volunteer's first three or four sentences, I use my Benign and Solicitous Teacher Voice to say "Very good!" I also find two or three occasions to require the volunteer to repeat after me some different way of saying what he/she has just said, as though I were correcting a mistake in language. The reaction to my work with this second volunteer is generally quite strong on two levels. On one level, the volunteer's position is very much like that of a language student, and the onlookers also feel themselves vicariously to be in his/her shoes. On this level, the reactions are generally annoyance, resentment, even anger. On the other level, both the volunteer and the onlookers are teachers who can imagine themselves doing what they see me doing. On this level, the reaction of the onlookers is generally shock at the difference between my handling of the two volunteers, and at the suspicion that they themselves may be more accustomed to using the second style than the first. I myself can remember using the second style both when teaching and when training teachers. I have seen others also who used the second style, even while they were conducting training sessions in various "humanistic" approaches to teaching.

Finally, I ask for a third volunteer. This time, as soon as the volunteer has said anything at all about his/her picture of the building, I go off on a long and enthusiastic monolog of my own, talking about something that the volunteer's description reminded me of, and leaving the volunteer no chance to continue. Here, in the terminology of Transactional Analysis, I am playing the Child. A few people seem to recognize themselves in this third style, through it is apparently far less common than the Parent.

This apparently simple technique can be much more powerful than it looks. Jean Bodman has told me of an incident in one of her classes. The student who was doing the visualizing was a young man, and what he was visualizing was not a building, but his "dream car." After he had described its lines, and its power, and its accessories, he let the rest of the class try to guess its color. (People do not always visualize the green rod as something green!) They guessed one color after another, and finally learned that it was gray. The elegant appropriateness of this color apparently struck them, for with one accord they let out a spontaneous "Aaahhh!" of admiration.

The "Little Green Rod Technique" became the basis for a more elaborate one which came to be called "The Islamabad Technique." The name came from the fact that the first student who served as "originator" in using the technique talked about Islamabad, the capital of Pakistan.

There are four basic steps in the Islamabad Technique.

1. A student agrees to serve as originator. The originator describes a city (or other place) which no one else in the room has ever seen. This guarantees that what is said will be genuine communication. It also means that the listeners will not be tempted to superimpose their own memories on what the originator says, and therefore distort it.

The originator describes the city one sentence at a time. With each sentence, he puts one or more cuisenaire rods (algebricks) into place to represent what he has said. The rods, with their ten lengths and ten corresponding colors, soon form a striking pattern on the tabletop. (This is particularly true if the tabletop has been completely cleared beforehand.)

The originator speaks either in the target language or in his native language or in both. Whatever the originator's language or combination of languages, the teacher gives for each sentence a "counseling response" in the target language. On the human level, this provides emotional support. At the same time, on the linguistic level, it gives the originator and the other learners the information they need in order to know what is correct and what is not. With beginning students, the form of the teacher's response follows the form of the originator's sentence as closely as possible. Otherwise, it might create confusion. With more advanced students, the response should usually be more flexible. Otherwise it may become monotonous.

During this first step, the other students simply watch and listen. (They frequently report that the concreteness and color of the rods provide a helpful visual focus for their concentration and their imagination.)

In some classes, the students develop their own unspoken (or even spoken!) rule that the originator must stick to the target language and, worse yet, that he should try to originate without errors. I have even seen some students who spent hours preparing at home when they knew that their turn as originator was coming up the next day. Such classes grow tired of the Islamabad Technique after using it a few times, and no wonder. The spontaneity and adventure have been drained out of the technique; instead it comes to be filled with perfectionism, competition, and inevitable anxiety.

2. The teacher retells the description in the target language. It is generally helpful to point at each rod as it is talked about. Some teachers like to retell the description in a more or less hesitant way. With their sentence intonation and their facial expression, they ask the originator to verify the *facts* in what they are saying. This contributes to the originator's feeling of status, and therefore to his overall confidence.

The teacher's retelling serves two purposes: (a) It allows all of the learners to hear the material again. In fact, by pretending to be confused or absent-minded, the teacher can provide any number of extra repetitions. (b) It gives the teacher a chance to speak more naturally and authentically than when responding one sentence at a time as in Step 1.

3. The other students take turns pointing to the rods and telling things that they remember from the account. It seems to be important that each student tell only one fact per turn; otherwise, this step can become a contest to see who has the best memory for this sort of thing. This may invigorate the best students, but it very quickly discourages the others. People seem to differ from one another less in their ability to remember *single* facts that they themselves have *chosen*, and to differ more in their ability to reproduce a *paragraph-sized* description that *someone else* (in this technique, the originator) has provided.

In Step 3, the students are meeting the same material once more. This time, however, they are recalling it freely from their own memories. At the same time, of course, they are now for the first time carrying responsibility for actually producing it themselves. They have a choice between saying something that they feel fairly sure of, or of trying something that they think they may need to hear again. As in Step 1, the teacher gives "counseling responses," not approval, correction, or praise. By listening to the "counseling response," the learners correct most of their own mistakes. At the same time, they are spared the deadening impact of the nonverbal messages that come along with conventional corrections.

4. In the last step of the Islamabad Technique, the other students ask the originator questions about the city (or other place) that he has described. Rods are added or moved to reflect new information. The teacher moves to the edge of the conversation, but is still available as a "counselor" to paraphrase questions and answers. Again it is essential that his nonverbal communications be such as to say, "I'm an interested participant in this conversation." Under these circumstances, students still notice and correct most of their mistakes, but the conversation continues. If the teacher's nonverbal communication says, "You've just made an error that you can correct by listening to me!" then the footmen turn into mice, the coach into a pumpkin, and the conversationalists into students who are trying to please their teacher.

This is the end of the basic procedure. In it, people have done something together. To this something, the originator has contributed facts; the teacher and the other students have contributed ignorance of and interest in the facts; the teacher has provided guidance and whatever words the originator needed. The teacher has also contributed to the security of the students, both by maintaining a "counseling" manner and by guaranteeing the authenticity of the language. (It would be disastrous if the students came away feeling, "Yes, we were fluent, but we may have been butchering the language!")

Obviously, the language that comes out of the Islamabad Procedure may feed into many other techniques. It may be recorded on tape, or written on a wall chart, or reproduced in handout form to be distributed at the next session of class, or used as material for dictation, or used in many other ways. The only limit is the imagination of the teacher. Sometimes at the end of the fourth step I scoop the rods into a pile at the center of the table. Then it becomes the job of the other students to reconstruct the model and talk about it while the originator watches and corrects errors of fact.

Taking into account the number of teachers who have used the Islamabad Procedure, and the number of languages in which it has been used, and the range of levels on which it has been used from near-beginning to advanced, it may be the most successful technique that I have ever devised. It has also served as the basis for a number of variations. Three such variations were reported by Larry Cisar in Japan (*TESOL Newsletter,* November 1978). He had evidently had an undistorted account of it from Betsy Bedell.

In one of the variations that Cisar's students came up with, the originator uses the rods to build the area around his own home. He then describes the area in detail, while the others listen and ask questions. After the listeners have understood the map, the originator gives directions for getting to his house. The listeners follow these directions, and try to put their fingers on the spot that corresponds to the originator's home. Finally, the whole group talks about why it was or was not easy to find the right place.

The second variation violates some of the rules of the original procedure, but in a very productive way. The whole group serves as originator in building a model of an area that everyone knows well. Here, the function of language is not to convey new external information, but to settle differences in how various students have seen and remembered things.

In the third variation, the whole group again serves as originator. This time, however, they do not talk about an actual place. Instead, they work together to design an ideal city. In this, as in the basic procedure and the other variations, (1) the students are given a clear but open-ended task, which (2) cannot be completed without everyone's help. (3) The rods serve as a visible, touchable, movable channel of communication which runs parallel to the verbal channel, and supports it. This seems to be terribly important to some students, less so to others. But in any case, (4) the rods serve as a central, shared object which serves as a unifying focus for the entire class. (5) The teacher's nonverbal behavior is that of a human being who is making a special contribution to the work of the group; it is not that of a drillmaster or a judge.

The principle of the counseling response can also be applied to the use of conventional materials, such as those in the audiolingual format. Here I will only sketch its use in pronunciation practice and in the learning of basic dialogs.

The audiolingual approach to pronunciation of a new language is summarized in the formula "hearing before speaking, speaking before reading." The procedure which I am about to describe reverses that sequence of activities. In the first step, the teacher writes on the board a column of words in the target language, and a parallel column of equivalents in the students' native language. (The writing system of the target language may be one with which the students are familiar, or it may be one that is new to them.) In the second step, the students take turns reading a word off the board. They may choose to read either in the target language or in their native language, depending on how adventurous they feel. (If the writing system is new to them, then their very first initiatives will of course have to be in the native language.) The teacher replies to each of these initiatives with a counseling response which consists of nothing but her own correct pronunciation in the target language. The student then has the option of remaining silent or of repeating after the teacher. I have found it best to have a student take two consecutive turns before going on to the next student. In the last step of this procedure, after the students have all had several opportunities in the second step, the teacher makes general informative remarks about any sounds that still seem troublesome for one or more students. She does not indicate how many or which students still haven't mastered the sound. This procedure activates the students' attention more fully than the standard audiolingual mimicry procedure does, and thus ensures that what they get from it will be more fully their own. I have found that it is not more time-consuming than mimicry, and I suspect that its results may be more enduring.

The procedure with dialogs begins with pronunciation, handled very much as in the preceding paragraph. When pronunciation has been satisfactorily established, the students take turns in telling what they already understand about the sentences of the dialog. The teacher is mostly silent but remains in the role of understander. Then the students ask whatever questions they still have. The teacher gives brief answers to any questions that they cannot answer for one another.

As a further way of bringing meaning into the dialogs, the students then make slight variations in the sentences. The teacher's counseling response takes the form of a (correct) repetition in the target language followed, if necessary, by a translation into the students' native language. The teacher must of course be sure that the nonverbal component of these responses is that of a counselor and not a critic.

In the final step, a student takes one of the roles in the dialog while the teacher takes the other. The teacher's book is closed, but the student's is open and he uses it as much as he needs to. In this way the students take turns "teaching" the teacher until she can do it satisfactorily. The teacher, through transparent but effective pretense, can "have difficulty" enough to keep this activity going as long as she thinks appropriate.

This chapter has ended with descriptions of one of my best teacher-training devices, and some of my favorite classroom techniques. I would remind readers, however, that the theme of the chapter has been the "counseling response," and not the techniques. Having seen the "counseling response" at work in these examples, the reader may get a better feel for how it can leave the psychologist's office behind and come into the language classroom. The best applications will be the reader's own.

CHAPTER 12

A ROLLER COASTER RIDE
TO SWAHILILAND,
OR NOBODY LOVES A SKELETON

Irene Dutra

Over the years, I have watched the Classical Community Language Learning method and numerous variations on it in the hands of many teachers. I have also used it myself with real students. Unfortunately, I have never had the time to sit down and write out step by step what happened in those classes. But I have also had about a dozen opportunities to conduct 6-to 15-hour language learning experiences for teachers using this method. Irene Dutra, who was a participant in the first of these, wrote an account of it from inside the skin of one "student." I sat down by myself and put together a description of a later experience. And in the summer of 1977, I had the help of my students in amassing an account of yet another experience from many points of view.

Teacher-participants in such experiences sometimes think that their reactions are quite different from those of "real students." I have not been able to agree with them. They have seemed to me very, very like "real students" of similar age and educational background. I therefore make no apology for recounting, in these next three chapters, how things happened in what some people would call "demonstration classes."

The first account shows me as a fledgling "language counselor." I placed great emphasis on giving the group as much responsibility as I could, as soon as I could, in the hope (I must admit) that a brilliantly beautiful community would spring to blossom in those two days and bear spectacular fruit in the form of language mastery. The language results were, in fact, very gratifying. But I was to some extent exploiting the group for my own purposes. I therefore failed to give enough attention to security, and so ran too many risks with the emotional ups and downs of the learners. This episode shows both the very positive results to which CCLL can lead, and some of the dangers that lie in it. (I am happy to say that I have never again given a class such an extreme roller coaster ride as I gave that first one!) EWS

Recently a group of New York ESL teachers participated in a Community Language Learning (CLL) workshop to experience learning a foreign language in a new way. We discovered that indeed "learning is persons" and that the skeleton (bare bones grammar) of a new language is lovable only when encased in a warm human body—first, in that of the teacher-counselor and then, as the learners grow in linguistic independence and peer interdependence, in the body of the learning community. The following is not meant to illustrate a *typical* CLL experience (each experience being *unique*); rather, it is a personal account of what happened when a teacher and a few learners came together for two days of Swahili and "let a community come into being."

The first morning the teacher-counselor, Earl Stevick, and five students boarded the roller coster bound for Swahililand. We didn't know we were climbing into a roller coaster; we thought we were boarding a relatively smooth-riding train—anticipating, of course, occasional jerky stops and starts.

Two days and 12 hours of Swahili later, with wobbly legs and emotions, students and teacher stumbled off onto level ground, murmuring "Wow!" What had happened on that ride? Well, we had learned (in passing) quite a bit of Swahili, but more importantly, we had learned something about ourselves, about our fellow passengers, and about the complexity and subtlety of the group learning process.

We started out, the first morning, five slightly apprehensive learners sitting in a circle with a tape recorder and a microphone. Earl, our Swahili teacher, stood outside the circle. Dave, a student, asked the group (in English) who was going to start. Earl moved behind him and in a low voice gave him the Swahili translation. Dave turned to the group, snapped on the mike, and asked: "Nani ataanza?" Lee responded: "You're going to start." Earl quickly moved behind her, lightly touched her shoulder and said: "Wewe utaanza." Lee took the mike, turned it on and playfully informed Dave: "Wewe utaanza." And so it went for about a dozen utterances, everyone taking a tentative whirl at the language.

I was feeling very good about myself, my peers, the teacher, and the Swahili language. This was going to be fun!

We then listened to the entire conversation on tape (only our Swahili, not the teacher's, was recorded). It sounded pretty good, rather "African." We smiled at each other in delight.

We listened a second time, sentence by sentence, with each student supplying the English translation of his sentence. We had no trouble recalling the meanings of our utterances.

We listened a third time while one student attempted to write a transcription of the Swahili on the blackboard, looking frequently to the rest of us for help. Earl verified the transcription. A student copied it on a sheet of paper, and carbon copies were given to each of us as page 1 of our "text."

Now with our first Swahili conversation transcribed, some students felt moved to analyze its grammar: "That must be a pronominal prefix." "*Nime* and *mimi* both seem to mean 1st personal singular, but when do you use one and when the other?"

My stomach muscles started tightening. I didn't want to look at the bony skeleton of Swahili. I was getting annoyed at my peers for performing this ghastly dissection and at the teacher for permitting it.

Only 45 minutes had gone by, and my emotions had run the gamut from delight to discomfort to annoyance!

The language learning round was over. Earl, in the role of counselor, joined us in the circle for a group feedback session (in English). It became clear that I was not the only one irritated by the grammatical dissection that had ended our first round of Swahili. One or two others admitted getting knots in their stomachs. Listening to them share their feelings lessened my own discomfort; I wasn't alone in my feelings. As we opened up bit by bit and as Earl reflected back our comments and tried to "catch" our underlying emotions in his counseling responses, it emerged that, to varying extents, four of the five students wanted to approach the language more intuitively. The fifth, however, expressed a strong need to approach it analytically. A definite conflict in learning styles had been uncovered in our small group.

A change in procedure was therefore proposed: the next time, instead of "attacking" the grammar as soon as the Swahili conversation was transcribed on the board, we would spend a few minutes silently "communing" with it, mentally noting any points that interested us, making any hypotheses we chose to make. After this period of silent reflection, we might (or might not) choose to share a few of the hypotheses we had formed. Finally, we would test our hypotheses (even if unarticulated) by generating new sentences, using the data we had before us.

Everyone agreed to give this new way of working a try; so we went on to a second round of Swahili, similar to the first but with the changed procedure at the end. As we generated new sentences, Earl gave us nonjudgmental feedback on the correctness of our hypotheses: "Yes, we could say that in Swahili" or "I would say . . . instead."

In the feedback session that followed we all voiced our pleasure with the new procedure. Susan, however, who had initially expressed her need for a more analytical approach, said she still felt the need for more explicit grammatical analysis. The four others outvoted her, and we broke for lunch.

I came back from lunch feeling too lethargic to jump into Swahili again. I was annoyed that my peers seemed peppier and more interested than I; *everyone* should feel logy after lunch. I sat there rather sullenly, barely participating in the Swahili conversation. In the feedback session I hesitantly expressed some of my negative emotions. Strangely, as I did so and as Earl "caught" my feelings in his counseling responses, I began to get a surge of energy, and by the time we began another round of the language, I was animated and interested again.

The value of having negative emotions understood and accepted by the teacher was becoming clearer.

And so it went for two days—a Swahili conversation followed by a feedback session, the group making slight changes in procedure as we felt and voiced the need to. In the Swahili conversations we were taking more risks, venturing more often into Stage II (the "kicking stage") and Stage III (the "birth stage") by trying to use words and structures from previous sessions. We were also looking more to our peers and less to Earl to supply a word or finish a phrase for us. At a certain point we invited Earl to sit in the circle instead of standing behind us. At the time it seemed spontaneous, but in retrospect the invitation might have been an unconscious acknowledgment of Earl's changing relationship to us. Yet even as we were trying to become more independent of Earl, we were aware that he was always there, warm and supportive, for the times we needed him, for the times we wanted to return to the womblike security of Stage I.

In the feedback sessions, too, we were taking more risks. Susan shared with the other students how rejected she had felt when they twice seemed to spurn her analytical way of learning. On the first day, she said, her emotions had gone up and down and up again—initial delight turning to feelings of rejection—near tears turning to contentment as she started feeling understood and accepted by her peers. I tried to express the awful tug-of-war I felt between my own needs and the needs of the group, having always to make the choice of subordinating one to the other or reaching some harmonious balance. Jean confessed she felt subtle group pressure to speak and participate more, which infringed on her learning space and made her feel crowded in. At times she wanted and needed simply to sit there in silence, letting the language "wash over" her.

By the second day we also felt freer to criticize the teacher in feedback sessions. Earl gave us understanding counseling responses as we criticized him: he had been rather authoritarian in abruptly starting off the class that morning; he had been brusque with Susan when she got off on a tangent. I said he broke off eye contact with me too soon when giving me new Swahili phrases, causing my mind to block completely; and that in his effort to be nonjudgmental, he was sometimes "inauthentic." I even criticized him for (innocently) greeting me in Swahili outside of class; as an insecure beginner I panicked at this intrusion of Swahili into the *real world*. (Surprisingly, a few days later when I again met Earl in the *real world*, it was *I* who initiated a Swahili exchange; my fears had totally vanished.)

Yes, we were all in this together—students *and* teacher. Our emotions were surfacing, our sensitivity to the dynamics of the group developing, our trust in and care for each other growing. We were allowing ourselves to become more vulnerable, more transparent. Our defenses were falling, our masks dropping. A "fragile community" was forming.

The strain of participating in this intellectual and emotional adventure began to show by the middle of the second day. At lunch, exhilarated after a good morning session, Dave, Lee, and I concocted a hilarious fantasy involving a pompous linguist and his microphone. (Did this reveal veiled hostility to the mike we used—and somewhat feared—in class?) There was much camaraderie and hysterical laughter; tears rolled down our cheeks. During the Swahili session after lunch, I started giggling every time I looked at the mike. Unable to suppress my giggles, I—a usually serious sedate adult—fled the room, feeling like a silly first-grader.

When I returned for the feedback session, I apologized for my childish (or was it childlike?) behavior and confessed I didn't understand what had happened to me. It emerged that most of the group had been feeling giddy since lunch, and that the giddiness was perhaps a release of tensions. No one in the group had been aware of great tension during the two days; for the most part it had been a pleasurable learning experience. Yet there were necessary tensions involved in learning a foreign language, in gradually opening up to each other, in coalescing as a group—even in realizing that our fledgling community would soon be disbanding.

Community Language Learning was much more complex than I had imagined.

Our last Swahili conversation was a breakthrough. For the first time, instead of safe, somewhat superficial topics, we chose to speak in the foreign language of our deeper concerns and feelings. We tried to make the same connections with each other in Swahili as we had made in English.

Time was running out, though we still had a little left. We didn't feel like learning any more Swahili; we were drained. The roller coaster was slowing down. Someone suggested that Earl teach us an African song, so he sang us a soft Bantu lullaby, and our roller coaster ride came gently to an end.

CHAPTER 13

A ONE-DAY WORKSHOP
WITH COMMUNITY LANGUAGE LEARNING

This chapter tells about an experience which took place at the School for International Training in Brattleboro, Vermont, on November 5, 1976. I have left it essentially the same as when I first wrote it. Rereading this account three years later and setting it alongside Chapter 12, I am struck most of all by how much more attention I paid to security this time. Perhaps as a result, the emotional ups and downs were relatively gentle—certainly no "roller coaster ride."

PROCEDURE

Preliminary contact. The members of the M.A.T.L. Program had already been introduced to basic concepts of CL by a resident staff member. On the evening before the Swahili course, I talked with all 56 members of the program for about two hours. One incidental effect of this session was, I hope, to reduce any general anxiety which the 12 prospective Swahili students may have felt with respect to me as a stranger.

On Friday morning, I began by reminding the learners of the first step in the procedure, which they had read about before my arrival, and with which they had already experimented on a small scale. My purpose in doing so was threefold. First, I wanted to be sure that they had the information fresh in their minds, so that the first step would go smoothly. On a deeper level, I wanted them to feel secure with respect to the way their time was going to be structured for the next few minutes. Deeper still, the content of what I said at this point was only a vehicle for a tone of voice and overall manner which I hope conveyed calm and self-assurance on my part. The first two of these goals could have been reached without the third. The third could have been reached without the first two by talking about some external topic such as the weather. By using the CCLL procedure itself as the content, I hoped that the three aspects of what I said would enhance one another.

From previous experience, I knew that people often become very anxious while making the tape-recorded conversation because they are aware that they can't remember what they have said. For that reason, I casually remarked that the learners were not expected to remember anything at this time, but that later steps would provide for retention.

I chose my clothing with the learners' security in mind. They were young adults in their twenties, living on a campus where life is quite informal. They therefore wore clothing such as blue jeans and sweatshirts. I could have tried to dress the same way. If I had, however, I would have felt that I was saying to them, "See, I'm one of you!" which would have been false. To have said that would have implied, further, "When I'm around you, I'm not comfortable with being a member of your parents' generation." If my way of dressing had in fact come across to the learners in this way, it would have had an unnoticed but not negligible effect on their security with me. And I was sure that, in any event, I would myself feel like a hypocrite in clothes like theirs. My own insecurity at this point would have been transmitted to them in subtle ways. I therefore wore wool slacks, a warm brown dress shirt, and a tweed jacket. As a symbol of informality, I did not wear a tie.

Investment: Making the recording.   The 12 learners were seated on simple metal folding chairs arranged in a tight circle. On the floor in the center of the circle was a cassette tape recorder with a start-stop switch on its microphone. I was outside the circle. I said that the conversation would continue for about ten minutes.

A learner who had something to say to another learner signaled that fact by taking the microphone in his/her hand. (Since most of the learners were women, I will use the feminine pronoun to refer to "the learner" from this point on.) I went and stood behind her, placing my hands lightly on her arms just below the shoulder, and my face about four inches from her left ear. When she said in English what she wanted to say to the other person, I gave her an equivalent expression in Swahili. I gave the Swahili one or two words at a time. My voice was loud enough for everyone in the circle to hear. As I gave each part of the Swahili sentence, the learner turned the tape recorder on just long enough to record her own repetition of it, and then turned it off again. When she finished the sentence, I increased the pressure of my hands slightly for an instant and then released them. This was my signal that her turn was finished, and that someone else could speak. Ten minutes of this kind of conversation produced a tape with a playing time of something less than a minute, entirely in the voices of the learners, and entirely in the target language.

Commentary on the making of the tape.
    1. The closed circle makes it easier for the learners to develop a sense of community.
    2. The vastly superior knowledge of the knower, necessary as it is to the learning process, nevertheless constitutes a potential threat to the learners. In addition, when a learner has tried to say something new, she normally looks at the face of the knower for some indication of how she did. Either approval or disapproval places the learner in the position of being evaluated, and an impassive face on the knower is more threatening still. It is for these reasons that the knower is outside the circle, and invisible to the learner.
    3. The knower's hands on the learner's arms convey, first of all, the fact that he is there. It conveys this information in a way which does not require

the learner to glance over her shoulder and thus break off eye contact with the other learners. It also conveys gentle support and, at the end, acceptance without either approval or disapproval.

4. The announcement that the conversation will last for about ten minutes seems to have at least two desirable effects. It directs the learners' attention toward the conversation itself, rather than toward a task of making up sentences for use in the next step of the procedure. It also means that there will be too many sentences in the conversation for each to be fully processed in the succeeding steps. The learner thus feels less responsible for each sentence as it is being recorded. In both of these ways, the announcement reduces the learners' self-consciousness and thus contributes to their security. When the learners are secure, they are less likely to produce perfunctory sets of unrelated sentences, and more likely to produce conversations that mean something to them.

5. At four inches from the learner's ear, the knower's face is well within the learner's personal space, yet not close enough to threaten physical contact. This, together with the knower's invisibility and the support conveyed through the knower's hands, sometimes produces one or both of two illusions. The learner may feel that the foreign words are originating within her own head. She may also be unaware of the knower's hands on her arms. Both of these illusions were reported during the Brattleboro experience.

6. In my first experiences as a language counselor, I tried to speak softly so that only the learner that I was helping at the moment could hear me. This proved to be both unnecessary and undesirable. My reason for keeping my voice down was that I wanted to help the learners to have the feeling that the sentences were coming from them rather than from me. It was unnecessary because even when I give the sentences aloud, learners sometimes report that they have been unaware of my voice, and aware only of each other as speakers. It was undesirable because when the sound of my words was not loud enough for people to hear clearly, they became anxious and annoyed.

People frequently ask whether the knower-counselor can in fact come up with adequate instantaneous translations of whatever the learners decide to say. Even a native speaker of the target language is likely to introduce at least subtle distortions under these circumstances, and a nonnative like me is likely to encounter gaps in his own vocabulary. Both of these things do happen. Neither causes serious trouble, however. The purpose of the translation is not to produce an exact equivalent, but only to provide for the learner a sentence in whose content he can feel some sense of investment. If the knower-counselor cannot come up with a word that is essential for even an approximate translation of the learner's sentence, he simply says "Blank," and goes on. This happens to me on an average of once in a ten-minute conversation, and the learners say that it doesn't bother them. The important thing seems to be that the counselor-knower himself, through his non-verbal communication, convey a sense that he himself is comfortable with the gap.

When the knower sees that the learner's sentence is very long or complex, he may quite properly convert it into a larger number of simpler sentences, either during the recording or while the sentences are being written. The important thing is that the learners recognize the result as something that originated with them.

7. In the first few conversations, the learners generally have trouble with the stop-start switch on the microphone. As a result, the first parts of some sentences don't get recorded; or the counselor's voice, or even the learner's native-language sentence may get recorded. In the succeeding steps of the procedures, these sentences will be treated exactly as though they had been perfectly recorded. In the meantime, it is important that the counselor avoid anything that could be interpreted as even joking disapproval or derision. This includes grimaces.

8. If the target language sentences are broken into the right size pieces, pronunciation is good. In fact, it is more faithful to the knower's pronunciation than I have heard by any other method. When, as rarely happens, syllables are transposed or there is some other gross discrepancy, I simply give the model again *in exactly the same tone as the first time.* Any change in voice, or in pressure of the counselor's hands, is likely to be interpreted as an expression of impatience, or as an expression of patience. (The latter, of course, is just one more way of expressing the same judgment that lies beneath impatience.) In the three conversations recorded during the Brattleboro experience, I can recall only one or two occasions when I needed to make a fresh presentation of the model. There were of course a number of times when a learner used the wrong phoneme. I ignored these for two reasons. First, I have found that this sort of thing usually clears itself up in the succeeding steps of the procedure, provided the learners feel secure. Second, I have found that too many corrections during the recording session can undermine security, thereby reducing the spontaneity of the conversation, and even making it less likely that the error itself will remain corrected for very long.

9. When there is a pause between one learner's turn and the next, I stand back away from the circle, with my eyes averted. I do this in order to avoid putting nonverbal pressure on the learners.

Reflection: Understanding the learners' reactions.   Immediately after the end of the ten-minute recording session, I seated myself in the circle and invited the learners to voice any reactions that they had at the moment. The verbal part of my response to what they said was intended to verify for them and for me that I had understood what they had said, together with any non-verbal expression of their feelings. The nonverbal part of my response—tone of voice, posture, etc.—was intended to convey relaxation, acceptance, and confidence both in myself and in them. The only other content to my responses was an occasional very short answer to a question of fact.

Reflection: Listening to the tape.   We then listened twice to the tape, once without interruption, and once stopping after each sentence for someone to recall the general meaning of the sentence. On the one or two occasions when the group could not readily come up with the English equivalent, I gave it in a matter-of-fact way and played the next sentence from the tape.

Although this step and the preceding step are "reflection" on the recorded conversation, anything that a learner says during these steps is at the same time a venturing out, an "investment," of herself. This investment will be either punished or accepted, according to the quality of the knower's response to it. I think that this is especially true of the nonverbal component of the knower's response. To a large extent, the learner's security is made or broken during the two or three seconds following each of her self-investing acts, by things that she herself may not be conscious of.

Reflection: Writing the conversation down.   Playing the tape a third time, I filled one sheet of a large lecture pad with sentences taken from the conversation. I did this as rapidly as possible, without asking the learners for any help. (Swahili is written with the roman alphabet, and is a highly "phonetic" language.) After going through several conversations, some groups have voluntarily assumed responsibility for copying the conversation off the tape. They could probably do rather well at it even with the first conversation. But to do so would leave a few relatively quick and articulate individuals feeling elated, with the others feeling slow and stupid by comparison. The cost in security and community feeling would be prohibitive.

A blackboard was available, but I did not use it for this step. The lecture pad or the overhead projector makes a record which need not be erased. An additional advantage of the lecture pad is that the sheets can be taped to the wall for ready reference.

During this step, the learners were completely secure as far as any overt demands from the knower were concerned. In one respect, however, the appearance of the written words seemed to be regarded by some as a statement of an obligation on them to learn what had been written down. On the other hand, the written words were obviously a great relief to those who regarded themselves as "eye-minded."

Nobody tried to make private copies of the sentences at this time. I would not have allowed it in any case. The sentences were readily available on the pad, which was community property. To have made individual copies now would have broken up the group into twelve isolated people. It would also have interrupted the pace of the class. Anyone who really wanted her own copy could make it during the break.

The writing of the conversation was at the same time a further form of "reflection," and also a first step toward retention.

Discrimination: Identifying the meaningful parts of the conversation   I asked for and received the English equivalent of the first sentence. Then, using a contrasting color, I underlined one stem or one prefix at a time. In almost all instances, someone very quickly gave me a correct English translation for it. As soon as I heard the correct translation, I wrote it under the corresponding element of the Swahili sentence. In the few cases when the needed element did not come readily from the group, I wrote it myself and went on to another element of the Swahili sentence.

With regard to the security of the learners during this step, I suspect that: (1) The knower should choose first those elements which he thinks will be easiest for the learners to guess, rather than going through the sentence in linear order. (2) The knower should look at the written sentences rather than at the learners. (3) Those learners who are less quick and less articulate are likely to feel a bit insecure as a result of this step. This insecurity must be balanced against the security that even these quieter learners may derive from having dealt successfully with a set of exotic linguistic structures.

I repeated the preceding step and this step for a few more of the sentences from the conversation. I deliberately avoided writing all of the recorded sentences, for two reasons. The most important reason is that since I have stopped writing all of the sentences, the learners have seemed much less self-conscious about recording further conversations. The other reason is that to process all of the sentences from a 10-minute conversation would produce a sluggish rhythm for the total procedure. And a shorter conversation would not give the learners sufficient opportunity to get involved in what they were saying.

Reflection and discrimination: Silent contemplation.   I then asked the learners to sit in total silence for a period of three minutes. I announced the length of the period and timed it with my watch. The thinking that individuals were able to do at this time of course had considerable value from a purely cognitive point of view. The opportunity to sort things out free of distraction from knower or other learners, and safe from competition from other learners, was evidently a very welcome relief to many. In these ways, it helped to maintain a relatively high degree of security. Announcing the duration of the silence, and sticking to it, presumably contributed toward confidence in the knower-teacher. Finally, the announcement itself was one more occasion for using a tone of voice which was either calm and strong, or otherwise.

Discrimination: Small-group discussion.   In the next step, I broke the class into groups of three and told them they had three minutes to ask one another, within these small groups, for clarification of anything they didn't understand. This led to a quiet buzzing which answered many questions, at the same time dramatizing both their dependence on one another and their relative independence of me.

Discrimination: Verification of conclusions.   Sitting in one corner of the room, as inconspicuous as possible and invisible to some of the learners, I invited them to say aloud whatever they had concluded about Swahili. This produced quite a few statements, most of which I could confirm by a quiet "That's right." Where a conclusion was wrong, I gave additional information, with the restriction that none of my replies lasted more than 5 seconds. To have talked longer would have meant that I was giving them, out of my own world, new information that their hypotheses had reminded me of. This would have damaged the security level because many of the learners would have felt responsible for understanding and remembering what I said. Even from a purely cognitive point of view, this new information would probably have been an overload. By staying within the five-second limit, I hoped that I was filling in blanks in their world(s) rather than trying to pull them into mine. My reasons for remaining physically inconspicuous were that (1) the sight of me with my vastly superior knoweldge of Swahili might be discouraging or threatening to some learners; (2) seeing my face might have made many learners feel subject to my expectations of them; (3) I wanted to foster the feeling of community and interdependence among the learners (This last reason also accounts for my saying "That's right" quietly rather than enthusiastically.); (4) my face would have conveyed either approval or disapproval, either of which would have established a climate of evaluation.

Discrimination: Answering questions.   There were still a few questions that people wanted answers for. I dealt with them in the same way as in the preceding step, paying strict attention to the five-second limit on my replies. Where learners needed more information than I could put into that amount of time, they were free to ask supplementary questions. These questions were an additional form of "investment." I assume that the quality of their attention to my replies to their self-invested questions was superior to the attention they would have given to my most polished mini-lecture on Swahili grammar.

Reflection: Passive listening.   The next step was one which I had never used before. It was inspired by what I had read of the "concert pseudo-passive" sessions in Lozanov's method. I should emphasize, however, that what I was doing was at most a crude approximation to one step in the complex and carefully integrated methodology called Suggestopedia.

I told the learners that now I was going to do something that would allow them to absorb the sentences that we had been working with. I asked them to try not to think about me or what I was saying, and not to look at the written sentences. I said that if they had favorite ways of relaxing, this might be a good time to use them. I said I would read each sentence for them three times in Swahili. The first time, I would read it in a matter-of-fact voice, and follow that with a word-by-word literal translation into English. The second reading would be animated, much as the sentence might sound in actual conversation. The third reading would be in a very positive, optimistic tone of voice. I gave this information in a very relaxed way.

In reading the sentences, I left after each voicing of each sentence a few seconds of silence. I also left 30 seconds of silence before the first sentence and after the last sentence. I noticed that most or all of the learners had their eyes closed during the reading.

Reflection on the experience   As the final step, I invited their reactions to the experience so far. As before, my responses were intended primarily to verify my understanding of what the learners said and my acceptance of their reactions. Their reactions at the end of the first cycle were highly and almost uniformly positive. They seemed particularly happy with the passive listening. Their comments indicated that quite a bit of sorting out had gone on in their minds during the reading, and that it had left them in a relieved, optimistic frame of mind.

The total time from the beginning of the first cycle until the end was about 1½ hours. After a 20-minute break, we began the second cycle, which lasted until noon. The second cycle again involved seven active speakers, including the five who had been inactive the first time. The second cycle was conducted in the same way as the first, except that I allowed a little less time for the silent period and the small-group work. My reason for this was my desire to complete the second cycle by the scheduled lunch hour. Reacting to this, and possibly to related nonverbal cues which I was not aware of putting out, the learners reported that they felt rushed during those steps, and that this bothered them.

During the reflection period at the end of the second cycle, there was some evidence of discomfort within the group, particularly across the line between the relatively ready speakers and those who needed more time before bringing something out. Both sides expressed their own feelings on this issue, with me reflecting whatever they said. There was some criticism of me, which I also "understood." Then we went to lunch.

At the beginning of the third cycle, one or two of the learners said they didn't want to do a new recorded conversation because they had already been exposed to more than they could digest. I "understood" this, but then asked them to go ahead anyway, and they agreed to. The third cycle followed the same procedures as the first two, except that all twelve of the learners were active during the recording. This change was suggested by the learners, and I agreed to it. Some fatigue was evident in some of the learners at the end of the third cycle, though not in all. Otherwise, spirits were good.

In addition to the procedures used during the first two cycles, I added two more:

Discrimination: Tabulating verb prefixes   I drew two vertical lines on the blackboard, thus forming three columns. I put a subject prefix at the top of the first column, a tense prefix at the top of the middle column, and a verb stem at the top of the last column. Then I relinquished the chalk to one of the learners, who agreed to serve as secretary for the group. The task was to fit the verbs from their sentences into these columns. I sat at the back of the room and made occasional interventions or answered questions, but at least 95 percent of the talking was done by the learners.

The overall effect of this step was the learner's discrimination of prefixes and stems. My staying physically out of their way contributed to their security from me and their confidence in themselves. My drawing the lines on the board and dissecting the first verb contributed to their security by giving them a clear framework within which to proceed. On the other hand, leaving the initiative to them allowed them to invest themselves by contributing data to be fitted into the diagram. My asking for someone to serve as "secretary," rather than calling on someone to "recite," protected the security of that person and of anyone who might take her place.

I used the blackboard for this activity, rather than the lecture pad, because incorrect guesses could easily be erased and forgotten.

Discrimination and investment: Writing sentences.   I divided the learners into groups of three, and gave blank 3 by 5 cards to each group. The group was to write an original Swahili sentence on each card, without English translation. I circulated while this was going on, looking over people's shoulders to see the sentences as they were written. Most of them were correct, but I suggested changes where necessary. When each group had at least three sentences, they passed their cards to the next group, which figured out what the sentences meant.

The small-group format contributed to security, while still allowing even the slow talkers plenty of air time. In this way, they were able to take apart the sentences on the wall (discrimination), and participate in making new ones (reinvestment).

Reflection: Monolog by the knower.   After a break, I told the knowers that I was going to talk to them for a few minutes in Swahili, just so they could get some idea what connected speech sounds like. I told them that I would not question them or otherwise put them on the spot with respect to what I was going to say. I said that while they might recognize some things that I said, I would make no attempt to stay within the vocabulary that they had been exposed to.

My monolog lasted for something over five minutes, with great animation and continuous eye contact. I sat where I could see the sentences that we had written from all three cycles, and drew on them, but said whatever else I felt like saying. I repeated myself frequently, but in ways that would be appropriate to a similar monolog where no foreign language is involved.

Following the monolog there was a long silence, at the end of which people began telling me what they thought I had said. They were usually right, and among them they retrieved most of what I had said. I confirmed or disconfirmed their guesses with brief, matter-of-fact replies.

This step seemed to leave the group with some feeling of elation.

Since much of what I said was based on what had been in their recorded conversations, the monolog was in some sense a diffuse "reflection" of all that the learners had done up to that point. I have done this same kind of thing with several other groups under similar circumstances. Both the learners and I are always amazed at how much they have understood. I suspect that this result could not have been obtained if I had not maintained their security by (1) assuring them that I would not quiz them; (2) refraining from quizzing them; (3) acting casual about the successes and occasional failures of their guesses. These guesses were, after all, a further form of self-investment, which could have dried up immediately in an atmosphere of evaluation.

Reflection, discrimination, and investment: Dialogs with the knower   As the last activity of the day, I engaged in two or three minutes of vigorous conversation with each of the learners. Before I began, I told them that whoever I was talking with was free to ask help from the others, either in figuring out what I had said, or in deciding how to reply; and that if they didn't feel ready to reply in Swahili, they could always reply in English.

During the conversations, I spoke rapidly and with great animation at all times. If a learner didn't understand something, I was willing to repeat it, but not to slow it down. My part of the conversations consisted almost entirely of (1) questions based on sentences they had met earlier in the day; (2) my "understanding" responses to their replies to my questions; (3) my "understanding" recapitulations of what the learner had said during the entire interview.

Like the monolog, these conversations were a diffuse reflection of what the learners had created earlier. My questions required the learners to make appropriate discriminations in order to understand and reply. Their replies, in turn, became new investments, which I had to meet with nonthreatening responses in the form of Swahili-language reflection. These responses, together with the privilege of replying in English if they needed to, seemed to keep their security at a fairly high level.

GENERAL COMMENTS

I suspect that the end of the morning was a crisis in two respects: (1) The learners expressed discomfort with each other, and some criticism of me. I think the afternoon would have died (a) if I had not given them a chance to air these things, or (b) if I had taken sides, or (c) if I had become defensive when I was criticized. (2) A few students came back from lunch with a request that we continue to work on the sentences from the morning, rather than starting a new conversation. My decision not to follow this suggestion was a way of reminding them that I was ultimately in charge of format, and not they. To that extent, it presumably contributed to their security. If I had turned out to be wrong in my decision—that is, if the third conversation had in fact swamped them—the net effect of this decision would have been to damage their security on several levels.

I denied the request for three reasons: (1) I thought that they could handle the additional input. (2) To have continued chewing over the earlier conversations would have implied that the whole day was a cognitive, academic exercise, rather than an experience with self-invested communication. (3) Moving ahead maintained progress and enthusiasm.

Note that I did accede to their suggestion that all 12 learners participate in the third conversation.

Some of the techniques which I have described in this chapter will show up again in Chapter 14. To remove one or another of two similar descriptions would, however, force the reader to flip back and forth between chapters while trying to read one of them, and would destroy the integrity of the narrative.

CHAPTER 14

COMMUNITY LANGUAGE LEARNING IN HONOLULU

In Chapter 6, I reported on an experience in teaching Turkish with the Silent Way at the University of Hawaii. The same class of over 40 then went on to learn some Swahili by an adaptation of the Classical Community Language Learning technique (Chapter 8). As before, six people per day were assigned to hand in short papers summarizing what we had done, and their reactions to it.

As in Chapters 5, 6, and 13, I would urge readers to focus only secondarily on what I *did* in these classes, and primarily on the reasons behind the choices that I made.

First day.   Before class, I made out a new roster for the small groups. First, I took one person from each of the Silent Way groups and put them into a new group. Then I made a few changes to ensure that no group would be made up entirely of men or women. My reasons for mixing the class at this time were to give the feeling of a fresh start, to exert authority in a way that people would be comfortable with, and to broaden each person's range of acquaintances in the class.

In the past, I had always started a CLL class by having six people do a 10-minute conversation, during which the students' Swahili was recorded. The recording was then played back and processed more or less as I have described it in Chapter 13. In this session, I departed from that procedure in three ways. (1) I did not use a tape recorder. The reason was the size of the room and the number of people in the class. I felt that to go through the entire procedure with one group would leave the remaining 85 percent of the class too far distant from the action, psychologically as well as physically. Besides, the use of the tape recorder can produce its own anxieties: (a) The mechanics of passing the microphone around and turning it on and off at the right time are unfamiliar and frequently troublesome. (b) Some people are uncomfortable at hearing their own voices in a recording. (2) I kept the conversations relatively short: about five minutes apiece for each of five groups. This again was to ensure that as many people as possible would get a chance to participate. (3) I postponed all of the comments from the students until after the last group had had its conversation. I did this in order to keep the comments of one group from contaminating the experience of the groups that followed it; and to give greater unity to the overall experience with the conversations; and to make certain that everyone had a chance to participate.

My overall goal for this first session was to leave people comfortable with having talked with each other in Swahili, in spite of whatever feelings they might have had about "exotic" languages in general or Swahili in particular; and in spite of the strangeness of talking with the help of a knower-counselor.

Because the seats were bolted together in threes, we were unable to form a tight circle of six students. Instead, we used a large triangle with nine places in it.

I began by describing the CCLL procedure briefly, and outlining what we were going to do this morning. I included a warning that the part of the procedure that we would use today was not likely to lead to much retention of vocabulary or structure, but I assured them that retention would be taken care of later on. I did this because I have found in the past that anxiety about lack of retention is a regular feature of the initial steps in CLL.

I then invited each group to send at least one representative to the nine-seat triangle, to form a temporary conversation group. I did this instead of working with one of the established groups after another for three reasons: (1) I hoped in this way to keep the entire class involved in the entire series of conversations through vicarious participation in what their representatives were doing. (2) I was able in this way to reduce the number of conversations, with nine people at a time instead of six. (3) I wanted to prevent the individual groups from splitting off, psychologically, from the class as a whole on the basis of the content of their separate series of conversations. I felt that this would lead to chaos. The price, of course, was slower formation of an esprit de corps in the newly formed working groups.

Some of the written comments had to do with details of technique. One of the students reported that she would have preferred to get the sentences with the counselor facing her. By contrast, another said that although she could not see my articulation of the sounds, she was "glad that I could hear his sounds better behind me." Along the same lines, one person said that the experience was "very agreeable to me as I felt someone was behind me to help me."

On a few occasions during the conversations, a student's repetition was so far off that I had to give the model again. The only person who referred to this indicated that my re-presenting of the model had come across just the way I wanted it to: "He would repeat the phrase in such a way that he seemed to be thinking, 'Well, maybe she didn't hear me,' and not as a correction."

Although I knew that touching the learners' shoulders was less acceptable in some cultures than in others, I decided to use it at least in this opening session. There was only one written comment on it, by an Asian woman: "As for the teacher's hands on students, I was not bothered."

Other comments had to do with the method as a whole. Two people expressed uncertainty about its general efficacy. Four were uneasy with the structurally and topically random nature of the conversations. Two felt some frustration because they had retained so little Swahili from the morning's activities. It may be worthwhile to quote one of these papers at length, with my own comments:

"It was hard for me to remember what was said. The conversations were too loose. There was no continuity between statements. I suppose that if today's class were a real language class proceeding toward real goals, then the students would have slowed things down and concentrated on one or two points until everyone had mastered them." I have heard many people express similar reactions to a first exposure to the group conversation step in the CCLL procedure. It is in fact mistaken: "real students" begin by fumbling just as much as "demonstration students" do. What caused the "looseness" and "discontinuity" to which this writer referred was not any lack of serious purpose or long-term commitment. It was the unfamiliarity of the procedure itself, complicated by the fact that the individuals involved were strangers to one another. The resulting uncertainty produced insecurity, which kept everyone more or less wary, and narrowed the scope of their cooperation.

The same writer continued, "I couldn't help feeling that I was part of a team of linguists sent out into the middle of nowhere to crack a previously unknown language." This, too, is a frequent reaction of people who have had a brief exposure to CCLL. It comes, apparently, from the fact that this procedure does not start from preexisting lesson material: the language is, at the beginning, totally unknown; what the students learn of it in the CCLL procedure comes from what they hear during the procedure; and what they hear in the target language depends on what they ask for through their native language. The same things are true of elicitation procedures in linguistic field methods.

But there are also important differences: (1) Students in CLL are allowed to consult conventional grammar books outside of the CCLL procedure itself. (2) Even within the procedure, during the "reflection phase" (which was not included in today's experience), the teacher may give brief answers to questions about structure. (3) What the knower provides in the target language is not necessarily a close or even an exact translation of what the learner has said. The knower is obligated only to provide something which the learner can feel that he, the learner, was the source of. (4) Most important, the essential part of the conversation is the developing communication among the learners, and not the "linguistic field work." If the learners treat what they are saying as just a series of linguistic objects called sentences, they lose a whole dimension of personal involvement; learning becomes verbal and cognitive, without the emotional and practical content that lets the language permeate the whole learner.

The writer concludes, "It seemed to me that a teacher could have directed our conversation along lines that would have been more profitable. The teacher could have anticipated sticky linguistic situations and steered the conversation away from them until such time as we could deal with them." At this point, the writer is evidently still thinking of "profit" in the same terms in which conventional lessons succeed: words, sounds, and/or structures retained, real-life situations (banks, hotels, restaurants, etc.) with which the learner can now cope, and so on. He appears not yet to have noticed either the dimension of personal depth or the dimension of community interaction, in both of which important things had begun to happen.

He was also unaware that there were at least two layers of protection between the class and linguistic matters that were "too sticky to deal with" in this initial lesson: (1) The students were asked neither to reproduce nor even to retain any of the material. "Stickiness" becomes a problem only when the learners are asked to make the discriminations among sounds, among morphemes, and/or among sentence patterns which are necessary for reproduction or retention. (2) Even after students do begin to work with the material in ways that require some discrimination, the teacher has broad powers of selecting, simplifying, and/or suppressing material from the original conversation. In this last statement, the writer is feeling the absence of the accustomed security-giving restraints that the teacher and the text-book have imposed, and has not yet discovered the limits which the counselor-teacher provides. He therefore feels anxious. This is a very common first reaction to CCLL.

Finally, another writer comments, "It seems to me that the teacher has to have great confidence in himself and in the system." This is true. I would add that the teacher must have equal confidence in the learners, and in what they will do in a secure and rich learning environment.

A contrasting reaction to the same session read, in part, "The teacher filled a much more traditional role in this method than in the [Silent Way]. There was less student frustration, since the teacher provided a more immediate model for the student to follow. . . . Students could be more 'creative' in the new language right from the beginning, and this no doubt makes the method more intrinsically satisfying to the students."

Second day.   The procedure was as for the first day, except that after the last conversation, I wrote a few of the sentences on the board. I then guided the students in identifying the meaningful parts of these sentences, quickly supplying, in a nonobligating tone of voice, whatever they could not guess. I did, however, ask the students not to copy what was on the board.

During the conversations, a few students said sentences or parts of sentences in Swahili on their own. If I happened to be near when this happened, I gave a slight squeeze to the student's shoulders with my hands, just as at the end of a sentence a student had gotten from me. If I happened to be on the other side of the room at the time, I merely nodded and smiled slightly. My purpose was to convey acceptance without approval. If a sentence that a student volunteered was seriously wrong, I went to him, stood behind him, and gave him the sentence exactly as if he had said it in English.

The session ended with me understanding several student reactions, and silence.

One of the written comments mentioned my statement that the students were not expected to retain anything yet. Two others explicitly recognized that for the time being, the goal was only for them to become comfortable with the language and with this first part of the procedure. Nevertheless, there was widespread uneasiness over the small amount that was remembered, and over the fact that what one remembered, others could not remember, and sometimes could not even recognize. This is hardly surprising: students cannot be expected to accept immediately a set of goals that they have never before seen pursued systematically, or recognized academically.

This feeling of malaise was probably the principal source of several of the written comments. One person felt "dumb, awkward, slow and frustrated" whenever she found that she had forgotten something that she thought she had "learned." Another person was restive under my request that they not copy today's sentences from the board "so as to make them more permanent in my own mind." This restriction certainly produced a certain amount of anxiety. On the other hand, whatever is copied down constitutes, by universal academic custom, an obligation; failure to fulfill (their own interpretations of) these obligations would have produced even more anxiety. Another felt that the system was hit-or-miss in introducing the various parts of the language, and that it consumed too much time for the amount that was retained.

Under these circumstances, three people were moved to compare their experience under CLL with their experience under the Silent Way. Two of these found in favor of the Silent Way: "I cannot help but think how reassuring and comfortable it was in the Silent Way. . . . From the first day, I came out of each class feeling that I had definitely learned something, however little. That positive feeling about oneself is important, and I do not yet have it in CLL." "Whereas I felt in the Silent Way Turkish that my retention was excellent, CLL Swahili seems to be going in one ear and out the other. It is frustrating to feel no results from the time invested." The third person had a different view: "In these first two sessions of CLL Swahili, I have felt more secure and comfortable than in the Silent Way, partly because I always know the meaning of what I am saying in CLL, and partly because I am corrected only with the instructor standing behind me and using a tone that conveys 'warmth, acceptance, and understanding.' "

One person said he thought it would have been easier to improvise conversations in a group where he knew the other members. He said that in a group of strangers, "there wasn't really anything I wanted to say." This statement, by implication at least, supports the importance of the community-building goal in CLL (or in many other systems).

One person commented on the fact that he derived a feeling of security from my hands on his shoulders, and also from my calling the students by their names in dealing with them. Another said that the general lack of pressure was "comforting." A third reported that the periods of silence in the group activity "were in fact moments of intense mental activity. . . . I found myself verbalizing to myself the sentences that I heard from other people."

One paragraph out of one of today's comments has provided me with food for many rethinkings: "Not being bound to written formulas for memorization is a great aid to 'just letting what sticks stick.' When something does stick, however, my tendency is to push it to its limits and discover if what is sticking is sufficient or if there is something I haven't yet discovered." [This illustrates the way in which a student who is feeling secure will go instinctively from "Retention" to "Discrimination," and on to further "Investment."] "This causes anxiety, especially in a group where many members experience the language as happening to them, as opposed to them making the language happen. Still, this anxiety is healthy and good, and exists not as a state but as a goad. If we were able to give ourselves completely and simply to 'play,' *this anxiety would then manifest itself as play.*" [Emphasis added.]

One of the people who compared CLL to the Silent Way wondered "whether the two methods might not be good complements for one another—SW as a means for drilling structures, CLL for building vocabulary and realistic communication. Each seems to fill a gap in the other. Combined, they would be dynamite!" I have heard this comment in the past from many people, including myself. I think, however, that the teacher-student relationships are so different that the *methods* could not be combined, or merged. This is not to say, however, that a teacher using one of these methods could not borrow techniques from the other, with appropriate modifications.

Third day.   Today, we had only two group conversations. After each conversation, I understood student reactions from the participants, and then from the onlookers. (I gently declined questions and comments which I felt to be from the point of view of a teacher.) Then, I asked the participants to call out sentences from the conversation, either in English or in Swahili, or in a combination of the two. I wrote these sentences on the board in correct Swahili, editing or abridging them as I did so whenever I felt that a sentence as it stood would be too cumbersome. I even reserved the right to omit a whole sentence on the same ground.

I did without the tape recorder once more because I still thought that the mechanical operation of it, and some students' self-consciousness about hearing their own voices, would do more harm than good. On the positive side, I saw value in the students' having the experience of serving as their own playback mechanism. In doing so, (1) they discovered in themselves a power that would otherwise have gone unnoticed; (2) they had the benefit of doing delayed free recall; (3) they selected those parts of the conversation that had meant most to them; (4) they made a further "investment" of themselves without having to expend any further inventiveness; (5) they saw me accepting the imperfections as well as the successes of their recall, and providing a target-language "reflection" of it.

After the sentences were on the board, I went through them, underlining each successive meaningful element (prefix, stem, etc.); and then writing a simple English equivalent underneath it. I did this even to a prefix that might be occurring for the fifth time. I did it in order to maintain the security of those who might not be quick at looking back and/or remembering. But even for the quicker ones, I wanted this to be a smooth, rhythmic experience. Having to look back, either on the board or in their brains, would have detracted from the quality that I was after.

This simple parsing of the sentences was similar to what I had done with many previous classes. There was, however, a difference in timing. On this occasion, I paused only slightly before writing the English equivalent. Previously, I had paused until someone guessed the correct equivalent. But student reactions in the earlier groups had shown that, while the experience of translating a brand new language with almost no help was exhilarating for some students, it produced great anxiety in those who weren't able to contribute. Shortening my pauses was intended to do away with this effect. Leaving short pauses instead of eliminating the pauses entirely still allowed people's minds to work along with my chalk.

When the parsing was completed, I announced that we would take two minutes by the clock just to look at the sentences—without writing them down. When the announced time period was ended, I erased the sentences and invited a new group to come and go through the same procedure.

The reason for the silent contemplation has already been discussed. Announcing and adhering to a fixed period of time reduces the discomfort of anyone who is uneasy with silence; more generally, it contributes to security by structuring time. On the other hand, however, I feel perfectly free to "fudge," and reduce an announced 2-minute period to 90 seconds if I feel that the silence is getting too long.

I omitted some of the other steps that I had used in Brattleboro and elsewhere (Chapter 13) for a number of reasons. Most immediately, this was the last day of the academic week—the day on which I had promised to deal with questions and comments from the participants' point of view as teachers. Time was therefore at a premium. But in addition, I felt that too much analysis would create more anxieties than it would relieve. This was also the reason for not allowing people to make private copies of the sentences.

After the second conversation had been processed in this way, I gave the students a few minutes to work in pairs and produce Swahili sentences of their own. We then wrote a few of these sentences on the board and translated them before going on to deal with the "teacher-questions."

Producing new sentences in a group of peers is more secure than producing them alone for at least three reasons. (1) The student is not working under the watchful eyes of teacher and classmates. (2) Many errors are corrected before a sentence is exposed for public scrutiny. (3) Responsibility for the final product is shared. Having only two people in a group gave maximum time for each individual.

The Swahili-learning part of today's session lasted about 50 minutes.

The people who handed in accounts of today's session seemed less worried about "retention" than the people who reported on the second day. One person commented that imperfect retention didn't bother her. Two people commented that they would have liked to write the sentences down for study at home. On the other hand, one person said explicitly that he "really didn't feel any need for writing yet, even with the large number of sentences that came up." Another person said that just seeing the sentences written on the board helped in remembering, but that at the same time it tended to "freeze" his pronunciation so that he was no longer open to improving it.

Three people remarked on how far the class had come in the language in a relatively short time.

One person lamented that the participants in the conversations still tended to "go off on tangents" and thus to produce material that was not as useful as it might have been. By contrast, another found a satisfying degree of "focus" in today's conversations. A third person reacted against the repetitious, "focused" quality of today's conversations, saying he would have preferred to break new ground rather than reworking the old.

Two people commented favorably on the working of the small groups. "Among the six of us, we have usually been able to come up with anything we need." "[As in the Silent Way] I found myself interacting with my classmates to check meanings and practice pronunciation. Even when the teacher was translating my English sentences, my attention was directed within the circle, and not to the outside where the teacher was standing." Another person, however, felt that exposure to the group was perhaps "intimidating" and "not too different from classroom techniques of bygone days. In this, I feel that the Counseling-Learning technique is not living up to its reputation as I had understood it."

Two people commented that it was occasionally hard to hear what was going on in a distant part of the room.

One person said that not writing all of the sentences on the board, and not asking the class to do the parsing, made it easier to just listen and "flow with the sounds." At the same time, she felt satisfaction that she had been able to do some of the parsing before I wrote the English on the board. ·

Fourth day.   While the class was gathering, I wrote on the board a few sentences which were recombinations of what the class had met on the first three days. I then parsed them with the class, as we had done before. The purpose of this was simply review and warmup after the weekend. When the parsing was completed, I set aside a minute for silent contemplation.

I then asked nine people to come to the central triangle, and we went through the same procedure as on the third day. At the end of that procedure, I asked people to put their minds in neutral, closing their eyes if they liked, and to listen to the sentences that were on the board. I then read the sentences with the three different "intonations," as described in the Brattleboro experience (Chapter 13).

At this point, I felt that the conversations were more cautious than they needed to be; that people were fabricating them only as an academic exercise; and that I had more confidence in the students than they had in themselves. Therefore, when the second group came forward, I sat down with them and engaged them in lively conversation, concentrating on one person at a time. This was a "mask-change," conducted very much like the final activity at Brattleboro (Chapter 13).

The oral reactions at the end of class showed some enthusiasm for this last procedure, and for what it had demonstrated about the students' ability in Swahili.

The following are excerpts from four of the written reports:

"When I came to class, I felt very frustrated because I could remember only four very simple Swahili sentences, and thought that the others knew much more than I did. Toward the end of the hour, I felt much better because I found that I was not really far behind my classmates. I could understand most of the conversation, and could even say some simple things in Swahili by myself! But when I left the classroom, I again felt a lack of self-confidence. I wish the teacher had let me write down all the sentences in my notebook so that I could review them at home, and come to class the next day with more confidence."

From my point of view, this student *might* have concluded from this session that she had a surprising ability to understand and to say things in Swahili, beyond what she had thought she had before she came to class; and that this ability would be available again in the next class session. She did not in fact reach this conclusion. Instead, she reached out for traditional sources of confidence (the written word, and homework) to prepare her for a traditional goal (smooth recitation in the next sessions). In fairness to this student, I must admit that a single day's experience, no matter how encouraging, is not usually a sufficient basis for reorganizing a complex set of expectations.

Another person wrote, "I can honestly say that I was learning and absorbing Swahili almost every minute during class, except when I'm asked to go to the triangle. Something happens to me when I'm in the triangle. My mind can't seem to function. . . . Although the teacher is at all times very supportive, I get very tense. To me, taking part in the conversation in the triangle is like being put on the stand in a courtroom where the other people in the triangle are like prosecuting attorneys, and the people outside of the triangle are like members of the jury.... Yet I'm amazed that when I'm not actively participating, I can remember almost all the words we've said so far. This surprises me because, based on previous experiences, I consider myself to be a poor language learner."

Here is a graphic statement, both of the agony of feeling "on the spot," and of the difference between learning as a direct participant and learning as an observer.

A third person commented on the passive listening to the three intonations: "This is quite a contrast to what I'm used to. Who in audiolingualism would allow the student to close his eyes and *listen* while the language was slowed down? I always resented the fact that audiolingualists were reluctant to let the student hear the language at anything less than rapid native-speaker speed. I felt that if I could hear everything slowly, I could learn to apply the rules of contraction and deletion and thus speed up my utterance *later!*"

This was the first time that I had not found almost unanimous enthusiastic response to the three-intonation technique. Perhaps it was overshadowed by the more dramatic technique in which I conversed with the students.

Concerning the latter, one person wrote, "It gave us a sample of hearing Swahili in a very natural environment. It was also encouraging to see how we could pick up certain meanings even though we hadn't heard the word before." Another person, one of the veterans among the teachers in this course, wrote at length:

"[The first group] went to the center of the room and conversed with the help of the teacher, as on the preceding three days. But this time, a lot of the talking was originated by the speakers in Swahili instead of English. People were still talking not because they wanted to say something, but because they were expected to say something; but now they were doing their hunting more from among the things they knew how to say.

"Then I took my turn in the center group expecting more of the same. But this time, the teacher jointed us an immediately started a spirited conversation at good speed with various members of the group. I don't know how much Swahili I actually learned in those few minutes, but the psychological impact was tremendous. I had actually experienced at a very early stage in language study, and *in class,* one of the basic preconditions of "real" (non-classtime) language learning. ... The teacher used all of the techniques that a 7 year old native-speaking friend might have used in trying to communicate with us: non-identical repetitions, high redundancy, simplified grammar, and lots of action; but it was always *natural* in both speed and feeling.

"The psychological impact arose not just from the skillful use of real conversation (I had seen many cases of this before), but from the great apparent distance between what the teacher was doing and what the students thought they were ready for. It was truly a great manifestation of 'faith in the ability of the learners.' "

Fifth day. At the beginning of the session, I handed out three hecto-graphed sheets with sentences from the preceding days, and with a fragment of a verb paradigm. The groups examined these sheets together for a few minutes and discussed them. The purpose was review, aided by the written form of the language. I hoped that people would find it reassuring, both emotionally and linguistically, to have their own copies.

Then we turned to group conversations, but we did them in a way that was very new to the class, and partially new to me. The differences were (1) We used the tape recorder, because by now the class was beginning to feel at home with the other parts of the CCLL procedure, and I wanted them to hear their conversations in connected form. (2) I did not stand behind the speakers, but sat with them in the circle. The reason for this was purely mechanical: there was no start-stop switch on the microphone, so I had to sit beside the tape recorder to turn it on and off as necessary. (3) The writing on the board was done, not by me, but by pairs of student volunteers. I clearly referred to these volunteers as "secretaries," who were acting *on behalf of* everyone. I did not want anyone to feel that these students were in any sense either being tested or being shown off. I used the volunteers, instead of doing the writing myself, for three reasons: (a) Mechanical difficulties with the tape recorder would have made it awkward, though not impossible, for me to copy sentences onto the board one by one in the usual way. (b) I knew that many of the students were able to do this work, as long as they worked in pairs. (c) It saved time.

At the end of each conversation, I went to the board, corrected and com-pleted the transcript, and then parsed it as I had on previous days. I worked quickly and as unobtrusively as possible, in order to avoid making the "secre-taries" feel uncomfortable about the imperfections in their work. As I produced the corrected version of each conversation, a third student copied it down so that I could use it in preparing an edited version for duplication and distribution. My goal here was to maintain the students' feeling of security relative to a large amount of conversational material which we would then examine and work with on the following day. (We will see, below, that I did not altogether realize this goal.)

By working in this way, we were able to complete five conversations. I used one of the existing small groups at a time, instead of drawing repre-sentatives from them as I had on previous days, because I wanted to enhance esprit de corps within the groups. This time the students originated many of their sentences entirely or partially in Swahili.

Today, the period of reflective silence preceded the understanding of student reactions, instead of following it. The oral reactions revealed one group of students who felt an intense need to analyze some of the existing material and practice it before going further, and another group who wanted to continue immersing themselves in conversation. This second group was repelled by the idea of stopping to take things apart. In addition to understanding the individual reactions, I highlighted this split within the group. (Compare the experience of the students in my first Swahili weekend, Chapter 12.)

The written reactions were mixed, but generally favorable. One person said that she was amazed at how much Swahili people had been able to use. She continued, "For a while, I was feeling confused by all the new words and patterns. Now I feel that they are coming to me as well as to the other students." Another said, "Certainly there has been a great deal more language learning going on than previously. . . . I think students are enjoying their language lessons much more." But a third student said, "I don't feel I'm progressing as I normally would. I was very bored and I don't know why. I feel that what we are doing now is very far away from the idea of Counseling-Learning. It feels as if we are rushing to get certain objectives out of the way. There has been almost no counseling, and there is no more reassurance from the teacher's being behind me." On this last point, another person regretted that I had stopped placing my hands on people's shoulders while giving the new Swahili sentences.

One person felt very nervous at having to record his voice, and found it hard to say anything. But "when you played the tape, I felt much better, because the conversation ran smoothly. I felt good about the conversation."

One person commented that she appreciated the silence at the end of the session, but suggested that I might say two or three of the Swahili sentences during the silence, so that she could remember them better. I interpreted this as an indication that yesterday's reading of sentences with the three "intonations" had been effective for this person.

Someone else said that, although she had really liked the silence on other days, today's silence was a time when something that had been bothering her during the lesson "boiled up" and made her even more uncomfortable.

One person would have liked me to give lists of supplementary vocabulary related to words that had come up in the conversations: "north," "south," and "east" to go along with "west," for example. I see this suggestion as evidence of a conflict which this person was feeling between the familiar academic-verbal style of learning on the one hand, and on the other hand a still-unfamiliar style of learning through whole-person investment in the setting of a community.

Two other people similarly expressed discomfort at trying to meet demands which CCLL *does not place* on learners, and which may have been carried over from earlier language study. One of them felt bad about originating sentences in English during the conversations, instead of in Swahili as many of the others had done. The other felt "pressure to produce natural conversation *which will add something easily grasped to the class' knowledge of Swahili.*" [Emphasis added.] What CCLL asks, of course, is only that the students converse with each other as naturally as possible. The structures will take care of themselves under the guidance (and editing) of the teacher.

Sixth day.   My general strategy for today was to take the large amount of material that we collected yesterday and help the students to begin to digest it. Yesterday was primarily devoted to the "AA" of the SAARRD model; today the focus shifted to the "RR."

I began by distributing handouts based on yesterday's tape. I had the students first look at them silently, and then ask questions of one another in the small group. As they did so, I could hear that they were making slow progress, and getting bogged down in structure. In terms of the SAARRD model, what I had intended to be an exercise in "Reflection" was requiring more "Discrimination" than they were ready for. I had overestimated them at this point. Therefore, I took the center of the stage and read the sentences aloud slowly, giving a literal morpheme-by-morpheme translation of each. In so doing I was taking back onto myself the responsibility for "Discrimination." This was right because it was necessary; if it had not been necessary, it would have been wrong.

When I had gone through all of the sentences in this way, I again had the students look at the handout in silence and then ask each other questions. After a minute or two of this, I invited people to state any tentative conclusions they had reached, so I could verify them. When there was only a little response to this, I invited questions about the language. I answered these questions very briefly, so as to avoid straying from the world of the questioner into the world of my own knowledge and thereby losing my hearers. As an added support for the students' security, and also to utilize the visual as well as the oral channel, I wrote on the board all of the Swahili that occurred in the students' questions and in my answers.

During this activity, I could again see that many people were feeling overwhelmed, so I put that observation into words. This was what C-L theory calls a "counseling response," which appeared to be on target for quite a few.

Next, I had the class go back into groups of two or three, and write their own sentences or dialogs based on the handout. I can't justify this in terms of the SAARRD model, for in so doing, I was asking "Discrimination" of a class which wasn't even feeling very "Secure" at the moment. Perhaps I thought that trying to do something concrete would be easier for them to focus on than just looking at the sheets and trying to understand them in general. And, socially, the small subgroups of two or three people seemed to offer the best combination of linguistic and personal security.

In any case, after they had had a few minutes to work on this, I invited them to read out some of their sentences. I stood at the front of the room with my eyes closed and repeated the sentences, first in correct Swahili, then in English. My purpose was to give them informative feedback on their work. I kept my eyes closed in order to reduce the element of personal confrontation, either in seeming to demand sentences from them, or in giving back to them Swahili that might be very different from what they had given to me.

As the last activity of the session, I did a monolog of exactly five minutes duration, very much as described in the account of the Brattleboro experience. The first person who asked to try to guess what I had said turned out to have missed most of the meaning. The next one, however, gave it back almost completely. Others also seemed to have followed most of it. I asked for a quick show of hands, and most people felt that they had gotten "over half" of what I had said.

In the oral feedback at the end of the hour, there seemed to be wide agreement with one person who said that the monolog was "just what she needed at this point." One can only speculate as to why people felt this way. The obvious guess, and the one supported by the written comments, is that they were surprised and delighted by how much they were able to understand. In addition, however, this was their first experience with Swahili which did not require productive effort on their part. It was therefore able to become a fully communicative experience—one which involved them and me intensely, and thus became an experience in "acquisition," and not just "learning."

Written comments on the first part of the hour indicated that it had achieved its purpose, at least for some people: "It was a great help to me. I had a chance to do some *sorting out*. . . ." "It made me more confident, as it gave me the chance to *sort things out*." "Today was more or less a *sorting out* session." [Emphasis added.] For a few people, however, the handout represented "new things," and there were "too many of them."

One person pointed out that when I kept my eyes closed, I was unable to respond to the raising of hands. Another would have liked me to say the Swahili again after giving the English translations of the students' sentences.

One person who did not get much from the monolog reported that she had been trying to listen to it "analytically." By contrast, one person who had understood most of it said, "I just lay back and floated. . . . I intentionally tried not to digest the story word for word." The student who had summarized the monolog successfully in class wrote, "I was not paying much attention because I was still trying to work out the dialog we had been writing. . . . But my attention was grabbed, and I got caught up in the story. I guess that being caught up in the story is paramount to understanding it." On the other hand, one student who understood much of the monolog felt that it required a lot of work. And one who didn't understand much still was able to enjoy the "sounds" and the "drama."

One student commented that he could see how "the Counseling-Learning teacher does not give in to the whims of the students, but uses strategies to get things happening the way s/he wants them to. . . . Today, you were in control of the class; we were being aimed, not just flying off every which way." I would rephrase this last comment to say that the CLL teacher "varies the activities in response to changing needs, so as to keep learning focused in a productive way."

Seventh day.   At the beginning of the period, I put up large sheets of newsprint on which I had written sentences from the previous day's conversations. One sheet also contained a partial verb paradigm, showing how affirmative and negative forms differ from each other in Swahili. I allowed a few minutes for the students to study these sheets in silence. My purpose was to refresh people's minds and give them something to work from in today's conversations, and also to start them off with a feeling of security. I did not invite questions or comments. My reason was that I did not want people to get sidetracked into Discrimination activities, at the expense of further self-investing conversation.

Before we began the audible portion of the activities, I commented on the difference between students' reactions which had surfaced at the end of yesterday's sessions. I summarized both the logical and the emotional sides of these reactions, and also commented that these differences were neither unusual nor unexpected, but that the experience of overhearing one another's reactions might make it easier for both sides to deal with the differences. This was intended as a kind of two-way counseling response, which might drain off some of the emotion on both sides so that it would interfere less with the cognitive work to be done.

I then asked for two volunteers to sit in the circle and converse. By using volunteers, I could ensure that no one who was not ready for conversing would be under pressure to do so. By using only two people, I hoped to get a conversation that was very clearly focused. In this I was successful. The conversation, furthermore, was largely originated in Swahili, and with relatively little help from me. I personally felt that the content of the conversation was a little pedestrian. Evidently the speakers were being adventurous in their exploration of their independence rather than in the content of what they said. This was probably the very best thing they could have done, from the point of view of the needs and readinesses of their hearers. Nevertheless, I remember being concerned lest the dullness of this conversation diminish the level of enthusiasm.

Parts of this conversation were written on the board, and the meaningful parts were identified in the usual way.

In the next conversation, I sat down in the circle with three volunteers, and conversed with each of them in much the same way as in Brattleboro. There had been no overt invitation for me to join the group, but I felt that these three volunteers were ready for it.

Again, parts of the conversation were written on the board and analyzed quickly.

In the written comments, the only thoroughly negative point was that, on a previous day, a new person (probably a visitor) in one of the groups had aroused the competitive nature of one student in a way that that student had thoroughly disliked.

Otherwise, the written comments were quite favorable. Several people appreciated the opportunity to overhear conversations for a change, rather than having to participate in them. In this respect, my conversationally authentic repetitions of what people said in the second group were welcomed as a way of slowing the exchange down without making it seem less real. Two people said that they enjoyed hearing the language in large chunks, even when they didn't entirely understand it. Three people expressed desire to have a transcript of these conversations, either written or tape-recorded, to work with between classes. This would probably have been a good idea.

Two people reported that they found themselves recalling Swahili expressions spontaneously outside of class.

Two types of internal conflict emerge in the comments of one person who participated in neither conversation: "Today, I was caught between wanting to converse and not wanting to be under pressure to perform. Just listening to the two conversations was very helpful, though. . . . I understood most of the second conversation, though much of what you said about being in Africa I didn't understand. I didn't ask for a translation because I didn't want to interrupt and I thought I could guess."

Finally, one writer observed that, "These two conversations show that the teacher's role may shift from informant to participant, but in neither case does he take the initiative away from the student."

Eighth day.   My overall goal for today was to continue exploiting the conversational material generated on the fifth day, and to use it as the basis for further self-investing conversations. I was aware of what seemed to me an important conflict, between having conversations that grew out of and contributed to the small-group communities on the one hand, and having material that the entire class could relate to on the other. I was also concerned that the range and variety of the activities that I had been using might lead to confusion, and thence to insecurity, on the part of some students.

I therefore wrote the following outline on the board before class:

0	silence
7	cards
8	concentration
1	compose
2	complete
3	copy
4	contemplate
5	combine
6	confirm

The meanings of the words in this outline were as follows: *Compose* a new conversation, working together as a small group. *Complete* the conversation by checking it with me. Each member of the group may then *copy* it, and a little time should be set aside to *contemplate* the new text in silence. Then the group is to *combine* in new ways the material that they have at their disposal, and *confirm* the recombinations with me. Then each new word or affix is to be written on its own *card,* and an English equivalent on another card. (These were 3 by 5 cards cut in half.) Ten pairs of such cards were then turned face down and used for a game of "*concentration.*" The group was then to allow a minute's worth of silence before going on to the next cycle. I put 7 and 8 before 1 to 6 because I wanted the class to begin today with the new activity, which was the game of "concentration."

In this game, each player turns up two cards, and gives the opposite-language equivalent of each. In this he is checked and, if necessary, assisted by the rest of the group. If the two cards happen to correspond to each other, the player keeps them and takes another turn in the same way. Otherwise, he puts them back, face down, and the next person plays. The object of the game is to match and remove all the pairs of cards as quickly as possible, by remembering which of the face-down cards is which. As played in a CLL class, it is more cooperative than competitive, although both elements are present.

The obvious question is, "Why bother playing this game? Why not let the students spend the same amount of time working individually with conventional flash cards?" I can see at least three reasons: (1) The game produces social support where the cards produce social isolation with whatever anxieties that may tend to aggravate. (2) The game turns the paired-associate learning into a means toward a (simple) end that lies just beyond the language itself; flash cards focus on a purely cognitive goal, and make the paired-associate learning an end in itself. (3) In concentrating on remembering locations, the student can allow the target proficiency to develop just outside the center of his attention. In this sense, the location task is a useful "distractor."

I was not completely satisfied with the way this procedure worked, particularly in the "compose" and "combine" steps. Most simply, since all groups started at the same time with the same step, they tended to "compose" and "combine" at the same time, so that I was wanted in several places at once. If I had foreseen this, I could have dealt with it by devising alternative activities for them to engage in while they were waiting for me.

More troublesome, I found some groups to be very aggressive in eliciting new vocabulary and even structure from me during the "compose" step, while others were very cautious. I saw that this could very quickly lead to linguistic diversity and social division among the groups. Again, if I had foreseen this obvious certainty, I could have taken care of it with a few simple guidelines to limit exploration.

Most troublesome of all, I sensed that these two steps were raising the overall level of anxiety. I can see two reasons why they ought to have done so: (1) I was not providing enough guidance to keep the students' learning space clearly structured in these two steps. (2) I was asking the learners to engage in more Discrimination than they were ready for.

About 15 minutes before the end of the hour, we were visited by an East African whom I had met a few days earlier, and to whom I had issued a general invitation to "drop in any time." I let the students listen to us talk for about five minutes, and then invited them to talk with our guest themselves. Several of them did.

The game of "Concentration" received several favorable comments: "I found this to be an excellent way to help me review the words I had just learned. Whatever I didn't know or wasn't sure of, I could learn from the others in my group." "It was a respite to play Concentration. It helped me to learn words without . . . pressure. It was a group study effort."

The eight-step procedure for small-group activity, for one person, was "enjoyable, because I was able to feel relaxed—I didn't feel under pressure as I usually do when I am being observed. The people in my group created a friendly atmosphere of mutual help and encouragement." Another person, however, found that "making the dialog was a bit more difficult. It was hard to include five people in a conversation and yet keep it to a manageable size. [Nevertheless,] I found it useful for two reasons: (1) Everyone had a chance to insert something that s/he wanted to learn. (2) I felt a sense of accomplishment in seeing that I could use Swahili in a conversation."

A third person was more critical: "Although composing our own conversations allows us to explore new territories in the target language, I personally feel that I would have been gaining more if I had been using the language more in class-wide activities during this time. We were told that we would not be held responsible for whatever was developed in the small groups. But class time is so limited and so precious that I don't think it should be given to tangents in groups that divide the shared knowledge of the class. . . . This could lead to stress and anxiety—something I thought CLL was trying to avoid." I share the views of this writer. Looking back, I think it would have been better to take the "Compose" step out of the small groups, for the time being at least.

Three people expressed great pleasure at the feeling that they had been able to understand, and even to communicate with, an East African who had never seen them or heard them before. One writer went further: "The reward, in fact, continued on into my next class where I spent some time (at the expense of the lecture) making up questions I would have liked to ask the visitor. For example, in class I had asked him, 'Where are you from?' He had answered, 'Me? I'm from Tanzania,' and continued on with particulars. In my silent rehearsal in the next class, I followed this up with, 'In your country—in Tanzania—what language(s) do they speak?' and imagined an answer with several other languages as well as Swahili. This rehearsal was done with real feeling, including imagined tone of voice and gestures, and with the remembered gestures and facial expressions of the visitor. *That silently rehearsed sentence, in fact, became more real to me than any I had actually heard or used in class.* I would be able to use it, given the opportunity, more readily than any sentence I had learned in class. And I thought, '*Maybe this silent rehearsal is the biggest part of language learning.*' Classtime activities had provided the ingredients: (1) the words and patterns to work with, and (2) the motivation (from speaking with the visitor). *The payoff came in my imagination*—where I wasn't encumbered either by anxiety or by muscle lag." [Emphasis added.]

I expect to reread this last quotation many times, thoughtfully.

Ninth day.   I hoped that the eight-step routine that we had established yesterday could continue through one or two new cycles. That was therefore the procedure for today. The only innovation was to add a new game with the cards. In that game, each player had his share of the cards in his hand, and they took turns calling on each other for cards that matched the ones they had. This game seemed to me to work only moderately well.

One person felt that this was "a most enjoyable way to learn a new language. The game seems to achieve that delicate balance between familiarity and variety which leads to rapid second language acquisition." Another writer emphasized the role of the group in the games: "The reasons why I was able to learn more words in the group were (1) The steps enabled me to see all the words and their meanings more than once. (2) I was able to ask questions whenever I needed to. I had no hesitation in asking because I knew the people in the group. (3) The people in my group were the only ones who knew about my questions and my mistakes. I didn't have to worry about outsiders."

Thus the community was, for this student, a source of liberating security. The Discrimination and reinvestment activities, for which he did not yet feel ready, had the opposite effect: "I found it difficult to construct new sentences with the words we had. *There were so many things that I had to consider* in order to construct a new sentence." [Emphasis added.] The value of the group again: "But with the help of my group I was able to construct a few."

Some of the written "Teacher-Questions" at the end of last week had expressed concern that the class was being exposed to pronunciation (mine) that was nonnative. I felt that this concern was irrelevant in a course where languages were being learned purely for the study of method. Nevertheless, I felt that to say so would sound defensive on my part. I therefore assured the class, near the beginning of this session, that my pronunciation of these two languages was actually good enough so that they need not worry on this score. One of today's respondents expressed continued skepticism about learning from a nonnative. He also was skeptical about the value of learning in a schoolroom. In his own previous experience, even being taught by a native speaker had been of limited value. He felt that he had not begun to learn until he was set down in a community where the language was spoken. He did comment, however, that "the games we played in class were a good review, and a relief from the unnatural way we have been learning Swahili."

In contrast to this writer, who wanted natural language learning in an authentic setting, another student said she was relieved that the class had had an opportunity to "practice Swahili composition without introducing more new rules and patterns." She listed several things that she still wanted to get thoroughly "figured out" before going further.

One person commented that the times when I spoke Swahili rapidly to/with the class were "both challenging and frustrating."

All in all, I came away from this session with the feeling that enthusiasm was less than it had been, and that I must make some changes. Yet I felt that a *total* change would be upsetting for many.

Tenth day.   The groups began the session by continuing to work through the cycle of activities from where they had left off on the preceding day. After about 10 minutes, I brought one group to the central triangle for a CCLL conversation. As the conversation progressed, it was written on the board by two "secretaries." At the end, I went to the board and quickly completed and corrected what was there. I then allowed a minute or two for the groups to deal with questions that the members might have about the new material, and briefly answered any questions that remained. Next, I went to the back of the room and read the sentences with the three "intonations," as on the fourth day. Then I allowed time for people to make their own copies. Finally, the groups made their own cards for "Concentration," and went back to work on the regular cycle of activities that we had been following all week.

The only new element in today's session was that I allowed people to write the new sentences down for themselves. This was intended to contribute both to their language study per se, and also to their feeling of security.

There were several favorable comments: excitement about how much Swahili was being understood, both from my monologs (on earlier days) and from the conversations themselves; one person who found himself spontaneously repeating Swahili phrases in his head outside of class, with a feeling that the language was on the verge of "dropping into place" for him; a feeling that "a great deal of learning is taking place."

Nevertheless, there were also several signs of malaise. Some seemed very specific: the difficulty that one group was having because it had had to take in a newcomer as a seventh member; and the difficulty of doing group work in a noisy room. Others were more general, and caused me more concern. Although one person found that "oral composition within the group is very effective and interesting," a time of mutual help and real learning, another felt that the group work was relatively inefficient—that it turned Swahili into a game played in English, which actually separated the students from the language.

A second person reported that, although I myself remained "very supportive and nonjudgmental," her attempts to compose new sentences left her feeling "frustrated and stupid." This indicated to me that, for this student and possibly for others, I had rushed too quickly to activities that required "Discrimination" among the various words and prefixes that they had been exposed to.

Even the "Concentration" game was the occasion for a partially negative comment: "I found the game very helpful with new or unfamiliar words. When we used cards with old, familiar words, however, it was just a game of spatial memorization. The people who were good at remembering the arrangement of the cards tended to do a lot better than the others. Those who did poorly could very easily become discouraged. Nevertheless, the game really helped me. Even the spirit of competition had a good effect on my motivation and ability to remember, as nasty as that may sound to some people."

My own overall impression, based on oral and written reactions, was that though spirits were not low, they were certainly leveling off.

Eleventh day.   Before the students arrived, I wrote on the board a note instructing them to resume work in their groups, and to call on me when they needed me. After they had worked in this way for a while, I brought a group to the center of the room for a conversation. As on earlier days, student "secretaries" wrote on the board a rough draft of the conversation. I corrected it and helped the class to identify the meaningful elements. Then I read each sentence with the three "intonations." Since this was the last day of the week, the last half hour was given over to questions which the students had from their point of view as language teachers. The session closed with silence.

One person said that she wished there could be regular opportunities to copy the sentences down. Other than this comment, most of the written and many of the oral reactions bore in one way or another on interpersonal issues.

One person remarked that she liked the directions on the board, because "that takes the focus off you as the teacher, and leaves the responsibility with the students to make their group work successful." At the same time, however, she indicated that her own group had not yet resolved some matters of mechanics, and some that related to attitudes. Another person, from a different group, implied a similar feeling on his part when he suggested that the membership of the groups should have been rotated from time to time so that "we might have more chance to encounter the possible difficulties and frictions, as well as rewards." Another person found the correction by fellow members of the group to be frustrating [even though from my own point of view as teacher it was highly satisfactory]. The same person who had said she liked my note on the board also said later in her report that she would have liked more of a reaction from me when I visited her group: "This week when you came to our group, you simply gave the information asked for, without any comment or reaction. I'm not sure [how much the teacher should react]. A lot depends on the situation. Sometimes, I'd like more of a reaction than you give, at least during group work. On the other hand, during the conversation it's more comfortable not to see your reaction. I need different kinds of support at different times."

All of the above quoted reactions point fairly openly to unresolved issues of who to depend on—an essential element in security.

This general incipient malaise may have been one source of one person's comment that the recombining and reworking of material in the groups was for him the least effective of all the CLL procedures he had met. Somewhat in the same vein, two people expressed a readiness to get back to more conversation.

Although I at no time set out to provide the students with deliberate frustrations or to make them uncomfortable, I think I would have done them a disservice if I had shuffled the groups every few days. For one thing, to have done so might have created its own new insecurities. More important, *in a course for training teachers*, it might have blurred some of the very issues which came to the surface today. It might have prevented one person from concluding: "I've learned a lot this week about being a whole person in the classroom. There's a lot of group work in the classes I teach. I've been thinking about my awareness of myself and of what's happening with the people in the class. My own experiences as a student and as a member of a group are very helpful and useful."

One person wondered whether I had been surprised at some of the negative comments at the end of class today, and asked what would have happened if no one had spoken up. This is for me the distinctive value of the intermittent "counseling" segments in Counseling-Learning. Equally severe stresses and strains are almost inevitable *in a class taught by any method,* but unless they reach an explosive level, they are usually kept submerged, exerting an unrealized, pervasive, and destructive influence on learning. Today's negative reactions were, from this point of view, an indication that I had established with the class the kind of relationship that I had hoped for.

Twelfth day. This last day of language learning was spent entirely in conversations by one group after another, with help from student "secretaries," and with completion, correction, and parsing by me. We moved rapidly enough so that almost all of the groups had a chance to come to the center triangle and converse. The only unusual feature was that when someone asked a question about why a word that was the same in English could begin with a number of different consonants in Swahili, I gave a very short exposition (between 1 and 2 minutes) which showed the principle of "concord" as it is used in Swahili (and other Bantu languages). I was careful not to include enough material to make the students feel "responsible for" concord—just enough to prevent unsatisfied curiosity from turning into anxiety.

Today's reactions were strikingly different from last week's. Words such as "gratifying," "successful," "welcome," and "pleasant change" were used. One person did remark that, "The game of Concentration is a useful and interesting way to review vocabulary, but to my way of thinking, it does not give the kind of individual experience and therefore satisfaction that [this] does."

RETROSPECT

Looking back on these twelve days of CLL in Honolulu, I am generally quite satisfied. To judge from the anonymous evaluations written after the course had ended, the students felt the same way. Nevertheless, this experience suggests several things that I might do if I were ever to teach a similar class under similar circumstances.

There are some things that I would not change. Three of them were innovations. The one that the students were most aware of was the short period of silence at the end of the sessions. I would also use brief formulaic sentences to introduce and to close this period, as I did in Honolulu. (This I learned from Lozanov.)

I would also lead the class gradually into the group conversation routine, instead of plunging immediately into the full procedure. That is, I would not write anything down after the first conversation, but would only understand and reflect the reactions of the students. After the second conversation I would write a few short sentences on the board and quickly identify the meaningful parts. Only with the third or fourth conversation would I use the tape recorder. I also think that I would write the first few conversations in chalk, to be erased. Later, I would switch to felt pen and paper. The trick, I think, is to steer between letting the students feel more responsibility than they are ready to handle, and leaving them frustrated at not being able to refer back to material that is within their range.

Third, I think I might again minimize the use of the tape recorder in a class of this size, even if a suitable one was available. The mechanics of recording, plus the mechanics of playing back, create a drag both on the time and on the emotions of all concerned, or so it seemed to me. It also seemed to me that the effect of this drag increased with the size of the group, and with the awkwardness of the physical arrangement of the classroom.

There are, however, at least six ways in which I would do otherwise than what I did in Honolulu.

My largest-scale error, I think, was in the emphasis on having the students produce new sentences by recombination of elements from old ones. They were not ready for this linguistically, because there are many mechanical details to control when one tampers with a sentence in Swahili. In terms of the SAARRD formula, I was rushing them to D without sufficient RR. They were thus unprepared not only linguistically, but also emotionally, in terms of their general security with the language and with the method. The language mistakes that resulted from their attempts further diminished their security.

Next time, I would have more confidence in the ability of the rest of the class to identify with the group that is originating a conversation, and to profit from what that group is doing. The small-group activities for processing one conversation before going on to another would be briefer, and would concentrate on Reflection and Retention, with minimum demands for Discrimination in these early hours.

I would also be more ready to allow the making of individual written notes at some clearly designated time in the schedule. These qualify, after all, as Reflection and Retention devices par excellence; they also relieve the anxiety of many people, provide visual input when needed, and involve the writing muscles, which is an important aid to memory for some learners.

A more localized but equally serious error, I think, was to have concentrated so much conversation on the fifth day, and then to have spent most of the time on the days that followed in small-group work. There were obvious cognitive difficulties that followed from this decision. Even more serious, I suspect, this arrangement prevented the learner-clients from regular and frequent contact with me *in my role of knower-counselor.* This was probably detrimental to security.

If we had generated a small amount of new material per day, using one group per day in the central, active role with the others participating vicariously during those five or ten minutes, and if the students had had access to written records of that work, they might have assimilated more between classes, either through memorization or in other ways. The opportunity to do this certainly would have contributed to the security of some students. On the other hand, it would have opened a new arena of competition, and so might have had the opposite effect for some other students.

I would like to try using the "three-intonation" reading of the new material at the very end of the session, just before the final silence. I think it might be more productive in that setting. In addition, doing so would enhance the "ritual placebo" effect.

Finally, I would be less willing to accept a classroom without tables and fully movable chairs.

CHAPTER 15

COMMUNITY LANGUAGE LEARNING IN TWO VERY DIFFERENT SETTINGS

In the course of the past six years, a number of other teachers have sent me accounts of their experiences with Counseling-Learning in foreign language classes. This chapter consists of two such accounts which contrast with each other and also with my narratives (Chapters 12-14) in age of student, institutional setting, and target language.

Stroinigg's article is all the more convincing to me because three months after the end of the program that he describes, I had an opportunity to talk with two of the people who had been in it. (They did not know of my own connection with Counseling-Learning.) Their enthusiasm about the experience was still high, and they were obviously well-satisfied with what they had learned.

Bedell's account has been particularly instructive to me because of the great care and apparent candor with which the writer has recorded her experience.

COUNSELING-LEARNING
A practical application in foreign language learning
by *Dieter Stroinigg*, Miami University, Oxford, Ohio

In this article I would like to stimulate interest in a relatively new and little known method of language teaching called Counseling-Learning, a program which promises to do justice to the psychological and emotional needs of students at a time when they no longer can be disregarded. In the past, the traditional approach has generally underestimated this aspect of learning. Various means of dealing with it have included the adjustment of technique in an attempt to entertain or inspire, the introduction of cultural material and the use of visual aids. All too often the goal becomes simply trying to cope. The Counseling-Learning method takes the opposite tack, relying on the untapped resources within the student, including the innate desire of each to learn, as positive factors. This approach frees the desire to learn and vitalizes it by removing the psychological blocks inherent in the authoritarian nature of the normal classroom situation.

For a year now I have been experimenting with this "Whole-Person Model for Education," developed by Curran, applying it to first- and second-year German courses at the university level, and in particular to the special requirements of the six-week Intensive Summer Language Program for first and second year offered at Miami University's branch campus in Luxembourg. On the basis of this experience, I would like to highlight in this paper the general principles, method and success of the Introductory Intensive German Course.

The first class period began with an informal meeting where everyone introduced himself and I stated the general goals and guidelines of the Counseling-Learning approach, after which we casually began a tape-recording session, which the students only later recognized as the basic technique of each class. We formed a circle with a tape recorder in the center and the microphone easily accessible to the participants. Each was encouraged to begin a conversation in German with anyone in the group. He first spoke in English, while the instructor standing behind him as his counselor whispered a close equivalent of the utterance in his ear. The student then repeated the sentences in German, speaking into the tape recorder, so that his words would remain for later inspection. The students soon realized that they should abbreviate their sentences in order to remember the strange combinations of sounds long enough to repeat them into the microphone. After each had the opportunity to record a few of his "German" sentences, the recorder was stopped, rewound, and replayed at intervals. Each student was asked to refresh the memory of the others and repeat in English what he heard himself say in German. Some could not remember their sentences, but there was always someone else in the group who did and was able to give the English equivalent, so that no sentence went unremembered and unrepeated. In this basic model, which I had the opportunity to observe at a workshop on Community Language Learning at Ann Arbor in May, 1975, I felt that the role of the instructor at the beginning is simply to repeat the original sentence if requested by the student. Practical experience with this method showed me how well this method lends itself to building *confidence* rather than inhibition during the students' first encounters with a new language and, indeed, throughout the program.

A *reflection* period immediately follows each recording session. When students are asked to express their feelings regarding their experience with total frankness, the overwhelming response is surprise, pleasure and a sense of accomplishment for having remembered so much in the short period of time and actually having spoken German. A grammar lesson of a different breed concludes the period. From the material just recorded, the instructor writes sentences on the board in order to familiarize the students with the proper spelling and the capitalization peculiarities of German. In my experience, the students notice the capitalized nouns and are curious about them without prompting on my part. If students feel the need to know about these or any other points, they are encouraged to ask about them. Since the sentences are their own creations, they feel a personal involvement and a closer affinity for them than for something contrived by the instructor or the author of a textbook. It is impossible to cover all of the recorded sentences in the time available, so I naturally choose those sentences containing particular ideas or grammar which demonstrate potential for the students' investigation. In effect, the students are "set up" to ask specific content or grammar questions. If they respond to the stimuli and question aspects of the given material, their questions are to be answered; if they do not, I assume that they are not ready to progress to something new.

The results in the Luxembourg program soon become apparent. Some of the students clearly advanced more quickly than others. The group relationship provided that the faster students could advance on a nearly individualized basis, yet without making the slower students ill-at-ease or resentful of their slower progress. Members of the group helped each other when there was a need for encouragement, clarification or information, leaving the teacher free to observe the learning process without having to direct or even seek out reinforcement activities. To a considerable extent, the group provided this by itself and for itself.

Using this method I discovered that the need for a published textbook played a secondary role, since the group in effect wrote its own. The students were encouraged to copy sentences written on the board into their notebooks, in order to have a record of the material and grammatical points brought out by the group members. Their notes could be used later to refresh memories and fulfill the need for more information.

Since each student had a hand in writing his notes, he was more familiar with all the material. He could refer to them with ease. I discovered that most of the students carried these "textbooks" wherever they went so that they could refer to them as soon as a question arose. Published material which proved helpful included a reference grammar and a pocket dictionary containing basic information on the principal parts of strong German verbs, plural forms of nouns, etc.

One of the students approached me at the end of the first week to boast that he had already learned 800 words in that short span of time. I must admit that even I was surprised at this number. This student's experience illustrates the fact that he was not being stifled, but was encouraged to develop his potential as rapidly as he was able.

A primary characteristic of the Counseling-Learning approach is the feeling of trust among members of the group, resulting in a mutual and open exchange of ideas. Its origin is the self-identification and self-realization which the student develops when he is in a stable and productive relationship with others. He no longer needs to learn on a *competitive* basis, but wants to satisfy curiosity by exploring the language and culture in question.

Of necessity, the role of the teacher is modified. He is no longer the prescription-giver who proclaims, "You should study chapters 1 and 2. This sound is pronounced differently in German, John; why don't you repeat it for Mary. This is a good review, and remember, you will have a quiz on these chapters at the end of the week." Instead, the instructor is a resource person who provides necessary information; he functions as a counselor. In practical terms, it is the student who, in his desire to learn what is meaningful or necessary for himself, determines his own needs and thereby the pace and presentation of subject matter. For instance, it would not be unusual for questions about the tenses in German to arise even in the first class session. But such questions might also not occur until the end of the first, second, or even third week. The subjunctive mood, traditionally taught at the end of the first year, was discussed in this group at the end of the first week, because the students felt they should know about it. When some of the students would not accept "Was möchten Sie zum Frühstück?" as a mere idiom, it was time to discuss the use of the subjunctive. I did not try to console the students, as one traditionally does, with the statement: "That is a very interesting question. 'Möchten' is a subjunctive form; however, that is too advanced for you at this point. Would you please hold off with this question until we reach it in our textbook?"

Student-directed learning implies that the teacher must be prepared at any moment to explain any given point. A well-organized planning book or the practice of keeping one lesson ahead of the students are neither desirable nor possible with this method. In the learning process, the student holds most of the initiative in his hands. A reversal of the conventional teacher-student role has taken place. The students actually prescribe the lesson plan and raise questions for which they seek answers; the teacher is obligated to fulfill the student's needs. Learning becomes a group effort with a minimum of competition and "allows each student to grow in self-worth and self-understanding and in appreciation of himself and others as he increases in knowledge." (Curran, Intr., p. 2)

During the course of the program, the first phase was to teach the students *how* to learn with this method, and then *what* to learn, according to their own choice and interests.

My experience in the Luxembourg course as well as in regular campus courses has convinced me that the method displays great flexibility and effectiveness in language classes of widely differing size. If the class is fairly large, it is best to divide it into small groups of five or six, the optimum size. The counselor's function is then filled by the more advanced students, one in each group. The instructor becomes the resource person and responds directly to the counselors' questions. A very sound and effective application of the Counseling-Learning method, this distribution of responsibility is a further means of diminishing inhibitions. Its success was apparent in my students' active participation and enthusiasm. The gratifying results of the program as a whole demonstrate that the students' technical knowledge of the language after six weeks was on a par with that of students completing a regular first-year university program. In addition, they had developed a feeling of satisfaction and self-reliance and discovered their own capacity to relate their thoughts and emotions to the German language. The students were elevated from the all too common level of "thinking machine," when they were encouraged to involve their whole persons in this decidedly humanistic approach to learning.

COMMUNITY LANGUAGE LEARNING IN THE CLASSROOM—
Evolution of a teaching approach
by *Betsy Bedell*

From February 25 to March 25, 1977, a group of six foreign language instructors (candidates for the MAT degree at the School for International Training) were hired to teach in the annual Immersion Program at the Miami Valley School, a private school in Dayton, Ohio. The students involved were seventh and eighth graders who had elected to study either French or Spanish. Within each language group, the students were divided into three subgroups: the A group, all beginning seventh graders; the B group, consisting of high-aptitude (beginning) seventh graders and eighth graders who had studied the same language in the previous Immersion Program; and the C group, composed of the more advanced eighth graders.

The Immersion Program was an intensive program involving approximately four and a half hours of language instruction per day, five days a week. In addition to a forty-five-minute lunch period, the remaining two hours of the school day included a sixty-minute gym period and a fifteen-minute café break during which the students were encouraged to use the target language. The four-week period was structured so the groups would rotate among teachers after the first two weeks and again after the third week, providing exposure of each group to each teacher, and vice versa. A language coordinator from the school handled administrative details for the six teachers, served as their liaison with the administration, met with them daily as a group after school, and visited classes daily to observe and make suggestions.

This report of my experience as a Spanish teacher in the Immersion Program focuses on some of the more salient aspects of the experience and on the conclusions I drew from it.

My first class was the B group. It did not take long to spot potential problem areas: among them, the students' disparate experience with Spanish, and the fact that this was a notoriously disruptive group. In addition, I was expected by the administration to cover a very specific list of grammar points and culturally related material. This particular combination of factors, coupled with my inexperience with students of this age level, resulted in my decision to approach the task in a basically authoritarian manner. That is, I was the one who determined what material was to be covered and assumed the responsibility for its presentation. My approach to discipline became increasingly firm during the two weeks I spent with this group.

Since each day began with a grammatically based drill, my approach with the B group could perhaps best be described as a variation of the audio-lingual method. Each day's lesson was built on the work of the preceding day(s), with cultural and grammatical material closely related. The emphasis was on developing a Hispanic identity for each of the students in the group. Hence, the first day, the students were assigned Spanish names; the second day, addresses; the third day, professions; and so on. Grammatically, they were working on variations of "¿Cómo te llamas?" on the first day; "¿Dónde vives?" on the second day; "¿Quién eres?" on the third day, and so forth. The answers to these questions were cued by small yellow cards that were passed out to each student at the beginning of class. Homework questions and other exercises were personalized by further use of the same information. Apparently the students did accept these new identities as their own; at one point, when it was facetiously suggested that they switch names, they were quick to protest.

The most successful experience with this class began the second day when a unit on street names was introduced. Students were divided into two groups and asked to design maps of their own based on a previous examination of Mexican and Spanish maps and a discussion of their distinguishing features. Their maps showed a lot of detail, and the students expressed an interest in continuing the project over several days' time. While they were involved in this particular project, they worked attentively and cooperatively. I developed a variety of ways to work with the maps; so during the course of the project the students increased their vocabulary, learned how to give directions in Spanish, and explored an area of cultural differences as well. Furthermore, the map work reinforced the grammatical material the students were working with.

Throughout the first two weeks, however, I was aware that not all the students were assimilating the material adequately. Although some caught on rapidly, others were struggling to keep up, while still others evidenced a complete lack of interest. It appeared that the dynamics of the group were closely related to this variety of learning rates. Those who learned quickly seemed to tire of the classroom activities; those who were having difficulty (or thought they were) were often not persistent in their efforts; and those who were most disinterested or uninvolved generally required more individual attention than I was able to provide. As a result, these factors were manifested behaviorally in the classroom.

From the outset I had hoped to establish a sense of community among the students. It appeared, though, that such an aspiration was too idealistic with this particular group, perhaps as a result of the method employed. For most activities, the students did not interact cooperatively in smaller groups or pairs (total class size was eight). They expended a lot of energy breaking pencils, shooting orthodontic rubber bands, taunting each other, and otherwise expressing their disinterest in the class. Attempts to have the students work together often did not alleviate the situation but had the opposite effect instead, especially with certain combinations of students. However, it was not always possible to predict such results. The second week, two students were gained and one lost, further affecting the dynamics of the group.

At one point during the first week I resorted to sending one of the students to the office in response to his test of my authority. This action did have an effect: since a trip to the office meant an hour's worth of work on the campus (picking up litter, for instance), the students did settle down somewhat. However, in opting for this type of disciplinary action, I had set myself up for a power struggle with the students. Much of the time spent with this group therefore involved an exhausting attempt to cover material while keeping the students "under control."

On my last day with this particular class, I asked the students for their evaluation of the class. During this open discussion I "reflected" the students' comments and took notes. Some of the more salient remarks were that I had tried to cover too much material, that there had been too much work, that more time should have been spent on verbs, and that I had used too much spoken Spanish. In regard to the first three comments, I recognized that the problem was more likely inadequate exploitation of the material. Comparatively speaking, I had felt that I was actually covering less than the other teachers. Yet I was frustrated at not "getting through" to the students. Basically I was responding to the objectives of the program and not as much to the needs of the students. I also realized that my use of Spanish was not effective in clarifying grammar points, whether it was used to explain or to give simple examples. A short explanatory response in English would probably have answered the students' questions much more rapidly and efficiently in a number of instances.

Because the first two weeks in Immersion had been so exhausting and frustrating for me, I resolved to change my approach completely with the advanced C group. These students had just been involved in a very challenging learning situation, were a stimulated and eager group, and demonstrated a strong sense of community. During my transition between groups, I had reevaluated my own goals and decided it would be much more effective to give the students an active hand in their study of Spanish. Therefore, in closer accord with my own feelings about teaching and as a result of my experience with the B group, I chose to focus my attention more closely on the structuring of class activities while giving the students more responsibility for the content. The most logical way to approach this aim seemed to be through Community Language Learning.

After talking briefly with the group to establish my expectations of them and to discuss their expectations of me, I asked the students to tape-record a conversation and explained how this would be done in accordance with the CLL model. The first tape consisted primarily of Spanish expressions that the students already knew and of other very basic words or statements that contained little analyzable grammar. However, one item of significance arose from the making of this tape: the fact that one of the students did not know the days of the week. Since there were seven students in the class who as yet had not been given Spanish names for that week, I suggested that each select a day of the week as a name. This idea met with great enthusiasm until two students decided to be "Jueves." In order to resolve the conflict, I suggested taking the matter "to court" in Spanish. Thus an entire court scene, including appeals, was enacted and recorded. I encouraged the students to use me as a resource when they needed help with vocabulary. The tape was then treated like a usual CLL tape, written up and analyzed for grammatical elements and vocabulary. For homework, I asked the students to summarize the day's events using past tense, which they had begun to study the week before. The next day they shared their summaries, using their new vocabulary to ask and answer questions about their court scene.

Late in the morning a new tape was made, this time following a different format. I asked the group to make up a chain story, each student contributing one sentence and following in order around the circle. Again we used the CLL model, and I provided correct Spanish when necessary. This activity, being more structured than the original two recordings, appeared to foster a greater sense of security among the students. No attempt was made to limit the content of the story. The result was a tale about rocket ships and little green men, but the content, being a product of the students' imaginations, was much more vital to them. Again, we followed the same procedure of writing up and analyzing the tape.

The idea of producing a group story rather than taping a conversation resulted from my observation that the social maturity of the students was perhaps not at a level that would ordinarily permit free discussion. There was a divisive element in operation between the boys and the girls which seemed to inhibit their talking freely together. However, within the structure provided, they functioned together cooperatively and imaginatively, and appeared to enjoy the recording process.

By Wednesday the students were working with some of the distinctions between past and imperfect tenses. However, after their break they expressed their confusion and frustration with my approach. In part they felt estranged from their first teacher, with whom they had established good rapport. But on the other hand, they were making some very valid and articulate criticisms of my way of dealing with the material. During the first few comments, I felt a need to explain myself but quickly realized that the situation could be handled much more effectively by reflecting back to the students what I heard them saying. This change in attitude produced a feeling of security among the students and a willingness to continue expressing their feelings. In fact, they continued to "feed back" for about forty-five minutes, until it was time for their gym period. (The coordinator, who had come into the room during this discussion, later expressed her surprise and pleasure at how openly the students had talked.)

As a result of the students' feedback, I structured the rest of the day's activities in a way that would make the learning situation more immediate to the students' needs. When they returned from gym, I allowed time for reflection by reading their story aloud sentence by sentence, slowly and with a variety of intonations. This exercise enabled the students to focus back in on the story and helped to solidify it in their minds. Then, distributing a set of

cuisenaire rods among the students, I asked them to use the rods to reconstruct and talk about the story. Thus the students had something very
tangible to work with while speaking Spanish; in fact, their story became
much more vivid through the use of the rods. At this point the coordinator
happened back into the classroom, providing a perfect audience for a
recounting of the tale. Further work with grammar points continued in the
afternoon, and a short feedback session at the end of the day indicated that
the students had benefited from the shift in emphasis and felt good about
their learning experience of the day.

The next day I selected a different sort of exercise for the class. Knowing
the capability of the C group, I wanted to expose them to some Latin American literature. To begin, I presented a dictation exercise, a slightly modified
paragraph taken from Gabriel García-Márquez' *El Coronel no tiene quien le
escriba*. I chose this particular passage because the verbs were all in past
tense, which the group had been studying; there were a large number of
cognates; and the subject matter was very simple. Thus the content of the
paragraph was not intended to threaten but to reinforce what the students
already knew and were familiar with. Then I asked the students to work in
groups to perfect their versions of the paragraph and upon completion to
compare their work with the correct form which I had written on the board in
the meantime. After they worked among themselves to clarify any questions
they might have had about the passage (content, vocabulary, grammar, etc.),
one person from each group underlined on the board the parts of the paragraph they were still unsure about. I then responded to these remaining
questions with very brief explanations. Often only a translation of a word was
required. The students then used the elements of this paragraph as a basis
for a new tape-recorded story. Activities similar to those employed earlier in
the week were used for working with the new story.

By the end of the week, this group had demonstrated improved
competence in their use and understanding of the Spanish language. Their
performance, from my point of view, had in fact been excellent, and there
had been a minimum of behavioral problems in the class.

Having witnessed some really positive results from the CLL-based
approach employed with the C group, I decided to work with the A group in
much the same way, modifying and revising what had been done in the C
group. We spent the first thirty minutes on Monday morning outlining the
procedure and generally helping the students to feel at ease in their "new"
environment. Then the students taped a chain story and worked with it in
much the same way the preceding group had done, using rods and asking
each other questions about the story. Then I asked the students to divide into
small groups to practice specific grammatical constructions extracted from
the story, after having developed an understanding of their meaning and use
in the large group. Each group was given six index cards on which to write
sentences using the expressions, and I circulated among the students, offer-

ing help when needed. The students then shared their sentences with the rest of the group. Even though the students had been dealing with a specific subject matter throughout the day, their feedback at day's end indicated that they had maintained their interest in the work and felt good about their use of several language skills, as well as about what they had accomplished that day.

Tuesday, using the same story, I introduced the past tense, but rather than engaging in an involved grammatical explanation, I simply posed the question "¿Qué hicieron los niños?" in contrast to the present "¿Qué hacen los niños?" and let the students work to understand the distinction. In fact the group caught on very quickly; I encouraged those who were first to grasp the distinction to share their understanding with the others. Thus the students relied on and learned from each other in dealing with a controlled stimulus that I had presented. To reinforce this introduction of past tense (third person plural), I asked the students to break into groups and write on index cards three questions and answers using "¿Qué hicieron. . . . ?" They then asked these questions of the other groups. Later in the morning, after gym, we followed the same procedure with "¿Qué hizo?" to distinguish between singular and plural forms. At the end of the day the students expressed satisfaction with the amount they had learned; they felt successful and their enthusiasm was high.

My rationale for this particular handling of past tense was this: First, the students had shown their readiness for it. They were doing well with what they had already covered, and several past tense verbs had appeared in their story. Rather than give them too much to handle at once, I felt it would be better to deal with one inflection at a time. That way, the students would work to master one discrete element before going on to another. For the most part, I remained silent during this exercise so as not to interfere with the learning process. Thus the students were allowed more freedom and more responsibility for their learning. Their response was very positive. They accepted the challenge and felt rewarded for having done so.

The next day's work focused primarily on further practice of the past tense through the use of different types of question-and-answer forms. Again these activities involved small-group work with index cards. The remainder of the week was devoted to review, preparation for the all-school fiesta, and testing.

Homework assignments for the entire week were kept simple and served as a review of the day's activities. Generally the assignment was to write six questions and answers using a particular grammatical construction. These were used to initiate the next day's work after being checked quickly at the beginning of class.

About the middle of the last week it became clear to me that certain administrative expectations were in conflict with the CLL-based approach. These related both to content and to the fact that the students were to be given a comprehensive examination at the end of the week. Here, even though I felt comfortable with the work I was doing and with the progress of the students, the coordinator's personal doubts surfaced. Her questions focused on specific grammatical objectives (e.g., "What if the students don't learn how to use "gustar'?") and on how the students were being prepared for the final examination. Not only was it the end of the week, but it was the end of the program, and these questions inspired a serious reassessment of Immersion on my part. My feeling was that language learning as a cumulative process was reflected as such in whatever work the students did. Furthermore, by choosing to follow the CLL model, I had already acknowledged that from the teacher's point of view content was secondary to other factors. My interest was in the students' learning, in their working together as a group, in their increasing ability to use Spanish, and in their feeling secure and satisfied with their own efforts. In addition, I believed that if the students could be helped to feel a certain degree of success with their study of Spanish, this attitude might persist and their interest in Spanish might continue to grow.

Despite the coordinator's hesitations about the CLL-based approach, I felt that CLL had been much more effective in accomplishing not only my own goals but also those of the Immersion Program. I noted at the end of the third week that group C had actually covered more vocabulary within the CLL format than might otherwise have been expected. In fact, many of the vocabulary items that came up were not words a teacher would make a conscious effort to introduce and yet they were words the students needed or wanted to know. In addition, the students covered a variety of grammar points that would not normally have been introduced until much later.

Although with the first group preparation had been thorough and lessons well organized (this belief substantiated by the coordinator's observations), I had not been satisfied with the students' progress, nor apparently had the students. The most effective work with them, as with the other groups, was that which had required them to exercise their own creativity and assume responsibility for their own learning. On the other hand, when I exercised my "authority" with them, the results were much less desirable, both academically and behaviorally.

It was also evident that when the students were dealing with their own content they were much more invested and interested in the learning process. Thus they were more willing to continue working with the same subject matter over a period of two or sometimes three days. In such cases it was my responsibility to structure classroom activities around this content so as to tap and sustain the students' interest. This goal was most adequately met when we dealt with the grammar in very small units. In addition, the use of the rods provided a further means of investment in the material which I found to be particularly complementary to grammatical and cultural material.

The selection of activities which stimulated the students' interest while requiring that they work cooperatively together also had another significant effect. That is, as long as the students were working together on something that held their interest, behavior problems in the classroom were kept in check. In fact, the A group observed that they felt good about helping each other learn. Even with group B, the group which had gained notoriety for their disruptive tendencies, certain activities absorbed them thoroughly enough that they made few attempts to distract each other or me.

In general, students in the last two groups were much more attentive. A variety of factors might account for this fact, even though it is probably not possible to identify a specific reason for it. First of all, the composition of the groups was different; thus the dynamics were different in each group. Second, the previous teacher(s) may have had an effect on the dynamics of the last two groups in that a working relationship was already established among the students. Third, a different approach was taken with the last two groups as opposed to the first. Since Community Language Learning is based on the idea that security in the classroom is the first need which must be attended to, the result is a noncompetitive atmosphere in which the students feel comfortable working together. Given such an environment, it is not surprising that the C and A groups did not manifest the same needs for attention or otherwise disrupt the class as had the B group.

One of the significant contributors to such behavioral and attitudinal differences seems to have been the use of feedback sessions in the classroom. Such discussions proved to be a very effective tool not only for establishing an atmosphere of acceptance but also for informing me of ways to work more effectively with the group. The importance of reflecting the students' comments during feedback was readily apparent: this indicated to them that I was listening and was interested in what they had to say. It also added an element of order to the feedback sessions. Furthermore, in acting on the students' suggestions where appropriate, I was able to reinforce their sense of contributing to the class.

I did find it essential to listen to the students' comments with a critical ear. Since they were not sophisticated language learners and often not very articulate, it was important to interpret their remarks and understand the basis for them; hence my close assessment of the situation when the B group said too much material had been covered. I evaluated this to mean that the material which had been presented had simply not been exploited fully enough. It was also important to ensure that the students were not trying to gain favor through their more positive comments. Thus, when the students in the A group said, "You're just right for us," I felt it was necessary to reflect this statement back to them as impartially as possible.

It is also possible that my attitude affected the performance and behavior of the various groups. As I became more confident in relation to students of this age level, I relaxed in certain respects while also becoming more attentive to the students themselves. I found that it was essential to discuss with each group our mutual expectations. In order to do this, it was necessary to have my own goals clearly defined. As I clarified my own approach and expectations, I found each successive group easier to relate to. Certain external factors, such as living situation and health, also affected my work and relationship with the students. When these elements improved at the end of the first two weeks, a corresponding change in outlook resulted.

Although there had been a few differences of opinion between the coordinator and me as to teaching philosophy and method, these were generally minimal. I was fortunate to have a free if not always supportive atmosphere in which to work. Thus it was possible to explore a variety of techniques and approaches to language teaching.

Through these explorations, both individually and with other teachers in the group, I came to the following conclusions as a result of the teaching experience. First, it is necessary to accept the creativity of students as a positive factor to be utilized as much as possible in the classroom. Second, by allowing students to work with content of their own choosing, the teacher can attend more closely to sequencing of material and structuring of the class, while assuring a higher interest level on the part of the students. Third, by listening to what the students have to say through structured feedback sessions, the teacher can establish an atmosphere of security and acceptance in the classroom while also better evaluating his/her effectiveness. Fourth, an open, cooperative atmosphere created as a result of the teacher's sensitivity to the students can help to minimize behavior problems. And fifth, Community Language Learning is an approach that may best satisfy all the above conditions.

CHAPTER 16

MATERIALS FOR THE WHOLE LEARNER

In June of 1975, I read a paper to a group of ESOL teachers on the topic "Materials for the Whole Learner." In what I said, I was trying to apply Counseling-Learning principles primarily to published textbooks rather than to the materials that teachers put together for their own classes day by day. Looking back on that paper after four years, I find that I would still treat textbook writing in much the same way. Since 1975, however, I have also come across an increasing number of published lessons which do meet the criteria that I listed then. I will describe some of those books in a postscript to this chapter.

In some years of asking what the "whole learner" is like, I have come across at least four thinkers who have explored the same question. Each has his own system of thought and practice, and each has helped me greatly both in thought and in classroom practice. I have not yet been able to integrate in my own mind what I have gleaned from these sources. I shall therefore have to be content to list and juxtapose some of their principal concepts.

First for me, chronologically, was the fact that learning is something that the learner does, and that he does it best when the teacher does not stand over him, breathe down his neck, jiggle his elbow, and chatter into his ear. The second fact is that the so-called physical, emotional, and cognitive aspects of the learner cannot in practice be isolated from one another: what is going on in one of these areas inexorably affects what is possible in the other areas. In the same way, and this is the third point, the people in the classroom are not separable from one another: they inevitably make up a more or less successful community. Fourth, the needs of the whole learner go beyond the need for achievement and approval, which are central in the minds of most writers of textbooks. They also include needs for security, predictability, group membership, and the feeling that what one is doing makes sense in terms of an overall and deeply satisfying life pattern. Human beings fulfill these needs principally by the ways in which they interact with one another. People are conscious of some of the ways in which they affect other people and in which other people affect them, but many of the most powerful ways in which we affect each other lie outside of the focus of our conscious awareness.

But what has this to do with the design of relatively permanent, publishable materials for foreign language courses? Let's take a look at the traditional—and almost universal—relationships among textbook writer, teacher and student. In describing these relationships, I would like to use a pair of terms that may need some explaining. The first of these terms is "investment." "Investment," as I shall be using the word, means making a choice that leaves one committed irrevocably; it therefore includes the taking of a certain amount of risk. Clearly, there are all kinds and all degrees of risk. Accordingly, the quality and quantity of "investment" may vary from negligible to complete. Clearly also, "investment" with its associated risks can involve any and many of the levels at which we experience need, and at which we are therefore vulnerable to loss and anxiety.

The second term is "yield." This refers to one person's response to another person's "investment." The quality of the "yield" that one gets in return for a particular act of "investment" has a powerful effect on one's readiness to "invest" further. "Investment" and "yield" thus are two parts of a single pattern of rhythmic alternation whenever and wherever two people interact. Teacher and language students, or the writer and the users of a textbook, are no exceptions.

In the traditional relationship, dominated by textbook and teacher, the writer "invests" by making choices of what and how to write, with the risk that the teacher may not adopt the book, or that students may not learn from it, or both. The teacher in this relationship invests by making choices of what she tells the student to try to do; the teacher's risk is that the student will not perform in a way that will bring to the teacher a sense of achievement, or prestige among her colleagues. The student invests by choosing among alternative ways of trying to do what the teacher has told him to try to do. The usual risk for the student is a low grade, possibly accompanied by the displeasure of the teacher and the disdain of his classmates. In this model, the teacher holds power over the students, and to a large extent over the textbook writer as well. As long as teachers can influence the selection of the materials they work with, they will continue to have this power over the writer. They will force the writer to collaborate with them to maintain their chosen power relationship with the student. What the writer can do for the teacher depends on what the teacher intends to do with the students.

But the student is not entirely without power over the teacher in this relationship. If the teacher has a personal need to have successful students, then each student can reward or punish the teacher by doing well or poorly. And in schools where enrollment is voluntary, the student favors one course by signing up for it and dooms another by avoiding it.

The title of this paper is "Materials for the Whole Learner," yet in this traditional model of foreign language instruction, we never see the whole learner at work. Or, to say the same thing in another way, the whole learner is present in every one of his acts, but in the traditional model the parts of the learner's mind and personality are not working in harmony with one another. Some parts may be relatively inert, and some may even be working at cross purposes with each other.

This assertion on my part requires illustration. Let me begin with an example taken from something that I published almost 20 years ago. As a part of one lesson, I gave the populations of five medium-sized cities in the United States:

Nashville	173,000	St. Louis	852,000
Denver	412,000	Cleveland	905,000
Memphis	394,000		

with the purpose that the student should substitute this information in the original sentence *Columbus has a population of over 374,000*. Obviously I wanted the student to "practice the pattern" *X has a population of Y*. The learning theory on which that drill was based has of course been seriously questioned in recent years, but that is beside the point that I want to make here. The question that I am concerned with is: What are the various parts of the learner likely to be doing during a drill of this kind?

Assuming that the content of the drill is not information that the student has already mastered, his intellect will be fairly busy. He must remember to say *has a population of Y* and not *has the population Y*. He must remember how to pronounce the names of some unfamiliar cities, and he must get his tongue around some relatively long numbers. If he does well, he receives the usual approval—from the teacher, from himself, and possibly from a few classmates—that accompanies a right answer in a classroom. If, in addition, he happens to believe in the efficacy of the method, he also gets the feeling that he has taken one more step toward whatever long-term goal brought him into the course in the first place.

Looking first at this drill in a framework borrowed from Transactional Analysis, the teacher and the textbook together are in the classic stance of Teacher-as-Parent, saying to the student, "Now try to do this, so that I may tell you how you did." The student, in turn, plays the Adapted Child, trying to do what the Parent demands of him so that he can get what he wants from her. Other than that, there is nothing in the drill for the Child part of the student's personality: no physical activity, no fun, no aesthetic pleasure. Nor is there very much for the Adult part of the student's personality, which is the part that is concerned with forming and maintaining an accurate picture of the world as it is. The population figures given in this drill were correct according to the most recent census, but I doubt that these particular facts fitted into any very urgent gaps in many students' maps of reality.

Shifting away from the Transactional terminology, we may say that in this drill the student's soma remains almost completely inactive, while at the same time there is nothing much for his psyche to make an investment in. The only choice is in which answer to give, and the only risk is that the answer may be wrong.

To look at the same drill from still another point of view, the student's need for security is met to the extent that the format of the materials and the actions of the teacher lead him to feel that he is in firm and competent hands. There is, on the other hand, nothing in this sort of activity to foster the growth of group feeling among students, and thus to contribute toward meeting each individual's need to belong. The need for esteem is met only with regard to the correctness of the answers: the student has no opportunity to explore and enjoy his own powers of originating and of judging for himself. Finally, the need to feel that this drill fits into a total and satisfying life pattern is met only to the extent that this is one more small step toward a linguistic competence that for some reason the student wants.

All in all, then, this drill is hardly an activity in which the whole learner is involved in any coordinated, internally harmonious way. In the terms that I used in my 1971 book on materials, it is "light" enough, and "transparent" enough, but it is almost completely lacking in "strength." I have taken it from my own work in order to avoid the unnecessary embarrassment of pillorying somebody else. But I would not have used your time and mine in this way if I did not believe that essentially the same personal dynamics are present in more recent and more highly regarded materials by other authors. Where those materials go beyond what I have outlined, they seldom go very far beyond it. Sometimes they do provide humor, or attractive pictures, or subject matter especially chosen to fit the student's professional interests, or a carefully limited amount of freedom for the student to devise his own responses. But the overall message to the student remains the same: "Try to perform this linguistic task so that we may tell you how well or how poorly you performed it." This message is at the heart of the generally "confrontational," or "judgmental" style that too many teachers and too many students seem to take for inevitable.

The materials that I have been describing, then, are definitely not what I would call "materials for the whole learner." Let's turn now to the positive side, and see what such materials might be like. First, a list of five desiderata:

1. There should be something for the emotions, as well as for the intellect. That something may be beauty or humor, but it may also be controversy or apprehension. Or beauty and controversy may occur together.

2. The materials should provide occasions for the students to interact with one another.

3. The materials should allow students to draw on present realities, as well as on their distant future goals.

4. The materials should provide for the students to make self-committing choices in the areas covered by 1 to 3 above.

To summarize 1 to 4, "whole-learner" materials allow and encourage students to make a much fuller self-investment than other materials do. But will students actually welcome these opportunities for self-investment? Some will, but others won't. The student's ability to participate in and enjoy this kind of risking commitment will depend on how safe he feels on each of the levels that I mentioned earlier. If he expects that linguistic errors will bring unpleasant consequences, he will be cautious with the form of his sentences: instead of experimenting with them, and instead of using them for the purpose of saying something, he will pick his way through them as if they were a minefield. If he feels uncertain about his place in the group, he will be careful to reveal nothing about his activities and his preferences that might lead to rejection by teacher or classmates. If he finds insufficient structure or clarity in the materials, he may either rebel or withdraw. In any or all of these ways, he avoids the kind of investment that I have been talking about.

There is, therefore, at least one additional desideratum:

5. Design of the materials should contribute to the student's sense of security.

We have already seen that the quality of the "yield" that a student gets back after making an "investment" is one important source of security. The materials themselves are the other source. *The extent of security limits the depth and intensity of investment, and the depth and intensity of investment are the principal determinants of the quality and the quantity of learning.*

Up to this point, I have been talking largely in abstractions. It is time to look at some concrete ways in which my five desiderata may be—and occasionally have been—realized in nonephemeral, publishable materials.

The security need, represented by the last of my five desiderata, is fundamental. It is also complex. The student needs to feel that whatever he is learning from is strong, and that it is strong in a number of different ways. He needs to be able to say at least three things about the textbook:

1. "This book contains something that I want to know." Insofar as what the student wants to "know" is "a foreign language," published materials need to give some evidence that what is in them is authentic. This is why publishers mention the native competence of the authors, the academic and literary attainments of those who have contributed, and the careful checking of the manuscript by numerous experts.

2. "This book can give me access to something that I want." This is why we write phrase books for tourists, and special language courses for engineers or for students of literature or for air traffic controllers. The specially selected vocabularies are undeniably of some practical advantage to the various users. But I suspect that a large part of the value in studying from a textbook aimed at one's own special field of interest lies in its placebo effect.

3. "This book gives me clear directions what to do." This is surely a large part of the reason why materials ought to be fairly "transparent," as I used that term in 1971.

There are additional ways of helping the student to feel secure in working with a set of materials: claiming that the materials are in harmony with the latest linguistic and/or pedagogical thinking; associating the name of the author with fascinating, widely publicized experiments in which pigeons have been taught to seem to play ping-pong; use of carefully selected typography and paper, and so on. None of these is new; publishers have used them for centuries, and I list them only for the sake of completeness. The trouble is that in all of the centuries that publishers have been using them, they have seldom gone beyond them.

One way in which most textbooks could contribute more to the student's sense of security would be to change the Suggestions to the Teacher, printed before Lesson 1. Any set of materials can be used in a variety of ways; and, in the sense that I specified a few minutes ago, some ways of using materials are more "confrontational," or "judgmental" than others; and the ways that authors recommend are commonly near the more confrontational end of the spectrum.

The Suggestions to the Teacher can also contribute more than they usually do to the student's need for belonging if they place suitable emphasis on work in small groups. Sometimes authors do not mention small groups at all. When they do include them, they often treat the group merely as an expedient for giving each student more air time at the cost of having his mistakes less dependably corrected. They almost always ignore at least five important features of groups: (1) A group of even three or four people is likely to be more reliable than any one of its members when it comes to recognizing which of a set of alternatives is the correct one. (2) A correction from a peer is more telling because it comes from someone who has had the same amount of exposure to the language, and not from someone with professional qualifications. (3) At the same time, a correction from a peer is generally less threatening, both because the one doing the correcting is not the person who gives out the grades, and because the correction is less likely to come in a reproachful or other judgmental tone of voice. (4) Competition between groups is less threatening to individuals than competition between individuals is. At the same time, it can be just as exhilarating. (5) Working, risking, and suffering together for even a short time can produce noticeable feelings of mutual loyalty.

These, then, are two ways in which an author can improve the whole-person effectiveness of his textbook before the reader even gets to Lesson 1.

In writing the lessons themselves, the author will be less preoccupied than we usually have been with the sequencing and presentation of discrete units such as grammatical structures and lexical items. There is a place for these concerns, of course. But the first and central aim of the writer of whole-learner materials will be to say something—or better, to help the student to say something—that is worthwhile and interesting. Within that framework, but only within that framework, he will take care to see that the linguistic elements do not get out of hand.

There are at least three well-known paradigms—well known but under-used—which lend themselves to "whole-learner" materials. The first we may call "The Lady or the Tiger," after Frank Stockton's well-known story with that title. Let's take a look at this story in terms of our desiderata:

1. The story contains plenty of color and emotion to interest the Child part of the student's personality.
2. The question contained in the title leads naturally to discussion and debate among students.
3. The story is interesting in itself: it does not depend for its interest on the fact that questions about it will appear on the final exam.

4. Expressing and defending one's own answer is a self-committing choice.
5. The story contains plenty of linguistic ammunition for use by both sides.

It is of course true that this particular story requires the student to have an advanced level of reading comprehension, and anyway, not many such stories exist. Let me comment on these two points in reverse order. First, although few stories end with the outcome so uncertain as this one, there are many stories that lend themselves to discussion in terms of "What if . . . ?" and "What should. . . ?" "What if Tom had not stayed at home with a cold that day?" "What should Helen have done when she noticed that the porch light had been turned off?" Much fiction—and some nonfiction as well—is suitable for this kind of use, but not all of it is. "Whole-learner" materials will contain more of this sort of text than do materials which ignore this point of view. Once again, the criteria are that the text should carry intrinsic interest for the emotional as well as for the intellectual side of the students, that it should lead to self-committing interaction among the people in the class-room, and that it should supply plenty of raw material for that interaction.

The same model may be applied not only at the advanced level, but also in very elementary lessons. Take, for example, the set piece in which a city or a town is described. This is commonly done in a style which is linguistically antiseptic and emotionally sterile. I used to write things like this for my students:

> Mr. Smith lives in Pleasanttown. Pleasanttown is located in the northeastern part of the state. It is not very large, but it is not very small, either. A river flows through the center of Pleasant-town. On the banks of the river there are a park, and the campus of Pleasanttown College. Mr. Smith teaches English at Pleasanttown College. The college is near the center of Pleasanttown, but Mr. Smith lives on the southern edge of the city. He usually goes to work by bicycle. He has to ride through the business district and across a bridge.

This description is followed by a series of "comprehension questions":

> Where does Mr. Smith live?
> Where is Pleasanttown?
> Is Pleasanttown large, or small?

and so forth. These are followed by questions like:

> What does Mr. Smith do every day?
> Describe Pleasanttown.

and the like. Finally we reach the culmination of the lesson, "real communi-cation practice":

> Where do you live?
> Is your town large, or small?
> How do you come to class?
> What do you pass by on your way?
> Do you cross a bridge on your way?

All of us, I'm sure, recognize the author's goals in writing this lesson: Stick to the simple present tense, introduce vocabulary for points of the compass and for assorted landmarks, and provide further practice with "there are" and "has to," which were introduced in earlier lessons. All of this will be useful in the "communication phase" that ends the lesson.

I'm also sure that I don't need to point out to this audience the generally musty odor of this reading passage, which could hardly have originated anywhere but in an ESL textbook. The content itself is cloistered, probably originating in a security fantasy of the author. Now, I believe that this passage is not much worse than much of what we find in many published materials that we see every day. Yet it fails all five of the criteria that I have set in this paper: There is a minimum of color or emotion; the material has no intrinsic interest; it does not lead to discussion, debate, or self-investment; it does not even contain the raw materials for any of these. At best, it can lead to what Eric Berne calls a "pastime," and a rather perfunctory pastime at that: "I come by subway; you come by bus; she usually walks but sometimes she takes a taxi; they come by car."

Whole-learner materials on this same topic would be different in at least four ways:

1. They would be written in a style that had some currency outside of language textbooks.

2. They would convey some emotion, whether enthusiasm or despair or amazement or anger or whatever.

3. They would be less bland in their content. Some neighborhoods in Pleasanttown might turn out to be run-down, and certain parts of town might actually be dangerous.

4. They would provide alternatives. There might be two or more descriptions of the same place from different points of view, or there might be descriptions of different towns. Either would enrich the student's vocabulary, but more important, materials of this kind provide what Keith Sauer called a "basis for disagreement," and therefore for nonperfunctory interaction.

A second paradigm is one that we may call "Twenty Questions." The game called "Twenty Questions" is, as we know, an old standby for language teachers. I would like for our purposes today, however, to let it stand for a much wider range of activities, in which factual information is unevenly distributed, and in which there is some reason why the participants want to redistribute the information, and in which there is at least one objectively correct solution waiting to be arrived at. One team of students trying to duplicate another team's configuration of cuisenaire rods through use of language would be an example. Asking one another about weekend activities is another example, and the accumulated techniques of language teachers down through the centuries could supply many more.

From the "whole-learner" point of view, some of these "Twenty Questions" activities are much better than others. All of them, of course, provide occasions for students to interact with one another. But they differ widely in their aesthetic and emotional impact, in the immediacy of the interest that they arouse, and in the scope that they provide for student investment beyond a relatively shallow intellectual level. Obviously they differ also in the amount of linguistic raw material that they provide.

In illustrating some of the possibilities in the paradigm of "The Lady or the Tiger," we looked at alternative treatments of the "Our City" topic. To explore some of the potential in the "Twenty Questions" paradigm, let's turn to an equally ubiquitous theme: "My House/Apartment."

One kind of lesson on this theme could be drawn from the real estate or apartment rental advertisements. The task given to the students might be to read a series of five or ten advertisements with the prices deleted, and try to rank-order the advertised properties according to cost. This can be done by teams of three or four students, with the winning team determined by reference to answers printed in the back of the book. With students for whom accurate knowledge of the housing market is a valued survival skill, this exercise meets the five desiderata for "whole-learner" materials. So far, so good.

But remember that we are talking about publishable, nonephemeral materials. A column of ads taken from the *New York Times* may be highly suitable for students who are living in the New York City area, but they will have less appeal in Miami or Cairo. Even in New York, ads that are a year or two old are of less interest than ads that came out this week. The very process of publication places a limit on freshness.

This brings me to an observation about authors of textbooks, and about what they expect of themselves. They seem to think that it's up to them to provide everything that the users are going to need. This is a big part of the freshness dilemma that I have just mentioned. What they might better do, it seems to me, is to provide a full-sized sample of lessons based on apartment ads, or supermarket ads, or weather forecasts, or sports stories, or what-not, and give the basic vocabulary, and outline a number of suitable techniques, but not think that they have to go on and fill up a whole book in the same format. Instead, they might supply a few examples, with sufficient vocabulary and technique to meet the security needs of the users, and then invite the users to make up similar lessons, as many or as few as they need, from local and current sources.

Incidentally, and outside of the "Twenty Questions" paradigm, a column of apartment ads can provide quite a range of activities, which involve many different parts of the student's personality:

In appealing to the student's curiosity or to his desire for achievement, we might ask him to make a list of all the words that occur only once in the column, or of all the words that occur five or more times. The former would be a basis for vocabulary expansion, while the latter would provide information about the core vocabulary for this particular subject matter. Or we might invite the student to rewrite the ads in complete sentences, with all of the function words, and with all of the abbreviated words written out in full. In this way, students could verify their comprehension, and at the same time get practice in guided composition. This activity is suitable for small-group work, with the teacher or a paraprofessional native speaker serving as referee only when needed. A further activity, also suitable for small groups, might be to compare the prices given in the sample with local prices for similar accommodations. Students could draw upon both the local newspapers and their own experiences. This would work equally well whether the students are in the same currency area as the sample advertisements or in a different area. Finally, students might look at the ads with the eye of a detective, or of an anthropologist, to see what inferences they can draw about life among the people by whom and for whom the ads were written.

Moving now from the practical to the realm of daydreams, which of these apartments would you want for yourself, or for yourself and your family, and why? Or suppose that you were advertising your own house or apartment for rent. What might the ad say?

Some students might want to move from the verbal to the graphic, drawing pictures or floor plans to correspond to printed ads. Other students might then interpret these productions back into words.

In the time that remains, let's take a quick look at a third paradigm, which is probably the most powerful one of all. Remembering that on one occasion, when people were still using a single language to coordinate their efforts, they almost solved their real estate problems permanently, we can call it the "Tower of Babel" paradigm. In a "Tower of Babel" activity, the goal is not to express and defend a point of view, or to solve some problem for which a right answer exists. Instead, the participants are using language in order to do something that they want to do for reasons that are independent of (unrelated to) their study of the language. Some examples that I have actually run across in other people's programs around the world, are:

Teaching the teacher and fellow students how to make linoleum block prints.

Teaching others how to lay bricks.

Planning a religious service for the end of the language training period.

Sharing memories of early experiences related to rain, bread, etc.

Learning to convert mentally between the English and metric systems of measurement.

Published materials can contribute to many of these activities of teaching, learning, planning, sharing, and doing together. Instructions for knitting, or paper folding, or writing Chancery Cursive script, can be cast into language that is suitable for the ESL classroom, so that a person who already has one of these skills can teach it without unnecessary linguistic impediments.

In summary, then, materials for the whole learner will aim first of all at helping the learner to make self-committing choices in the new language. These choices will involve as much of the learner's personality as possible, and not just the verbal part of his intellect. To this end, whole-learner materials contribute to the security of learner and teacher, both by providing adequate linguistic models, and by suggesting techniques that make for wholesome interaction among the people in the classroom.

POSTSCRIPT

More and more books are breaking the bonds of what is safe and emotionally sterilized. The first such book that I came across was *No Hot Water Tonight*, by Jean Bodman and Michael Lanzano. My own first real teaching experience was in Manhattan, and I remember the difference between life as we described it in our lessons and life as we and our students lived it in the slums and the subways. In *No Hot Water Tonight* we find a central character who is an elderly, sometimes lonely widow; a mother who as a single parent faces uncertainty about whether her teenage son is on drugs; and young single adults who do or do not pick up dates—or get picked up—in a bar. The book's pedagogical format is not unusual, though some of its vocabulary has an authenticity that ours lacked thirty years ago. The important contribution of the book is the way in which, by its own example, it invites students to talk in class about the realities of their own lives. Many other books, by their example, have warned students that the painful and the seamy sides of their lives have no welcome place in the language classroom.

Another book which grew out of Manhattan Island was *Getting Into It: An Unfinished Book*, by Dave Blot and Phyllis Berman Sher (Language Innovations, Inc., 1978). It contains 13 brief "stories," written mostly in the first person. Each story tells how one student or teacher sees the study of English, and some of the things that have happened to him or her in the use of the new language. Following the story are a few discussion topics and writing assignments designed to get the students talking with one another as well as with the teacher.

Recently Francis Ricciardone brought to my attention L. G. Alexander's *For and Against*, which he had used with great success overseas. Each lesson is on one topic that people are likely to disagree about. It provides a full statement of one point of view on the question, and then outlines, in fragments of sentences, two sides of a possible argument. The grammatical incompleteness of these two outlines forces the students to contribute at least some connecting words, and from there it is only one step to developing the ideas further, changing them and adding new ones.

A more recent set of materials is constructed on a much larger scale. It is titled *Challenges*, written by Brian Abbs, Karin Beier, Christopher Candlin, Christopher Edelhoff, Jan Maulden, Terry Moston, and Malcolm Sexton, and published by Longmans in 1977.

These materials call themselves "a multimedia project for students of English." They consist of:

1. A 100-page paperback book, with many black-and-white pictures.
2. A series of 35-mm slides.

3. A number of short films.
4. Tapes, which contain:
   a. Short programs.
   b. Exercises or drills.
   c. Stories or other comprehension material.
(I myself have seen only the book.)

The "project" is divided into six parts. Each part has its own *theme*. The themes are:

> Somewhere to Live
> Someone to Love
> Somewhere to Work
> Somewhere to Go
> Something to Say
> Something to Do

Each of the six parts is divided into half a dozen "chains." A "chain" is made up of three to seven "steps." Generally, each chain begins with a step which presents interesting, culturally authentic information. It ends with one or more "tasks," in which the students do something which is like what they might need to do one day in an English-speaking country.

Some features of these materials.

1. Each of the six themes is a need which everyone has, and which underlies everything that we do. These themes are therefore able to catch and hold the student's interest. At the same time, they are broad enough so that a wide variety of material can be included under each theme.

2. The student often has to use more than one medium at a time. For example, he may find a series of questions in the book. The information which he needs in order to answer the questions may be found in a conversation on one of the tapes. But the questions are not on the tapes, and the book does not contain a copy of the conversation.

3. Some steps take a single goal of communication and pull together a number of ways—grammatically quite different from one another—by which people commonly reach that goal. Thus, for the goal of "Making a tactful suggestion," the book offers:

> Let's . . .
> What would you think of. . . ?
> What about. . . ?
> Perhaps the best thing would be to . . .
> Why don't you/we. . . ?
> Can't we. . . ?
> etc.

4. Free discussion is frequently helped by charts which give it a "notional" or a grammatical outline, but which still allow the students to say things that they really want to say.

5. The book, tapes, and visual materials contain some English which is more complex or idiomatic than the students are ready to produce: "Here we lived and fed in a family fug. . . ." Or it may be in a style for which the student is not likely to find much use: "What's the magic ingredient for the party of the year? An army of waiters? An expert chef? No, it's you alone with Kitchen-made Electric Blender." There are examples of newspaper headlines, obituaries, and application forms. Here the writers are taking advantage of the fact that people can understand far more than they would be able to say by themselves. Students are allowed and expected to get the meanings from context, from asking other students or the teacher, from guessing, or from using the dictionary. They are even allowed to miss some of the details. But what they are expected to say and write is carefully planned so that they can work successfully within their limits.

This gap between what people are supposed to understand and what they are supposed to produce has several good effects:

1. It allows the writers to include culturally authentic and lively materials: genuine, unrehearsed conversations; brochures; literature; advice columns.

2. The liveliness and authenticity of the materials help to remove some of the student's feeling of having severe limitations on his language and on his ability to learn.

3. The liveliness and authenticity also awaken parts of the student's personality which are ordinarily asleep in a language class. Language practice therefore comes closer to language use.

4. Students may actually pick up some of what is there—things too complicated for explanation or formal presentation.

At the end of each "chain" the student finds one or more realistic "tasks" which are to be performed. These tasks pull together the activities of the earlier steps in the chain, and they also show the student why the earlier activities were worthwhile.

In some of the steps, students work individually; in others they work in pairs, and in still others they work in small groups. The materials therefore do *not* depend on the personal energy that is set free in only *one* of these patterns.

Because these materials draw energy from so many different sources within the student, my guess is that more energy will be available for use in learning. It seems to me also that the cross-cultural content of this course gives life to its grammatical and notional machinery, while at the same time the machinery helps the student to work his way through the cross-cultural content without getting lost.

Incidentally, I have recently talked with one person who reports that he has used ideas out of *Challenges* successfully in developing materials in a non-Western language for English-speaking students. The book by itself, without the accompanying tapes and visual aids, is a concentrated package of stimulating ideas.

The books that I have described up to this point are books to be placed in the hands of students. But the past few years have also brought an increasing number of what we may call "idea books" for teachers. Though these books may contain a certain amount of general discussion about teaching, their most important feature is a list of techniques from which teachers may choose and adapt to suit their own needs.

One such book is *Drama Techniques in Language Learning* by Alan Maley and Alan Duff (Cambridge: 1978). In spite of its title, this is *not* a book about putting on foreign language plays. As the authors explain in their opening paragraph,

> Let us be clear from the start what we mean by "dramatic activities." They are activities which give the student an opportunity to use his own personality in creating the material on which part of the language class is to be based. These activities draw on the natural ability of every person to imitate, mimic and express himself through gesture. They draw, too, on his imagination and memory, and on his natural capacity to bring to life parts of his past experience that might never otherwise emerge. They are dramatic because they arouse our interest, which they do by drawing on the unpredictable power generated when one person is brought together with others. Each student brings a different life, a different background into the class. We would like him to be able to use this when working with his fellow students.

They also assure us that their "drama techniques" are not a substitute for the psychoanalyst's couch.

Maley and Duff have divided their manual into two parts. In the first, which covers fewer than 30 pages, the authors set out their thinking about what they have done, and why they have done it as they have. At the same time, they give us a highly readable overview of what language teachers will find useful in much of the research of recent years: research on language-in-society, language-between-people, and language-beyond-the-sentence. This section of the book could, in fact, easily stand by itself as a short, nontechnical introduction to that research.

The second part of the book lists and describes five dozen techniques, most of them with variations. The first 10 are built around the student's powers of *observation*; the next 24 enlist the student's powers of *interpretation*; in the remaining techniques, students *interact* with one another and talk about their interactions. Within each of these three groupings, the authors present first those activities which make the smallest demands on the student, and move gradually to activities which require more and more from the student, either of language or of imagination or both. Under each technique, they first tell us "What to Do"; they then offer a few "Remarks," in which they share with us their own experiences, or give us hints about the purpose and the principles behind the technique. The language is straightforward, mercifully clear, and appropriately colleague-to-colleague in its tone. This latter part of the book, like the first, could stand by itself.

All of the techniques follow a single dependable formula:

1. The teacher sets the activity up. In setting any activity up, the teacher must be sure to do two things: (a) Establish some area of tension or

uncertainty—something for the students to work out in their own way.
(b) Make clear what the students are to use in resolving the tension or the
uncertainty, and the rules that they are to follow. The "tension or uncertainty" is not limited to the cognitive plane, and does not depend entirely on
uneven distribution of information among the students. Most of the activities
include a strong aesthetic or emotional component.

2. The students use the resources that the teacher has given them, and
work within the rules, in order to reach the goal. At this time, the teacher
largely withdraws from the center of the stage and gives only as much help as
is absolutely necessary.

3. Students discuss what they have done, among themselves and
sometimes with the teacher. (This third step is not stated explicitly with every
technique, though it is stated with most and is possible with the rest.)

Two examples will illustrate how this formula works itself out in Maley and
Duff's techniques. In one of the activities in the section on "Interpretation,"
the entire class is given a fragment of a conversation, such as:

> A. A man came to see you.
> B. Oh? When?
> A. While you were out.
> B. What did he want?
> A. He didn't say.

The students are to work in twos. Each pair is to imagine who the speakers
are, and where, and what they are doing. Then they go through the dialog,
adding to the beginning and the ending, but leaving the original lines as they
were. Finally, they try out their versions on other pairs of students. The five-
line fragment quoted above shows how *very common words, in short and
structurally simple utterances,* can set up uncertainty—even uneasiness or
dread—while at the same time they give to the students a nucleus of language around which they may gather their own ideas and put them into
words. This is one of several techniques which show students, without telling
them so, that the meaning of what is said comes mostly from the context, and
only partially from what they can look up in dictionaries and grammar books.

In one of the "Interaction" techniques, the students work in groups of
three. Each group decides on a situation that involves some tension: the
wives of trapped miners waiting for news, lovers having a quarrel, etc. They
work out a *silent* scene to show what the tension is about. Then each group
pairs off with another group and tries to guess the meaning of the other
group's scene. The guessing, discussing, and commenting, of course,
produce a great deal of language. Finally, each group takes the silent scene
of the other group, puts words to it, and acts it out before a *different* group.

As described in the preceding paragraph, this technique seems to need a
class with a certain amount of imagination and fairly good control of the
language. Or perhaps we would be surprised at how much a class could do
with this technique after a few weeks or months of study! In any event, if

students need more to work with, it can be given in the form of "briefing papers," one for each of a set of situations that the teacher has thought out ahead of time. The "briefing paper" need not be in dialog form.

In ordinary "free conversation," and in some language games, the students are expected to give birth to ideas ("what to say") and to clothe those ideas in words ("how to say it") at the same time. In most of the techniques which Maley and Duff offer us, this is not the case. In the miming activities, the ideas may be brought forth in silence, so that the inventing of thoughts and of words are completely separated from one another. But even in the other activities, emphasis falls first on "talking about what to say," and then on "saying it." It seems to me that there is value in protecting the student from having to fight a two-front war, or from having to juggle two quite different sets of objects, at the beginning of an activity.

Maley and Duff emphasize that their "drama" activities are only one side of a complete course. The other side may contain quite a bit of fairly conventional presentation and controlled practice. Even in the "drama" activities themselves, the authors provide a clear structure with its own "electrical charge," its own life. These activities will become productive only when the students add their own "charge," something from themselves. After all, an electric current flows between positive and negative terminals; both sperm and egg must be alive if anything is to come of their union. So the authors avoid the trap of throwing out drilling altogether in favor of "doing," or of assuming that a classroom deserves to be called "humanistic" only to the extent that the students have been given responsibility for their own learning, or of seeming to say that telling a student what to do—on some level, at least—may not be a necessary part of helping that student to grow.

CHAPTER 17

CONTRASTING EXPERIENCES WITH COUNSELING-LEARNING IN TEACHING WITH VERSE

During the autumn of 1976, I came up with several bits of verse in relatively simple English. Dot Carhart, a colleague from the Middle East Institute, used three of them in a language-learning experience that she conducted for a group of teachers who were native speakers of other languages. The method that she used was drawn entirely from the principles of Counseling-Learning. Later, I put eleven of these verses together into a small booklet and distributed copies to a number of ESOL teachers with a request for information on how they did (or did not) work in their classes. I received rather full replies from Dot Carhart, and from Joy Noren, who was teaching evening classes for adults in New Jersey. I also received briefer replies from a number of English teachers in Barcelona.

This chapter consists of (1) the booklet; (2) a slightly edited version of Dot Carhart's letter to me; (3) a summary of the comments by Joy Noren and the Barcelona teachers. (Joy's report was on a tape cassette which got mislaid or misappropriated. I regret the loss of a long, interesting, and very encouraging account!) It begins with a lesson plan consistent with Counseling-Learning:

UNDERSTANDING THE WRITER

LANGUAGE: Silent reading. Reading aloud by the teacher. Members of small groups try to clarify meanings for one another, referring to the teacher whatever questions they cannot answer.

IDEAS: What was the writer trying to say? On how many levels? Write a paraphrase. (Much of this may be done in small groups.)

FEELINGS: How did the author feel as he was writing? What makes you think so?

UNDERSTANDING ONE ANOTHER

FEELINGS: How do you feel after reading this text? What in the text makes you feel that way?

IDEAS: Do you agree with the ideas in the text? Why (not)?

RELATED EXPERIENCES: What does this text remind you of? Can you provide illustrations that agree with, or that contradict, what the writer was saying?

Note that in both halves of this lesson plan, whatever a student says constitutes an "investment" of him/herself, which may receive a supportive, understanding response from teacher and/or fellow students.

These texts are only a start. The ones you write yourself will be more suitable for your classes.

Good luck!

INVOCATION

Sand has dark yellows and light blacks.
The night is not different.
Here, the two are
One,
And so, now,
Are we.

FIRST LEAF

Easily,
The autumn sun
Falls through this leaf
And turns a glad golden orange,
While the leaf hangs, calm,
Waiting these last few days,
Drinking the warmth that gave it life.

Still green,
Its neighbors look as they looked
Three months ago,
But they don't let the light through.
And the warmness of the sun
In the cool air
Means less to them.

SNOWFLAKE

The first snowflake,
Black against the gray sky, but
White against the maple's winter black,
Brings us to the window where,
Framed against the panes,
We stare, and talk about
The first snowflake.

Nobody talks about the million-and-first snowflake,
Yet without it there would be no million-and-second snowflake,
And without the million-and-second snowflake,
The first snowflake would have been, at most,
Part of a flurry.

I'm the one-million-and-second person
In a city of three million.
I'm the two-billion-and-third person
In a world of four billion.
Without me,
What would the rest of you be?
(I'm glad I'm not the first snowflake.)

No flake is exactly like any other flake.
I am the first son of these two, and not those two.
I have lived at 1805 Grand Avenue and 120 N. Clinton.
Nobody else has.
I am the only person in this room who plays the baritone.
And the only one I know who likes madeira.

But every flake is partly like the others:
We've all come here today for about the same reason;
We pay the same sales tax when we buy a cake of soap;
We breathe the same dirt;
We can hum many of the same good songs;
And at the end, each snowflake either melts or turns to ice.

FOOD

The Norwegians eat herring, and thrive.
The Egyptians don't eat herring, but they thrive too.
The best thing in Cairo is a ripe black olive,
But they don't have to have olives in Oslo.

What the Koreans thrive on is kimchi,
While the Brazilians eat a lot of beans.
(I can't think of eating kimchi and beans together,
I'd expect to feel bad if I did.)

Someone has said that you are what you eat.
If that's true, then the Koreans
Must be very, very different from the Cairenes,
And it's a long way from Stockholm to Santiago.

But maybe it's the other way round.

Maybe I can turn borscht into the bones of an American,
And you can make bratwurst into the blood of Ghana.
Maybe a Greek who eats cheeseburgers
Is just as Greek as one who eats souvlaki.

Or maybe not!

DOCTOR!

Doctor!
I'm afraid of you!
What will happen if I let you inside the world of my body
With your needle, or with your pill?
Something good may happen, something you and I hoped for.
But something else may happen, and whatever happens
Will be inside my body, not inside yours.

Doctor!
Are you afraid of me?
You let me tell you where it hurts, and when it began,
But often, if I tell you more than you asked, if I speak my own thoughts,
Your ears close, your eyes turn away,
You go on with healing my body, but leave me.
What happens inside your gut when I tell you
More than you understand?

ADVICE

If you try to pull a stamp off of an envelope,
You are likely to tear it.
But if you hold the stamp, and pull the envelope away from it,
The stamp will not tear.
This really works.
Try it sometime!

People are like that, too.
You can take a lot away from me
If you will leave me as I am,
But if you try to pull me away
From something that I have stuck myself to,
It will be hard for you, and very hard on me.

I hope that you won't forget this next time.

CITY DWELLER

With its clucking of turnstiles,
Moo of passing trains,
Squeal of metal brakes,
The subway is a barnyard.

The city is a stockyard.
The subway stairs are chutes
Through which I shuffle every day,
Going to be killed a little,

Giving my meat to my employer,
Skin to my lover,
My guts along with other people's guts
For making dogfood,

Of which, on my way home from work
Daily, or almost every day,
I buy a can
For supper.

INTERFACES

Pure silk,
Brown, yellow, red, and a little dark green,
In buying this tie, I said to myself,
"You deserve a pat on the back!"
When I wear it, I say to the world,
"Somebody likes me, and
You can like me, too!"
    When I wear an old tie, I ask myself,
    "Does this one go with my suit?"
    And I say to the world,
    "Here I am as you expected me."
Giving you a tie, I say, "I think you ought to like this."

A jacket is much bigger, and takes more money.
When I wear a new one, I say to myself,
"Here is something that you may become,"
And to the world I say,
"Aha! There is more in me than you knew!"
Wearing my old brown tweed, I feel safe.
It has become what I am, and the world knows it can trust me.
    I wouldn't want to wear your jacket,
      even if it fitted me.
    If I did, I would see everything two ways
    at the same time, and the world would
    know, without knowing it, that something
    was wrong.
I'd never give you a jacket. Don't you give me one!

Shoes are something else.
My shoes are the only thing between me and what I stand on.
If you look at my shoes, you will know
What I think is going to happen to me today.
Heavy or gentle,
Sober or silly,
Careful or carefree,
You will know me by what I have on my feet.
Shoes are something one person can't buy for another.
    When you meet someone new, the neck-
    tie or scarf, the jacket or blouse, will
    be what they are showing you,
But always look first at the shoes.

PROTEST

My eardrum is a trampoline.
The notes of rock and roll jump up and down
Like happy eight-year-olds,
Pounding out a pattern *I* don't understand,
Straining my springs, and
Making my frame creak.

That I can take.
That's all in a day's work for an old trampoline.
What slashes through my canvas
Is the hobnail boots some of the notes wear—
The words, words for stomping over
Another person's needs
To meet the singer's own.

TIME

"Yesterday" is what was before the small hand of
    my watch went round these last two times.
"Tomorrow" is what will be after the same
    hand goes round twice more.
"Now" is what would be if my watch stopped.
That's why I'm careful to wind it every morning.

And if I had no watch at all,
Who would I be?

GENOCIDE

In the yard behind my house there stands a tree.
It's an oak tree, and because it *is* an oak tree,
It makes acorns.
Every autumn, it makes 521,376 acorns
(Give or take a thousand),
And throws them on the ground.
I wish it wouldn't!

What good are all these acorns anyhow?
We can't eat them.
The squirrels can eat them, and do,
But nowhere near that many.
If it's for making new oak trees, why
A couple of dozen acorns, in the right place,
Would be enough.

Don't get me wrong! Some of my best friends
Are oak trees.
I have one right outside my window,
And as a boy,
I helped my father to plant three of them,
Lovingly,
Just where we needed them.

PARENT

Don't set tomatoes on top of the automatic dishwasher.
The heat will come up through
And get to them,
And they will go bad.

Don't put lettuce on the bottom shelf of the refrigerator.
That's the coldest part.
The lettuce will freeze there,
And nobody will want to eat it.

Don't leave me, either, where I am nothing to you
Or to anybody.
I won't like what happens to me then,
And neither will you.

DOT CARHART'S ACCOUNT

What follows is a partial description of what we did with the poems in my English class, and what came out of the group. I include some of my own reflections and observations, and some of my experience as the "teacher."

I tried throughout to understand and respond to what they said and did (their investments) and to encourage them to share their questions and thoughts with each other. I occasionally answered a direct question. I began to learn when to "stay out" if they were involved with each other, even if they were making errors. If I constantly "understood" everybody, the focus was too much toward me; the key seems to be to focus on the material or communication at hand. Yet there is another element: as the group became more of a community, I was in it too, and was no longer just the "knower" trying to keep out of their learning space. This became possible (in part) through my interest in them and what they were expressing. After a while, they were interested in what I thought, too. (In the middle of some discussions on interpretation, someone would turn to me and say, "Do you think he meant..." or "What do you think?") I guess this was a real live experience of a stage 3–stage 4 situation!

I provided structure for the class (and thus security) through: (1) providing them with copies of the poem (Snowflake) at a certain time; (2) suggesting activities to do with it (silent reading, my reading aloud, looking at meanings, group work on summaries to be presented to the other groups, eliciting and writing down how the writer felt, comparing experiences); (3) establishing break times; letting them know we would continue with the poem in the morning (we started it about 3 p.m. on Wednesday the 29th); letting them know some limits (e.g., copies had to be returned but they could keep them overnight).

I had a dictionary available which they used on their own (especially one person who was fairly reticent) and also at my suggestion when I too was unsure of exact meaning (does a "pane of glass" include the "frame"?) or origin ("madeira").

A note on overall structuring of the class: the poem was introduced at a good point in terms of class spirit, after use of the Islamabad procedure (2 to 3 p.m. Wednesday) in which Mr. C _____ had told his version of "The Tortoise and the Hare." There had been a lot of self-investment during that activity and after, including personal thoughts on the moral of the tale, sharing of similar stories in the students' native countries, and Mr. C_____'s (personally very important) reasons for telling the tale. We had a real community at this point; interest and involvement were high.

One of the first reactions was excitement about reading poetry in English. Some had never done this; it was something new and special and engaged their interest. When one expressed this, others came in with similar self-investments. I said it was from Dr. Stevick. This could have been for the sake of my own insecurity (invoking authority from above because I didn't always feel comfortable introducing new activities). I think I also wanted to arouse their curiosity. They were curious—"Do you think he wrote it himself?" I kind of admitted that you had and Mrs. F. _____ identified the handwriting as yours. So there was the added element of personal interest and curiosity.

First they read it silently. When most had finished, one had not, so I said we would take a few more minutes to look it over. I hope the one who had not was not made to feel too self-conscious at that point; she was the quietest in the class and I was quite concerned about her.

I asked if they would like to hear it read aloud, and they were quite eager. I tried to be clear and to be careful about phrasing. Later, when we had a short time to go over the other two poems, they requested to hear them read aloud.

The poem is long, but the division into sections is quite helpful. This gives students a feeling for verses in English, a concept which may not be the same in their native poetry. The division lent itself to convenient paraphrasing, looking at the poem one section at a time, etc. During the summarizing activity in which groups compared their summaries with other groups, the idea of "development" or "progression" came up. There were different interpretations, and individuals wanted to see how theirs were borne out as the poem developed. This might be a new concept for many foreign students. (In Persian at least, each line of a poem can stand by itself and yet illumines the others; the order can change and there is no "development.")

There was some speculation as to whether this was prose or poetry. I said it was called free verse. This was not pursued; I could have explained further but that would have been too much from my world. Most of them just accepted that it was poetry. Later they will have something to compare to.

We started out looking at meanings of words or sentences they were not sure of, and very quickly got into the poet's meaning and underlying meanings. As I mentioned before, someone looked up "pane" and "madeira" and read the definitions to the class. There were questions on "flurry" and "flake." Someone didn't understand "maple's winter black"; Mr. D _____ explained that it was a poetical way of putting it, and someone else described the black tree trunks. There were questions about "framed against"; Mrs. B _____ described the scene in her own words and others added their ideas. Mr. C _____ had a question on the long sentence in the first verse—it was broken by a phrase set off by commas. Someone else came in and explained what was referring to what. They were using each other's resources quite a bit, and sometimes referring to me for confirmation.

Immediately we got into deeper meaning. Mr. M _____ got so involved in what he was trying to express about the mood of the poem (dark/light imagery, sadness/excitement) that he forgot about his English. (He had earlier admitted his self-consciousness about speaking.) He also identified the scene described in the poem with his own first experience of snow. Others came forward with similar experiences. There was excitement about this. I don't know if M _____ was so involved with his idea that he didn't pick up anything from my responses! But I think he did correct himself; sometimes he just didn't have the words to express his idea and I helped him out, hopefully not too much.

Someone brought up the use of "I" and "we" in the poem, and to whom they referred. Some considered "we" in the first verse a poetical usage, and then reconsidered on closer examination of the context. They figured it had to be a number of people, inside a house.

There was also a lot of discussion around the grand numbers: million-and-first, million-and-second. Some were confused, and others compared the large ordinals with "first, second, third" and identified the connectors. Mr. C_____ wondered about the function of the parentheses ("I'm glad I'm not the first snowflake.") There were comparisons to people living in cities; Mr. D_____ talked about the universe. The idea of the relation of the first to the second or the one-million-and-second to the first really captured their minds. The idea of importance came up quite a bit (the importance of the first one.) They touched on ideas related to the "flurry" business (if it hadn't been for... it might have been only...) but didn't pursue it. That sentence may have been confusing. Later, though, there was some discussion started by Mrs. B_____, concerning the attitude of the poet toward the first snowflake with special reference to the second verse.

This brings up something significant. Certain questions came up on the first examination, with resulting discussion, clarification, etc. Later in the paraphrasing and writing down stage, students discovered and revealed further points about which they were unsure. Mrs. F_____ came and asked me again about the "million-and-first" snowflake during the paraphrasing phase. I tried to determine if she was comfortable with the large ordinal; it seems she was more concerned with the meaning of that verse.

The last three sections are more straightforward; the students didn't discuss them as deeply as the others—though they did wonder if you really collect stamps! (They were sure you did when they read the next poem—the personal interest again.) They compared the experience in the poem to their experience in a Big City. Most of them mentioned New York and their feeling of being insignificant there. Again their common experiences came out; one investment would spark another in someone else in the room.

In the paraphrasing stage, Mrs. F._____ brought a question to me on "I am the first son of these two and not those two." I tried out the concept of "firstborn" and "eldest" on her; she identified the parents and the whole thing made sense to her.

The ideas of "uniqueness" and "sameness" (oneness) were pretty apparent and didn't elicit a lot of discussion. No one mentioned the concept of two worlds introduced in the seminar earlier. Many noted "we all breathe the same dirt"; "dirt" made a real impression.

The last line, about melting or turning to ice, aroused their interest. The two most outspoken, Mr. D_____ and Mrs. B_____, had their ideas. In the paraphrasing stage, a few of them said not to talk about it (i.e., death)!

They expressed their discomfort. (One of the interpretations had to do with the legacy men leave behind, with "ice" representing great lasting contributions; another with the cycles of nature: water vapor, rain, snow, melting, etc.) No one explicitly said, "We all die in the end," though later when we talked about the poet's feelings "uncertainty about the future" was mentioned.

As people came forward with their ideas, more discussion revolved around meanings of poetry in general. Does a poet have a specific meaning in mind, can there be a variety of interpretations, does a poet even know his meaning? Some wanted to ask you what you had in mind! The fact that they recognized the legitimacy of multi-interpretations was significant: they were recognizing each other's investments and learning something about poetry.

I have already mentioned a number of points that came up in the paraphrasing stage, which occurred the morning of the second day. At the beginning of that day, we had a short feedback session, established break times, filled Ms. H _____ in on the previous afternoon's activities, and gave her time to read the poem. (She missed a few hours.)

I divided the class into three groups (three, three, and two); the three "shy ones" who had been sitting together on one side of the room were together. (I think it helped them not to have someone in the group who would dominate things too much.) After a period of quiet, things began to hum—they were working hard. In the group of two, they kept to themselves for a while and then began comparing notes. I was called for questions a few times; once for clarification on what I expected, and the other times for help with the meaning of the poem. I had let them know beforehand that I would be available to help them.

This phase took some time; at a certain point I had to establish some limits. I asked each group to present their summary to the others. Once this was started it was decided by the group to go verse by verse, rather to summarize the whole poem. There was considerable discussion at this point, and more interpretations. I tried to encourage their understanding each other, rather than just agreeing or arguing; meanwhile *I continued to understand them*. We could have summarized some of this further in writing, but we had already spent a good deal of time, and *I didn't want to run a good thing into the ground.* [Emphasis added by EWS.]

As a final activity, we tried to understand how the writer felt. I gave them examples. I would get their consensus, or weigh the different opinions, and write them in full sentences on the board. I allowed myself to come in a little here; I didn't write up everything which was said, and tried to put some responsibility on the group for what we were going to write down. I can't remember everything we came up with. I do remember "contentment" (w/ being himself) and "he feels the anguish of uncertainty"; others felt that was too strong (some needed to know what "anguish" meant) and felt that "uncertain about the future" was better. (This provoked discussion on the difference in usage between "uncertainty" and "uncertain.") Someone also thought the writer felt resigned (to his fate). Someone didn't feel sure about the meaning of "resigned"; others provided her with examples and distinguished this from resigning from office. This activity did call forth further investments and reflection.

At this point I asked if anyone had had a similar experience. They had already come forward with quite a few; so asking this at this juncture was probably not a good idea. This drew a blank; so we left it at that.

I had been considering splitting the class into groups again and giving a choice of topics to consider (experiences of their own, their feelings about the poem, lines of the poem meaning the most to them). I wanted to give them more opportunities to understand each other. But as stated above, we had done so much already, they had invested so much of themselves already, and it was time for a change.

We had a short time left before a break (about twenty minutes), and I gave them a choice of activities including a chance to see the other two poems. They really wanted to see the poems. They read them; we discussed meaning and pronunciation of words; they asked to hear me read them. This much seemed satisfying.

Having a Greek and a Korean in the class was neat. A number of experts were helping me with pronunciation of foreign words (kimchi, souvlaki, Santiago, Oslo, etc.). It helps if the teacher is not the Expert at all times.

I had assumed that everyone realized that these were two poems on one sheet. When one member of the class mentioned this fact, others expressed their relief—they had felt confused, thinking this was one long poem on pulling stamps off of envelopes and eating different foods! Again, one investment calls forth another.

This should give you a good idea of what we did with the poems and what came out of the group. What I cannot measure is how much the students felt they "learned," since we had little feedback of that sort. I can only guess that their close scrutiny of the language and meaning of the poem ("Snowflake") and their involvement in sharing meanings and ideas with others gave them insights about English, either consciously or intuitively.

Based on my one-and-a-half-day's English teaching experience, I think the poems are great for English learners. They are clear and straightforward, but have sufficient challenges at the linguistic and meaning levels to involve even more proficient students. The subject matter is very appealing and very human; everyone got involved in a personal way. The poems can be taken in many ways and can call forth similar experiences on the part of the learners; there are many opportunities for investment, at least in classes based on a CL model. I think the poems will help any teacher and group of learners involved with CLL to know that "learning is persons."

Just one more note, brought to mind by the excitement in our English class about reading English poetry. If one's language learning experiences can affect one's attitude toward learning language so much, the same might be true for the first poem. Perhaps if learners' first engagement with poetry is deeply satisfying, or at least not frustrating or merely at the superficial level, they will be more open to poetry, literature, and learning in general later on.

From Joy Noren's tape two points stand out in my memory. The first has to do with procedure: when the students seemed shy about saying what they thought the writer had in mind, Joy just stepped across the hall for a few minutes, and soon she heard the sound of animated discussion.

The other point that I remember has to do with results: after a session on "Doctor!" a woman student stayed after class to tell Joy somewhat of her own experiences with doctors and hospitals.

Dot's and Joy's experiments with these "short texts" had overwhelmingly positive results. The reports from Barcelona, by contrast, were mixed.

One of the Barcelona teachers used the "short text" on *Food.* He reported some positive things, particularly the fact that the students became more aware of the existence, and the value, of differing individual interpretations. But the students generally seemed quite uneasy at the fact that there was not just one simple meaning. There was a gratifying amount of mutual help in clarifying some vocabulary items, but "the main problem is to overcome fear of appearing ridiculous in interpreting someone else's production."

It is impossible to be sure why the same text that worked well in one class did not go over in another. Perhaps overall linguistic proficiency, or age (the Barcelona students were apparently younger), or cultural traditions for dealing with poetry. What *is* clear is that the Security level in this class was low, and that the amount of Assertion was small.

Another teacher used the text on *Genocide* with two different small classes. In both, it seemed to provoke a good amount of thinking and discussion. The negative things happened at the end. In one class, the teacher asked the students how they felt about what they had been doing. They said it had been enormously difficult. One complained about her education in a convent school, "where opinions were frowned on and feelings were almost taboo." In the second class, the teacher's last question was, "How did *you* feel reading this?" This produced an awkward moment and very little response. Perhaps the students were being asked to make an Assertion on a level where they lacked Security.

A third teacher used *Invocation* and *Snowflake* with a class that had had 70 hours of English by the Silent Way. The teacher began by generating the whole of *Invocation* from the first word charts (Chapter 4). [This was made easier by the fact that I had written it as part of a creativity exercise which Lee Gillespie had conducted using those same charts.] This led to a bit of poetry writing by the students themselves. The teacher felt that this was a very positive experience, but one that was difficult to continue.

The same teacher tried *Snowflake* in a CLL-type class that had had 125 hours, but concluded that "poetry just isn't their thing; they prefer politics."

A fourth teacher tried *Advice* with a second-level class, but found that some of the vocabulary was too confusing, and that in general no one seemed to identify with the text.

A fifth teacher gave *Doctor!* to a class which she felt had been falling apart as a group. The result was an hour-long session discussing the text *in Spanish.* The teacher felt that this discussion achieved her purpose because it improved the spirit of the group.

A sixth teacher gave *Advice, City Dweller,* and *Snowflake* to a class that had had nearly 500 hours of English. During the hour, the teacher himself kept a very low profile. After some discussion of the texts one at a time, the class turned to consideration of the question, "What must the person be like who wrote these?" (And I would not say that their conclusions were far from right!)

A seventh teacher used *Advice* with a 250-hour class. It seems to have worked fairly well, leading to perhaps 25 minutes of discussion, after which the class "ran out of steam."

The eighth teacher gave her class *Invocation,* but without its title. She had them read it, think about it, and then suggest titles that might fit it. This apparently led to some contributions, after which the group claimed they were "too realistic to imagine any more poetic images." (Again, as in two other groups, an expressed uneasiness with this *kind* of material. Age? Cultural background? Coincidence?) There was some discussion of this reluctance, and also a unanimous rejection of the teacher's introduction of the word "love." Here, the class may have been finding out more about themselves individually and collectively than about the poem, but that of course is at least as good—perhaps better.

The class then asked the teacher to read the text aloud. The reaction was "an absolute *storm!*" The discussion of meaning then resumed with more confidence than before the oral reading.

To judge from this account, the text had richly accomplished its purpose! Then the teacher asked whether they had liked the text, and the majority came back with an emphatic "No!" One area of objection to it had to do with discomfort at working with poetry in general, and the absence of clear meaning, rhyme, and rhythm in particular. (Two people seemed to believe that one is not qualified to like poetry until one has had special "training.") Another objection was that nothing in this 30-minute session bore directly on the public examination which was coming up a month later.

This series of accounts illustrates what we already knew: that the same material in the hands of competent teachers works more or less well according to the interests of the students and their inhibitions, as well as their level of proficiency and the way the teacher runs the class: "What goes on inside and among the people in the classroom" again. Beyond this general observation, however, I think it is fair to say that this material worked best when the teacher seemed to be using it because (s)he thought it was worth using, rather than trying it as an experiment, and when the teacher had some skill in and commitment to a simple form of "counseling," as that term was used in Chapter 8.

PART IV

A THIRD WAY: SUGGESTOPEDIA

CHAPTER 18

THE WORK OF GEORGI LOZANOV*

It has been five years now since I first heard of Suggestopedia, and I have yet to view a significant amount of learning by this method. The results which it achieves are reported to be outstanding, yet the way in which the results are reported has sometimes left them less than clear. In 1976, I wrote all that I knew about the procedures of Suggestopedia. Since that time, I have talked with three people who have had firsthand experience with the method, including one who went through the two-month training period which Dr. Lozanov recommends for foreign teachers who want to use his system. I have also just read Fanny Saféris' account of Suggestopedia and her own experiences with it. Jane Bancroft has provided some details in a recent article in the *Modern Language Journal*, and the *Journal of the Society for Suggestive-Accelerative Learning and Teaching* is largely concerned with this approach to education. Dr. Lozanov's own recent book *Suggestology and the Principles of Suggestopedy* will be indispensable, of course. Yet I am still unable to give an authoritative account of what is done and what makes it succeed. Why then am I writing about Suggestopedia again here?

For three reasons. (1) The ideas behind Suggestopedia seem to fit in with the ideas I have talked about in earlier chapters, even though they are in some ways quite different from them. (2) Reading about Suggestopedia has set me to doing some things that I'm glad I did even though they themselves could never be called examples of Suggestopedia. (3) Reading about Suggestopedia has helped me to make sense of some of the things that have happened to me as student, teacher, or supervisor of teachers in language classrooms.

Anyone who wants a readable, lively, and stimulating description of Suggestopedia at work should read Saféris' book. The course consists of ten units of study, each of which takes exactly six hours of class time and (by some accounts) a little student time just before bedtime and just after getting up in the morning. The day's study consists of four 45-minute periods. Each unit consists of a long dialog, a bit of explanation, and many activities that

---

*On his visit to Washington in April–May, 1979, Dr. Lozanov very kindly read the penultimate draft of Chapters 18 and 19, and also permitted me to observe a full three-hour session near the end of an Italian course which was being conducted under his direction. I have made some changes as a result of talking with Dr. Lozanov and watching Suggestopedia in operation. I would still emphasize, however, that Suggestopedia is not a fixed system, but an area of Dr. Lozanov's ongoing research; and that these chapters of mine are accounts of my own thinking, and not definitive descriptions of his method.

draw on ("elaborate") what was in the dialog. The dialog itself is introduced during the third period of one day. During the fourth period of that day, the teacher reads the dialog aloud twice to the students as they sit back and listen to music (the "concert" session). The whole of the next day and the first half of the third day are devoted to activities of many other kinds.

I have not tried here to give a complete description of how Suggestopedia is used for teaching languages. I have even avoided trying to give a description that could be used as directions for organizing a course, because to do so would almost certainly be misleading and therefore destructive. Although this chapter is based on some of Dr. Lozanov's writings, and particularly on a speech he made in 1976, it will not really be a discussion of Suggestopedia either. It will be only an account of my own thoughts, and some of my actions, that have come out of my contacts with Lozanov's work.

In a bird's-eye view of what I have to say, twelve points stand out. I will number them so that we can refer to them later.

To begin with, I see Suggestopedia as being based on three *assumptions*: (1) That learning involves the unconscious functions of the learner, as well as the conscious functions; and (2) that people can learn much faster than they usually do, but (3) that learning is held back by (a) the norms and limitations which society has taught us, and by (b) lack of a harmonious, relaxed working together of all parts of the learner, and by (c) consequent failure to make use of powers which lie idle in most people most of the time.

The *strategy* of Suggestopedia, therefore, is to (4) remove these norms and (5) these tensions, and to (6) avoid introducing other limiting norms or inhibiting tensions in their place.

For these purposes, the teacher has *tools* of three kinds: (7) psychological, (8) artistic, and (9) pedagogical.

The guidelines for using these tools, and the *criteria* by which success is judged, are (10) the principle of "joy and easiness," (11) the principle of the unity of the conscious and the unconscious, and (12) the principle of "suggestive interaction." Lozanov has emphasized again and again that teaching which does not meet *all three* of these criteria will not achieve the results of Suggestopedia and should not be called Suggestopedia.

Let me then set forth my own thoughts and my own experiences in relation to these twelve points.

(1) *Learning involves the unconscious functions of the learner, as well as the conscious functions.* One part of the meaning of this sentence has to do with what it is that a learner remembers. When one "studies" a particular word, for example, one may think consciously only about its translation equivalent in one's own language, or about a picture that the teacher has pointed to in presenting the word. At the same time, however, and without thinking consciously about them, one may be aware of many other things that are connected with the word: other ideas, other words, other objects or actions that are frequently associated with that word in real life; emotional

impacts that the word has had on oneself or on groups that one has been in; the way the teacher acts and what the teacher seems to assume is going to happen; all of these things and many more. The same range of unconscious associations exists for individual sounds, and also for larger units of language such as sentences, games, conversations, and stories.

Lozanov's point, as I understand it at least, is this: that whenever a student is consciously dealing with the overt content of a lesson—the part that he and the teacher are focusing their attention on—he is at the same time dealing unconsciously with other things which lie just outside, or far outside, the center of his awareness; and that what happens on the unconscious level affects what can happen on the conscious level. This much of what Lozanov is saying is receiving much more attention nowadays than the bare lip service that it was given at some times in the past. The "humanistic" methods place particularly strong emphasis here. This observation—that the best learning takes place when what is happening on each of these two levels supports what is happening on the other—is approximately what the word "double planeness" refers to in English translations of Lozanov's writings.

But Lozanov goes a step further. In Suggestopedia it is not merely a matter of having things generally pleasant on the unconscious level so that things will be sure to go smoothly on the conscious, cognitive level. That is to say, it is not just a matter of the one level serving as a foundation or support for the other, as lath supports the plaster of a wall. It would be more accurate to say that the two are constantly being woven or knitted into each other. To take only one example, this interplay of the two levels shows itself in the names and identities which the students take on when they enter the classroom, and which they keep until the end of the course. The name, occupation, and home of each character provide multiple examples of some one sound that the students need to learn. Thus in the English course "Robert Fox" is "a doctor from Oxford," and "Shirley Burton" is "a journalist from Birmingham." This by itself is merely a cute device on the cognitive level. But the assonance, rhythm, and (in some cases) rhyme of these identifying formulas give to them a primitive but very real aesthetic quality to which students will respond even if they never think about them—echoes and drumbeats which speak to the student's body more than to his mind. The fact that these aesthetic qualities show up dependably in all of the characters implies further that the people behind the course know what they are doing. If the student draws this conclusion *unconsciously and for himself,* it will be vastly more effective than if the same idea were stated in so many words on the first page of the textbook.

Each of the occupations is also prestigious or interesting in some way, and may even be glamorous. Since the student's "real" identity is entirely excluded from the classroom, he receives from this new surrogate identity—largely on the unconscious plane—a number of positive, pleasant associations that go with that occupation. He will thus feel good about this fictitious

Self, and in that *Self* will be more ready to enter into whatever is happening on the conscious level. In this character, he may take roles in dialogs which involve a whole new set of temporary characters which are being played not by his real Self, but by his surrogate Self.

If Lozanov is right about the importance of "double planeness," then a Suggestopedic teacher needs to know what is going on on both planes at the same time. But in most kinds of teaching, the teacher is not much more aware of this detailed interaction between the two planes than the student is. The training of a Suggestopedic teacher therefore involves learning to be conscious of, and to control, some of the things that the teacher does which affect the learner mostly on the unconscious plane.

(2) *People can learn much faster than they usually do.* This is the side of Suggestopedia that catches the attention of the public: the claim that experimental subjects have in some sense learned the meanings of 1000 foreign words in one day, and that even in the classroom students absorb 2000 words in 60 hours of instruction. The term for this phenomenon is "hypermnesia"—"supermemory." Yet I think that Lozanov would insist that "hypermnesia" differs from what students are usually capable of not only in the amount of the material that they hold onto. The basic difference is not quantitative, but qualitative. Hypermnesia depends on activating different *kinds* of powers within the student—powers which ordinary teaching leaves untouched or even blocks off. I regret that I cannot tell the reader exactly what these "reserve powers" are, much less give instructions on how to bring them to life. But I am fairly sure that Eric Berne, in writing about the wonderfully flexible and creative potential of the Child ego state, had seen something of what these powers can do. And Schaefer (Chapter 11) may have seen some of these powers emerge during "Regression in Service of the Ego."

(3a) *Learning is often held back by absence of psychic relaxation.* I am sure that I do not understand all that Lozanov means by this point. Quite possibly it refers to what happens biochemically inside the brain, and even in parts of the body outside of the brain. But it may also be saying that when the student is unconsciously resisting something that comes along with the new word, sentence, or whatever, he cannot at the same time welcome the word or sentence into his total system of memories. Imagine a guest at a party, a person of some charm and even of some importance, but who insists on bringing with him his pet boa constrictor. He is less likely to be kept on the list of prospective guests for future parties than is a person of comparable charm and importance who does not bring a boa constrictor with him.

In a language class, then, many of the student's resources, and much of his energy and attention, will be used up—or tied up—in defending himself from whatever is causing the "psychic tension." From this tension and from the student's efforts to deal with it, there may come not only inferior learning, but also psychosomatic disorders: drowsiness, headaches, digestive discomfort, and the like. One of the hallmarks of genuine Suggestopedia is that the students have fewer such difficulties.

Here, I suspect, is a large part of the reason why the schedule of a Suggestopedic course is so rigid, and why the teachers take charge so briskly, and why the students are not invited to contribute to decisions about what to do next. It may also account for the fact that students have absolutely no social contacts with the teacher outside of class, even during breaks. What is wanted is an image which is clear, self-consistent, and self-assured. This must be an image which will not provoke conflicts either within the student or between students—one which will not even raise in the student's mind any alternatives that are not necessary to the progress of the course.

(3b) *Learning is often held back by norms which the student learned as a part of his upbringing in society.* The destructive effects of "psychic tension" have at least been mentioned by other writers. The emphasis which Lozanov places on this second limiting factor, however, is one of the distinctive features of the Suggestopedic point of view. We have been told over and over from an early age, directly and by implication, that learning a language is hard work, or that only a few people can do it as adults, or that we ourselves at least are not cut out for it, or that twenty new words a day is about all that anyone can hope to hold onto. As Lozanov tells us, the earlier an idea comes to us and the less conscious we are of its coming, the more power it will wield in shaping our thoughts and in controlling our actions. So most of us are more or less "born losers" (or at least born underachievers) even before we first set foot in a language classroom.

In this context, the large number of words per day in Suggestopedia is not only an *outcome* of the method. It is also an important *tool* of the method. The very size of the demand blasts the student out of the small orbit that was determined by what society had persuaded him were his limitations. It forces him to grasp for, and find, and use, and rely on powers—modes of learning— which he did not know were in him. The demand also implies—"suggests"— confidence in the learner and in his powers. Needless to say, an apparently unrealistic demand does not by itself lead to success. It must be one part of a total system in which the student finds out fairly soon that the demand is not impossible after all, and that he himself is able to meet it. Otherwise, it is worthless and even disastrous.

Those of us who teach non-Suggestopedic courses also have, on a smaller scale, our own opportunities to "suggest" and "desuggest" limitations on the powers of our students. One area in which this is true is in our explanations of grammar. I think we have much to learn from Lozanov here even if we are not using his method.

An example of what I mean cropped up in my own work just last week. A student who was having to leave for Turkey halfway through the Turkish course was sounding distressed because she had not yet come to the passive forms of verbs. I doubt that such situations ever arise in Dr. Lozanov's courses, and I do not know what he would do if they did. Nevertheless, the thought struck me that this student's ignorance about the passive voice was really a small matter. What was of great urgency (and here I think that Dr. Lozanov was whispering in my ear) was her idea that the passive was some mysterious forest, or some treacherous bed of quicksand, through which she could pass safely only with the help of a licensed guide and an officially published chart. To have answered her question as I used to answer such questions would have been a service to her in the short run. In the long run, however, it would have been a disservice, because I would have implied— "suggested"—to her once again that her own powers were very weak.

Instead, I said to her in Turkish, "Oh, it's not all that difficult." Then, turning to a Turk who was with us, I said, as if I were uncertain, "*Vermek . . . verilmek?*" ("to give" . . . "to be given"?). After another example or two of this kind, all without English translation, the student saw for herself what we were doing, and began to contribute examples of her own, complete with correct vowel harmonies in the suffixes. I had been right in guessing that she would be able to do this. If I had not been right, I would have had to change my technique quickly, and without her noticing that I had changed it. Otherwise, I could have ended up having conveyed the ideas that (1) she was as limited in her ability to deal with these things as she had thought she was, and that (2) she was in the hands of an incompetent teacher.

Once I saw that the student was playing happily with the kind of passive that I had introduced her to, I gave her the other essential fact about Turkish passives: "It's not all *that* simple." Then, as we had done earlier, we gave her a few examples of another passive-like suffix and let her play with it. Finally I said in English, "So you do have to know which verbs form the passive in which way. But from what we've done here, you can recognize passives when you run into them from now on, and you also know that no one way of forming passives is hard."

In earlier days, I would have responded to the student's question quite differently. First, I am sure, I would have picked up the nearest piece of chalk and made for the blackboard. Once arrived there, I would have outlined what I knew on the topic, as simply and clearly as I was able. My central purpose would have been to prepare the student for understanding and producing correct passive forms in her future encounters with the language. If I did the kind of job I was trying to do, I would leave her feeling that she now understood Turkish passive verbs, and feeling relieved from her earlier anxiety on the subject, and grateful to me for having relieved her from her anxiety by putting this new knowledge into her hands. As I gave the explanation, I would have been aiming for exactly this kind of result, and so my facial expression, my tone of voice, and all the rest would have automatically begun to convey earnest messages like, "Now always remember. . . !" and "Are you *sure* you understand. . . ?" And when, as is almost inevitable, she someday failed to apply her new knowledge correctly, she would say to herself (or she would hear me saying), "You've forgotten. . . !" We would be back to the chain, as old as the Garden of Eden, in which knowledge leads to responsibility, and responsibility leads to guilt, and guilt means that one can get no good thing except by the sweat of one's brow.

Let me say again, I do not offer this as an example of what a Suggestopedic teacher would do. It is merely one instance of conveying—"suggesting"—to the student, in an atmosphere of "joy and easiness," that her powers were greater than she had thought. This contrasts with suggesting to her what she already believed: that she was in fact dependent on me, in an atmosphere of earnestness and responsibility.

(4) *The strategy of Suggestopedia includes removing the psychic tensions that would interfere with learning.* There are two obvious channels through which to reduce tension. One is the design of the materials and the other is the behavior of the teacher. Suggestopedia is concerned with both, sometimes in ways that would surprise the rest of us, or which violate some of our dearly held principles.

The best-known rule of the Direct Method, for example, is to speak to the students only in the target language. This allows, or forces, the students to figure out the meanings from the context. This can be exhilarating and deeply satisfying for some students, but seriously frustrating for some others. Almost any student under these conditions will feel at least a little tension. Suggestopedia avoids this tension both by allowing the students to follow the printed text in parallel NL and TL versions, and by allowing the teacher to give *sotto voce* translations when needed. (In the current version of Suggestopedia, the translations are given on separate strips of paper which can be inserted into the book when needed, and then removed later on.)

A quite different source of tension is the contents of the dialogs themselves. So, on the smallest possible scale, a student of Portuguese who expects to go to Portugal may be annoyed when one of the speakers in the dialog calls a railway train a *trem* (the Brazilian term) instead of a *comboio* (the word used in Portugal). On a larger scale, a person headed for Ouagadougou may wonder whether his precious time is being well spent in a course that is set in the shops and restaurants of Paris, and an electronic technician will not feel at home using materials that concentrate on history, politics and the fine arts. The language professional may remonstrate with the student that the pronunciation and basic grammatical structure are the same, and that the specialized vocabulary for any particular purpose is small and easily learned. The fact remains, however, that students do become uneasy about these matters, and this kind of uneasiness can spoil the Suggestopedic environment, just as it can reduce the effectiveness of methods which are less highly coordinated than Suggestopedia.

Another source of anxiety is one that we explored thoroughly in Chapter 1: the very fact of being a student who is ignorant, powerless, and under evaluation every time he opens his mouth. An additional source of conflict, which we have generally taken for inevitable, lies in the custom of having each student take each part in each dialog. Related to this is the fact that the cast of characters changes entirely, or at least partially, from one lesson to the next. Under these circumstances, no student identifies himself or herself very strongly with any of the fictional characters in the book. Speaking their lines for them becomes at worst a sterile mouthing of words, and at best an enjoyable moment of amateur theatrics.

I am beginning to see how the design of a Suggestopedic course reduces all of these tensions. Most conspicuous is the *surrogate identity* which the student receives upon entering the course. This goes far beyond the ancient practice of assigning a foreign name. This identity has depth and continuity, and emotional content relative to the identities of the other students. The "world" of the classroom can therefore take on a complexity and a (provisional) credibility which are lacking in most other classes. This complexity and this credibility allow for (provisionally) real communication which for language-learning purposes is as effective as communication among students in their permanent and public identities. Communication among the surrogate identities has the further great advantage that it does not bring in any of the problems and anxieties which the students have outside the classroom. The same is true for the plays-within-the-play—the characters in the long, interesting dialogs on which the ten lessons are based. In assuming this identity and in playing these roles, the student is less likely to fret about whether the vocabulary of the course is exactly right for his own specialized needs.

At the same time that the student uses the person of "Dr. Robert Fox" as a vehicle for entering the new language, he can also use it as a mask to hide behind. Suggestopedic teachers do not say "No," and never say "That was a mistake." So the student is safer from feeling evaluated than he would be in most courses. Nevertheless, if he notices that he has said something that the teacher would evidently not have said, it was Dr. Fox who "made the mistake," and not he. Suggestopedia thus effectively (deliberately?) blurs the boundary between fact and fiction, so that the student can drift back and forth between them.

Unlike the reality of the student's life outside the classroom, this "fictitious reality" brings with it no embarrassments, no conflicts, no anxieties. On the contrary, it brings a series of enjoyable experiences.

Suggestopedia thus agrees with some other systems of teaching which avoid the danger of setting up an evaluative atmosphere in which people have their mistakes pointed out to them as "mistakes." It also avoids praising people because they have succeeded in doing something "difficult." To describe something, or to treat something as "difficult," is in itself "negative suggestion," which curdles the atmosphere and makes Suggestopedia almost impossible.

Suggestopedia also concurs with many other methods in the belief that it is good for the teacher to be lively, cheerful, and efficient. A difference, however, is that most other methods seem to regard the liveliness, cheerfulness, and efficiency of the teacher merely as a plus factor—important and desirable, but something that the teacher brings *to* or adds *to* the method. For Suggestopedia, these qualities in the teacher are integral parts *of* the method.

(5) *The strategy of Suggestopedia includes removing the limitations which society has suggested to the student.* The trick is to lead the student to forget about or to ignore the limitations. But before he can allow himself to do so, he needs an excuse, a justification for venturing outside of the old fence even after the gate has been opened. A doctor sometimes sees that a patient's body could cure itself, except that the patient is convinced that his illness requires help from a professional. So the doctor gives the patient a prescription which costs money, and which has a scientific-sounding name, but which is made of nothing but sugar or cornstarch. The patient gets well after taking these pills, not because of any chemical action, but because the person has now used his own powers—powers which he did not know he had—to cure himself. A medicine of this kind is called a "placebo."

Lozanov makes much use of placebos in Suggestopedia in order to "desuggest" the undesirable social norm, and to leave the student open to other, positive suggestions. Virtually every element in a Suggestopedic course has, in addition to its overt effect, also a "placebo" effect.

According to Lozanov, every healthy person has three barriers to suggestion from outside. We resist suggestions that don't make sense to us in terms of what we already know. ("It's obviously impossible for me to learn 100 words a day; in the past I've had trouble holding on to even ten!") We resist suggestions that undermine our feelings of confidence and security. ("Why should I sit back and close my eyes while the teacher reads the dialog along with the music?") We resist suggestions that we do something which we think is morally or ethically wrong. ("We shouldn't be playing all these games in class—we should be working!") Lozanov recognizes that without these three barriers to protect it, any personality would very quickly be torn apart by all the disorganized and conflicting suggestions that constantly strike it from outside. So he does not set out to destroy these barriers, or even to attack them directly, for that would lead to more trouble, not less. He seeks only to circumvent them, to sneak around them, or to pass through them by blending with them.

The process of desuggestion and resuggestion requires the teacher to make deliberate and skillful use of the general atmosphere—the background against which the student will see and interpret whatever else the teacher does. Even the color of the classroom walls and the style of the furnishings may be taken into account in designing a Suggestopedic classroom. But what about those of us who are not pretending to use this method in any authentic way, and who in any case are not in a position to redecorate or refinish our rooms? None of my friends would accuse me of being compulsively neat in the way I keep my own office. Yet when I walk into a classroom and see students seated around a table that is loaded down with clutter—clutter than is permanent, and unrelated to what they are doing at the moment, I wonder what kind of "suggestion" this clutter is broadcasting to the students as they try to learn.

The most important background element, though, is not paint, or armchairs, or a clear table. It is what Lozanov calls the "authority" of the teacher. By "authority," Lozanov means much more than the ability to issue instructions that will be carried out. The central element in "authority" is the teacher's apparent competence—her competence in the eyes of her students—and her reputation for being able to produce amazing results. People will not trust themselves even to a strong bridge if it looks flimsy, and if they do not set foot on it they will never arrive at the place to which it leads. As in the case of liveliness, cheerfulness, and efficiency, Suggestopedia differs from other methods in that it considers the authority of the teacher (and of the school, and of Suggestopedia in general) to be an integral part of the method, and not just a desirable characteristic of the teacher.

We have seen this same principle at work in the history of language teaching outside of Suggestopedia. At least a portion of the early successes which swept audiolingualism to a dominant position in some parts of the world in the 1950s must have come from the well-publicized exploits of the linguistic scientists in teaching seldom-taught languages during World War II. And at least some part of the success of programmed instruction must rest on what people have read about those pigeons who were taught to appear to play ping-pong. This is not to belittle either of these methods or the sources of their success. But the same kind of "authority" which these methods have profited from generally and in haphazard fashion is in Suggestopedia developed consciously and painstakingly, and used with great efficiency.

The desuggestion-resuggestion process also requires the teacher to make deliberate and skillful use of the conscious and unconscious elements in whatever she does against that general background of authority, pleasant decor, and all. This brings us back to the subject of "placebos." Specific combinations of objects, actions, and words used over and over again can become rituals, and Lozanov sees "ritual placebos" as among the most powerful tools of the Suggestopedic teacher. I have already described (Chapter 6) my own use of silence, and of an unchanging set of words that introduced the silence, which seemed to have something of this effect in a non-Suggestopedic course. The difference, once again, is that what is used as an isolated technique in other methods is used systematically in Suggestopedia, and woven into the very fabric of the course. The trick is to choose elements, and to combine them, in ways that will fit with—and will therefore help to join together—both the expectations of the students and the pedagogical aspects of the course.

(6) *Once the tensions and the negative suggestions have been removed, it is necessary to be sure that they do not creep back in.* They sometimes sneak back in subtle ways. For example, one of my own frequent goals both as a writer of materials and as a teacher has been to break into small pieces whatever I was trying to teach, and to give it to the student in very gentle gradations so as to maintain his self-confidence and leave him with a feeling of success. Lozanov points out that this may leave the student with the impression (i.e., it may "suggest" to the student) that the language, relative to his own powers, must be very hard. In other words, his own powers relative to the task of learning the language must be weak. It is true that by our careful sequencing and grading we have left the student with a feeling of confidence. But it is confidence in power which is much narrower than what lies hidden in him. And the success which he has achieved in this way only persuades him further that the ceiling which society has placed on his rate of learning is a realistic one.

Once the student has concluded that he should not expect to learn rapidly and easily, the natural result is that he will not learn rapidly or easily. Even with the best of Suggestopedic materials, details of the teacher's tone of voice or body language may convey the impression of difficulty, unsatisfactory progress, danger of mistakes, and failure. Materials and procedures must therefore be carefully designed, and teachers specially trained, in order to maintain the conditions under which Suggestopedia will be possible.

(7) *Some of the necessary tools used in Suggestopedia are psychological.* These include the means by which the teacher makes use of emotional stimuli, and not just cognitive ones, including those that come in around the edges of awareness. We have already seen what some of these are: liveliness, cheerfulness, efficiency, the teacher's evident self-confidence and joy in what she is doing; the making of demands that imply that the student has great powers which he has never before used; the happy, successful lives of the people in the dialogs, and so on. The reader should turn for further detail to the books by Dr. Lozanov and others. But I suspect that full understanding of this point will require firsthand training which I have not had.

(8) *Some of the necessary tools are artistic.* They make use of what Lozanov calls "certain harmonious art forms," which certainly include music. Some reports also speak of special, stylized, almost "balletesque" body movement on the part of at least some teachers. It is after all in the nature of art (as contrasted with mere illustration or decoration) that it speaks to us on two levels—or on many levels—at once. This may be what Lozanov has in mind when he speaks of the "liberating and stimulating character" of the arts in Suggestopedia. The most conspicuous artistic medium, and the one which has received the most publicity, is the music which forms a part of the "concert sessions." After a new dialog has been presented and before going home at the end of that day, the students have two of these sessions, one "active" and the other "passive," in which the teacher gives a highly skilled and somewhat dramatic reading of the new dialog against the background of

recorded music. The actual musical selections are chosen largely for the deep messages that they convey—certainty and deep but controlled emotion in the "active" sessions; order, stability, and completion of the task (of memorization) in the "passive" sessions. It is not necessary that the student be an enthusiast for music of the classical and baroque periods; the important thing is that he receive the underlying messages which they carry. Or so some of my sources report. Once again Suggestopedia differs from other methods in that the art forms are integrated into it, rather than being used as supplements for the purpose of illustrating the course or brightening it up.

(9) *Some of the necessary tools are pedagogical*: materials, techniques, and so on. I am afraid that I have no very exact information concerning the pedagogical tools beyond what I wrote in 1976. Having seen videotapes of Suggestopedic classes in the Soviet Union, Canada, and the United States, and having watched a very few classes taught by people trained in Sofia, and having seen copies of a few of the dialogs, I still have not seen anything that was greatly different from what I have seen good language teachers do in non-Suggestopedic classes. This is not to say that Suggestopedia is not greatly different from other systems. It is only to say that the difference lies, not in any one element, but in the extraordinary care with which the elements are integrated into one another. The goal is to produce consistently the effects that in most methods come only at "peak moments."

One very important "pedagogical tool" is the "global" nature of the dialogs themselves. Compared to other dialogs I have seen, they are long, rambling, and variegated—Victorian mansions compared to the neat, manageable tract houses that we so often construct for our students. The purpose is that the whole will be full of life, and that each person will remember what his or her own background, interests, etc., cause to stick. No two people will hold onto exactly the same things. Yet little or nothing will be lost, because in the "elaboration" sessions the teacher is working with the collective memory of the whole group, rather than testing the memory of individuals.

In this connection, Lozànov emphasizes the importance of maintaining in the students' minds the vividness of the meaning-bearing whole, shifting away from it to analysis of details only briefly, and then coming back to the synthesis of form, meaning and feeling.

The three principles that guide this integration are covered in points 10 to 12:

(10) The first is sometimes translated from Bulgarian as "*the principle of joy and easiness*": the students should enjoy what they are doing and not see it as something hard. This implies an absence of any destructive or inhibiting tension. But psychic relaxation does not mean inattention or laziness. There are two kinds of "concentration." One is the care-full kind, the kind that

teachers so often demand of their students and that the students soon come to expect of themselves. This is the "concentration" in which the student is apprehensive lest he miss something, or in which he thinks (or mutters) a new item over and over rapidly as soon as it is introduced. This kind of concentration, says Lozanov, does indeed lead to education, but to a "false education." The other kind of concentration is relaxed and care-free, yet without being care-less, and so allows learning to go on in a way that is not tiring. The principal source of tension in the former kind of concentration is the student's lack of confidence that he can do what he is asked to do. This lack of confidence is therefore a chief target of the Suggestopedic teacher's use of materials, pedagogical techniques, and artistic media. The principal source of joy in the carefree concentration that Lozanov is talking about lies in easy assimilation and easy use of the language.

A few other methods place emphasis on relaxed concentration, and some of the best teachers by almost any method help their students to reach that kind of concentration at least part of the time. But Lozanov emphasizes that a teacher whose students are working in this way is not necessarily "doing Suggestopedia," or even "doing 1/3 of Suggestopedia." This criterion must be met *along with* the two that follow.

(11) The second principle that guides the integration of the various means to Suggestopedia is that *the conscious and the unconscious reactions of the student are inseparable from one another.* This is a partial restatement of point (1), above. Here, it becomes a criterion which demands that the teacher use overt means of which the student is conscious in order to pursue goals of which the student may not be fully conscious, as well as to pursue those goals that do occupy the center of the student's attention: confidence, physical enjoyment, etc., as well as accuracy, fluency, and vocabulary.

(12) The last principle is what Lozanov calls "*suggestive interaction.*" He says that the level of such interaction can be measured by how fully the "reserve powers" of the learner have been mobilized. These powers are qualitatively different from those used in ordinary learning, and can lead to a new, less tiring, and more permanent type of learning. (Looking ahead to Chapter 21, one cannot help wondering about the relationship between this "qualitative difference" and the qualitative difference(s) between what in that chapter are called "acquisition" and "learning.")

For genuine Suggestopedia, then, not one and not two but all three of these criteria (points 10 to 12) must be met simultaneously and continuously. When they are, the students become more and more able to teach and help themselves as the course goes on. But this freeing process must not be limited to the cognitive level alone, says Lozanov; freedom in the process of instruction must go hand in hand with freedom from the inner fear of one's own limited powers of assimilating new information.

SUGGESTOPEDIA AND CHAPTER 2

Suggestopedia, with its carefully prepared materials and its emphasis on the authority of the teacher, is anything but a power vacuum. Yet it also requires the teacher to be warm and supportive, and to refrain from talking about "mistakes." In this way, it avoids the "evaluative paradigm." While it does try to give the student full-time security as far as the teacher's competence is concerned, it certainly does not intend to protect him from making errors. What it does produce, according to all reports, is people who enjoy using the language.

In its look inside the learner, Suggestopedia sees a person whose physical, emotional, and intellectual sides are closely intertwined. The learner-anxiety with which it deals most directly is that which arises from uncertainty about ability to handle the course and the language. The other anxieties that we looked at in Chapter 1 are apparently expected to wither away naturally in the wholesome light of "joy and easiness" and "desuggestion-suggestion."

Teacher "*control*" is firm throughout the six-hour cycle. To judge from what I have seen, the teacher also exercises much of the "*initiative*" in the beginning, but allows the students a great deal of "initiative" later on. Many of the later activities involve considerable cooperation among the students, in such activities as preparing skits. But even in the earlier and more tightly structured activities, the teacher may address her questions to the class as a whole, rather than putting one individual on the spot at a time. By doing so she appears to assume (i.e., she "suggests") that the class is a functioning *cooperative* unit, and so the students act as one. In a group of 10 to 12, moreover, there is almost certain to be someone who can come up with the answer. As a result, the "principle of joy and easiness" is maintained, and at the same time an extraordinarily strong feeling of *community* arises.

"Good vibes" are of course at the very heart of Suggestopedia, in the unnoticed positive messages which the teacher sends out at all times.

I am not sure what to say about "mask changing" by the Suggestopedic teacher. I do know that—presumably to protect the teacher's aura of authority—teachers do not fraternize with students outside of class. On the other hand, my best firsthand source reports concerning his training in Sofia, "My guide rewarded me when I relaxed into playfulness and chided me only when I undertook any exercise that smacked of drilling. I must admit I did notice a change of expression on the students' faces at such times. The sunny looks became clouded for a moment and the wary expression appeared that is seen so often in conventional classes." Perhaps the meaning of "double planeness" is precisely this: that at all times the teacher wears both masks— the mask of the director of learning, and over it the warm, engaged mask of one human being in happy relationship with another.

This guess is consistent with my brief observation of the Italian class.

During the "concert" session, as she read the new dialog against a background of classical music, the teacher looked for all the world like the soprano soloist in an oratorio: confident and in charge of her audience, but performing in a way that gave to them what they had come to the concert for. Also as in an oratorio, her voicing of the language was highly stylized. During the "elaboration" session, there was constant give and take of one kind or another between teacher and class. In this activity, I felt that I was watching people play with a frisbee. For example, when the teacher threw out a question, she did so like a person who is sharing in a game. When the answer came back, she received it with the same gusto, very much as if she were snagging a well-placed toss of a frisbee. She very clearly did *not* do what we so often do: when the response came back, she did *not* step from in front of a target and then announce how close the student's shot had come to the bullseye.

My guess is that the Suggestopedic teacher would be a good model for the student's "Self 1" to pattern itself after.

Apparently the Suggestopedic teacher does not invite students to express their reactions to the course, at least not while it is in progress. To do so would at the very least take something away from the teacher's status as someone who has no doubts about what she is doing. And if the students expressed any serious discomforts or doubts, the schedule would be thrown off. The whole Suggestopedic basis for success might even crumble.

CHAPTER 19

SOME SUGGESTOPEDIC IDEAS IN NON-SUGGESTOPEDIC METHODS

I said in Chapter 18 that nothing I have ever done could properly be labeled "Suggestopedia." I have never even attempted such a thing. One reason why I have not done so is that I take Lozanov seriously when he says that Suggestopedia requires the teacher to have kinds of training that I have not had. Nevertheless, certain of my experiences may cast light on the description in Chapter 18, just as the theory has helped me to understand the experiences better. I will relate them in chronological order.

THE SWAHILI MONOLOGS

From time to time, as a methodological experience in Counseling-Learning for language teachers, I have taught 10 to 20 hours of beginning Swahili. This book contains accounts of three such experiences, in Chapters 12–14. The third time I conducted a short course of this kind (not one of the experiences described in Chapters 12–14), one of the students said, after about four hours, "These conversations among us are all very nice, but I'd like to hear how the language sounds when it's really spoken." I decided to provide a sample of fluent Swahili after the next break.

My reason for doing so was not simply to comply with the student's request. It was that I felt that we were all of us ready for a change of pace before going on with what we had been doing—an interlude which would provide relief from routine without departing altogether from what we had been trying to do.

Since this was an experience in Counseling-Learning, I was particularly concerned that what I did should not diminish the students' sense of security. I therefore began by saying, "I'm going to let you hear a sample of Swahili as it might be spoken rapidly outside the classroom. All you need to do is listen. I won't ask you any questions about it when I have finished." Then I talked to them for about five minutes. When I began talking, I had no clear idea of what I was going to say. I talked *to* the students, not just in front of them, and I spoke with considerable animation. I used gestures, and some of the words that they had been exposed to, as well as two or three proper names. But whenever I needed words that the students had not met, I went ahead and used them. In using them, I was not apologetic, but continued to act as though I thought my meaning was getting across. I was garrulous and somewhat repetitious, but the repetitions were of the kind that might come up in normal discourse between speakers of a language. They were not the kind of thing that a teacher uses in order to "be helpful."

When I finished, I left a few seconds of silence, as though I were catching my breath before going back to the scheduled activity. Before I spoke again, one of the students said, "Do you mind if we tell you what we understood?" I was a bit surprised, but of course invited them to go ahead. As it turned out, both they and I were amazed at how much they were able to recount in English from what they had heard in Swahili. Among them, they brought back virtually everything I had said. And so a new procedure was born.

Since that incident, I have used this procedure with numerous other classes. The results have always been at least as good as the first time, and sometimes better. One of these occasions was on the sixth day of the class on which I have already reported in Chapter 14. Some of the written comments of students in that class were the following:

> It was just about the most exciting thing that has happened in the class so far. . . . It did not seem contrived. . . . I was amazed that I could follow the story after a scant six or seven hours of study.

> I didn't understand much, but the sounds were beautiful, and the gestures and facial expressions were fascinating. It was good communication. It was a beautiful drama.

> I was not paying attention because I had something else on my mind, yet the story was told in a highly animated way, and was addressed to us as if we had been speaking Swahili all our lives, so that I became caught up in the story. [This comment was from a student who had reproduced in English almost everything that I had said in Swahili.]

> I just let my brain go limp and let it take the story in without too much backtracking. . . . It was exciting to realize how much the human brain can piece together with very little information.

If we look carefully at these four quotations, I believe we will recognize some bits of the ore which, if refined, purified, and crystallized, might become the stuff of which Suggestopedia is made. Pleasant, relaxed emotions are evident in all of them. The unspoken attitude that I conveyed by talking to the class "as if we had been speaking Swahili all our lives" indicates that the peripheral ("suggestive") communication was consistent with my purposes, and this fact also fits Suggestopedia. All quotations but the second display success far beyond the student's expectations or previous experience. The last two show evidence of the kind of "pseudopassive" attention that Lozanov talks about. The very last sentence sounds very much like a reference to "the normally unused reserve powers of the mind." It is as though the very impossibility of coping with the rapid flood of language in the usual way had forced the minds of these people into a new and (to them) surprising mode of operation.

Most of the forty-some students in this class had the feeling of having followed "more than half" of what I had said. Nevertheless, there were some who felt that they had understood very little, and one reported that he felt uncomfortable because most of the others seemed to understand so much more than he had. These facts alone would be enough to keep this episode from being called an example of "Suggestopedia." In addition, the material that I used lacked careful integration of the "three tools" to the degree that Lozanov seems to call for. Even so, my contacts with Lozanov's thinking have helped me to recognize these good things when they happen; recognizing them, in turn, makes it easier for me to do them again in other classes, on other days.

It may be worthwhile to distinguish two sides of this episode. One was the relaxed way in which many of the students were able to catch and use, amid the flood of language, those bits of Swahili that they had been exposed to. No more need be said here about that side. The second side was the way in which I was apparently able to "desuggest" the limitations which could have kept the students from even trying to do such an "impossible" thing. In ordinary classroom use, these two move along together, and may seem to be parts of the same thing. But as we try to understand them so that we can learn to achieve these effects in our own teaching, it would be helpful if we could see one of them separated from the other. The following episode seems to show just that.

In September of 1976, I found myself facing an audience of about 50 people in a two-hour time slot directly after lunch. I had had two other sessions with the same audience on the mornings of preceding days, so that we were to some extent comfortable with each other. But the hour, plus the fatigue which the audience had accumulated during a week-long training program, made it clear that I could not get away with just another lecture. So I began by writing on the board two vertical columns of English words:

hairs	toiling
annulled	udder
furry	warts
starry	warts

First, I had the audience read the list aloud one word at a time. Then I recited it myself, with the intonation of someone who is telling a story: "Hairs annulled furry starry, toiling udder warts, warts welcher alter girdle deferent former wants inner regional virgin." The listeners, who were native speakers of English, found themselves *hearing* this meaningless series of *words*, but at the same time *understanding* the *message*: "Here's an old fairy story, told in other words—words which are altogether different from the ones in the original version." I then went on to tell them the entire story of "Ladle Rat Rotten Hut" (Little Red Riding Hood) in this way. The entertainment value of this stunt is greatest when the story is told at just the right speed, allowing the listeners to be equally aware of the actual words and of the message, and to enjoy the discrepancy.

On this occasion, however, my purpose was to do more than just keep the audience awake after lunch. At the end of the story, with almost no comment, I went into a monolog in Turkish. This monolog was conducted in the same manner as the Swahili monologs that I have already described, but this audience had never before been exposed to any Turkish at all. As a minor placebo, I drew a very rough map of Turkey on the chalkboard and made occasional references to it. At the end of the monolog, many members of the audience felt that they had understood much of what I had said. For those people, it was apparently an experience like the one that Alice had when she read *Jabberwocky*: "It fills my head with ideas, but I'm not quite sure what they are." One interpretation of their reaction is that I had "desuggested their limitations," but without going on from there and actually teaching them something. I had unlocked a door that opened on a blank wall. The experience seemed to have been a pleasantly exciting one for this audience.

The major placebo which made this possible was of course not the map. It was the story of Ladle Rat Rotten Hut. With it, the hearers had suspended their normal way of listening, and had found themselves "understanding the unintelligible." I suspect, therefore, that this was an example of the third aspect of Suggestopedia—the aspect to which language teachers least often give their attention. This episode took place in a training seminar. What we hope for in a real class is that the students will combine this feeling and this openness with some actual resources in the target language. When they do so, their progress should be many times greater than what we are accustomed to.

In connection with a Counseling-Learning episode, I have already (Chapter 13) described a technique for reading aloud to students the same sentences that they have already studied cognitively, using three different styles of speaking. As I said there, this technique was quite frankly based on my attempt to understand what Lozanov meant by the three "intonations," in his description of the "concert pseudopassive" sessions of Suggestopedia. The aspect of that technique that I wish to comment on here, however, is not the reading itself, but the way in which I introduce it. My formula goes something like this: "Now I'm going to read you the sentences in a way that will help you to absorb them. I'll read each sentence three times." I then give a brief description of the "intonations" and continue by saying, "If you have a favorite way of throwing your mind into neutral and not trying too hard, you may want to use it. I will also ask you not to look at the written words. You may want to close your eyes as I read." In reciting this formula, I use a quiet but firm voice, which is intended to convey the impression that I have used this technique in dozens of classes and that it has always worked. I leave about 15 seconds of silence before the first sentence and after the last one.

My most recent information indicates that my understanding of the "intonations" was mistaken, at least in terms of present-day practice. Nevertheless, the technique does work well. I think that its success may depend on several factors, all of which are related to Suggestopedic theory: (1) The peripherally conveyed confidence. (2) The use of an unchanging formula—

almost an incantation—which becomes one part of a "ritual placebo." (3) The readiness of young adults these days to accept the value of mind-quieting exercises such as yoga and meditation. (4) The possibility that some students actually draw on their own earlier experiences in those areas. Negatively, (5) I did not use music in these sessions because I was fairly sure that my choice of selections would be more or less inappropriate, and that my handling of the tapes would be more or less clumsy, so that the overall effect would be amateurish. I am sure that music done well would have enhanced the effect still further, but done poorly it would have damaged my aura of confidence and competence (my "authority"), and so would have spoiled the overall effect. (6) For similar reasons, I did not engage in a formal, overt procedure aimed at inducing physical or psychic relaxation.

I believe that Suggestopedic factors also play a role in the success of many other methods and techniques which in themselves have nothing to do with Suggestopedia: the conversations described at the end of Chapter 13; my choice of clothing to be worn to class; the reputed miracles wrought by linguistic science in language training during World War II, as a factor in the success of the Audio-Lingual Method.

In Chapter 22, we will look again at the place of "miracle" in our profession. Here, however, I would like to comment briefly on two kinds of activity. One is rapid-fire choral and individual "mimicry" drill which is so characteristic of orthodox audiolingual teaching. The other is the explanation of grammar, which we find somewhere or other in most methods though not in all.

The basic technique for the beginning stage of one kind of audiolingual instruction is massed choral and individual repetition after the teacher. Details vary, but in a typical procedure the teacher would say the last part of the first sentence and have the whole class say it after her. She would do the same thing again, and then go on to add another part of the sentence. She would continue in this way with larger and larger parts of the sentence, giving each part twice and having the class repeat it after her until finally they had reached the whole sentence. Then she would treat each successive sentence in the same way. At the end of the choral repetition, she would switch to repetition by individual students, correcting their pronunciation whenever she thought it was appropriate to do so. After a heavy dose of this kind of thing, students went on to try to produce the sentences by themselves, and eventually to memorize the dialog which was made up of these selfsame sentences. What I have given in this paragraph has been a simplified description of a relatively primitive and unsophisticated version of "mimicry-memorization." My purpose here, however, is not to write a manual on the use of that technique. It is, rather, to point out one potential strength in it—a strength which I have come to see more clearly after reading about Lozanov's work.

When I first used vigorous and protracted repetition, I thought that it worked because it helped to "burn the sentence (or the grammatical pattern) into the brain." Then I noticed that this kind of activity didn't work for everyone, although it certainly worked for many. So I had to change my theory. I guessed that the technique worked best for people whose minds took the noises and the muscular feelings that were there fresh in their immediate memory, and worked with these noises and feelings, looking at them from one point of view after another, even while the words remained the same, repetition after repetition. In this way, a sentence would enter the student's memory with a richer set of associations. For this reason, the student would find that the sentence came back to him more readily when he needed it.

I still think that both of these theories may be partly right. But while I was conducting some intensive "mim-mem" drill recently, a third explanation came to mind.

An ordinary, old-fashioned radio signal uses what is called "amplitude modulation" (AM). The sound of a voice or of a musical instrument comes to us as vibrations of the air. These vibrations are at relatively low frequencies—some hundreds or a few thousands of vibrations per second. The designers of early radios wanted to take these vibrations out of the air and change them into electromagnetic vibrations so as to send them over long distances without wires. Unfortunately, however, electromagnetic waves which are of the same shape and frequency as sound waves do not travel very well. Then the engineers hit on the idea of using electromagnetic waves that vibrated at some unchanging frequency of at least half a million cycles per second. These radio waves travel very well, but they are at frequencies far above what anybody can hear. The trick was to make this "carrier frequency" stronger or weaker (in technical terminology, to "modulate" it); *and to do so at a rate* which corresponded to the shape of the sound waves:

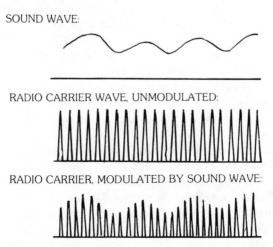

SOUND WAVE:

RADIO CARRIER WAVE, UNMODULATED:

RADIO CARRIER, MODULATED BY SOUND WAVE:

This was the job of the transmitter. The receiver's job was just the opposite: to filter out the radio carrier frequency but hold onto its shape, and to convert this *shape* back into sound waves by means of some sort of headset or loudspeaker.

This has been a long explanation of a matter which is not directly a part of language teaching. I apologize to those readers who understand radio principles better than I do. But I need the concepts of "carrier" and "modulation" in order to explain my third theory of how "mim-mem" can work.

If a dialog is well chosen, and if the teacher breaks the sentences into pieces of the right size, then the rhythm of modeling by the teacher and repetition by the students becomes both rapid and quite regular. Such a rapid, regular rhythm can be soothing to the students and (in the everyday sense, not in the technical sense) almost hypnotic. This is like the radio carrier frequency, which can go places that lower, less regular frequencies cannot go. It makes its way around and past the anxieties that the student would feel if he focused on each sentence as a separate problem or set of problems. It carries with it the unspoken ideas (i.e., it "suggests") that the teacher is competent; that the teacher is in charge; that the students are "in good hands"; and that since things are going so smoothly the students themselves are also competent. Keeping up with this kind of drill can thus give to the student a general sense of personal adequacy, even elation. The bodily participation in the physical rhythm must also be a part of the total effect. (This is close to the experience that students and teacher share in Carolyn Graham's "jazz chants.") The overall result, then, may be to "desuggest" many of the limitations that the students thought they had.

At the same time, the teacher may superimpose other ideas on this stable and rapid rhythm, just as a radio transmitter modulates its carrier frequency to carry the shapes of sound waves. Slight changes in technique, or in facial expression or body language or tone of voice may carry such messages as, "We're making a little game of this," or "I'm enjoying myself," or "Aha! Since you did that so easily, let's move on to this new variation!" Yet if the teacher tries to transmit messages like these directly, in words like the ones I have quoted here, they will not come through as effectively. They may run afoul of the "antisuggestive barriers." If they arouse suspicion or misgivings, their net effect may even be the opposite of what the teacher intended: "Is she trying to *encourage* us because she thinks our performance must be *discouraging* to us?" and so on.

Of course, the "modulation" which the teacher applies to the rhythmic "carrier" may be undesirable to begin with: messages like "I'm the slave-driver and you are the slaves," or "Why can't you get it right?" or "Don't let me down in front of our visitor(s)!" Any and all of these messages can come in along with the words, are stored in the student's memory along with the words, and color the student's feelings toward the language and its speakers.

Before leaving the topic of "mimicry-memorization," I should remind readers that this technique is *not* a part of Suggestopedia, for Lozanov seems to avoid mechanical drilling of any kind. I have discussed it here because I think Lozanov has helped us to see why one and the same technique can be either heavy and deadly, or light and lively.

Let us turn now to look at ways in which a teacher may "explain grammar." My own basic insights on this topic come out of Counseling-Learning, so that it might have been discussed in one of the chapters on that approach. It has been postponed to this chapter because those insights are also consistent with my understanding of Suggestopedia, while at the same time Suggestopedia makes some things explicit which are only implied in Counseling-Learning.

The explaining of grammar fills more than one of the student's needs. Most obviously, it helps him to see how the words, the endings, the phrases, the sentences on the mechanical side of the language all fit together. It casts light on the unfamiliar pathways and the arbitrary obstacles through which he must eventually be able to run back and forth with his eyes shut. It can thus save him a certain amount of time, energy, and barked shins. It is for this reason, of course, that the teacher needs to know these same pathways and obstacles—not only to run back and forth in them for herself, but also to see them as they look to a newcomer. On top of this are the skills of knowing when to turn on the spotlight of explanation and when to turn it off, and knowing just how to aim it so that it will help the student instead of blinding him. Everything that I have said in this paragraph is, as I said at the beginning, obvious to any experienced teacher.

But I think that the student has a second need which he hopes that grammatical explanations will meet. This is the need for power—symbolic power, almost mystical power—to protect him amid the chaos of an alien and inhospitable (language-) universe. My guess is that this second need of the student's comes into being somewhat as follows:

1. Some people, by accident of nature or training, recognize and work with tastes (or spatial relations, or musical tones) better than other people do. In the same way, some people recognize and work with grammatical distinctions more readily than others do. We may call these people "Group G."

2. Group G people do relatively well at most tasks that language teachers set for them—the same tasks that non-G people find most mysterious and therefore most difficult. These tasks include the memorizing of verb paradigms and the like. They also include becoming accustomed to the fact that in one language English "I have _____" is literally "there is to me," in another "I am with _____," and in a third "there is my _____." This part of their success comes from the fact that they perceive directly the abstractions with which they must work in order to perform these tasks.

3. Group G people also do relatively well at understanding grammatical explanations; because they understand them, they also do relatively well at remembering them; and by remembering they make more effective use of

them. This again helps these people to be relatively successful in language courses. But these two kinds of success are different from each other: the first (point 2, above) is like the ability of a person with mechanical aptitude to know instinctively how the parts of a disassembled bicycle must fit together; the second is the ability to make sense out of the printed instructions.

4. Group G's ordinary classmates (Group O) notice both kinds of success, but without distinguishing between them. They see Group G doing well, and they hear Group G talking about rules. They conclude that the former follows as a result of the latter, but this conclusion is valid only in a limited sense. They do not see that to a large extent both kinds of success grow out of the same basic ability to deal with a particular type of data. It is as though I, with some but very modest musical ability, were to conclude that if I were to read the same books on musical theory that professional musicians read, my own performance would improve greatly. That conclusion might not be entirely false, but it could be bad for me if it aroused false hopes or led me to misdirect my efforts to play better. We are dealing here with something akin to gnosticism, an early Christian heresy which held that salvation was to be gained through a certain body of secret mysterious knowledge.

The first need for grammatical explanations was a straightforward and relatively unemotional need. This second need, by contrast, can be highly charged with feelings, both positive and negative. It is for this reason that I have brought this topic in after discussions of both Counseling-Learning and Suggestopedia. Here is a scenario that plays itself out all too often:

a. A student in Group O has difficulty with something.

b. He concludes that the solution to his difficulty is greater knowledge.

c. He assumes that the best way to knowledge is to get someone to give him an explanation.

d. Someone gives him an explanation.

e. He understands the explanation to some extent, at least for the moment.

f. He feels (i) grateful to the person who provided the explanation, (ii) confirmed in his assumption (c, above), and (iii) responsible for holding onto the explanation and using it to improve his performance.

g. When performance time comes, he still makes mistakes, either because he has forgotten the explanation, or because he never had understood it fully, or because the explanation itself had been less than adequate. (Many errors in language use are in matters which are simply too complex or too subtle for ordinary explanations.)

h. The disappointing performance leads to (i) feelings of resentment toward the teacher or the book that provided the explanation, or (ii) feelings of guilt and/or personal inadequacy, or (iii) demand for additional review of the explanations or others like them. Steps d through h of this scenario can repeat themselves indefinitely. Too often, each repetition intensifies the negative feelings.

I have written the scenario from the point of view of an ordinary student (Group O). The students in Group G generally make the same assumptions as Group O concerning what happens and what needs to happen and why. Since they succeed, however, they are spared the negative feelings (h in the scenario). This reinforces their own belief, and the belief of their Group O classmates, about the scenario and the assumptions which lie behind it. As for the teacher, she is almost certainly an alumna of Group G. She understands the grammar, but she does not understand the fallacy which lies behind the scenario. If she has a personal need to "shine," or if she has a personal need to feel that she is responding to needs that the students express, or if she has a need to "give" the students information that she will later be able to grade them on in tests—*if, that is, she has her eye on anything except the students* and how her words are affecting them as she speaks— then she is likely to launch into an inappropriate kind of explanation, or an excessive amount of it. In this way, she uses her spotlight to blind the students, as we said above, or to burden them, rather than to help them.

(The gathering, studying, forgetting, and reviewing of vocabulary lists may follow a similar scenario, except that the absence of "rules" removes some of the tendency to depend on explanations.)

From the point of view of Counseling-Learning, the grammatical system of a language is like a picture, or a series of pictures. To the teacher who knows and loves the grammar of her language, it is a wonderful, fascinating, and inexhaustible museum. The students are visitors to the museum and she is its curator. She takes a visitor by the elbow and leads him to one of the paintings on the wall. As he gazes at it and attempts to make sense of its unfamiliar style, she points out an important feature of it. Then she steers him across the room to another, somewhat different painting. There, she points out a related feature in the second painting and asks the visitor whether he sees what she has pointed out to him. Either out of politeness, or because he does see it at least halfway, he says, "Yes, of course!" The tour continues in this way, with the visitor half-comprehending each point as it is made, perhaps making careful entries into his notebook on "Art Appreciation," and ending the tour full of gratitude to the curator and admiration for her erudition. In the terminology of Counseling-Learning the curator has been attempting to "pull the visitor into her world." Unless the visitor has unusual ability or previous training in looking at paintings, however, he is likely to feel bewilderment, discouragement, and intellectual fatigue along with his gratitude and admiration.

In teaching English, for example, the teacher may start out to explain the tense of the verb in the sentence:

I'm going to do it tomorrow.

This could lead to the morass of trying to explain just when to use each of two similar tenses:

> I'm going to do it tomorrow.
> I will do it tomorrow.

and from there to the difference between *shall* and *will*. Other wilderness paths may beckon:

> I'm going to do it tomorrow.   or: I'm going to do it tomorrow.
> I'm willing to do it tomorrow.   I'm to do it tomorrow.

Even if the teacher sticks to one point—or if the curator explains only one painting—it may not be one that the student/visitor was ready for. The teacher/curator has still pulled the guest into her own world.

From the new learner's point of view, the grammar of the new language is not like a museum at all. It is an alien and perplexing object which has been set before him in the midst of his own world—more like a jigsaw puzzle than it is like a meaningful collection of paintings. Counseling-Learning would urge the teacher to try to enter into this world of the student's, and to look over his shoulder, and to see which gap he is trying to fill at the moment. Then the teacher, who knows what the completed puzzle will have to look like, may pick out that one piece. She will not set it into the puzzle herself, but will leave that work (and that pleasure) to the student. Or, instead of pointing out the missing piece, she may only provide the smallest hint that will help the student to locate it for himself. Exactly what she does will depend on her sensitive awareness of the student's world and where he is in it.

The place where Suggestopedia illuminates the explaining of grammar (and where I believe it can further illuminate Counseling-Learning in general) is in its careful attention to the unspoken, unrecognized, and therefore powerful messages that ride along with the words of an explanation. Some of them that I have "heard" from time to time (and I suppose that, as a teacher, I have also transmitted the same messages) are:

"*My museum is so rich and subtle that you will never be able to see and appreciate everything in it.*" [The full grammatical structure of any normal language is this complex—so complex, in fact, that none has ever been completely described even by scholars. The trouble with this unspoken message is that it emphasizes the hopelessness of getting the whole, rather than the easiness of getting any one part. I think of the solicitous visitor in the hospital, who sympathetically exclaims to a patient, "Oh, you poor dear! You look terrible! You look just like Uncle Henry did just before he passed away!"]

"*This particular point is very hard!*" [Any one point of grammar is easy. What pass for "difficult" points are actually clusters of related points which the teacher, operating in her own world and not in the world of the student, has never bothered to pick apart from one another. For example, "formation of the plural of English nouns" consists of a number of relationships: *key–keys, dot–dots, face–faces, house–houses, ox–oxen, woman–women,* and so on. A wise colleague of mine used to tell his students that French has 70-some classes of regular verbs—and no irregular ones! To dismiss his statement as mere playing with terminology would be to overlook the difference between his unspoken message and the message that most of us send out when we are lecturing our students on such matters.]

"*Don't ask questions. I want to move ahead with the rest of my explanation.*" [The words that often accompany this unspoken message are "Okay?" or "Right?" or "Do you have any questions?" But something about the speaker's nonverbal or supraverbal communication says, "I'm on a fixed track, and I'm moving. If you actually ask any questions now, you may derail me. One or both of us may be slightly bruised as a result."]

"*Now that I've explained this to you, remember it!*" [This is a "laying on of expectations." (Chapter 7). A student who continues to make errors in the matter that has been explained is thus invited to feel either guilty or inadequate. Some manage to feel both ways at the same time!]

"*See how much I know, and how expertly I have set it out for you!*" [The implication is: "You could never have done this for yourself. In understanding things like this, you depend on me."]

I suppose that most teachers would agree that all of the above "messages," as I have stated them, are undesirable. Many of us, however—students as well as teachers—assume that they are unavoidable. As I try to transmit these messages less and less, I find certain tricks useful:

Find out first from the students what they already know about the point. This is quite different from asking them what their questions are, and then setting out to answer those questions. In the former, the students show us the pieces of the puzzle that they already have before them. We can then see exactly where the empty space is.

This is also different from starting out with examples taken from material to which the students have already been exposed. They may even have memorized parts of the material, but that does not guarantee that they have it alive in their minds at the time we begin our explanation.

Paraphrase many of the questions before answering them. This "counseling response" (Chapters 8 and 11) is useful in three ways: The teacher's tone of voice can imply that the question was not a stupid one, and that the mental activity which produced it is welcome. It makes the teacher less likely to answer some question which is a little different from the one that the student had in mind. It increases the likelihood that the other students will know clearly what question it is that is being answered.

Say as little as possible. Students remember what they have phrased for themselves, no matter how clumsily, better than they remember our most elegant summaries. I try to say just enough so that the "spark" (Chapter 2) can jump across the gap. Saying just enough without saying too much is a skill at which nobody can be successful all of the time. This is another example of constantly "learning the students" even while one is helping them to learn the language.

Hold each answer by the teacher to no more than 5 or 10 seconds as measured by a clock. Each time a student does something with an answer, or asks a further question, the clock starts again. This is just one more device to keep me from dragging visitors through more of my museum than they were ready for.

No matter what the length of the explanation, omit all information that is not demanded by the student's question. For example, in giving the past tense of the English verb *shine* in a sentence about shoes, I would simply say "shined." I would restrain myself from loading onto the students the additional fact that we say, "The sun *shone* all day," not "shined," but that we do not say, "I shone my shoes." This fact is quite interesting to me, and it might even be interesting to some of my students. If my purpose is to entertain or amuse or impress my students, rather than to provide the missing piece that the student needs, I may even give them this extra information. But if I mix purposes carelessly, I confuse and discourage my student. So as a teacher I need to see my purposes for what they are. I also need to discipline myself in choosing among them.

If something needs to be written on the board, get a student to do it on behalf of the class. Once we get the chalk into our own hands, it is all too easy for us to leave most of the students behind, even if we do toss a few questions like "Okay?" and "Right?" over our shoulder as we fill the board with examples. Then we are dragging the students through our own museum, rather than helping them to fill holes in their puzzle.

Invite the students to try out their new knowledge, to see whether it works as they hope it will. This calls for the students to make up their own examples. It is quite different, however, from saying, "Now everybody make a sentence using this tense, or this construction." In the former, emphasis is on activity by the student, directed at a goal which has importance for him. In the latter, it is on producing a linguistic artifact with minimal depth of meaning: another instance of "Now try to do this so I can tell you whether you did it right." In the former, the teacher is a source of needed information; in the latter, she is a judge.

Leave time and opportunity for students to answer one another's questions. Often this means nothing more than just hesitating a second or two before giving one's own response to a question. It does not mean staring expectantly at the students and saying, "Figure it out for yourselves!" The latter asks the students to act like linguists doing field work. It may be very appropriate at some times in some classes, but it is not the kind of exploration that I have been describing here.

Appear interested, but nonchalant. This is the students' quest for information, and not my quest for success in explaining.

By following these rules of thumb, I hope to convey unspoken messages that are different from the ones that I listed earlier. Some of the conclusions that I want the student to draw for himself out of this kind of "explantion" are:

"*My mind is O.K. at handling this kind of thing!*"

"*This new thing turns out to be a special case of what I already knew!*"

"*My classmates and I can depend on one another for much of what we need in sorting these matters out.*"

Several months ago, a colleague came to talk with me about a class she was teaching. The class consisted of four adults, nonbeginners, all of whom spoke the same native language. None was a highly experienced student of foreign languages, and their "aptitude" for this particular type of academic undertaking was not high. Their progress in the course had been slow, and seemed to be slowing down even more as the days went by.

What my colleague and I came up with was a set of materials which we described as "long, narrow dialogs." As of this writing, those materials have been used for 80 class hours. So far, the results have been all that we could have hoped for: fluency and accuracy have increased sharply, and so have morale and creativity. I will describe these materials briefly in the next few paragraphs, but in so doing I do not mean that I think I have found the (or a, or another) final solution to my own teaching problems or anyone else's. My purpose in describing it is only to illustrate how the three "ways" may intersect in, or may interpret, a method that does not completely belong to any of them.

We call the dialogs "long" because each one contains at least 75 sentences. Moreover, each dialog leads into the next, so that they form a connected series of episodes. We call them "narrow" because few sentences have more than five words and most have fewer. The dialogs contain one role for each student, with the teacher taking bit parts such as waiter or taxi driver. Each student stays in his/her own role, rather than exchanging roles as is done in most courses that use dialogs. All of the characters in the dialog are natives of the target culture, and all are happy, well-adjusted, and successful. Their occupations were chosen to be relevant to the student's own, though not identical with them. The events find the characters resolving uncertainties, making choices, and overcoming difficulties, but the choices are pleasant ones, and the difficulties are both minor and short-lived. The native-language translation is readily at hand in a parallel column. In all these respects, the "long, narrow dialogs" are patterned after Suggestopedia, and particularly after the sample dialog in Saféris' book.

The techniques which my colleague is using with these materials are partially like those which have been described for Suggestopedia, but only partially. As in Suggestopedia, the students start out with activities which allow them to listen and understand without the need to produce anything at first. They are then asked to read through the dialog once before retiring, and once on arising. As in Suggestopedia also, any drill-like activity is made into games, or at least is carried out in a manner that is gamelike. The style of dealing with mistakes is nonevaluative. And like Suggestopedic lessons, these lessons end with the students putting together their own skits.

But these lessons are quite clearly not Suggestopedic. Most conspicuously, there is no music, no "concert session," no drama or contrasting intonations in the teacher's reading of the dialogs. And, significantly, the lessons take about 20 hours apiece, much longer than the six hours in which Suggestopedia covers a comparable amount of material. We might have tried to use the dramatic and musical components, but neither of us has had that kind of training. We also lack the equipment for playing the music.

As I have watched some of these classes, and particularly as I have talked with the students on several occasions, certain points have stood out very clearly:

1. The students are happy. This method provides an extraordinarily high degree of security for the student, from at least three sources: (a) The fictitious character that a student has assumed, and not the student himself, is felt to be responsible for any errors. (b) The teacher's nonevaluative style minimizes the student's need to defend himself by avoiding things that he is not sure of. (c) The materials themselves to prevent the anxiety that can arise from having to originate one's own conversations (as in Community Language Learning) or from feeling that what one is studying is ephemeral, nebulous, and possibly unsuited for actual use in the target culture. On the positive side, these materials contribute to security by being easy and by consisting of happy adventures involving people who have no serious anxieties or internal conflicts. The student is thus able to leave aside many of his own anxieties about language study, about living in the target culture, etc. (I suspect that this format would be an excellent one for doing cross-cultural training, since the students are open and receptive, and the presentation is (quasi-)experiential.)

2. The continuity and the length of the dialogs effectively provide the student with a fictitious world which is large enough and vivid enough so that he can improvise within it. This is the "self-investment" which Counseling-Learning and other research (*Memory, Meaning, and Method,* Chapter 3) have seen to be so important for whole-person learning. The "self" that is "invested" here is a fictitious one, to be sure, but the investing is still *done* by the *real* self—the same self that has to do the learning. Meantime, the irrelevant conflicts and anxieties that the student brought with him are left with no *persona* through which to speak. They therefore are unable to arouse each other, to call each other forth, to build upon each other.

3. As in most methods, there is considerable reiteration and reworking of the new material. As in Community Language Learning, this new material in some sense represents "self-investment" of the students with whom I have talked. But because the material was made up ahead of time, the teacher is

not in the position of having to take fresh, unpredictable conversations and shape them on the spot into a sufficient quantity of games, drills, or whatever. She must still respond moment by moment to what she sees the students are ready for, of course. But by working from existing materials, she can prepare more fully. This contributes to her own feelings of stability and security. This stability *and* the teacher's feelings become unspoken messages which the student receives, and so they contribute in turn to the security of the student—to his confidence in the teacher and in himself.

4. These students have shown a clear increase in their ability to handle the phonological and grammatical differentiations which they need for correct production of the target language. Of particular interest was a technique for introducing some verb forms which past students have generally found to be more or less mystifying or esoteric or threatening. The teacher simply talked with the students about material in the dialogs from earlier lessons, except that she worked many examples of the new verb form into what she said. This proved to be painless and highly effective. It appears that the context, though fictitious, had come to life, and that it was rich enough to allow these new grammatical seeds to take root in it.

This "long, narrow dialog method" appears, then, to have been a successful way of meeting the difficulties that had been troubling my colleague's class. Let me repeat what I said above, however: I do not think that in this little fragment of method I have found the (or a, or another) final solution to my own teaching needs or anyone else's. Nevertheless, it does appear to have taken account of the many sources of anxiety and alienation about which I have written in the earlier chapters of this book; and to have provided security against them; and to have drawn the students out of their shells and into self-asserting activity; and to have reused the material systematically, allowing the students' minds to work on it in enough ways so that they could hold onto it; and to have produced a growing degree of accuracy alongside a gratifying increase in fluency. It seems to have followed the formula and achieved the goals (SARD) of Community Language Learning but without the features of the latter method which cause such strong anxiety in some students.

I have gone on at length about "mim-mem" drills and the giving of grammatical explanations, both of which lie outside of Suggestopedia proper. Few of us will be able to be trained for two months by Dr. Lozanov. If we try to "do Suggestopedia" without such training, we are doing a disservice to our students, to ourselves, and to the reputation of the method. Yet this does not mean that we must throw up our hands in despair: though we cannot "do Suggestopedia," we can at least try, as with the "long, narrow dialogs," to "see Suggestopedically" the methods that we do use. This may, in the long run, prove to be Lozanov's greatest gift to the worldwide profession of language teaching.

PART V

PART I, CONTINUED

CHAPTER 20

ONE TEACHER'S VIEW
OF THE THREE "WAYS"

In the first two chapters, I began to talk about one "way" of looking at the teaching and learning of languages. In Chapters 3 to 19, we examined three unconventional "ways" of teaching: the Silent Way, Counseling-Learning, and Suggestopedia. We saw that each of them agrees, largely but not uniformly, with a set of general principles which were stated in Chapter 2. Now it is time for me to come back to my own "way"—my own view—to see what I have added to it by standing on the shoulders of those three thinkers (helped up, as I was, by the hands of many friends, colleagues, and students!). Finally, in Part V I shall develop this "way of seeing" against the background of two more theories, one of them contemporary (Chapter 21), the other a hundred years old (Chapter 22).

Let me begin this brief chapter by saying in as few words as possible how these three ways look to me, and then guessing at how they might look to one another.

The Silent Way sees the Self of the learner as isolated and independent. It also sees the splendid power which that Self can have—can develop—when it comes to know itself and so to shape itself. It is the "Invictus" of William Ernest Henley's well-known poem, who thanked "whatever gods may be/for my unconquerable soul," and who in triumph and defiance cried out to the world that "I am the master of my fate!" This finally and fiercely lone Self, as it develops, may come to give something of its own to the world in which it finds itself and to some of the other Selves around it. Among them, a group of such selves may attain a degree of "community."

The stance of Counseling-Learning is in some respects exactly opposite. It, too, sees the individual as alone. But where the Silent Way affirms the aloneness of the learner, and pushes him to come face to face with that aloneness and to live through it and beyond it, Counseling-Learning begins by reducing that aloneness through the warm, total, womblike support of the counselor-teacher. In addition, the lonely Self of each learner receives support as it finds its place in a developing community of other learning Selves. As it progresses through the five "stages" of Counseling-Learning, however, it becomes less and less dependent—more and more self-standing. In both of these "ways," the path that the learner follows runs between independence and community, but it runs in opposite directions.

These two approaches differ also in what they see as interfering with the learner's progress as he moves along that path. The Silent Way, at least in the books that are addressed to language teachers, focuses mainly on the cognitive work—the cognitive *adventures*—that meet the learning Self. Counseling-Learning gives more explicit attention to interpersonal and intrapersonal forces of all kinds. That is why it was able to help me to make sense of the differences in outcome between my two experiences as a language student in Silent Way courses (Chapter 5).

I have less to say about Suggestopedia because my experience with it is so small. It does appear, however, that Suggestopedia makes explicit many details of peripheral communication, an area in which Counseling-Learning has very little to say, and which the Silent Way seems to ignore altogether. It sets the individual down right in the middle of the community-individuality path that we talked about above. The community (at least in the beginning) is prefabricated and totally synthetic. As the days pass, however, Suggestopedia expects this plaster image of a community to come to life. It hopes that the real people who have lived in this community will leave the course better prepared for coping with the world outside.

A practitioner of the Silent Way might appreciate the detailed control and the constant initiative which the Suggestopedic teacher exercises in the first hours of each unit of study. She might also find compatible with her own outlook the absolute faith in the reserve powers of the student, and the effort to release those powers in ways that will produce extraordinary learning. On the other hand, she would not be comfortable with the fact that in Suggestopedia the learner is neither required nor even allowed to work out for himself the kinds of thing to which the Silent Way devotes so much time and attention. The Suggestopedic teacher, in turn, might note that the Silent Way teacher is making only partial and haphazard use of peripheral communication. She might also be alarmed at the way the student is so often thrown on his own resources in working with new material—a situation where struggle is likely to suggest inadequacy and self-doubt, at least in the short run. In place of "joy and easiness" we have earnestness and the Spartan acceptance of occasional temporary frustration.

Another striking difference between the Silent Way and Suggestopedia is the minutely meticulous presentation of one point at a time in the former, and the "global" deluge of new material in a Suggestopedic dialog.

The Silent Way teacher would note that the student in Community Language Learning, far from being forced to be as independent as possible, is allowed to remain as dependent as he likes, for as long as he needs. The conversations which the students originate in the first step of the "classical" procedure (Chapter 8) are certain to present them with new "challenges" (Chapter 3) which the Silent Way teacher (or any other kind of teacher who is concerned over grading and sequencing of structures) would find inappropriate for them at the time. Moreover, the students interact with one another as persons, and not just as language learners; this interaction exposes them to unnecessary distractions and anxieties. Finally, the large amount of "luxury" vocabulary (Chapters 3 and 4) even in the earliest conversations diverts energy from the learning of the more basic parts of the language. It is therefore an inefficient way of "paying ogdens" (Chapter 3).

The Counselor-Teacher, from her point of view, might feel that the Silent Way demands of the learner an openness and a fortitude which many will find impossible, at least at the beginning. It is as though the learner is being commanded to start out in "Stage 4" (Chapter 8). The Counselor-Teacher might also be uncomfortable with the degree to which her Silent Way counterpart holds onto the "initiative," and with the lack of warmth which some Silent Way teachers show. Finally, she might feel that at least in the beginning stages the Silent Way is overly cerebral.

The Suggestopedic teacher might feel that the CL teacher is making better use of peripheral communication than the Silent Way teacher is, but that she is still largely unaware of what she is doing in this respect. Two features of CLL—the lack of fixed materials and the opportunities for students to talk about their reactions to the course—would appear undesirable because they would waste time, interfere with concentration, and (worst of all) undermine the all-important "authority" of the teacher. The lack of obvious structure, and even (which is not the same thing!) the flexibility of the teacher, may in some learners create new anxieties which are as stubborn and as destructive as the anxieties which CLL is so good at reducing.

Looking in the opposite direction, the CL teacher might concede that the Suggestopedic atmosphere may temporarily anesthetize or neutralize some of the student's concerns, but she might go on to question whether it has not thereby limited the total scope of the learning experience.

The preceding part of this chapter was written a year ago. I still stand by it. I saw the excitement and the potential in each of these methods, but also the dangers. I saw the dangers, but also the possibilities for more life and better learning. I saw the Silent Way as elegant but austere. I saw "CL/CLL" as warmly human but sometimes hard to control. I saw Suggestopedia as powerful but also complex and inaccessible. Each of these three ways runs askew of the best-trodden paths that we know.

To produce satisfactory results always requires a certain degree of craftsmanship, even when one is following a conventional textbook in which everything is spelled out, and even when one is trying for nothing more than high test scores for one's students. I think that all three of the "ways" we have looked at would agree that sticking entirely to preexisting materials limits the depth of the goals at which one can aim, and that this shallowness in turn limits both the quality and the quantity of learning. But as we move away from readymade materials the demands on the teacher increase, and it is also true that as we aim for deeper goals the demands on the teacher increase. Any of the methods at which we have been looking therefore asks of the teacher a level of craftsmanship which must be unusually high, and which must be maintained day after day.

As I continue my own development in teaching, I find certain areas in which I would like to learn more from each of these methods. I am strongly attracted to the lean, logical elegance of Silent Way teaching, but I am also attracted to the rich sensory experience of Suggestopedia and to the full human relationship that often grows between Knower and Learner in Counseling-Learning. Certainly I could be more useful to my students if I had more of the discipline of the Silent Way; and if I were more expert at making Lozanov's two "planes" support each other through skillful orchestration of physical, verbal, and aesthetic elements; and if I had fuller, quicker insight into what from minute to minute my learner-clients are showing me.

Insight, technical skill, discipline. The fully ready teacher has all three. For me, though, insight is first. Without it, how can the teacher choose the method, the material, the technique that fits? These choices, and the skillful use of what is chosen, then come second. But without self-discipline, skill is only virtuosity—a show that enthralls students rather than setting them free. It is just here, in working toward the student's freedom alongside and inter-twined with his language skills, that the three ways find their common goal. The light they share is knowledge that of these two—the freedom and the learning—each can make the other stronger.

CHAPTER 21

THE MONITOR MODEL
AND THE LEVERTOV MACHINE

The purpose of this book, then, is not to set up a theory. It is rather to look at practice—at what has happened—in the hope of clarifying what has happened, and learning from it, and preparing to deal more effectively with what may happen in the future. I would therefore like to turn, in this next-to-last chapter, to a bit of theory which I think will bear some very practical fruits in years to come. This is an interpretation by Stephen D. Krashen and others of research on the relationship between "learning" and "acquisition" of foreign languages by adults. This interpretation has sometimes gone by the name "The Monitor Model."

I have already made brief references to the contrast between "learning" and "acquisition" (Chapter 1). In this chapter, I shall begin by summarizing very briefly the conclusions that the term "Monitor Model" stands for, and the evidence on which those conclusions are based. Then I will go on to outline some of my own reactions to the theory as it stood in the summer of 1978. Finally, I will explore the relationships among the "Monitor Model," my reactions to it ("The Levertov Machine"), and the "three ways."

The Monitor Model rests first of all on the assumption that there are two distinct processes through which we may gain more or less control of a language. The process which everyone uses to gain control of the first language is "acquisition." In "acquisition," one meets the sounds, the words, and the sentences along with the sights and actions and smells that are their meanings. The persons from whom one acquires a first language are parts of the social network that uses the language as one of its vehicles of communication. At the same time, one also "acquires" other vehicles of communication: body language and all the rest, and in the process one comes to be a member *of* the social network. Some people "acquire" two or more languages, of course, either simultaneously or one after another.

In later childhood, we become able to do something that we were not able to do when we were small. We can now focus on single elements in what is going on around us, and pull them out ("abstract" them) from the undivided web of experience, and hold onto them and move them around and pass them back and forth among us. In the realm of language, this means that we can compare words and classify them *as words,* and that we can see how the sentences in one list of examples are like one another but different from the sentences in another list. We can take what we have seen in this way and put it into a new sentence of its own: a "grammatical rule." We even come to where we can begin with a "rule" and use it to make up (or to understand) new examples which also fit the rule. Some of us are much better at this than others are, of course—at picking out and holding onto and shuffling bits of language—but this is for all of us a new ability which infants do not have. We also become able to think about the thoughts of others, and about their expectations. When a word that we had yesterday does not come to our tongue today, we nod to those who say we have "forgotten" it, and when our new sentence fails to fit the rules, we humbly agree it was an "error." In common speech, this process of picking out, and holding onto, and shuffling words is one kind of "learning," and "acquisition" is another. Krashen et al., however, use the word "learning" in contrast to "acquisition." For them, "learning" refers *only* to the picking-out-items-and-counting-mistakes process that adults, adolescents, and older children can engage in. For the purposes of this chapter, I shall follow Krashen in this distinction.

"Acquisition" grows out of the interchange between an infant and its total environment. "Learning" is pieced together through the interaction of one person in the role of "pupil" and another person in the role of "teacher." This "teacher" role consists in helping the pupil to pick out one thing at a time—or in picking it out for him; and in guiding him through—or compelling him to do—practice which will ensure that he holds onto it; and in notifying him—tactfully or harshly—of his mistakes; and in recording as a series of "grades" the pupil's progress relative to the subject matter—usually also relative to other pupils' progress. The word "teaching," as I shall use it in this chapter, refers only to these very restricted parts of what a teacher can do.

The proponents of the Monitor Model quote from the research on first-language acquisition two sets of facts. The facts in the first set have to do with the order in which children gain control of various features of their native language. Research has shown that almost everyone acquires certain features before certain other features; that is, there appears to exist a natural—though not inflexible—order of "acquisition" for children who are acquiring any given language.

Research is also casting light on a second set of facts about "acquisition": the conditions under which it occurs. In one formulation quoted by Krashen, when parents or older children talk to small children:

a. They talk about what is going on here and now, and about those parts of the here-and-now with which the child is actively involved.

b. Sentences are short and simple. As the child moves from one stage of acquisition to the next, the sentences become longer and more complex. The essential point seems to be that the sentences are on the level that the child already controls *or on the next higher level.* Sentences that are too difficult seem to be without effect.

c. Vocabulary is relatively simple.

d. Speakers repeat themselves in the syntactic patterns that they use.

e. When speakers find that they must slow down, they do so by inserting longer pauses, not by mouthing their words.

f. Speakers provide models to acquirers, by saying for them what the acquirers seem to want to say.

g. When they do any kind of correcting, speakers focus their attention not on the error, but on trying to communicate better with the child.

(As a working teacher, I have found this to be a stimulating checklist. I expect to look back at it often in years to come.)

We have sometimes assumed that at about the same age when we gain the power to "learn," we also lose the power to "acquire." The findings on which the Monitor Model is based say that this is not true. They indicate rather that both processes continue, to greater or lesser degree, side by side. The evidence for this conclusion comes from careful observation of errors made by various kinds of people under a wide range of circumstances, to see which parts of the language they control and which parts they do not. It turns out that under some circumstances the "natural order" of first-language "acquisition" is reflected also in the speech or writing of adults who are using a second language. Under other circumstances, the "order of difficulty" which is characteristic of "learning" shows up. The influence of "learning" is greatest when the person's attention is on linguistic form and when there is plenty of time for thinking. Then, for example, a nonnative user of English who had time to think might make very few errors in the third person singular present tense ending of verbs: *goes, sees,* etc. The rules for this ending are relatively simple to understand and to put into words. Some things, on the other hand, are almost impossible to put into rules and to learn: When should one use *a,* when *the,* and when no article at all? When does it sound better to use the future tense with *will,* and when the future with *going to?* Errors in matters of this kind follow the natural order of first-language "acquisition," even for people who came to the language as adults. Moreover, these adults' control of these matters does not change much even when their attention is directed to form and they are given plenty of time.

According to the Monitor Model, the "acquisition" process remains available to adolescents and adults, at least to some extent. Its availability, and also its results, may be obscured by the "learning" process, particularly when the new language is met in a conventional classroom. Nevertheless it is there. Not only is it there; it is the only path that can lead to control of those features of language that cannot easily be reduced to rules or to translation equivalents.

What we have "acquired" and what we have "learned" differ not only in how we got them into us. They differ also in how we get at them, to bring them out and use them when we need them. The Monitor Model holds that for the purpose of "creative construction" of what we want to say, we can draw *only on what we have "acquired."* We then run this new utterance past the Monitor, which includes what we have "learned." Then the Monitor, if it is in operation and if it has time to do its work, may make corrections in whatever came out of the "creative construction process."

In October of 1978, I had the privilege of speaking to the Los Angeles Second Language Research Forum on the subject of my thoughts about the Monitor Model. The next part of this chapter is taken from what I said there.

The title of my address was "The Levertov Machine." As I explained at the time, the "Levertov Machine" is a Rube Goldberg kind of diagram (see below). I called it a "machine" because I was afraid that if I called it a (theoretical) "model," people would take it too seriously. I wanted people to follow with me in what I was saying during that hour, rather than be preoccupied with deciding whether to accept or reject some new set of theoretical claims. It was more important to me that they should stay with me for that one hour than that they should remember my words after the hour was ended.

The "Machine" was named for Denise Levertov because she discovered, in a poetry course which she taught at Vassar, that people who had had little training sometimes *wrote* as good poetry as those with much training, but that those with more training had considerably better ability to *criticize* poetry. This seems to me to be another example of the same insight which underlies Krashen's "Monitor Model."

Unless I am mistaken, the distinction between *adult* "learning" and "acquisition" of language is potentially the most fruitful concept for language teachers that has come out of the linguistic sciences during my professional lifetime. Specifically, I think it may eventually prove to be of even more value to us than the phonemic principle or the principle of contrastive analysis. The Monitor Model has pulled together for me some of my own observations and experiences which had previously appeared to be unrelated to one another. I have also noticed that when I told some of my adult students about it, they took to it "like ducks to water," and spontaneously used the terminology in talking about what was going on with them from day to day. So I have read with special interest whatever I could find about the model and, moreover, I have thought about it actively, trying to push it still further without losing its basic insights. This paper on "The Levertov Machine," then, is simply a report on some of that thinking, and on some of the researchable questions that have grown out of it.

The diagram which Krashen and others have used as a picture of the Monitor Model looks like this:

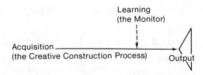

It is a highly (and, I think, wisely) simplified way of representing certain facts. In this paper, I propose to build from this diagram to the Levertov Machine one step at a time. As I do so, some of the evidence that I will use is evidence that Krashen and his collaborators have written about, but which they have not reflected in their diagram. Other evidence comes from my own observations.

One of the distinctions that must be preserved is the distinction between "learning" and "acquisition." As used here, "learning" is what has been consciously abstracted from experience, concentrated on and corrected, grasped, and stored against future need. By contrast, what has been "acquired" is what has come in as one part of a total experience, frequently at the edge of attention rather than at its center.

What has been "learned" and what has been "acquired" perhaps differ also in where or how they are stored, and in how we have access to them. We are all familiar with the person who has had four years of French in school and received all A's and B's (perhaps even a high score on the College Boards), but who arrives in France and is unable to use the language. This is a case of "learning" leading to (academic) performance, but no "acquisition" and therefore no practical use. A recent experience of my own seems to illustrate exactly the opposite. My son recently came home from college after a semester of Portuguese. One day, he asked me how to say certain simple things in Portuguese. I found myself feeling quite uncomfortable, and was unable to answer most of his questions. What Portuguese I know came from a little reading and a lot of talking with people. Recent experiences show that I apparently "acquired" a fair amount, and can "use" it with comfort and reasonable accuracy in conversation. But my son's questions were *about* the language, and so were directed to what I had "learned."

To the distinction between "learning" and "acquisition," I would add the claim which most clearly sets the Monitor Model apart from conventional thinking: that what has been "acquired" can be used directly in creative construction of utterances, but that what has been "learned" cannot be so used. A person who appears to be communicating through use of what he has "learned" but has not "acquired" is, in this view, assumed to be originating his utterances in his native language (or in some other language which he has "acquired"), and then transposing it more or less successfully into the target language by running the utterances through the Monitor and applying what he has "learned." This process accounts for many errors of the kinds that are predictable through contrastive linguistics: the error arises in the native language, and the Monitor fails to weed it out. In some cases, the learner's Monitor had not yet been developed to deal with the matter which caused the error. In other cases, the Monitor had the information that it needed, but for some reason it failed to operate.

This leads to another distinction which is characteristic of the Monitor Model, and which I want to preserve: the distinction between "Overusers" and "Underusers" of the Monitor. I am not certain whether an "Overuser" is just someone who uses the Monitor at inappropriate times, or whether an "Overuser" may also be one whose Monitor is too sensitive—is too easily triggered—or perhaps some combination of these. Anyone who is interested in pursuing the Monitor Model further may want to look into this question. Some parts of what Krashen et al. have said point to the former meaning, but as a card-carrying Monitor user of long standing, I have a strong hunch that the second meaning deserves some careful investigation too.

A native speaker sometimes makes slips of the tongue and then corrects himself. These corrections are clear evidence that the speaker has been "monitoring" what he has been saying. (And on the negative side, uncorrected errors by a native speaker are evidence that this kind of monitoring is not constant.) Yet the source of the correction could not have been anything that the speaker had "learned." The Monitor was clearly using material that had been "acquired." Krashen et al. comment on this phenomenon in a number of their papers, but have not represented it graphically in their picture.

This brings me to the first of my series of modifications of their diagram.

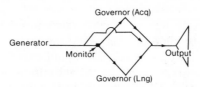

This diagram says that what is generated through creative construction out of the "acquired" resources may be sent by the Monitor through the "Learning" Governor, or through the "Acquisition" Governor, or through both of these, or through neither. At least that is the interpretation if we are willing to think of the Monitor as being at any given time either turned all the way off or turned all the way on. If, on the other hand, we think of the Monitor as varying in sensitivity, say from "slack" to "very careful," then we might do away with the line (ei) that bypasses the Governors. All utterances would then go through one or both of the Governors. What otherwise would be called "unmonitored" speech (or writing) would appear as lightly or slackly monitored.

The next evidence that I would like to introduce can be documented from everyday experience, but it has been substantiated by controlled experiments, some of which I cited in Chapter 4 of *Memory, Meaning, and Method.* It is the simple fact that, in our native language as well as in foreign ones, the internal "Generator" that does our creative construction operates sometimes vigorously and sometimes very faintly, and most of the time somewhere between. To use the language of recent years, some situations and some people "turn us on," while others "turn us off." This happens even with young children, who have "acquired" some language, but who have never had occasion to "learn" any. So my next addition to the diagram is a Rheostat, or variable resistor, of the kind used in volume controls of many radios or for raising and dimming the lights in a theater.

Acquisition Store   Governor (Acq)

Generator   Monitor   Output

Governor (Lng)

Another piece of evidence is also a part of folklore. I suppose we've all heard people say something like, "I speak my best Spanish when I'm angry." As a matter of fact, someone said exactly that to me not 48 hours before I left for Los Angeles, and I've heard very nearly the same thing from other people since I got back. The meaning of such statements is unclear, of course. They could mean that the speakers make fewer errors when they are angry, or that they are simply unaware of their errors, or that they are more fluent while making more, or fewer, or the same number of errors, or some combination of these possibilities. So we can hardly use statements like these as evidence for modifying our diagram. I mention them only because they tie in with an incident which I witnessed a few years ago, and which was witnessed also by one of the teachers with whom I work.

The class consisted of three people, enrolled for 700 hours of instruction. During the first third of the course, if performance were rated on a scale of 1 to 10, the first (the fastest) student performed consistently at about the 9 level, the third (i.e., the slowest) at a flat 1, and the second somewhere between 3 and 4. The style of instruction was what I considered to be an excellent variety of audiolingualism.

Then one day, the second student brought in an album of color snapshots from a holiday which he and his wife had spent in one of the most interesting cities in the world. None of the rest of us had ever been to that city. Student 2 amazed all of us by performing for a full hour at the 9 level as he told us about the pictures and answered our questions. Fluency had shot up, of course, but what the teacher and I noticed most was the dramatic increase in accuracy as well. The following day, the student was back to the 3 or 4 level, and remained there for some weeks more.

This anecdote is of some interest in relation to the Monitor Model because accuracy went up *and not down,* at a time when the student's attention was presumably focused on content *and not form.* But a single such incident might be only a flash in the pan.

By chance, however, a few weeks after this incident Student 1 was withdrawn from the course for reasons unrelated to his language study. The very next day, Student 2 began to perform at the 9 level, and continued in that way for the remainder of the course—some 200 or 300 hours. Our guess was that, although there had been absolutely no evidence of any animosity or friction between them, Student 2 had felt personally or intellectually overshadowed by 1. (Student 3, by the way, continued on the 1 level.) When the source of the shadow was removed, the second student's fluency, *but also his accuracy,* suddenly blossomed. For the purpose of designing the Levertov Machine, I am assuming that the departure of Student 1 allowed Student 2's Rheostat to be turned up. There is no reason to believe that Student 2 suddenly began giving extra attention to form. If anything, he was under *less* pressure in that respect.

This evidence obviously does not invalidate previous studies which have shown that accuracy for certain types of material increases when the speaker's attention is on form. We have already built that fact into our diagram in the form of the Monitor itself. But Student 2's accuracy increased at a time when his attention was off of form. *There must have been a second source of accuracy, other than the Monitor.* The obvious place to look for such a source is the "acquisition" store—that very same store which on the preceding and following days, aided by the Monitor and by attention to form and by ample time for the Monitor to operate, was not able to produce in Student 2 either the accuracy or the fluency of that one hour. This must be the source of those great tennis shots, as Gallwey describes them, made by a player who is "playing out of his mind," with the Monitor (Gallwey's "Self 1") switched off.

My speculation is that two things may be going on here. First, whatever the student is exposed to may be registered in the "acquisition" store even when it has been primarily "learned." The "signal strength" of such material might be much weaker in the "acquisition" store than in the "learning" store, however—too weak to be picked up and used by the Generator when the Rheostat is turned down. But (and this is the second half of my speculation) turning the Rheostat to a higher setting may enable the Generator to pick up and put out things that had been only faintly "acquired." If this is so, then we will not need to violate one of the basic postulates of the Monitor Model, which says that only what has been "acquired" can serve as input for the generator. The most efficient way to get new material into the "acquisition" store may still be through proper intake in communicative settings, but even in a classical "learning" situation, the same material that registers strongly in the "learning" store may still leave a trace in the "acquisition" store. As I said, this is pure speculation.

The results of a high setting on the "Rheostat" show up all around us. Not long ago, I went through a period of several months during which—without planning to—I wrote a bit of verse almost every day. I found that those verses with the strictest formal structure, such as sonnets, came at times when I was caught in some sudden and strong emotion. I was aware of the formal demands, but they seemed to fulfill themselves with little conscious effort on my part. I was of course only an amateur, but I think that what I felt was a distant cousin of what real poets call "inspiration." The "Monitor" is still at work. Yet the "correctness" of what comes out is not proportional to the strength of the Monitor. It comes, rather, from the power that has been fed into the Generator.

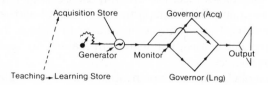

Another modification to the diagram requires no evidence beyond what has already been stated in existing discussions of the Monitor Model. If the Monitor and the Generator are distinct from each other, and if what has been "acquired" is used for monitoring as well as for generating, then there must be two lines from the "acquisition" store, one to the "acquisition" Governor and the other to the Generator. For analogous reasons, there is a line from the "learning" store to the "learning" governor, but there is none from there to the Generator, since by the basic hypothesis of the Monitor Model, what has been "learned" but not "acquired" cannot contribute to "creative construction."

I will also assert, without evidence, that the emotions connected both with "learning" and with "acquisition" have some effect on turning the Rheostat up or down. The fourth version of the diagram therefore looks like this:

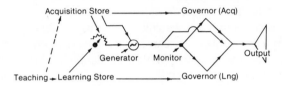

The next modification also draws on what is common knowledge and was assumed by the originators of the Monitor Model: that a person's command of a new language is built up of things that come in from the outside world. "Acquisition" comes from experience (which includes language), while "learning" comes through deliberate study, most often guided by "teaching." (I use "teaching" here in the narrow sense of singling out one item at a time, presenting it clearly, and correcting students' errors.)

I believe we are close enough now to the Levertov Machine so that further intermediate diagrams will be unnecessary.

I would like now to bring in a concept which is so vague that some will say it has no value in planning research: "social forces." I will not quarrel with anyone who labels it a *deus ex machina*. I will only say that this is a *deus* which we cannot exorcise simply by labeling it as such. And we are, I think, only beginning to do more than name and list some of these forces. I will do neither here. But I do think we need to go beyond a taxonomy of enzymes, as it were, and try following some of those enzymes through concrete and individual processes. I'm not sure myself what I mean to say in this paragraph, so I will not feel impatient with any readers who find it obscure. I have included it in the hope that at least a few will find in it a peg for meanings which are already theirs.

Be that as it may, my postulated "social forces" are partially determined by reactions to the speaker's own output. They come from many other sources, however. They provide the goals and the reasons, both conscious and unconscious, for "learning" (ac) and also for "acquisition" (ab). In addition, they act directly on both the Rheostat (ad) and the Monitor (af): that is to say, they "turn the speaker on" or "off," and also tell him how careful to be in weeding out mistakes before opening his mouth.

Here is clearly a prime area for research on the discourse and, more generally, on the interaction of the language classroom. I have seen descriptions of some systems for recording what goes on in class, but (as I read them, at least) their criteria are not subtle enough to pick up the differences between some "on-turning" and some "off-turning" kinds of teacher behavior. (Picking out these differences is made even trickier, of course, by the fact that two students may react quite differently to one and the same act on the part of the teacher.) If such a system is to be widely usable, it must be based on criteria which are simple enough so that two observers, after relatively little training, will score the same event in the same way. But if we chop the event into a series of segments, each segment to be daubed with one of the colors from the limited palette of such a system, then the system loses some of the judgments that a more skilled observer could make. It also sacrifices what even a naïve observer can see if allowed to record nonquantifiable aspects of the event. I am thinking particularly of the impact of the teacher's facial expressions, gestures, tone of voice, precise choice of words, and body posture. It may be that some of the preliminary research in this area will have to take the form of micro-case studies, as contrasted with application of questionnaires or other essentially taxonomic devices to statistically significant groups of subjects. I think that Curran in his way, and Lozanov in another way, have something to teach us in this area.

My next addition is a pair of dotted lines. One runs from the "acquired" store to the "learned" store (bc), and the other runs in the opposite direction (cb). The lines are dotted to reflect one of the key assumptions of the Monitor Model: that what is "learned" and what is "acquired" are essentially separate. Existing discussions of the Monitor Model allow for some connection from "acquisition" to "learning" in the " 'Eureka!' Phenomenon": when a student comes to a rule which pulls together many things which he has already "acquired" but never thought about, he may feel a sudden and pleasurable flash of insight.

I have not, on the other hand, found in the writings of Krashen et al. any provision for seepage from what has been "learned" into the "acquisition" store. I suspect, however, that such a seepage does take place, and moreover, that it may be of considerable importance for the design of methods and techniques.

Before I can explain why I hold that opinion, we need to take a brief detour into studies of human memory. The distinction between "short-term memory" (STM) and "long-term memory" (LTM) has been frequently cited and widely researched. STM is assumed to last only about 15 to 30 seconds, and to be able to hold only a relatively few "chunks" of information which are not somehow parts of larger storable configurations. In the experimental literature, material that is retained for two minutes or longer is generally assumed to have passed into LTM. This is certainly true for material that a subject can reproduce after two hours or two days.

A few writers on memory speak also of "tertiary" memory. Material in LTM (sometimes called "secondary memory") is gradually lost with the passage of time unless it is used occasionally. By contrast, material in "tertiary" memory is not lost, even if it is not used. Curran may have been talking about the same distinction when he contrasted "memor-izing" (temporary) with "psych-izing" (permanent). I am also reminded of Gattegno's distinction between "memorizing" and the establishment of "inner criteria."

What is tempting in the present context, of course, is to match up mere LTM with "learning," and "tertiary" memory with "acquisition." For the purposes of this paper, let's look at what happens if we yield to that temptation.

"Acquisition" comes through experience, I have said. But "experience" can make use of whatever is lying around handy, *including what has recently been memorized.* So it may prove very profitable to investigate, not only how to get new material from STM to LTM, but also how to structure and also to time "acquisitive" experiences so that they will derive maximum profit from recent "learning" activity.

Madeline Ehrman comments, "I suspect that this sort of thing will be very much affected by individual styles. What in this chapter has been called 'learning' may well be primarily a *sensitizer,* so that when we run across something in an 'acquisitional' setting we won't ignore it as part of an undifferentiated background. How much any one person can retain in a 'learned'

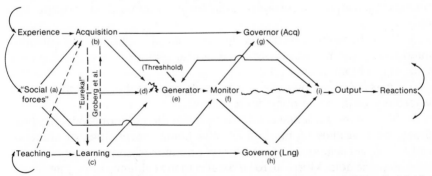

The Levertov Machine. "Social forces" work in "acquisition" (ab), "learning" (ac), and also in "turning on" the speaker (ad). Affect around learning may inhibit (cd), as in "lathophobic aphasia." The generator draws its power from the Rheostat (de); it draws content from acquisition (be), but not from learning (*ce). The output of the generator may come out as is (ei), or it may be monitored (ef), or both. Strength of the Monitor depends partly on "social forces" (af), partly on time. Correction may come from what has been learned (fhi) and/or from what has been acquired (fgi). An item may be both in (b) and in (c), but at different strengths. Weak items may not get through unless the Rheostat (d) is turned up. Some of the same "s.f." (a) that produce monitoring may also produce distortion (Gallwey) not correctible by governors (fi). Though learning and acquisition are qualitatively different, they may bleed into one another (bc, cb). Hence, try for social forces that will turn Rheostat up and at the same time keep monitoring at a desirable level ("infantilization" of Lozanov) (cf. also the five "stages" of Counseling-Learning). And find techniques which allow learning and acquisition to support one another.

store for eventual transfer to an 'acquired' store, and for how long, as well as the form of storage and the most effective technique for storing it, may well vary from person to person and from item to item."

The week before I delivered this address, I had occasion to discuss this question with a group of English teachers in Barcelona. Several of them reported instances where they had suddenly felt that a particular item—one which they had previously "learned"—slipped into a permanent place in what they had "acquired." I myself can remember where I was standing in Angola over 20 years ago when the three phonemic realizations of Portuguese final -s became a part of me.

The final line in the Levertov Machine (fi) stands for the fact that when we give too much of the wrong kind of attention to our output, we may actually get in our own way, and produce worse results rather than better. Gallwey, in his *Inner Game of Tennis* and elsewhere, talks about how the Critical Self can get in the way of the Performing Self and cause it to "choke." Some people speak foreign languages better after the Critical Self has been partially deadened by just the right amount of alcohol. A skillful teacher may produce the same effect without chemicals.

That completes my description of the Levertov Machine. The principal research areas that I see in it are the following:

1. Does material that we have met only in a "teaching"-"learning" situation also register, though faintly, in the "acquisition" store?

2. If so, can "turning up the Rheostat" really produce greater accuracy for that material, rather than less, even though the speaker is focused on content and not form? If so, under what circumstances?

3. What are the observable characteristics of high or low Rheostat settings? (galvanic skin response, syllables per second, body posture, etc., etc.)

4. What behavior which is under the control of the teacher (or other interlocutor) can raise or lower the Rheostat setting?

5. Is the Monitor ever totally off?

6. Does "Monitor overuse" mean using the Monitor too often, or too vigorously, or some combination of these?

7. Most of the evidence cited in support of the Monitor Model has been drawn from studies of mastery of inflectional morphemes or "function words." Would evidence from mastery of phonemic distinctions or of precise subphonemic details turn out to be parallel to the evidence from grammar? If not, how would it differ?

8. How does new material get into "tertiary" memory? What intermediate roles, if any, do STM and LTM play in this process?

9. What kinds of distortion are associated with extreme self-consciousness, or with extreme external pressure for accuracy, or with self-imposed perfectionism?

10. The Monitor may act on an utterance either before it is spoken or afterward. Are its pre- and postspeech effects alike, or how do they differ?

Those ten questions were the end of my paper in Los Angeles. But what will these "models" or these "machines" mean in practice? For one thing, if what we have "acquired" is what we know "just because it feels right," while what we have "learned" is what we know because we remember a rule or the back of the right flashcard, then these two sets of resources, the "acquired" and the "learned," can play back and forth on each other. I often have the impression that this is happening rapidly as I am conversing with someone in a foreign language. On one occasion, however, this process was slowed down so that I could watch it.

I had gone out to do a little running before breakfast on the day after I had finished reading Cecil Roth's *A Short History of the Jewish People.* For no particular reason, the phrase "history of the Jewish People" came into my mind, followed immediately by a (faulty) German translation: "Geschichte des Jüdische Volk." This didn't *sound right* (the Acquisition Governor at work?) and so it directed my attention to form. Since there was plenty of time, I activated my Monitor, switched to the Learning Governor, and started to run through what I could remember about adjective endings in German. This produced a revised version: "Geschichte des Jüdisches Volk." But then I seemed to remember that masculine and neuter nouns are supposed to take the ending -es in the genitive (possessive) case. This was the Learning Governor again, but it had forgotten some of the rules that I had learned in 1942, so it did not produce a clear output. I then decided that "Volkes" "sounded better" (back to the Acquisition Governor!). I settled on "Geschichte des Jüdisches Volkes," resolved to make a written record of the whole sequence when I got home, and went on with my running.

After breakfast, I wrote out what I remembered. Reading it over, however, I found that the German phrase still didn't seem right. The Acquisition Governor struck again! The word "Jüdischen" came from somewhere (Generator? Acquisition Governor?) and fitted a rule that I began to remember—a rule that had something to do with "weak" endings after a definite article. Accurate or not, this was the Learning Governor talking now! The final version, therefore, is "Geschichte des Jüdischen Volkes." For better or for worse I have left it as it came out of my Levertov Machine, unverified by grammar books or native speakers. Two points are of particular interest: First, the switching back and forth between what I had learned and what I had acquired underscores the fact that the diagram on page 270 is a rhetorically appropriate but also a great simplification of experience. Second, the two kinds of knowing were clearly present and clearly separate, each necessary to the final product and neither sufficient by itself.

THE LEVERTOV MACHINE AND CHAPTER 2

The Silent Way begins by presenting one small point at a time, guiding students through a variety of activities that it hopes will lead to retention, and (silently) pointing out errors ("places where the student needs to do more work"). It thus "sensitizes" the student (to use Madeline Ehrman's word) to a whole series of sharply delineated features, and in such a tightly organized way that there is no "undifferentiated background." All of this sounds like a description of purified, distilled, and concentrated "learning," and so it is.

Yet at the same time the Silent Way meets many of the conditions for "acquisition." In its insistence on never saying anything in the absence of the "truth" of what is said, it ensures that the beginning student will always be talking about (some sharply defined feature of) the "here and now." In emphasizing that the teacher must constantly be learning the students and staying "with" them, it guarantees that the level of new input will be right. Vocabulary is starkly simple, yet sufficient for endless creativity. Mistakes are dealt with, but not as "mistakes." Each new pattern is repeated a number of times.

There is one condition which is normally present during first-language acquisition but which did not show up in the list that I quoted from Krashen. This is the existence of a full, warm human relationship between speaker and acquirer. The most highly qualified Silent Way teachers that I have observed have come across as brilliant but remote and impersonal. Their teaching has appeared to concentrate on a highly cerebral presentation of the skeleton of the language, with little or no warm flesh to reassure the new acquirer. After the opening stages with the charts and the rods, the student meets pictures, printed sentences, and stories which make fuller communication possible. Even so, the steadfast concentration on one new language point at a time preserves an atmosphere in which "learning" seems to predominate. But perhaps a perceptive and imaginative teacher can build "acquisitive" opportunities on the foundation provided by these achievements of "learning."

In Classical Community Language Learning, the emphasis is in quite the opposite direction. The warm and supportive manner of the counselor-teacher provides a close approximation of a loving and attentive parent and an excellent backdrop for "acquisition." The teacher provides as many models as the student needs. Mistakes are not treated as "mistakes," but (if at all) as occasions for further communication with the student.

The technique also provides ample opportunities for short, simple sentences, within restricted vocabulary, about the here and now. This is where the teacher needs all her skills both as a pedagogue and as a counselor. When the students are uneasy with one another or with the teacher or with the method, they tend to sit in awkward silence or simply to make up sentences to appease the teacher—this instead of the self-invested conversation with which the technique is supposed to begin. Then their sentences become dead linguistic objects instead of being parts of themselves. The "here and now" is lost. The teacher sees this as her cue to work patiently to restore Security and so to improve the quality of Assertion. Otherwise, a key element of the "acquisitive" environment is missing.

But when the students do begin to chatter happily about their "here and now," a new danger arises. The teacher must now know how to use their conversations in such a way that the unrestricted syntactic patterns and vocabulary, which come out of the student's full control of his native language, do not accumulate so rapidly that the student gets in over his head. When this happens, two of the conditions for "acquisition" (b and c in Krashen's list) are lost. At the same time, of course, the student's feeling of Security is reduced.

Students in CCLL have access to conventional grammar books. Otherwise, however, "learning" activities are definitely subordinated to—are in fact developed out of—"acquisitive" activities. This calls for constant creativity on the part of the teacher. Without a certain amount of "learning," students become confused about what is going on and uncertain about what they are responsible for. When the teacher is able to guide the class through a suitably balanced course, however, CCLL can provide almost unrivaled opportunities for "acquisition" both of the rudiments and of the nuances of a language.

With regard to Suggestopedia, I must again point out that anything I can say is speculative. My firsthand experience has been with fragments of approximations to it, while my knowledge of the real article is secondhand. Its most conspicuous characteristic is the degree to which students do respond in an "acquisitive" way. At first glance it might appear that Suggestopedia violates the first three conditions (a, b, c) for "acquisition": talk is not about the here and now, but about a fictitious world; sentences are short, but structural gradation is very steep compared to most language courses; vocabulary is limited but again, by the standards to which we are accustomed, it is huge. I am fairly well convinced, however, that Suggestopedia does in fact meet those three criteria. The structures and the vocabulary are on a level that is suitable for the student, except that Suggestopedia sees in the student more readiness and greater powers sooner than the rest of us have seen. The dialogs by their length and their life provide a new "here and now" which is perfectly serviceable, and which at the same time is free of many of the conflicts and impediments that we find in the real world.

The "learning" activities in Suggestopedia are often (always?) conducted in the manner of other activities—activities which are not usually associated with the "learning" atmosphere of a conventional classroom. Thus one videotape showed a series of verbal interchanges which could have been classified as a fairly ordinary verb drill. As they spoke, however, teacher and students bounced a large ball back and forth among them. The "concert sessions" themselves are another example of this principle.

Krashen has said that both "learning" and "acquisition" are possible for all of us. He also believes that the two can support each other; that except in the short run, "acquisition" is more important than "learning"; that "learning" needs "teaching" (in the narrow sense), but that "acquisition" does not need "teaching" and does not profit by it; that premature emphasis on "learning" may stifle the ability to "acquire"; that while "acquisition" may not need "teaching," it does require more than merely being set down in a country where the language is spoken.

These conclusions of Krashen's fit well with my own experience. They certainly apply to the "three ways" that I have described in this book. I think that they apply equally to any other method I have seen.

CHAPTER 22

THE LANGUAGE TEACHER
AND
DOSTOYEVSKY'S "GRAND INQUISITOR"*

In the other chapters of this book I have recorded what went on in certain classes, and we have looked together at certain theories. I hope that what happened in those classes has lent color to the theories; at the same time I hope that the theories have made out of my narratives more than anecdotes.

But an event is just one foothold in the rock; a theory is a thin cable that ties events together—that lets us climb from one foothold to another with less risk of falling off the mountain. Theories do not tell us where the trail leads, or why one should try to climb it, or anything about the ethics of being a guide to those who climb. The answers to these larger questions come not from observations of events, and not from theories. A current TV commercial tells us that "without chemicals, life itself would be impossible." It is certainly true that any form of life as we know it has its chemical side—it uses chemicals. But it is also true that *human* life would be impossible without myth, and without metaphor. It is to these that we must turn unless we have decided to ignore issues which have lain just beneath the surface, especially in Chapters 2, 3, 7, 8 and 10.

Into *The Brothers Karamazov*, which was his final novel, Dostoyevsky placed one chapter that had no direct relation to his main story. It was about a long poem which Ivan, one of the brothers, had written or claimed to have written, and which he was paraphrasing for his brother Alyosha. The action of the poem takes place in Spain, in Seville, at the height of the Inquisition, a period when heretics were being sought out, and tried, and imprisoned, and many of them burned at the stake. At this time, according to the poem, the Son of God has heard the prayers of thousands who were begging him to come to earth again and he decides to visit his people, not in the long-prophesied and final Second Coming, but for a moment only. So he appears in the streets of Seville as an ordinary citizen, but people recognize him without naming him, and they are drawn to him, and he heals their sick, and raises from the dead a little girl whose coffin is being borne into the church. But as he does so, the Cardinal, the Grand Inquisitor, sees him. And the Cardinal sends guards, and has him seized and taken to an old prison, and there they lock him in. At night, in deepest darkness, the Grand Inquisitor

---

*The first draft of this chapter was delivered as an invited lecture at the first TESOL Summer Institute, on the campus of UCLA in July 1979.

enters the cell and the door closes behind him. The rest of the "poem" is a monolog which this old priest addresses to his Prisoner.

The Grand Inquisitor reproaches the Prisoner, even scolds him. The Prisoner had set out to give the whole human race something to live by, but also something to die by, something that would link, in meaning, the beginnings and the ends of existence, therefore quite literally a "religion." But, says the Inquisitor, the Prisoner had botched the job—botched it so badly that after some centuries a team of priests, acting in the Prisoner's name, had to assume control, and so replaced the Prisoner's work with their own.

What the Prisoner had hoped, says the Inquisitor, is first that all mankind would come to see the world—to see life—for themselves rather than letting someone else deliver them a simplified and printed map of it. Once they began to see for themselves, he hoped that they would then direct their own footsteps and choose their own paths, rather than waiting to be led like sheep. In doing so, each would become himself or herself rather than being a carbon copy of someone else. More, they would respect each other—see one another "whole against the sky," love one another even to the point, at times, that one would give up, to benefit another, what he himself most cherished. One more point: if this way is not to contradict itself—if it is not to lead to nowhere—then whoever follows it must choose it without bribery and without threat—must (as the Grand Inquisitor put it) be "great enough and strong enough" to choose it by his own free will.

"Are people truly like this?" asks the Grand Inquisitor, and answers, "No!" One in a million maybe, but for the rest in offering this freedom you have only added to their burden of anxiety and pain. They are in fact—except your very few—not strong but weak, not great but worthless, vicious, and rebellious. They crave two things and two things only: to go on living, and to find someone into whose hands they may entrust their consciences. So even while they are rebellious, they long to be controlled." So says the Grand Inquisitor. And this is the heavy task which the Inquisitor and those with him have taken on themselves: to bear responsibility for convoying, even with lies and trickery, their blind and frightened fellow humans from birth until the grave. The tools by which they will accomplish this, he says, are three in number: first "miracle," then "mystery," and then "authority." Mystery is the substitute for independent thought; authority is what imposes and enforces mystery; miracle is what assures the follower that he has in fact trusted his destiny into the right hands.

Language teachers live in this same world that Dostoyevsky was writing about. We too sometimes control our students (and even other teachers) through mystification: when we explain to them more than they are ready to receive; when our explanations use words that are ours, not theirs; when we tell them directly or indirectly that "Life is too short to learn German," or English, or Korean, or whatever; but most of all when we make them permanently our dependents by doing for them what they could do for themselves.

In our reliance on miracle we are not very different from the missionaries who won converts through their use of Western pharmaceuticals among the peoples of Africa and Asia: as linguists we have used minimal pairs of words (*beat* vs. *bit* in English, high tone *bá* vs. rising tone *bǎ* in a tonal language) to show those who had been baffled where to concentrate their efforts in pronunciation; we have awakened teachers to "the furious sleep of green ideas," and we have explained to anyone who would listen the reason why "the love of a good woman (or man)" is at least one-way ambiguous. As methodologists we have put our wares into the hands of gifted teachers who have conducted brilliant demonstration lessons that left onlookers convinced that they and their previous methods were inferior. I am not denying the validity of minimal pairs or the usefulness of transformational-generative understanding of how sentences are related to one another, and I am quite ready to admit that some methods may be inferior to others. Certainly I would not quarrel with having demonstration lessons taught by good teachers.

What I am saying, however, is that through our apparently miraculous ability to juggle minimal pairs or whatever, we have made converts to our own set of mysteries, and enticed people aboard our own methodological bandwagons; and that these miracles have often been as relevant to the true needs of teacher and pupil as aspirin and antimalarials are to true religion. And that through climbing the administrative ladder, or through gaining control over funds, or through exercising our prerogative to hand out grades, or simply through personal prestige or charisma, we have gained authority, and have used that authority to support and perpetuate our own brand of mystery.

The three "ways" about which I have said so much in this book certainly have not shrunk from the use of miracle. "Hypermnesia" as it is reported in the Sunday supplements has performed this function for Suggestopedia. So has Lozanov's success in using suggestion as the sole anesthetic for a patient during major surgery. Curran's ability to listen to a client in such a way that after only 5 or 10 minutes the client came out with important new insights, or with release from long-standing anxieties such as fear of flying, had the effect of "miracle." The first experience as a student in the Classical Community Language Learning format often produces such a blessed feeling of well-being and relief that people are disposed to accept uncritically whatever theory the demonstrator-teacher then proceeds to lay on them. Similarly, the first experience of watching as a flood of student language pours out in the presence of teacher silence sometimes leads onlookers to regard the teacher-demonstrator of the Silent Way as something of a "magician." And so on. I suspect that every method that has been widely used secured its first foothold in the attention of the profession through the efforts of talented snake-oil vendors who really believed in it.

Each method uses "miracles" to claim for itself, in the name of its originator or guiding figures, the territory which it proposes to civilize by subjugating that territory to its own particular "mystery"—to its own intellectual model of learning and teaching, or to its own insights and discoveries about language, or to its own "state-of-the-art" hardware and software—and sets out to make the local inhabitants fluent in the jargon which its initiates use for the Siamese-twin purposes of expounding the model and making the model difficult to challenge.

I do not mean to say that there is no place for "miracle, mystery, and authority." It seems clear that Dostoyevsky would not have said so either. After all, the Prisoner himself is reported to have made deliberate use of miracles; the religion which he left behind—indeed any religion—has its own essential mysteries; and it was said of him that he taught his hearers as one who had authority. The issue, then, is not "whether" miracle, mystery, and authority; it is rather "what kind of" miracle, mystery, and authority, or it is the place of miracle, mystery, and authority in education. It is this issue that I am trying to get at in this final chapter. I do not expect to settle the issue, but I do hope to open it for thinking and for discussion.

The word "authority" as we hear it every day has two meanings. One of these meanings carries with it the use of coercion; the second implies a relationship in which both parties believe that one of the parties is competent to direct, guide, or instruct the other. When Lozanov makes a great point of the importance of "authority" in Suggestopedia, he is pretty clearly talking about the second type. This second type of "authority," is what we have in mind when we say, "She's an authority on such-and-such a subject." I believe that it lies, unspoken but implied, behind the *successful* use of all other methods as well. The Grand Inquisitor with his police and prisons and autos-da-fé seems to have been talking about the first—the coercive—meaning of "authority." Yet how easily a taste of recognition as "an authority" can lead to an appetite for widening that recognition and, more pernicious, for perpetuating it. Here is where the benign authority of well-deserved recognition may develop into the malignant use of whatever power we have over our students or our colleagues: to cut the troublesome ones off from a chance to be heard, and from those who do not give confirmation to our own brand of mystery, to withhold the grades, tenure, money, status, or whatever symbols of recognition they must have to live.

I have just distinguished between two kinds of "authority." I think there may also be two kinds of "mystery." Some mysteries are made by human hands and human brains, formed to enhance the standing of their makers and maintained in order to keep their makers and their custodians one-up on those around them. Other mysteries are natural mysteries. Some natural mysteries lie in areas that we will someday understand but are still exploring: how people express and recognize interrogation or remonstrance, for example, or what rules account for the choice of high tone or low tone on a given syllable of a given verb in Shona (the first Bantu language I worked on). Other natural mysteries are those which we may explore but will never completely understand: how a particular learner's mind works, for example, or what it is that some people find so exciting in Elizabethan drama, or the landscape of modern Spain, or the discovery of rules that govern conversation in a particular culture. Natural mysteries are mysteries that we do not hold onto, but that we share with our students and with one another. But our theories—our tentative and partial maps of the natural mysteries—turn easily into artificial mysteries, and into weapons in a power struggle with those around us.

Let us turn now to "miracle." Surely in the task-oriented world of the foreign language classroom there must be place for some kind of "miracle," if only because students need to believe in what they are doing and in the people who lead them in doing it. Perhaps the distinction that we need to make here is not between two kinds of miracle, but between two ways of using it. Miracle may be used on a continuing basis as a means of compounding mystery and perpetuating authority. Or it may be used as a means of getting people's attention and showing them where the natural mysteries lie.

What I have been saying is tied in with three often-stated goals of education in general: the goal of freedom, the goal of uniqueness, and the goal of tolerance. If education is to be a liberating, or freeing, experience, then it must enable the students to see the world more clearly for themselves, so as to be able to choose how to use what energy they have, and act less impeded by blindness or by distorted images that do not correspond to reality. By choosing and acting more freely, we become, each of us, closer to what only we can become, not pounded or squeezed (or inflated!) into the same shape as everyone else around us. This is the uniqueness. But my uniqueness will be unlike yours (we saw this in Chapter 7), and the two may not obviously fit together. Each of us must allow the other some of this uniqueness, and that is what I mean by "tolerance." Tolerance allows the pieces of the puzzle, the students in a classroom, the people in a society, to fly off, each in its own direction. Authority—the coercive kind certainly, but also the noncoercive kind we talked about—is a force that draws the pieces back together. But what will the pattern be, the pattern toward which these pieces will be drawn? This brings us back to the issue of "what kind of mystery?" The artificial, synthetic, man-made kind of mystery stifles "uniqueness"—tells each person what to see, and how to label what he sees, and how to run it through his mind. In choosing which man-made mystery to follow, the miracle worker acts for the other person, and that is the end of "freedom." All of this brings to mind three other terms—Gattegno's—where he speaks of "independence," "autonomy," and "responsibility."

I have said that I see two kinds of "authority," though one kind sometimes corrupts itself into the other. I have said that there are at least two kinds of "mystery," though one of them may feed upon our exploration of the other. I have said that "miracle" lends itself to use in one way or in another. And so it may appear that I have been leading up to some sort of recommendation, if not indeed to an exhortation: "Let us strive to cast out from our teaching any unnecessary mystification of our students, and forego the power, security, personal gratification that synthetic mysteries can put into our hands. Let us employ miracles sparingly, just enough to direct our students' attention to the natural mysteries, and to make possible a relationship of noncoercive authority which rests on the students' recognition of our genuine competence. Then we will guide them in a shared exploration of the realities of the language, and of the natural mysteries of the learning process. We will make it easier for the students to become more and more free, and for each to realize his or her own unique potential. In imitation of our example, the students will treat one another as we have treated them, and so tolerance, our third goal, will be realized." This would, in the language classroom, have been not far distant from what the Grand Inquisitor said had been his Prisoner's dream. (I have long felt myself drawn toward these goals and I suppose I always will be. For just that reason, I must be all the more careful *not* to slip at this point into mere exhortation or inspiration. In this chapter more than anywhere else in the book, I am trying to see things as they are and to write about them with clinical objectivity.)

But the Grand Inquisitor raises again that question of his, this time not in the dungeon in Seville, but in our neat, bright, well-ventilated classrooms now, more than a century after Dostoyevsky wrote. His question is, "Are students really like this? Will students really stand to be treated in this way?" His own answer—that only one in a million will accept this kind of freedom— is in my own experience too pessimistic for a language classroom. Yet, although he may have misplaced his decimal point, my own experiences of the past six or seven years lead me to believe that he was at least partially right—that if he was not speaking the whole truth, he was at least speaking a half-truth, and that this truth or half-truth he was speaking is one which some of us who have explored, and committed ourselves to, the so-called "humanistic" approaches to language teaching have largely ignored or brushed aside. Some of us have assumed that if we provide a warm supportive environment and the information that people cannot supply for themselves, and if we guide them by presenting them a series of tasks or challenges which are neither too great for them nor too trivial, then they will learn faster and more fully, and that they will thank us for it. We have assumed that as they use powers they never knew they had and as they watch their minds—their whole selves—unfolding, growing, they will exult in this thrilling, never-ending voyage of exploration, and in the discovery that they have it in themselves to discover, and to discover how to discover further, and so on forever.

Perhaps we *were* right in that estimate of students, and the Grand Inquisitor was wrong. But if people *are* like that, they are not in my observation obviously like that, except a few. I have sometimes seen students, placed in a warm and accepting environment, given tasks which they were manifestly able to work out for themselves, and faced therefore with what was to all appearances a rich opportunity for all kinds of cognitive and personal growth, whose reaction was nothing but resistance and resentment. Like everyone else, I sometimes do things wrong, and some of this reaction may have been due to my own faulty techniques. But I am fairly sure that not all of it was. There remains, I am afraid, a residue—not universal but widespread—a residue of resistance and resentment against being given opportunities instead of rules and vocabulary lists—against being invited to explore one's own potential and to grow, rather than being immediately led to accrue some very specific communicative skills and repertoires for which one foresees a practical need. What most of us demand most urgently, it seems, is the means for meeting our most practical needs, and a leader whom we can follow without thinking, without wondering if we should have followed this one. The best leader is one who will keep us dazzled with miracles, who will guide us deftly but firmly to one concrete goal after another, and whose explanation of it all is both clear enough and vague enough so that we dare not question it. Here is the Grand Inquisitor with a vengeance!

But what of the teacher who does not follow the Grand Inquisitor? What of the teacher who, instead of offering (or claiming to offer) to the student exactly what he needs, offers instead to try to help him become able to get for himself five times as much? That teacher may be seen as undependable. What of the teacher who refuses to use the coercive kind of authority, who instead learns from her students what they can teach her, even as she invites them to learn what she knows but they do not. Such a teacher may provoke a feeling of uneasiness, for she is unlike the picture we have learned of what a teacher is. And what of the teacher who insists on telling her students that they have powers far beyond what they have dreamed about themselves? She will be punished for disturbing that safe dream, and for destabilizing a picture that had been learned at the cost of so much pain.

How many students can thrive—or how many students can coexist—with a teacher who does not follow the Grand Inquisitor? The answer may very well be different for different ages and for different cultural backgrounds. Certainly more than Dostoyevsky's one in a million. Certainly more than one in a thousand, probably more than one in a hundred, and perhaps even more than one in ten. But the Grand Inquisitor is still someone for any would-be "humanistic" teacher to reckon with.

Anyone who sets out to be a "humanistic" teacher—who offers to her students freedom and growth in addition to accuracy and fluency—needs all of the technical skills of a teacher who is not trying to be "humanistic" in this sense. She also needs some technical skills which are peculiar to one or more "humanistic" methods. In addition to all these skills, she needs greater flexibility in her use of them, for in making her choices and in determining her timing she will be taking into account much more than the students' accuracy and speed in mastering linguistic material. Most of all, however, she has to do without the Grand Inquisitor's "miracle, mystery, and authority" as means for controlling her students and for protecting herself against their attacks. All of this adds up to a tall order. It is no wonder that many teachers instinctively shy away from "humanistic" methods of all kinds. They see in their students, or in most of them, the human weakness and rebelliousness about which the Grand Inquisitor was so insistent.

We teachers, of course, are just as human as our students. This humanity can show itself in teacher-training courses and workshops. As proof of her qualifications for teaching the course or leading the workshop, the person in charge is expected to bring with her some miracles, in the form of a suitably impressive list of her publications, offices held, etc., and to produce a steady stream of new miracles in the form of brilliant lectures and amazing demonstrations of new techniques. Woe unto any leader who refuses to stand on past miracles, who offers to her audience as miracle to be explored only their shared humanity. If, further, she refuses to cloak herself in mystery and conceal her own relevant weaknesses, but instead addresses herself to the mystery of the relevant uniquenesses of everyone in the room, she may find that some of her audience will turn on her. If she uses authority only to organize the schedule and provide useful content, but holds herself back from posing as the all-sufficient director or answer-woman, then some of her hearers may feel cheated and resentful. She then risks rejection and repudiation. Feeling thus rejected and repudiated, seeing her best efforts lost and her words ignored, she wonders whether her audience would not have been better off if she had yielded just a little—if she had given them just enough "miracle, mystery, and authority" to pacify their craving. This dilemma is more poignant, and no less real, in a course or in a workshop whose purpose is to train teachers in "humanistic" methods. Here stands the Grand Inquisitor once more, just at the trainer's shoulder, certain that he, in the end, will win.

W. H. Auden once wrote two or three pages of free verse about a pair of characters who remind me a little of the Grand Inquisitor and his Prisoner. Two men pass each other at dusk on the edge of the city. One of them, the author, calls himself an Arcadian, and the other man a Utopian. As an Arcadian, the author inhabits an Eden where "one who dislikes Bellini has the good manners not to get born." Technology is represented only by saddle-tank locomotives, waterwheels, and other assorted "beautiful pieces of obsolete machinery." Since there is no technology, there are no mass media, so that the only source of political news is gossip. No one worries about a fixed code of behavior, but each observes his own compulsive rituals and superstitions.

The anti-type of the Arcadian is the Utopian. He, the author tells us, lives not in an Eden, but in a New Jerusalem. There, "a person who dislikes work will be very sorry he was born." Technology plays a central role in the New Jerusalem: even *haute cuisine* has been mechanized, and the mass media provide the news "in simplified spelling for nonverbal types." There is no religion, but the behavior of everyone exemplifies "the rational virtues." Again, as in the Dostoyevsky myth, we find freedom, uniqueness, and patience with individual differences on the one hand contrasted with clarity, order, and progress on the other. Just as there was no two-way communication between the Inquisitor and the Prisoner, so the Arcadian remarks of his meeting with the citizen of the New Jerusalem that "Neither speaks," for "what experience could we possibly share?" But where Dostoyevsky left the relationship at that, Auden went on to wonder whether their meeting had been, as it appeared, only a coincidence. Maybe, he speculated, this had been "also a rendezvous between accomplices who… cannot resist meeting," each "to remind the other of that half of [the truth] which he would most like to forget." They are anti-types, yes, Auden is saying. They are antipathetic and antithetical, yes. But they are also accomplices: neither can totally condemn the other without condemning himself for what he has omitted and yet depends on.

To carry this observation one step further, Auden wrote in the first person as the Arcadian. But he could not have written this particular bit of verse if he had not caught with great precision the other point of view as well. In order to do that, he must have had within him at least a tiny bit of the Utopian. (I doubt, however, that a Utopian with only a trace of the Arcadian temperament could have written anything comparable to Auden's poem!)

What, then, are we to make of the confrontation between Inquisitor and Prisoner, or of the uneasy meeting between Arcadian and Utopian? Here is not only a gap. Here is a gap which bears on either side of it one or the other charge of two primal, opposed polarities, just as the earth and clouds gather their static charges that will become lightning and make the thunderstorm. In the electrostatic analogy, they provide a theoretical—a pencil-and-paper— short circuit across a gap that still bears its unseen but no less heavy charge.

We can say, as I said a minute ago, that the two points of view are just "accomplices," halves of a larger truth—a truth too large for one person to contain it fully. Or, as I also put it a minute ago, we may see them residing side by side, in one proportion or another, within each person. Either of these views is partially right, of course. I believe, however, that they offer solutions which are too facile.

For a mythology that fits, I think we must concede that it was right to show the Grand Inquisitor and his Prisoner, or the Utopian and the Arcadian, as separate persons. In the real world of the classroom and the faculty lounge we meet these issues in the give and take among flesh-and-blood people—in what goes on between us and those around us. And a part of what goes on between us turns on this issue: How much freedom shall we offer to our students, and how independent can we ask them to be?

In the practical, task-oriented, real world of the language classroom, we cannot allow ourselves to go to either extreme, of course. If the teacher maintains complete control and totally monopolizes initiative, then at best the students come out as automatons who go through their paces nicely on the exam, but then have trouble "transferring" their skills to the job or the taxi or the restaurant. To turn all of the control over to the students and to insist that they exercise all of the initiative, on the other hand, would almost surely be disastrous. To cut people adrift from the structure and the guidance *that they truly need* is irresponsible, whether done to salve the conscience or to inflate the ego of the teacher. (I know of no method that asks teachers to go to either of these extremes.) We must walk the fine line between too much latitude and too little. But that is a truism.

Here I think we need to draw yet another distinction, this final one between two kinds of "freedom." When we use this word we most often have in mind the absence of restrictions or limitations imposed by people or by conditions which are not really part of the person who is "free." So we talk about "freedom *from*" slavery, or from poverty, or from tooth decay, or from an officious or tyrannical teacher. In this first sense, "freedom" is indeed something which we teachers may offer or withhold.

The second kind of "freedom" dwells within the person who is "free." When the moving parts of a mechanism get in each other's way, the mechanism begins to wobble, or slows down, or jams altogether. Then someone may go in and try to "free up" the parts where the trouble lies. In somewhat the same sense we sometimes say that an artist paints "with great freedom." This does not mean that the artist works carelessly or hastily. To be "free" in this sense requires both that one have considerable inner resources, and that these resources work smoothly with each other. The raw material for an inner resource can come only from outside; that is why *total* external freedom would make further growth of internal freedom impossible.

This latter is a "freedom" which is not ours to offer. What we teachers do and what we don't do may make it easier or harder for this inner freedom to develop. But there is no simple formula either for implanting it or for converting one kind of freedom into the other. We may smother the internal kind by failing to allow enough of the external kind, of course. As I said in the preceding paragraph, we may also starve it by bestowing too much external freedom at the wrong time. Mostly, though, our part of the enterprise is to watch for signs of internal freedom among those who have put themselves into our hands; and from our glimpses of it to guess what it is like in each class or in each student; and to remember where it was when last we saw it; and to work with it as best we can.

But if we do succeed in catching sight of this internal freedom, and in guessing what it is like, and in remembering where it was, and if we go on to work with it, we then—by that very seeing and guessing and remembering and working—help it to grow. We find that our fingers—whether we intended them to or not—have touched what Buber called "the special connexion between the unity of what [the student] is and the sequence of his actions and attitudes." We may have started out to be "humanistic" teachers primarily because in that way we could get more language across to our students, and make it stick longer. But now (again in Buber's words) we suddenly find ourselves engaged, wil-we nil-we, in "education of character." Insofar as this *is* what we are doing, or insofar as this is what we *appear* to be doing, we may meet resistance that does not arise from any "weakness, viciousness, or rebelliousness" on the part of our students. The strongest among them and the most mature know already, from within themselves, that this undertaking is far from easy; that it is not accomplished overnight by some magical technique leading to a pat list of "desired outcomes" whose desirability has been only half thought out; that finding the right goal and finding a right way to it lie just at the farthest edge of human reaching. These "strong and wise" ones, far from begging for someone to lead them by the nose, absolutely refuse to let even the best-intentioned someone-else grant to them or instill in them—with "lighthanded paternalism," as Ann Diller called it—something that they know must come from within themselves.

We must also recognize that.even those whom the Grand Inquisitor called "the few, the strong," who spend their lives alive in growth and in a search for inner freedom—even they have this searching and this growing as only one part of their daily cycle. Some of them will eagerly accept a "humanistic" language course as an arena, or as a medium, in which to find new adventures in discovering themselves and other people, and in which they can go on to become more than they had been before. Others of them, however, may decide that the language class is not a place where they choose to confront issues of alienation, or of personal values, or of restructuring cognitive strategies. They may just want to be taught well, by a method that they know already. We must respect this decision. Nevertheless, those issues still remain active in the classroom just as they are active everywhere, and they still continue to affect what goes on among and within the people in the classroom, to enhance or to reduce or to distort learning. So the "humanistic" teacher must face these issues whether or not her students are ready to face them along with her—whether or not they are willing even to know that she is facing them.

The difference between the Grand Inquisitor and his Prisoner, between the Arcadian and the Utopian, and between those of us who take after one or another of them, does not lie simply in the giving or withholding of external freedom. The difference is not even in whether the amount of freedom is allowed to increase as time goes on. The difference lies in whether an internal freedom comes alive which grows not by some teacher's sufferance and schedule, but on its own. If that is to happen, then sometime, somewhere along the line, and likely early, the teacher offers to the learners, not more external freedom than they can handle, but more than they *thought* they could handle—more than they had a comfortable and well-tried way of dealing with. One of the marks of a fine teacher is exactly this ability to see the gap between the far-possible and the near-comfortable, and to be the kind of person in whose company many learners reach the far side of that gap. This is the teacher who is more like the Arcadian or the Prisoner than like their adversaries. And here is where this kind of teacher finds herself in trouble.

For remember that it is the Prisoner and his ilk that fall into the hands of the Inquisitors of this world, and not the other way around. Auden tells us that the Arcadian looking at the Utopian feels alarm, but the Utopian looking at the Arcadian feels contempt. The one dreads whatever brings sterility;

the other is ready to destroy what leads toward instability. So a would-be "humanistic" teacher who offers freedom and demands independence *beyond custom* is the natural, predictable victim of punishment at the hands of those who guard custom and feel themselves guarded by it. (This in addition to whatever penalties she may have to pay for ordinary technical flaws in her teaching.) I have already mentioned some of the forms this punishment can take: resistance, resentment, rage, abandonment.

I think that here I am close to a point that Carolyn Hartl made recently. She began by saying that "the humanistic approach to teaching is based on [more than]superficial sentimentality." I would agree, and I would add that repeating "humanistic" slogans and adopting an assortment of pedigreed "humanistic" techniques, or having students talk about their feelings, dreams, and preferences, does not guarantee that a teacher is not in the tradition of the Inquisitor or of the Utopian. Nor does the use of an ancient conventional textbook necessarily mean a non-"humanistic" teacher. The three "Ways" that I have described in this book are "humanistic" in their intent and in their respective views of what goes on inside and among people; it is here rather than in their techniques that we may find hints for our own development as teachers. What is necessary, says Hartl, over and above the theories and the techniques, is "the ability to model convincingly" in one's own person "the outcome" of this kind of teaching. To do so, she says, a teacher must be "willing and able to share the most important aspects of life, to give freely of self." Beyond that, if what I have been saying in this chapter is true, the teacher must be willing to become vulnerable, taking risks with the clear knowledge that "risk" by definition means occasional painful losses. Hartl suggests that this kind of teaching may not be for every teacher. I think she may be right. We saw in Chapters 1 and 2 that the "heavy-handed authoritarian," and the "Grand Inquisitor" may be feared and disliked by their students, and may seriously limit their own effectiveness, but through using their "miracles, mysteries, and authority," they are usually able to keep any corrosive effects bottled up inside their students, so that those effects do not spill out on them.

Why then undertake a kind of teaching which is so demanding of skill and at the same time so risky? To risk and lose means among other things to die a little: to see one's ties with the outside world severed by just that much, and within, to feel that Self out of which one's future messages to the world must rise called into question—called into question not only before others but before oneself, never being quite sure where this loss, this particular failure, came from, whether merely from some error of technique, or from having guessed wrong about what this particular student truly could have done, or from having opened for the student a door through which in fact he might have stepped but which he has slammed shut in our face. In addition, we meet the dying out of that echo from our colleagues that tells us, "Yes, you are on the right track. You are one of us." Not least, there is also the basic physical loss in slipping, by the amount of any failure, that much closer to unemployment—to economic death. Remember Eric Berne's way of putting it: that when we don't get the strokes we need, "our spinal cords shrivel up."

Once more, then, why not avoid this deadly risk? Perhaps the answer to this question is one of the permanent natural mysteries. For some people, the answer to this question lies in the nature of life itself. In earlier chapters I said that when we say that something—a person, an animal, a vegetable, a microorganism even—is "alive," we mean that it is able to take into itself new things that it needs, and to use them, and to get rid of what it no longer needs, and to grow (in size or in other ways) into the world around it; and that in doing all these things it continues to be itself even as it changes. "Life" in this sense has not only length and breadth, but also depth. The same person who is physically sound and economically prosperous may on other levels have stopped taking in the new, and letting go of what no longer fits, and changing: may, for the sake of hanging onto the Self that is, have given up knowledge of, and further unfolding of that very Self. This grinding to a halt, this digging into a permanent position, this inflexibility is a loss of life, therefore a kind of death on the one level—the symbolic level—which is available only to human beings and not to animals or plants.

This is what the would-be "humanistic" teacher sees. But the very seeing of it is an act—or better, it is a process—which is going on at the deepest, most uniquely human level, inside the teacher. Therefore, to withhold what flows out of this insight—that is, to fail to offer more and deeper "life" to her students, would for the teacher be a contradiction of her own life process, and a denial of it: therefore a termination of it. So the teacher risks one kind of death for the hope of a different kind of life within herself as well as in her students.

What this kind of teacher tries to do—exchanging life on one level for life on another by helping her students to find in themselves a freedom which is their own, an understanding and a self-understanding which will go on growing of itself—this is impossible. Yet it does take place.

So it is because she has seen the impossible event take place—because she knows that the process, incredible as it is, can still continue—it is out of this knowledge, this experience, that this kind of teacher takes up her authority with not a little reverence, and bears it with a natural humility, handling with courage the mystery-behind-mystery, playing out her part in simple, daily miracle.

EPILOG

This book has in it several methods and many techniques—all of them *ways* of helping people to learn languages. But throughout, it sets before the reader only one *way*—only one man's *way*—of looking at the methods and using the techniques. No one else will see in exactly this way, or follow the techniques precisely as they have been laid out here.

What I have sung to you is not me,
But it comes from where I have come from.

And who I have sung to is not you,
But someone I hope is within you.

We will go, you and I, late or soon,
But the singing was here, like a rope—
like a bridge—
And we were the ends of it.

Singing is all there is.

Sing to me!

In 1979 John Haskell, editor of the *TESOL Newsletter,* circulated a questionnaire asking the respondents to name ten books that they would recommend as a basic library for new language teachers. Here is the reply I made then:

"It's hard to know where to stop in such a list. I will therefore attach great weight to two words: a *basic* library for *new* teachers. On that ground I have eliminated much that I consider to be merely 'excellent,' 'invaluable' and 'indispensable' for the fully formed teacher.

"I would begin, as I have said several times in the past, with a book which sets out what a teacher or a learner may (and may not) reasonably try to do, and which does so without distracting the reader's attention from essentials by talking about language classes: W. Timothy Gallwey's *The Inner Game of Tennis.*

"Second, I would move to a book written by a gifted language teacher, but written long enough ago so that it would not immediately draw the reader into present-day issues and controversies: Otto Jespersen's *How to Teach a Foreign Language.*

"Third, I would go to something which is more recent, but which is old enough to give a longish perspective on what we are doing now: Wilga Rivers' *The Psychologist and the Foreign Language Teacher.* The issues that Rivers deals with in this book are no longer the focus of attention in the profession as they were when she wrote, but they will always be with us, and the clarity of her treatment is exemplary.

"Fourth, I would ask a new teacher to read the introduction to Maley and Duff's *Drama Techniques in Language Learning.* These few pages are unmatched, as far as I know, for brevity and clarity in sketching what there is to be taught and learned besides sounds, words and grammar.

"By now, I think the reader would be ready for a book which describes one good solid method, and describes it with both clarity and conviction. One such book is Paulston and Bruder's *Teaching English as a Second Language: Techniques and Procedures.*

"Then a sampling of what can be done with live and lively bits of communication by and for native speakers: the *Student's Book* written by Abbs and Sexton for the *Challenges* course published by Longman.

"About here, the reader-teacher ought to look at something by Krashen that draws a distinction between adult 'learning' and adult 'acquisition' of a second language, and lists some of the characteristics of 'acquisition': probably his 'Adult second language acquisition and learning.'

"This would be a good time for the new teacher to go on and sample the multiple techniques which make up the bulk of the Maley and Duff book.

"Then s/he might look at a clear and clarifying treatment of theory: Diller, *The Language Teaching Controversy;*

"and at her/himself in relation to teaching, through Jersild's *When Teachers Look at Themselves*;

"and last, at teachers and learners as human beings, through Martin Buber's essays "On education" and 'On the education of character' (in *Between Man and Man*).

"As I said in the first paragraph, I have taken you literally and concentrated on 'basics' that have been of help to me. From these, the new teacher may go on to books that provide an introduction to such essentials as phonetics, grammatical analysis, and testing.

"I need hardly point out that these books are 'basic' only for people who would like to become the kind of teacher that I would like to become."

The books that I have drawn on in the writing of *Teaching Languages: A Way and Ways* are the following:

PRINCIPAL SOURCES

General

Auden, W. H. 1957. Horae Canonicae: Vespers. In *Selected Poems of W. H. Auden*. New York: The Modern Library.

Becker, Ernest. 1968. *The Structure of Evil*. New York: The Free Press.

———. 1973. *The Denial of Death*. New York: The Free Press.

———. 1975. *Escape from Evil*. New York: The Free Press.

Buber, Martin. 1924. Essays on "Education" and "The Education of Character." In *Between Man and Man*. Macmillan.

Dostoyevsky, F. *The Brothers Karamazov*.

Gallwey, W. Timothy. 1974. *The Inner Game of Tennis*. New York: Random House.

Krashen, S. D. 1979. Adult second language acquisition and learning: a review of theory and applications. In R. Gingras (ed.) *Second Language Acquisition and Foreign Language Teaching*. Arlington, Va.: The Center for Applied Linguistics.

Krishnamurti, J. 1969. *Freedom from the Known*. New York: Harper and Row.

The Silent Way

All of these books are by Caleb Gattegno and are published in New York by Educational Solutions, Inc.

1972. *Teaching Foreign Languages in Schools: The Silent Way*.

1975. *On Being Freer*. (One of the principal sources for Chapter 3.)

1975. *The Mind Teaches the Brain*. (For me personally this was the Rosetta Stone that enabled me to understand parts of Dr. Gattegno's writings that had previously seemed cryptic.)

1976. *The Common Sense of Teaching Foreign Languages*.

1977. *Evolution and Memory*.

1977. *The Science of Education*.

1977. *On Love*.

1978. *On Death*.

1979. *Who Cares about Health?* (Beyond its immediate topic, this is an excellent summary and updating of some things that appeared in early books by Dr. Gattegno.)

And the series of videotaped records of a pair of actual classes, to which I referred on page 46.

Counseling-Learning

The following books by Charles A. Curran are available from Apple River Press in Apple River, Illinois:

1968. *Counseling and Psychotherapy: The Pursuit of Values.*
1972. *Counseling-Learning: A Whole-Person Approach for Education.*
1976. *Counseling-Learning in Second Languages.*
1978. *Understanding: A Necessary Ingredient in Human Belonging.*

Suggestopedia

Bancroft, W. Jane. 1978. The Lozanov Method and its American adaptations. *Modern Language Journal* 62:4, pp. 167–174.

Journal of the Society for Suggestive-Accelerative Learning and Teaching.

Lozanov, Georgi. 1979. *Suggestology and Outlines of Suggestopedy.* New York: Gordon and Breach.

Saféris, Fanny. 1978. *Une Révolution dans l'Art d'Apprendre.* Paris: Robert Laffont.

OTHER REFERENCES

Abbs, B. and M. Sexton. 1977. *Student's Book* for *Challenges.* London: Longmans.

Alexander, L. G. 1968. *For and Against.* Langenscheidt-Longman.

Berne, E. 1964. *Games People Play.* New York: Grove Press.

Blot, David and Phyllis Berman Sher. 1978. *Getting Into It: An Unfinished Book.* New York: Language Innovations, Inc.

Bodman, Jean and Michael Lanzano. 1975. *No Hot Water Tonight.* Collier Macmillan.

Carter, T. P. 1974. The imaginative use of projected visuals. *Foreign Language Annals* 7:314–324.

Curran, C. A. 1961. Counseling skills adapted to the teaching of foreign languages. *B. Menninger Clinic* 25:78–93.

———. 1966. Counseling in the education process: a foreign language learning integration. Unpublished.

Diller, Karl. 1978. *The Language Teaching Controversy.* Rowley, Mass.: Newbury House.

Hartl, Carolyn. 1979. Review. *Modern Language Journal* 63:4, p. 228f.

Jesperson, Otto. 1904. *How to Teach a Foreign Language.* (Republished in 1940 by Longmans.)

Jersild, Arthur. 19755. *When Teachers Look at Themselves.* New York: Teachers College Press.

Maley, Alan and Alan Duff. 1978. *Drama Techniques in Language Learning.* Cambridge University Press.

Maslow, Abraham. *Motivation and Personality.* Second edition. New York: Harper and Row.

Paulston, Christina Bratt and Mary Bruder. 1976. *Teaching Foreign Languages: Techniques and Procedures.* Cambridge, Mass.: Winthrop.

Rivers, Wilga. 1964. *The Psychologist and the Foreign Language Teacher.* Chicago: The University of Chicago Press.

Rogers, Carl R. 1951. Chapter 2 in *Client-Centered Therapy.* Boston: Houghton Mifflin.

Rowe, Mary Budd. 1974. Pausing phenomena: influence on the quality of instruction. *J. Psycholinguistic Rsch.* 3:203–224.

Schafer, Roy. 1958. Regression in the service of the ego. In G. Lindzey (ed.) *Assessment of Human Motives.* New York: Holt, Rinehart and Winston.

Stevick, Earl W. 1974. Language teaching must do an about-face. *Modern Language Journal.*

Stevick, E. W. 1971. *Adapting and Writing Language Lessons.* Publ. by Superintendent of Documents, but most readily available from TESOL.

———. 1976. *Memory, Meaning and Method.* Rowley, Mass.: Newbury House.

Whitman, R. M. 1964. Psychodynamic principles underlying T-group processes. In K. D. Benne, L. P. Bradford, R. Lippitt (eds.) *T-Group Theory and Laboratory Method.* New York: John Wiley & Sons.

INDEX